Seasoned
Judgments

BOOKS BY LEONARD W. LEVY

The Law of the Commonwealth and Chief Justice Shaw *(1957)*

Legacy of Suppression: Freedom of Speech and Press in Early American History *(1960)*

The American Political Process *(1963), ed.*

Jefferson and Civil Liberties: The Darker Side *(1963)*

Major Crisis in American History: Documentary Problems *(1963), ed.*

Congress *(1964), ed.*

The Judiciary *(1964), ed.*

Political Parties and Pressure Groups *(1964), ed.*

The Presidency *(1964), ed.*

American Constitutional Law: Historical Essays *(1966)*

Freedom of the Press from Zenger to Jefferson: Early American Libertarian Theories *(1966), ed.*

Freedom and Reform *(1967), ed.*

Origins of the Fifth Amendment: The Right Against Self-Incrimination *(1968)*

Essays on the Making of the Constitution *(1969)*

The Fourteenth Amendment and the Bill of Rights *(1971), ed.*

Judgments: Essays on Constitutional History *(1972)*

The Supreme Court under Warren *(1972), ed.*

Blasphemy in Massachusetts *(1973), ed.*

Against the Law: The Nixon Court and Criminal Justice *(1974)*

Jim Crow Education *(1974), ed.*

Treason against God—A History of the Offense of Blasphemy *(1981)*

Emergence of a Free Press *(1985)*

Constitutional Opinions: Aspects of the Bill of Rights *(1986)*

The Establishment Clause: Religion and the First Amendment *(1986)*

Encyclopedia of the American Constitution *(1986), ed.*

The Framing and Ratification of the Constitution *(1987), ed.*

The American Founding *(1988), ed.*

Original Intent and the Framers' Constitution *(1988)*

Supplement One: Encyclopedia of the American Constitution *(1992), ed.*

Blasphemy: Verbal Offense Against the Sacred from Moses to Salman Rushdie *(1993)*

Encyclopedia of the American Presidency *(1993), ed.*

Seasoned Judgments: Constitutional Rights and American History *(1994)*

Seasoned Judgments

The American Constitution, Rights, and History

Leonard W. Levy

Transaction Publishers
New Brunswick (U.S.A.) and London (U.K.)

Library of Congress Catalog Number: 94–11046
ISBN: 1–56000–170–4
Printed in the United States of America

Library of Congress Cataloging-in-Publication Data

Levy, Leonard Williams, 1923–
    Seasoned judgments : the American constitution, rights, and
history / Leonard W. Levy.
        p.   cm.
    Includes bibliographical references.
    ISBN 1–56000–170–4
    1. United States—Constitutional history.   I. Title.
KF4541.A2L3735   1994
342.73'029--dc20
[347.30229]   94–11046
                                                        CIP

Contents

II   Constitutional History

III   The Marshall Court

Preface

This book is a compilation of some of my writings on American constitutional history, a subject that is fascinating for several reasons: the achievements of the founding generation were titanic; the Constitution itself possesses delphic qualities; and the interpretations of it by its oracle, the Supreme Court of the United States, are as controversial as they are significant.

The founding generation, especially the framers and ratifiers of the Constitution, believed in a political philosophy of social compact, natural rights, and limited government. That philosophy yielded the most enduring, important, and creative constitutional achievements in our history. The Declaration of Independence, with it majestic preamble, was merely the beginning. Within only thirteen years, Americans invented or first institutionalized written constitutions, a bill of rights applicable against all branches of government, the device of a constitutional convention, popular ratification, a federal system, the practice of judicial review, and a solution to the colonial problem—admit territories to the Union as states fully equal to the original thirteen.

Religious liberty, the separation of church and state, political parties, separation of powers, an acceptance of the principle of equality, and the conscious creation of a new nation were also among American institutional "firsts," although not all of these initially appeared between 1776 and 1789. Yet in that brief span of time, America created what is today the oldest major republic in the world, and created as well political democracy, the first state constitutions, and the United States Constitution. These unparalleled achievements derived not from originality in speculative theory but from the constructive application of old ideas, which Americans took so seriously that they constitutionally based their institutions of government on them.

Despite its imperfections, the Constitution was the product of a nation conceived in liberty, as Lincoln said, and dedicated to the proposition that all people are created equal. The Philadelphia Constitutional Convention of 1787 suffered the continued existence of slavery because a strong union was not otherwise possible. Moreover, slavery would have flourished even in the absence of that union. Creating an effective national government that allowed the growth of liberty and equality was far more preferable than framing a constitution that outlawed slavery, because such a constitution would never have been ratified. An antislavery constitution would have led to the balkanization of the continent.

Ours is a world of supersonic aircraft, recombinant DNA, robots, computers, microwaves, gene splicing, space stations, a global village ecology, and an interdependent world economy. Yet on crucial and fundamental matters we still give our allegiance to the principles of those who framed and ratified the Constitution. It is a remarkable fact that we continue to live by a federal system, a representative government, the separation of powers among three branches or tripartite government, a system of checks and balances, elections at fixed intervals, and a political ideology based on liberty and equality.

Chief Justice Roger B. Taney, in the *Dred Scott* case, declared that the Constitution must be construed "as it was understood at the time of its adoption. It is not only the same in words, but the same in meaning." Taney was wrong. Our Constitution is a brief document framed by men trained to believe that a few comprehensive and expansible principles, supplementing a structural description, will be greatly malleable and will provide a guide that can serve to answer virtually any questions that might arise on a case-to-case basis. Edmund Randolph of Virginia, one of the framers, observed that two matters demanded attention when drafting the Constitution: "1. To insert essential principles only, lest the operations of government be clogged by rendering those provisions permanent and unalterable, which ought to be accommodated to times and events, and 2. To use simple and precise language, and general propositions . . . ."

When Chief Justice John Marshall reminded that "it is *a constitution* we are expounding," he meant that the Constitution marked out only the great outlines and designated only the important objectives, leaving the rest to be deduced; he understood that the Constitution grows in meaning, which is why it is regarded as a "living" Constitution. In that respect it is similar to Magna Carta, now approaching its 800th anniversary. It was originally "reactionary as hell," to quote a former chief justice of West Virginia, but the feudal barons who framed it could not control its evolution. It eventually came to signify many things that are not in it and were not intended. Magna Carta is not remotely important for what it intended but for what it has become. It stands now for government by social compact, for fundamental law, for the rule of law, for no taxation without representation, for due process of law, for habeas corpus, for equality before the law, for representative government, and for a cluster of rights of the criminally accused, especially trial by jury. The Constitution is comparably dynamic.

Although the Constitution is conventionally regarded as a bundle of compromises, we can discern with ease many matters of the foremost magnitude on which the framers agreed. Consensus existed at the Constitutional Convention on fundamentals, outweighing in importance the conflicts, compromises, and ambiguities that characterized both the convention and the Constitution. The framers undoubtedly intended to establish a stronger Union with its own sources of revenue and with authority to impose certain limitations upon state powers. They meant to limit powers, distribute powers, fragment powers, separate powers, and stymie powers, as well as to mix them. They believed in measuring the powers of government, not the rights of the people. They understood that government should never be trusted, which is the reason they placed systematic and regularized restraints upon its powers. They were committed to a natural rights philosophy. They concurred on the supremacy clause, on the enumeration of congressional powers, on the need for adding to that enumeration the necessary and proper clause, and they also concurred on the need for adding the Bill of Rights to the Constitution. The Constitution is certainly a principled document that reflects a coherent political philosophy. But none of this requires or enables judges to reach a decision favoring one side of an issue rather than another in real cases that comes before the Supreme Court.

"Tis funny about th' constitution. It reads plain, but no wan can underherstant it without an interpreter," said Mr. Dooley, the philosophic Irish bartender created by Finley Peter Dunne. This book is a small step toward that understanding. Of course, the Supreme Court is the official interpreter of the Constitution, even if a self-appointed one. From the beginning of the Court's history, disputes have raged about how it should interpret the Constitution. In its very first constitutional decision, on the question whether a state could be sue without its consent by a citizen of another state, the Court provoked a controversy that was resolved only by the framing and ratification of the eleventh amendment. The fact is that the framers who remained active in national politics divided intensely on one constitutional issue after another—the removal power, the power to charter a corporation, the power to declare neutrality, the executive power, the power to enact excise and use taxes without apportioning them on population, the power of a treaty to obligate the House of Representatives to appropriate monies, the power to deport aliens, the power to pass an act against seditious libel, the power of the federal courts to decide on federal common-law grounds, the power to abolish judicial offices of life tenure, the jurisdiction of the Supreme Court to issue writs of mandamus against executive officers, and the power of judicial review.

Judicial review, although not authorized by the Constitution, has been legitimated by the long acquiescence of the American people and their representatives. It never would have flourished had the people been opposed to it. The people have the sovereign power to abolish it outright or hamstring it by constitutional amendment. The President and Congress could bring the Supreme Court to heel even by ordinary legislation. The Court's membership, size, funds, staff, rules of procedure, and enforcement agencies are subject to the control of the "political branches," which are periodically accountable to the people at the ballot box. Judicial review, in fact, exists by the tacit consent of governed.

Judicial review, which is one of the subjects of this book, is at the core of the section on the Marshall Court, which focuses on problems of constitutional interpretation by the high bench. The period of the Marshall Court, ending in 1835, completes the formative era of the Constitution. All of the articles on the Marshall Court derive from my *Encyclopedia of the American Constitution*. Less than forty percent of the space in this book come from the encyclopedia, but the number of such articles dominates the volume. Their brevity, conciseness, and subject matter make them, I hope, eminently suitable as required reading in any number of courses dealing the American government and history. Bringing them together within the covers of a single book provides a useful service. Although the encyclopedia itself is easily available on the reference shelves of most libraries, using it is often inconvenient and from a librarian's viewpoint, required reading of the encyclopedia might be damaging to the set. I have selected for inclusion here only those articles of mine that I think suitable for a book that focuses on the foundations of American constitutional history and on rights. Thus, the reader will find articles on many basic concepts such as "social compact theory," "constitution," "constitutional convention," and "due process of law."

The initial section of the book covers a variety of constitutional rights. In our extraordinary system of government, the government has no obligation or power to tell people what to think or believe about politics, religion, art, science, literature, or anything else. American citizens have the duty as well as the right to keep the government from falling into error; the government cannot and should not keep the citizens from falling into error. Moreover the framers were deeply committed to a system of government that minimized the possibilities of convicting the innocent; but they were not less concerned about the humanity that the fundamental law should provided even to the offender. They believed that guilt or innocence should be fairly determined by just procedures that respect the individual. With good reasons, therefore, most provisions of the Bill of Rights deal with the rights of the criminally accused.

The criminally accused are but one of many kinds of minorities in our society. James Madison, the father of the Constitution, when introducing in Congress the amendments that became the Bill of Rights, declared that those amendments would prevent abuses of power by "the body of the people, operating by the majority against the minority." The Bill of Rights protects all kinds of minorities, but all of us benefit from it, because it helps keep us a free society.

Many of the rights of the criminally accused won acceptance much earlier than the First Amendment rights of free speech, freedom of religion, and separation of church and state. Indeed, many of the rights of the criminally accused came into existence because First Amendment rights did not exist, when government prosecuted critics and dissenters for crimes such as seditious libel or failure to observe the faith of the established church. The many articles in this book on rights help explain such vitally important matters of constitutional history. The broad sampling of my writings on rights also helps explain the provision of the Declaration of Independence that affirms that government in the United States was instituted to preserve the inalienable rights of citizens.

Leonard W. Levy
Ashland, Oregon

Acknowledgements

I am thankful for the following permissions:

All entires from the *Encyclopedia of the American Constitution* are reprinted with the permission of the copyright owner, Macmillan Publishing Co. The encyclopedia was published as a four volume set in 1986 and was followed by *Supplement One* in 1992, also published by Macmillan.

"The *Legacy* Reexamined," 37 *Stanford Law Review*, is copyrighted 1985 by the Board of Trustees of the Leland Stanford Junior University and is reprinted with the further permission of Fred B. Rothman & Co.

"On the Origins of the Free Press Clause," originally published in 32 *UCLA Law Review* 177, copyright 1984, The Regents of the University of California. All Rights Reserved," is reprinted by permission of both Fred B. Rothman & Co. and UCLA Law Review.

"The Right Is Wrong on Rights," 18 *Reviews in American History* 284 (1990), is reprinted with permission of the editor, Stanley I. Kutler.

"Property As a Human Right," 5 *Constitutional Commentary* 168 (1988) and "The Original Constitution As a Bill of Rights," 9 *Constitutional Commentary* 163 (1992), are reprinted by permission of the publisher, University of Minnesota Law School.

"The Fourth Amendment" and "The Ninth Amendment" are reprinted by permission of Macmillan Publishing Co. from my *Original Intent and the Framers' Constitution,* copyright 1988.

I

Rights

1

The Original Constitution As
a Bill of Rights?

The exclusion of a bill of rights was fundamental to the constitutional theory of the Framers of the Constitution. For that reason they deliberately omitted such a bill. Yet, no Framer opposed the rights conventionally protected by a bill of rights. As George Washington wrote to LaFayette during the controversy over ratification, "there was not a member of the Convention, I believe, who had the least objection to what is contended by the advocates for a Bill of Rights."[1] All the Framers were civil libertarians. Why then did they deliberately exclude an enumeration of the rights of the people, and why did they not prohibit the national government from abridging those rights? They believed that a bill of rights was quite unnecessary, because the Constitution, as they framed it, adequately protected the people's rights.

Thomas McKean, second only to James Wilson as an advocate of the ratification of the Constitution in Pennsylvania, explained to his state's ratifying convention that a bill of rights "is an unnecessary instrument, for, in fact, the whole plan of government is nothing more than a bill of rights—a declaration of the people in what manner they choose to be governed."[2] Alexander Hamilton made the point even more directly in *Federalist No. 84* when writing that "the Constitution is itself in every rational sense, and to every useful purpose, A BILL OF RIGHTS." Indeed, he added, the proposed Constitution "will be a bill of rights of the union."[3] But why was a bill of rights unnecessary, and why was the Constitution itself in effect such a bill, in the minds of the Framers?

Hamilton's explanation reflected the Federalist party line. Bills of

3

rights, he declared, originated as contracts between a king and his subjects, as in the case of Magna Carta, the Petition of Right, or the Declaration of Rights. Accordingly, bills of rights had no relevance to constitutions founded on the power of the people, who retained all rights and surrendered none. The preamble of the Constitution constituted "a better recognition of popular rights than volumes of those aphorisms" contained in the state bills of rights; those aphorisms "would sound much better in a treatise of ethics than in a constitution of government."[4]

Moreover, observed Hamilton, a bill of rights was not only unnecessary but would be "dangerous," because it

> would contain various exceptions to powers not granted; and on this very account, would afford a colourable pretext to claim more (powers) than were granted. For why declare that things shall not be done which there is no power to do? Why, for instance, should it be said that the liberty of the press shall not be restrained, when no power is given by which restrictions may be imposed?[5]

Similarly, James Wilson, the most influential Framer next to James Madison, sought to explain the Convention's omission of a bill of rights by observing that while the people of the states vested in their governments all powers and rights not explicitly reserved, the case was different as to the national government, whose authority rested on enumerated powers. Therefore everything not delegated to the United States was reserved to the people or the states. A bill of rights stipulated the reserved rights of the people; the Constitution, however, merely provided for the existence of an effective national government. An enumeration of popular rights not divested would, therefore, be "absurd."[6]

Wilson trumpeted the Federalist line when he made the argument that a bill of rights would be "preposterous and dangerous," would put rights at risk, and would augment national powers. He reasoned that a formal declaration on freedom of the press or of religion, over which Congress had no powers whatever, could "imply" that some degree of power over the press or religion had been granted because of an attempt to define its extent. Wilson also insisted on the impossibility of enumerating and reserving all the rights of the people. A bill of rights, he added, "is an enumeration of the powers reserved. If we attempt an enumeration, everything that is not enumerated is presumed to be given. The consequence is, that an imperfect enumeration would throw all implied powers into the scale of the government; and the rights of the people would be rendered incomplete."[7] (That argument eventually gave rise to the ninth amendment.)

The rights of the people, according to Federalist theoreticians, depended not on "parchment provisions," but on public opinion, an extended republic, a federal system, a pluralistic society of competing interests, and a national government of limited powers structured to prevent any interest from becoming an overbearing majority and to prevent any branch of government from exercising a power that could jeopardize liberty.

Personal liberty depended on public opinion rather than parchment guarantees because experience had revealed such guarantees to be ineffective when confronted by "public necessity." The Framers tended to be skeptical about the value of a bill of rights when confronted by what James Madison called "overbearing majorities." He had seen repeated violations of the bills of rights in every state. Recent history had revealed the futility of a bill of rights "when its controul is most needed."[8] In Virginia, for example, the constitutional protection of the rights of conscience meant little when the legislature had favored an establishment of religion; it was averted only because Madison and dissenters turned the tide of opinion against the bill. Any Framer could have cited examples of abridgements of civil liberties during times of popular hysteria.

Moreover, no state bill of rights was sufficiently comprehensive, and six states did not even have bills of rights. Virginia's highly praised Declaration of Rights omitted as many rights as it protected. It failed to protect against bills of attainder, for example, and the legislature had enacted them. A majority of states failed to protect basic rights; seven omitted a prohibition on ex post facto laws, nine failed to provide for grand jury proceedings, ten said nothing about freedom of speech, and eleven were silent about exposure to double jeopardy. Whether or not omissions implied a power to violate, omissions seemed to the Framers to raise a danger that could be prevented by avoiding the problem altogether: omit a bill of rights when forming a new national government of limited powers.

The fact that the government possessed only limited powers secured liberty. The fact that it was a government that was neither wholly national nor wholly federal also secured liberty, as *The Federalist* argued. The fact that the powers of government were divided between the United States and the states contributed to the same end. The fact that the powers of the government of the United States were separated among three branches that were capable of checking each other also made it more difficult for the government to repress individuals or minorities. The entire system of checks and balances (the Senate's confirmation of treaties and appointments, the bicameral system, the staggered terms of office, the periodic elections, the executive veto, the congressional controls over the judicial branch, the possibility of judicial review) worked against a tyranny of the majority. The fact that Congressmen represented large districts with diverse interests also militated against factional triumphs over the people. America's great diversity was the very greatest safeguard of liberty, an insurance that one class, or religion, or section, or interest, or faction could not become too powerful, jeopardizing the liberty of others. Diversity constituted a natural system of checks and balances, making for an equilibrium of powers contributing to the same end.

The argument that the Constitution adequately secured liberty and made a bill of rights superfluous, even dangerous, seductively attracted the proponents of ratification. But some of the points that they made were patently absurd, such as the claim that bills of rights were appropriate in England but not in America. In fact eleven states had framed written constitutions during the Revolution, and seven drew up bills of rights; even the four without such bills inserted in their constitutions some provisions normally found in bills of rights, as had the Framers when drafting the Constitution for the Union. To imply that bills of rights were un-American or unnecessary merely because the people in America were the source of all power was unhistorical.

Americans had become accustomed over a period of a century and a half to the idea that people created government by written compacts or constitutions that were fundamental law; that the government must be subject to such limitations that were necessary for the security of the rights of the people; and usually that the reserved rights of the people were enumerated in bills of rights. Yet, James Wilson had repeatedly informed the Pennsylvania ratifying convention that a bill of rights was unnecessary in America, even though Pennsylvania's state constitution had an elaborate Declaration of Rights. Governor Edmund Randolph of Virginia, another influential Framer, declared at the Virginia ratifying convention that the esteemed Virginia Declaration of Rights "has never secured us against danger; it has been repeatedly disregarded and violated." That was merely exaggeration, but

Randolph's rhetoric risked disbelief when he declared, "Our situation is radically different from that of the people of England. What have we to do with bills of rights? . . . A bill of rights, therefore, accurately speaking, is quite useless, if not dangerous to a republic."[9]

That supporters of the Constitution could ask, "What have we to do with a bill of rights" suggests that they had made a colossal error of judgment. They had omitted a bill of rights and then compounded their error by refusing to admit it. Their single-minded purpose of creating an effective government had exhausted their energies and good sense, and when they found themselves on the defensive, under an accusation that their handiwork threatened the liberties of the people, their frayed nerves led them into indefensible positions. Any opponent of ratification could have answered Randolph's question, or Wilson's speeches, or Hamilton's *Federalist No. 84,* and many capably did so.

If a bill of rights was unnecessary, they asked, why did the Constitution protect some rights? The protection of some rights opened the Framers and their supporters to devastating rebuttal. They claimed that because no bill of rights could be complete, the omission of a particular right might imply a power to abridge it as unworthy of respect by the government. That argument, in effect that to include some rights would exclude all others, boomeranged.

Hamilton, in *Federalist No. 84,* oblivious of inconsistency and illogic, had elaborately described the protections of particular rights in the proposed Constitution. Impeachments were regulated by guarantees of indictment, trial, judgment, and punishment according to law. No religious test could be exacted from office holders. Ex post facto laws and bills of attainder were banned, as were titles of nobility. Treason was narrowly defined, its proof regulated. In criminal cases trial by jury was guaranteed, and the writ of habeas corpus was protected too.

In Pennsylvania, Robert Whitehall answered James Wilson by noting the Constitution's protection of selected rights, and he called on Wilson to reconcile his argument with the Convention's handiwork. "For," declared Whitehall, "if there was danger in the attempt to enumerate the liberties of the people, lest it should prove imperfect and defective, how happens it, that in the instances I have mentioned, that danger has been incurred? Have the people no other rights worth their attention, or is it to be inferred, agreeably to the maxim of our opponents, that every other right is abandoned?" Stipulating a right, he believed, destroyed the "argument of danger."[10] Surely the Philadelphia Convention might have thought of some rights in addition to those protected in the Constitution. The ban on religious tests could have reminded them of freedom of religion. Did not its omission, together with the reasoning of proponents of ratification, necessarily mean that the government could attack freedom of religion?

What prevented enumerated powers from being abused by the new government, at the expense of personal liberties? Congress's power to tax, for example, might be aimed at the press or at religion, and therefore was a power to destroy or restrain their freedoms. Taxes might even be exacted for the support of a religious denomination. Tax collectors, unrestrained by a ban on general warrants, might invade homes and, as Patrick Henry feared, might search and ransack everything. Congress, he warned, might "extort confession by torture" in order to convict a violator of federal law.[11] Numerous opponents of ratification contended that Congress could define as crimes the violation of any laws that it might legitimately enact, and in the absence of a bill of rights, accused persons might be deprived of the rights to counsel, to indictment, to cross-examine witnesses, to produce evidence on their own behalf, to be free from compulsory self-incrimination, to be protected against double jeopardy and excessive bail, and to be exempt from excessive fines and cruel punishments.

Henry cleverly observed that the "fair implication" of the argument against a bill of rights was that the government could do anything not forbidden by the Constitution. Because the provision on the writ of habeas corpus allowed its suspension whenever the public safety required, Henry reasoned, "It results clearly that, if it had not said so, they could suspend it in all cases whatsoever. It reverses the position of the friends of this Constitution, that every thing is retained which is not given up; for, instead of this, every thing is given up which is not expressly reserved."[12]

Richard Henry Lee, also advocating a bill of rights, similarly scorned the ratificationists' arguments, turning them upside down. For example, he observed that a clause of the Constitution prohibited Congress from granting titles of nobility. If the clause had been omitted, would Congress have the power to grant such titles and create an aristocracy? "Why then," he asked, "by a negative clause, restrain congress from doing what it would have no power to do? This clause, then, must have no meaning, or imply, that were it omitted, congress would have the power in question . . . on the principle that congress possess the powers not expressly reserved." Lee objected to leaving the rights of the people to "logical inferences," because the Framers' principles led to the implication that all the rights not mentioned in the Constitution were intended to be relinquished.[13]

Abroad, two wise Americans serving their country on diplomatic missions appraised the proposed Constitution without the obligation of having to support a party line. John Adams in London, having received a copy of the document, wrote to Thomas Jefferson, in Paris, to say that he thought the Constitution was admirably calculated to preserve the Union, and he hoped that it would be ratified with amendments. "What think you of a Declaration of Rights?" he asked. "Should not such a Thing have preceeded the Model?"[14] Jefferson agreed. In his first letter commenting on the proposed Constitution, he wrote Madison that he liked the Constitution but concluded by saying what he did not like about it: "First the omission of a bill of rights." After listing the rights he thought deserved special protection, starting with the freedoms of religion and of the press, Jefferson dismissed as campaign rhetoric Wilson's justification for the omission of a bill of rights, and Jefferson concluded: "Let me add that a bill of rights is what the people are entitled to against every government on earth, general or particular, and what no just government should refuse, or rest on inference."[15]

Madison, who had long opposed a bill of rights, finally changed his mind—mainly for political reasons, but also because he came to understand that a bill or rights would complete the Constitution. When, in the First Congress, he introduced the amendments that became the Bill of Rights, he explained that all power is subject to abuse, which should be guarded against by securing "the great rights of mankind." The government possessed only limited powers but it might misuse them. He sought to limit the powers of all branches of the government, unlike liberty documents in Great Britain which operated only against the executive and left the legislative branch unrestrained. The great objective was to prevent abuses of power by "the body of the people, operating by the majority against the minority." He still believed that "paper barriers" might fail, but they raised a standard that might educate the majority against acts to which they might be inclined.[16] Moreover, he declared, if his amendments were adopted, independent tribunals of justice will consider themselves in a peculiar manner the guardians of these rights; they will be an impenetrable bulwark against every assumption of power in the legislative or executive; they will be naturally led to resist every encroachment upon rights expressly stipulated for in the constitution by the declaration of rights.[17]

Off the record, in his private correspondence, Madison revealed other motives for his unyielding demand for amendments protecting personal liberties. He knew that the amendments, if adopted, would kill the movement for a second convention, sought by opponents of the Constitution for the purpose of crippling the powers of the national government. He believed that the adoption of his amendments would appease the fears of the common people and give them confidence in the new government. He meant, also, to isolate the opponents of the Constitution from their followers; the adoption of his amendments, he said, "will kill the opposition every where," and put an end to disaffection to the new government.[18] Madison's political judgment was right. The Bill of Rights fulfilled the Constitution as a matter of political theory, and it also had the healing effect that he predicted. The Framers had rectified their great blunder of omission.

Notes

1. Washington to Lafayette, April 28, 1788, quoted in Charles Warren, *The Making of the Constitution* 508 n.2 (Little Brown, 1928).
2. Merrill Jensen, ed., *The Documentary History of the Ratification of the Constitution, Volume 2: Ratification of the Constitution by the States Pennsylvania* 387 (State Historical Society of Wisconsin, 1976) *("Documentary History")*.
3. *Federalist 84* (Hamilton) in Jacob E. Cooke, ed., *The Federalist* 581 (Wesleyan U. Press, 1961).
4. Id. at 579.
5. Id.
6. Jensen, 2 *Documentary History* at 390 (cited in note 2).
7. Id. at 388.
8. Madison to Jefferson, Oct. 17, 1788, Robert Rutland, et. al., eds., 11 *The Papers of James Madison* 297 (U. Press of Virginia, 1979).
9. Jonathan Elliot, ed., 3 *The Debates in the Several State Conventions On the Adoption of the Federal Constitution* 191 (Lippincott, 2d ed. 1891) *("Debates")*.
10. Jensen, 2 *Documentary History* at 427 (cited in note 2).
11. Elliot, 3 *Debates* at 448 (cited in note 9).
12. Id. at 461.
13. *Letters from the Federal Farmer,* Herbert J. Storing, ed., 2 *The Complete Anti-Federalist* 326 (U. of Chi. Press, 1981). Lee's authorship is highly probable but not positive.

14. Adams to Jefferson, Nov. 10, 1787, Lester Cappon, ed., 1 *The Adams-Jefferson Letters* 210 (U. North Carolina Press, 1959).
15. Jefferson to Madison, Dec. 20, 1787, Julian P. Boyd, et. al., eds., 12 *The Papers of Thomas Jefferson* 440 (Princeton U. Press, 1950).
16. Madison's speech of June 8, 1789 is reprinted in Bernard Schwartz, ed., *2 The Bill of Rights: A Documentary History* 1023–34 (Chelsea House, 1971).
17. Id. at 1031.
18. Madison to Richard Peters, Aug. 19, 1789, Rutland, 12 *The Papers of James Madison* at 347 (cited in note 8).

2

Property As a Human Right

In 1976, on the Bicentennial anniversary of our founding document, the Declaration of Independence, which celebrated life, liberty, and the pursuit of happiness, the Supreme Court decided the case of *New Orleans v. Dukes.*[1] One might think that liberty and the pursuit of happiness include one's right to a livelihood, but no such right exists under the Constitution, according to *Dukes.* The Constitution does not mention a right to livelihood, but it does not mention a great many other rights that the Court has been ingenious enough to discover: a right to abortion; a right to pornography; a right to travel; a right to privacy; a right to association; a right to free counsel for indigents; a right to spread hatred; and a right of free speech for corporations. A Court that is so imaginative should be able to find the right to pursue a livelihood in the same Constitution. That right seems fundamental to liberty, and it should be accepted as a protected property right, too.

Consider the facts in *Dukes.* They involved a woman who sold hot dogs from a pushcart in the French Quarter. If Nancy Dukes had been a nude dancer in one of the strip joints in the French Quarter and the City Council had put her out of business, she might have pleaded freedom of expression under the first amendment.[2] Nude dancing can be symbolic free speech, but selling hot dogs is just commerce, and therefore subject to little constitutional respect, even if it involves one's livelihood.

Dukes had operated a licensed pushcart in the French Quarter for two years when the City Council banned all pushcarts except those operated by their owners for at least eight years. This ordinance put only Dukes out of business but allowed two others to operate. The

13

Fifth Circuit thought that the exclusion of Dukes denied her the equal protection of the laws but the Supreme Court unanimously reversed. In an unsigned opinion the Court said that the ordinance was "solely an economic regulation" designed for safeguarding the tourist charm of the French Quarter and thereby aiding the city's economy. The Court did not explain why a third pushcart would offend tourists or hurt the city's economy, but the point of its decision was that no such explanation is required when a mere economic right is at stake. "When local economic regulation is challenged solely as violating the Equal Protection Clause, this Court consistently defers to legislative determinations as to the desirability of particular statutory discriminations."[3] The government regulation need only have some rational basis as a means of achieving some police power end. If an economic right is involved, the Court never questions the reasonableness of the government's means. Economic rights, especially those of individuals, are inferior rights.

By contrast, if some regulation seems to threaten first amendment rights or any of the rights of the criminally accused, or any of the rights that the Court has invented, like the right to an abortion or to travel, the Court subjects the regulation to strict scrutiny, reverses the presumption of constitutionality, and places upon the defender of the regulation the obligation of proving its constitutionality. In *Dukes,* however, the Court said that it will "not sit as a superlegislature to judge the wisdom or desirability of legislative policy determinations made in areas that neither affect fundamental rights nor proceed along suspect lines." Only once in the past half century had the Court held unconstitutional an economic regulation as a denial of equal protection,[4] and in *Dukes* the Court overruled that precedent as a needlessly intrusive judicial infringement on the state's economic powers. In the same half century, not one state or local act of economic regulation was held unconstitutional based on a violation of due process of law. Like the corpse of John Randolph's mackerel, shining and stinking in the moonlight, economic due process of law, the old substantive due process, is dead even as to personal rights in property. The Court has abdicated the responsibility of judicial review in such cases, although it has not in any other Bill of Rights cases.[5]

The rational basis test, used only when property rights are concerned and never for other rights, is inadequate. After all, the text of the Constitution explicitly protects property rights, not only by the fifth and fourteenth amendments but also through the fourth and seventh amendments, as well as with the contract clause and other provisions of article I, section ten. Yet the states can impose regulations on the entry of citizens into all sorts of jobs, requiring licenses from those who wish to be barbers, plumbers, masons, morticians, beekeepers, lawyers, bartenders, taxidermists, doctors, to name a few. Those who judge their qualifications are members of the guild or occupation, who prefer to keep competition down as well as standards up. About the only people who are unlicensed in California are clergymen and university professors, apparently because no one takes them seriously.[6]

At one time, the Court did respect occupational rights. In 1914, the Court held unconstitutional a statute that prohibited anyone who had not been a brakeman from serving as a freight-train conductor. The act put many experienced conductors out of jobs. The ground of decision was the liberty of contract doctrine from the fourteenth amendment, a judicial invention derived from substantive due process. Denial of equal protection also bothered the Court. It observed that depriving a man of his *"right to labor"* lessened "his capacity to earn wages and acquire property." Liberty, the Court said, means that "the citizen shall be protected in the right to use his powers of mind and body in any lawful calling." All men are "entitled to the equal protection of the law in their *right to work* for the support of themselves and their families."[7] In a 1923 case the Court expansively declared that the liberty protected by the fourteenth amendment denoted "the right of an individual to contract, to engage in any of the common occupations of life, to acquire useful knowledge [the right to an education?], to marry, to worship God according to the dictates of his own conscience, and generally to enjoy the privileges long recognized . . . as essential to the pursuit of happiness by free men."[8] That recalls a concurring opinion in the second *Slaughter-house* case, when Justice Joseph Bradley said that the right "to follow any of the common occupations is an inalienable right; it was formulated as such under the phrase 'pursuit of happiness,' in the Declaration of Independence. . . . This right is a large ingredient in the civil liberty of the citizen."[9] That is what the constitutional law of the matter should be. Bradley spoke of the rights of people, not corporations.

The Declaration of Independence is a starting point for measuring the legacy that we inherited from the founders. Some scholars argue that Jefferson and the Continental Congress discarded the Lockean trinity when they spoke instead of life, liberty, and the pursuit of happiness as unalienable rights—"the pursuit of happiness, mind you, not property or estate," said Harry Jaffa, that preeminent scholar of the Declaration.[10] But Jefferson did not break with Locke. Jefferson knew Locke's ponderous *Essay on Human Understanding,* which used the exact phrase "pursuit of happiness." In a chapter on the 'Idea of Power," which is really about freedom, Locke used the phrase no less than four times and also used close equivalents several times. Locke wrote:[11]

> Thus, how much soever men are in earnest and constant *pursuit of happiness,* yet they may have a clear view of good, great and confessed good, without being concerned for it, or moved by it, if they think they can make up their happiness without it. . . .
> A constant determination to a *pursuit of happiness,* no abridgement of liberty. . . .
> As therefore the highest perfection of intellectual nature lies in a careful and constant pursuit of true and solid happiness; so the care of ourselves, that we mistake not imaginary for real happiness, is the necessary foundation of our liberty. The stronger ties we have to an unalterable *pursuit of happiness* in general, which is our greatest good . . . we are, by the necessity of preferring and pursuing true happiness as our greatest good, obliged to suspend the satisfaction of our desire in particular cases.
> But as soon as any new uneasiness comes in, this happiness is disturbed, and we are set afresh on work in the *pursuit of happiness.*

The pursuit of happiness was the linchpin in Locke's political ethics.

The phrase, as a matter of fact, was not uncommon in England before 1776. An anonymous author used it in 1703 in a book entitled *Civil Polity.* William Wollaston, a rationalist writer, used it, and so did Francis Hutcheson the Scottish jurist, Oliver Goldsmith the novelist, Richard Price the nonconformist Whig, and even the anti-American Tory, Dr. Samuel Johnson, who used it at least three times. David Hume expressed a similar thought.[12] William Blackstone used a close equivalent of "pursuit of happiness" in his *Commentaries* in 1765, when he said that God interwove the laws of eternal justice with the happiness of each individual and reduced the rule of obedience to one precept, "that man should pursue his own happiness. This is the foundation of what we call ethics, or natural law."[13]

Closer to home, Richard Bland of Virginia, whom Jefferson knew and all patriot leaders read, cited Wollaston's use of "pursuit of happiness" in his 1766 *Inquiry Into the Rights of the British Colonies.*[14] Jefferson owned a copy of Wollaston. James Wilson in his influential essay of 1774, which Jefferson admired, wrote that "[a]ll men are, by nature, equal and free. No one has a right to any authority over another without his consent. . . . Such consent was given with a view to increase the happiness of the governed. . . . The consequence is, that the happiness of the society is the first law of every government."[15] In the same year Josiah Quincy wrote that the purpose of government was to promote "the greatest happiness of the greatest number,"[16] a thought expressed also by John Adams in 1776.[17] The most significant precedent besides Locke was the Virginia Declaration of Rights, written by George Mason a month before the Declaration of Independence and stating "[t]hat all men are created equally free and independent, and have certain inherent natural rights of which they cannot, by any compact, deprive or divest their posterity; among which are the enjoyment of life and liberty, with the means of acquiring and possessing *property,* and pursuing and *obtaining* happiness and safety."[18] That formulation is in many state constitutions, including California's. It was, in exact words, the first amendment proposed by James Madison in 1789 for a national Bill of Rights.[19] Some scholars, including Henry Steele Commager, are so eager to show that Jefferson broke with Locke that when they quote Mason's Declaration, they omit the property clause by using ellipsis marks.[20]

Jefferson's phrasing was more concise and felicitous than Mason's, but Jefferson followed, rather than broke with, Locke in the "pursuit of happiness" phrasing. John Adams wrote that "there is not an idea" in the Declaration of Independence "but what had been hackneyed in Congress for two years before,"[21] and Jefferson himself conceded that he had not intended to "invent new ideas"[22] "but to place before mankind the common sense of the subject . . . it was intended to be an expression of the American mind."[23] And so it was, including the familiar expression, "pursuit of happiness." If it meant an abandonment of the rights of property, Congress would not have accepted it. But it derived from Locke, whom Jefferson followed faithfully.

Harry Jaffa says that life and liberty were valuable natural rights "because they culminated in the enjoyment and possession of property."[24] That seems mistaken for two reasons. First, the proposition seems backwards: property, in the sense that Professor Jaffa uses it, was a means of enjoying life and liberty. But one cannot push the point because liberty and property were viewed as so interdependent that there is no knowing which was seen as a precondition of the other. As a writer in the *Boston Gazette* said in 1768, "Liberty and Property are not only joined in common discourse, but are in their own natures so nearly ally'd that we cannot be said to possess the one without the other."[25] And second, Locke did not mean property in the conventional way that Professor Jaffa does, namely, as one's estate or possessions with a market value. By property Locke also meant what Jefferson called the "pursuit of happiness." Locke was not consistent: he sometimes did mean the ownership of material things, but other times he meant by property a right to *anything,* not just a right to *things;* he meant a right to rights. In his *Second Treatise,* when he wrote that the chief reason that men made compacts for governance "is the preservation of their property"—a remark some conservative scholars quote out of context[26]—Locke did not mean assets with a cash value. He said that men "united for the general preservation of their lives, liberties, and estates, which I call by the general name—property." And, he added, "by property I must be understood here as in other places to mean that property which men have in their persons as well as goods."[27]

At least four times in his *Second Treatise,* Locke used the word "property" to mean all that belongs to a person, especially the rights that he wished to preserve.[28] Americans of the founding generation understood property in this broad Lockean sense, which we have regrettably lost. They regarded property as a basic human right, essential to one's existence, to one's independence, to one's dignity as a person. Without property, real and personal, one could not enjoy life or liberty, and could not be free and independent. Only the property holder could make independent decisions and choices because he was not beholden to anyone; he had no need to be subservient. Americans cared about property not because they were materialistic but because they cared about political freedom and personal independence. They cherished property rights as prerequisites for the pursuit of happiness, and property opened up a world of intangible values—human dignity, self-regard, self-expression, and personal fulfillment.

Political democracy cannot function without job-holding, property-owning, masterless citizens. Every time that a bank forecloses on a family farm, every time that an honest, hardworking shopkeeper goes into bankruptcy, and every time that some aspiring, able person loses his or her livelihood because some state-approved occupational board denies a license, political democracy dies a little. Private property owned by individuals, not corporations, is the bulwark of a free society.

Why then did the Declaration of Independence not say "life, liberty and property"? Why substitute "pursuit of happiness" for "property"? Aside from Jefferson's sense of style, he had two substantive reasons. First, he meant property in its broadest sense and he wanted to avoid ambiguity. Second, he was listing "unalienable" rights, and he did not believe in the unalienability of possessions, or property as estate. It was a natural right; it was indispensable; but it was not unalienable. Locke was no more a spokesman for corporate capitalism than he was for collectivism. He believed, and Jefferson agreed, that property had limits. When he spoke of a person gathering acorns or apples, and by his labor earning an entitlement to property, he was speaking of the state of nature, not of civil society.

Locke had little to say about property in civil society. When he concluded his chapter on property by referring to the emergence of money in civil society and to the legitimacy of heaping up money, he stated that communities regulated private property in civil society. "For in Governments," he wrote, "the Laws regulate the right to property, and the possession of land is determined by positive constitutions."[29] In a state of nature, property could not be bequeathed. The point is that property is a creature of civil society. Leo Strauss rejected that point, yet he acknowledged Locke's belief that "once civil society is formed, if not before, the natural law regarding property ceases to be valid; what we may call 'conventional' or 'civil' property—the property which is owned within civil society—is based on positive law alone."[30] But to acknowledge that Locke endorsed the right to accumulate as much property as possible in any way "permitted by the positive law" is to acknowledge that property is alienable.[31] Even in a state of nature, property rights had limits: a man had no right to own more than he could cultivate and consume, certainly not at the expense of others.

Whether or not Locke believed that property was alienable in civil society, Jefferson surely believed that property was the product of civil society and was alienable. In his *Tract on Property*, Lord Kames thought so, and Jefferson approvingly copied Kames in his *Common-Place Book*. Thomas Paine thought property was a civil right that could be regulated for the common good, and Jefferson agreed.[32] As he once said, ownership "is the gift of social law, and is given late in the progress of society," a reminder that we should not take literally Locke's social compact theory.[33] Jefferson did not believe in the theory that ownership derives from natural law and that government could not create and regulate it. Witness his successful assault on primogeniture and entail.

This view of property as a human right is the theme of a remarkable paper by the father of the Constitution and of the Bill of Rights, James Madison. In 1792 he wrote his essay on *Property*. In Lockean terms he described what he called the "larger and juster meaning" of the term "property." It "embraces," he said, "every thing to which a man may attach a value and have a right." In the narrow sense, it meant one's land, merchandise, or money; in the broader sense "a man has property in his opinions and the free communication of them. He has a property of peculiar value in his religious opinions, and in the profession and practices dictated by them. He has an equal property in the free use of his faculties and free choice of the objects on which to employ them. In a word, as a man is said to have a right to his property, he may be equally said to have a property in his rights."[34]

When agrarian capitalism predominated, the United States could easily celebrate property as Jefferson and Madison understood the term because most people were or meant to become independent freehold farmers who thought that they controlled their destiny. When industrial and financial capitalism became the governing institutions and the corporation became their major form, the meaning of "property" reverted to its cash nexus. The narrow, surviving meaning was the one that the Supreme Court adopted from the beginning. In 1795, Justice William Paterson, one of the framers, proclaimed the judicial power to hold unconstitutional any legislative act repugnant to the Constitution. In the case before him, *Van Horne's Lessee v. Dorrance,* he described the right to acquire and hold property, real or personal, as an unalienable as well as a natural right, the primary object of the social compact. He held that the power of government to take property when state necessity requires was "despotic." He censured the government's seizure of the land of one citizen, even for just compensation, to give it to others. It was immaterial to the government, he said, in which of its citizens land was vested; once vested, however, it was inviolable. "The Constitution encircles, and renders it an holy thing. . . . It is sacred."[35]

Within about a century a property-minded judiciary had run amok, inventing judicial doctrines to protect corporate interests from public regulation. Brooks Adams had good reason to say, in a 1913 book, that "[t]he Capitalist . . . regards the constitutional form of government which exists in the United States as a convenient method of obtaining his own way against a majority. . . . "[36] For a time the Court incorporated the contract clause, which was originally a limitation on the states only, into the due process clause of the fifth amendment. As a result, Congress had no constitutional power to require a corporation, to which the United States had lent money, to set aside a fund to repay its debt to the government.[37] The Court also incorporated the eminent domain or takings clause of the fifth amendment into the fourteenth, so that state regulatory commissions could not fix rates that significantly reduced corporate profits.[38] The Court dictated to administrative tribunals, state and federal, how to fix rates using absurd economic formulae. The Court invented the liberty of contract doctrine as a means of securing capital against state interferences with employer-employee relationships, and it struck down minimum wage and maximum hours laws as unconstitutional.[39]

By 1936 a conservative Court had created a twilight zone within which government power did not exist; neither states nor federal government could constitutionally enact regulatory measures to combat the Great Depression. Congress could not use the commerce power to regulate labor standards and labor relations because they were local matters falling within state jurisdiction. On the other hand, the states could not regulate those matters without violating the Court's liberty of contract doctrine.[40] The Court shaped constitutional law so that employers were free to exploit workers in accord with so-called laws of supply and demand and free competition, laws that never prevailed if they hobbled entrepreneurial profits.

The Court had discredited itself by its excesses and biases. Franklin Roosevelt blundered by attempting to pack the Court by statute, but his assault on the Court prompted the scales to drop from the eyes of Justice Owen Roberts. He simply changed his mind—the switch in time that saved nine. As a result, without a single change on the membership of the Court, a constitutional revolution was underway, and the rational basis test emerged as the dominating feature of constitutional law in any case involving economic regulation.[41]

Judicial irresponsibility had led to judicial abdication. Not even the most conservative Justices on today's Supreme Court question the constitutionality of government control of the economy. There are no longer any limits on the commerce power of Congress.[42] Whether we have a government-managed economy or even a socialist state is a question of *policy* to be decided by the voters at the polls; it is no longer a question of constitutional limitations. There are none in the economic realm. The government can take apart even the greatest corporations, like Ma Bell; if it does not proceed against General Dynamics or other giants, the reason is to be found in national defense needs and in politics, not in the Constitution. The states are supplicants before the United States government, beneficiaries of its largesse like so many welfare recipients, unable to control their own policies, serving instead as administrative agencies of federal policies.

Those federal policies extend to realms not remotely within the federal power to govern under the Constitution, except for the fact that the spending power, so-called, the power to spend for national defense and general welfare can be exercised through programs of grants-in-aid to states and to over 75,000 substate governmental entities; they take federal tax money and obediently enforce the conditions laid down by Congress and by federal agencies for control of the expenditures. Federalism as we knew it has been replaced by a new federalism that even conservative Republican administrations enforce.[43] The government today makes the New Deal look like a backer of Adam Smith's legendary free enterprise and a respecter of John C. Calhoun's state sovereignty.

Even conservative Justices accept the new order of things. Justice William Rehnquist spoke for the Court in *PruneYard,* and Justice Sandra Day O'Connor spoke in *Hawaii Housing Authority;* the Court was unanimous in both. In the first of these cases, decided in 1980, the Court held that a state may require a shopping center owner to allow solicitation of petition signatures on his premises. Rehnquist saw a reasonable police power regulation of private property and reminded us that the public right to regulate the use of property is as fundamental as the right to property itself.[44] One might have thought that as a matter of constitutional theory, the property right was fundamental and that the regulatory power was an exception to it that had to be justified. Rehnquist did not explain why the regulation was justifiable or reasonable; under the rational basis test the Court has no obligation to explain anything. It only need believe that the legislature had some reason for its regulation.

In *Hawaiian Housing Authority,* the Court unanimously held that the state could do the very thing that Justice Paterson had said it could not do—take property from one citizen, even at a just compensation, and give it to another at that price.[45] Land ownership in Hawaii was concentrated in a few people; to break the oligopoly of ownership the state fixed on a scheme whereby it took private property by eminent domain, lent tenants up to 90% of the purchase price, and arranged for transfer of titles. But the Constitution states that property may be taken at a just price only for a public use. Anyone who thinks that means an arsenal, a courthouse, a school, or a fire station is as naive as Justice Paterson.

Justice O'Connor identified a public use with a public purpose, equating the power of eminent domain with the police power. She proclaimed the need for judicial deference to legislatures, because legislatures are better able than courts to assess what public purposes should be promoted by eminent domain. Certainly an appropriation or taking of property for a public use may have a public purpose, like satisfying the need for an airfield or for a public dump, but vesting the title of land in private parties does not constitute a public purpose or a public use. The public use requirement, O'Connor said, is "coterminous with the scope of the sovereign's police powers." This case teaches that wherever an oligopoly exists, whether in the making of automobiles or disposable diapers, the voters can decide to transfer ownership to the workers in the industry by taking the property, selling it to the employees, and financing the loan they need to make the purchase.

On the Court's side is the fact that it made no new law in the 1984 case. The pre-Civil War history of eminent domain shows that the power was used to take property for railroads and other so-called public works or public utilities, which were privately owned.[46] But those companies were subject to rate regulation and government controls, from which other private property was exempt. Also on the Court's side is the fact that nothing was new in its equating the police power with the power of eminent domain. That foolishness had been going on since at least 1897. Whenever the Court used its own subjective standards and found that some regulation was excessive, it condemned the regulation as a taking.[47] In a case that shows how the Court abused its power for the benefit of utilities, it held that a schedule of rates that permitted the company to earn a profit of 6.26 percent was unconstitutional. The Court held that rates returning "7.5 percent, or even 8 percent" would be "necessary to avoid confiscation."[48] In these old cases, however, the Court held that the rate regulations were unconstitutional, amounting to an excessive use of the police power, rather than a violation of the eminent domain clause, which would have required compensation for confiscation or a taking.

Regulations designed to promote the public health, safety, morals, or interests should not necessarily be regarded as takings even if the regulation is excessive, so long as the government does not appropriate the property or make any use of it, and it remains in the possession of the owner, whose title has not been transferred or damaged. The fact remains, however, that the Court has long regarded excessive regulation as a taking. The striking difference between the early cases and the 1984 one is that the Court had invented its doctrine that an excessive regulation is a taking in order to protect rights of owners, whereas the Court in 1984 used the same doctrine against owners and in favor of the police power.

A Lockean liberal can accept the 1984 decision because it advanced the cause of individual ownership. What puzzles me is the failure of conservatives, on and off the Court, to criticize an opinion that is so hostile to property and that distorts the plain meaning of the constitutional text, which speaks of taking for a public "use," not for a public purpose. After all, conservatives supposedly cherish both the text and a jurisprudence of original intent.

We have arrived at a peculiar constitutional stance after two hundred years. Once we believed with John Dickinson and the founders that a free government is not one which exercises its powers reasonably but one that is so constitutionally checked that it *must* exercise its powers reasonably.[49]

Once, Jefferson and Madison, in connection with the bill to charter the Bank of the United States, had argued that if the power to spend were construed as independent of the enumerated powers, we should have a government of virtually unlimited powers. Hamilton did not argue the point on that occasion but did so later.[50] In 1935 Justice Owen Roberts for the reactionary majority of the Court, accepted Hamilton's argument on the power to spend, and in 1937 the liberals also embraced Hamilton.[51] There are no constitutional limits on the spending power today, and no power has more radically transformed American federalism.

Property rights have fallen from judicial grace, but not all property rights, because some are more equal than others. Corporate property is more equal than individual property. Purely private property is more equal than property affected by a public interest—a discredited term. Property deriving from fee simple or outright ownership is more equal than property deriving from statutory entitlement. Purely private property is more equal than private property publicly employed. Consider the case of the privately owned, powerful newspaper, the *Miami Herald,* which disparaged a person in print. The paper had a constitutional right to freedom of the press and no obligation to provide free space in its pages to its victim.[52] But when a small radio station, also privately owned, disparaged a person, its first amendment rights did not prevail and it had no obligation to provide equal time to its victim, apparently because the public owns the airwaves; the public does not own the *Miami Herald,* but neither does it own that radio station.[53]

Consider too the case of the welfare recipient whose home could be searched without a warrant and without probable cause if an administrative official decided to invade the premises to determine whether a welfare-assisted child was receiving proper care; refusal to admit a state official results in forfeiture of the entitlement.[54] The fact that the welfare recipient received government handouts should not make her property any less private than that of a farmer or a business receiving government subsidies. Nothing but a double standard explains the state of our constitutional law. The fourth amendment applied, as it should have, when an agent of the Secretary of Labor attempted to make a warrantless search of the property of a corporation in order to determine whether it was complying with standards of safety required by federal law. The Court held unconstitutional a provision of Congress's Occupational Safety and Health Act insofar as it authorized inspections without a warrant. The Court failed to explain why the welfare recipient's home was not entitled to the same protection against government intrusion as the business enterprise. The cases show that one must own property to enjoy rights, and, it seems, the more property one has, especially in corporate form, the more rights it buys. Constitutional law loves fictions, so it makes believe that the principle of equality has not been offended. For example, we can spend all we want to advertise or promote our views, and so can a corporation; the only difference is that we spend our own money and can reach few people, while the great corporations spend corporate monies in their exercise of their first amendment rights and can reach the nation.[55]

One who owns the right kind of property is freer than one who owns property but not the right kind. One who owns any kind of property is freer than one who owns none or very little. Property today, like 200 years ago, remains necessary for political liberty and individual independence. The Court made a mistake fifty years ago: it should not have employed the rational basis test in cases of economic regulation involving property as a human right. The Court should learn to distinguish the rights of people from the rights of business enterprises. Strict judicial scrutiny is called for when personal rights of property are at issue. Congress, for example, can regulate major league baseball if it wishes, but if it touches the free agency clause, crimping the right of the players to make top dollar, the Court should apply the same standard as it would in a first amendment case. Making a living is fundamental to one's personhood and stake in society. Free speech is of little value to a propertyless person. With the exception of freedom of religion, nothing is more important than work and a chance at a career or a decent living.

Every now and then we get some little case that shows astonishing perception, even if it is promptly forgotten. *Lynch v. Household Finance Corporation* in 1972 was such a case. A woman's savings account was garnished under state law for alleged nonpayment of a loan. She received no notice, no chance to be heard, obviously a denial of due process. She sued in federal district court but the court dismissed her suit, ruling that only personal rights merited a judicial hearing, not property rights. The Supreme Court, dividing 4–3, reversed the district court. Justice Potter Stewart for the liberal plurality (Douglas, Brennan, and Marshall), made this rare and wise observation:

> [T]he dichotomy between personal liberties and property rights is a false one. Property does not have rights. People have rights. The right to enjoy property without unlawful deprivation, no less than the right to speak or the right to travel, is in truth a "personal" right, whether the "property" in question be a welfare check, a home, or a savings account. In fact, a fundamental interdependence exists between the personal right to liberty and the personal right in property. Neither could have meaning without the other.[56]

Citing Locke, John Adams, and Blackstone's *Commentaries,* Stewart added: "That rights in property are basic civil rights has long been recognized."[57] If that were true, we would not have the double standard: strict scrutiny for all rights but property, a rational basis test for property.

No principled reason exists for the Court's refusal to ask whether a statute curtailing personal rights in property is in fact a significant means of achieving a legitimate police power objective, and whether it achieves that objective without unnecessarily burdening private rights. There is no legitimate basis for perfunctory scrutiny in such cases. Property owned by people should be accorded the same constitutional respect that courts give to other civil or human rights so essential to the pursuit of happiness.[58]

Notes

1. 427 U.S. 297 (1976).
2. *Schad v. Borough of Mt. Ephraim*, 452 U.S. 61 (1981); *see also Young v. America Mini Theatres, Inc.*, 427 U.S. 50, 62 (1976).
3. *Dukes*, 427 U.S. at 303.
4. *Morey v. Doud*, 354 U.S. 457 (1957).
5. Another little case in the festive year of 1976 again illustrates. By a 7–1 vote the Court held that a state statute compelling the retirement of uniformed police officers at the age of fifty did not deny the equal protection of the law. The officer who sued to be reinstated to active duty had just passed a rigorous physical examination, and the doctors had pronounced him to be in excellent physical and mental health. The Court, believing that fact to be irrelevant, held that its test of strictly scrutinizing a regulation applied only if a fundamental right was violated or if a suspect class was disadvantaged. The Court did not regard the right to work as a fundamental right, certainly not for a fifty-year-old cop if a legislature thought otherwise, regardless of individual differences. And that ended it. Justice Thurgood Marshall, dissenting, thought that the right to work ought not to be looked at in the same way that the Court looks at a mere economic regulation. *Massachusetts Retirement Board v. Murgia*, 427 U.S. 307 (1976).
6. Gellhorn, *The Abuse of Occupational Licensing*, 44 U. Chi. L. Rev. 6,6 n.2 (1976).
7. *Smith v. Texas*, 233 U.S. 630, 636, 641 (1914) (emphasis added).
8. *Meyer v. Nebraska*, 262 U.S. 390, 399 (1923).
9. *Butchers' Union Co. v. Crescent City Co.*, 111 U.S. 746, 762 (1884). *See also* Slaughter-House Cases, 83 U.S. (16 Wall.) 36, 109 (1873) (per Field, for four dissenters).
10. *Another Look at the Declaration*, Nat'l Rev., July 11, 1980, at 840.
11. 1 J. Locke, An Essay Concerning Human Understanding, 342, 345, 348, 355 (A. Fraser ed. 1894) (emphasis added); *see also* 2 *id.* at ch. XXI. Equivalents include "pursuit of our happiness," "pursuing happiness," "pursuit of true happiness," and "pursue happiness."
12. For the principal research tracing the pre-1776 uses of "pursuit of happiness," see Gantner, *Jefferson's 'Pursuit of Happiness' and Some Forgotten Men*, 16 Wm. & Mary Q. 558 (2d ser. 1936)."
13. 1 W. Blackstone, Commentaries on the Laws of England 40–41 (1765).
14. R Bland, Inquiry Into the Rights of the British Colonies 8–9 (E. Swem rev. ed. 1922).
15. Wilson, *Considerations on the Nature and Extent of the Legislative Authority of Parliament*, in 2 The Works of James Wilson 723 (R. McCloskey ed. 1967).

16. J. Quincy, Memoir of the Life of Josiah Quincy, Jr. 323 (1874) (quoting Observations on the Act of Parliament (1774)).

17. Adams, *Thoughts on Government,* in 4 Works 193 (C Adams ed. 1850–59).

18. 7 The Federal and State Constitutions, Colonial Chapters, and Other Organic Laws 3812 (F. Thorpe ed 1909).

19. 1 The Debates and Proceedings of the Congress of the United States 433 (June 8, 1789) (J. Gales & W. Seaton eds. 1834).

20. Commager, *The Pursuit of Happiness,* 49 Diogenes, 40, 53 (Spring 1965); Schaar, . . . *And the Pursuit of Happiness,* 46 Va. Q. Rev. 1, 5 (1970).

21. Letter from John Adams to Timothy Pickering (August 22, 1822), *reprinted in* 2 Works, *supra* note 17, at 512.

22. Letter from Thomas Jefferson to James Madison (August 30, 1823), *reprinted in* 15 The Writings of Thomas Jefferson 461–62 (A. Bergh ed. 1907) [hereinafter Writings of Jefferson].

23. Letter from Thomas Jefferson to Henry Lee (May 8, 1825), *reprinted in* 16 Writings of Jefferson, *supra* note 22, at 118–19.

24. H. Jaffa, How To Think about the American Revolution 44 (1978).

25. Boston Gazette, Feb. 2, 1768, *quoted in* C. Rossiter, Seedtime of the Republic 379 (1953).

26. *Charles R. Kessler,* in H. Jaffa, American Conservatism and the American Founding 7 (1984); L. Strauss, National Right and History 234, 245 (1935).

27. J. Locke, Two Treatises of Government §§ 123, 173 (P. Laslett rev. ed 1963) (3d ed 1698); *see also id* at § 87 11.5–6 and accompanying notes.

28. *Id* at §§ 27, 87, 123, 173.

29. J. Locke, *supra* note 27, at § 50.

30. L Strauss, *supra* note 26, at 235.

31. *Id.* at 241.

32. G. Chinard, The Common-Place Book of Thomas Jefferson 107 (1926); G. Chinard, Thomas Jefferson: Apostle of Americanism 80–83 (2d ed 1939).

33. Letter from Thomas Jefferson to Isaac McPherson (Aug. 13, 1813), *reprinted in* 13 Writings of Jefferson, *supra* note 22, at 333.

34. National Gazette (Philadelphia), March 29, 1792, *reprinted in* 14 The Papers of James Madison 266 (C. Hobson, R Rutland & W. Rachal eds. 1986).

35. 2 U.S. (2 Dall.) 304, 311 (1795).

36. B. Adams, The Theory of Social Revolution 214 (1914).

37. *In re* Sinking Fund Cases, 99 U.S. 700, 718–19 (1878); *Hepburn v. Griswold,* 75 U.S. (8 Wall.) 603, 623–24 (1869).

38. *Chicago, Burlington, and Quincy R R. v Chicago,* 166 U.S. 226 (1897).

39. S. Fine, Laissez Faire and the General Welfare State ch. 5 (1956); R. Hale, Freedom Through Law: Public Control of Private Governing Power (1952); C. Jacobs, Law Writers and the Courts (1954); A. Paul, Conservative Crisis and the Rule of Law (1960); B. Twiss, Lawyers and the Constitution: How Laissez Faire Came to the Supreme Court (1942).

40. *Carter v. Carter Coal Co.,* 298 U.S. 238 (1936); *Morehead v. New York ex rel.* Tipaldo, 298 U.S. 587 (1936); *Adkins v. Children's Hospital,* 261 U.S. 525 (1923).

41. *United States v. Carolene Products Co.,* 304 U.S. 144, 152 n.4 (1938); *West Coast Hotel v. Parrish,* 300 U.S. 379 (1937); Stern, *The Problems of Yesteryear—Commerce and Due Process,* 4 Vand L. Rev. 446 (1951).

42. Stern, *The Commerce Clause Revisited—The Federalization of Intrastate Crime,* 15 Ariz. L. Rev. 271 (1973).

43. A. Howitt, Managing Federalism: Studies in Intergovernmental Relations (1984); M. Reagan, The New Federalism (2d ed. 1981); D. Walker, Toward a Functioning Federalism (1981). The generalizations are mine; the works cited here supply the facts.

44. *PruneYard Shopping Center v. Robins*, 447 U.S. 74 (1980).

45. *Hawaiian Housing Authority v. Midkiff*, 467 U.S. 229 (1984).

46. Levy, *Chief Justice Shaw and the Formative Period of American Railroad Law* (pts. 1–2), 51 Colum. L. Rev. 327, 852 (1951). Part I of the article deals with eminent domain; Part II deals with railroads as common carriers or public works.

47. *Smyth v. Ames*, 169 U.S. 466 (1898); Chicago, *B&Q. R.R. v. Chicago*, 166 U.S. 226, 239 (1897). In *Pennsylvania Coal Co. v. Mahon*, 260 U.S. 393 (1922), Justice Holmes for the Court said, "The general rule at least is that while property may be regulated to a certain extent, if regulation goes too far it will be recognized as a taking." *Id.* at 415. *See also Berman v. Parker*, 348 U.S. 26 (1954), a direct precedent for sustaining an act that takes property from *A* and sells it to *B*. On the general subject, see R. Epstein, Takings: Private Property and the Power of Eminent Domain (1985); Dunham, *Griggs v. Allegheny County in Perspective: Thirty Years of Supreme Court Expropriation Law,* 1962 Sup. Ct. Rev. 63; Sax, *Takings, Private Property and Public Rights* (pts. 1&2), 74 Yale L.J. 36 (1964), 81 Yale L.J. 149 (1971); Stoebuck, *Police Power, Takings, and Due Process,* 37 Wash. & Lee L. Rev. 1057 (1980).

48. *United Rys. and Elec. Co. v. West*, 280 U.S. 234 (1930).

49. Dickinson, *Letters from a Farmer in Pennsylvania,* in 1 Writings of John Dickinson 356 (P. Ford ed. 1895) (1st ed 1768) (Letter VII in Vol. XIV of Memoirs of the Historical Society of Pennsylvania).

50. 3 Writings of Jefferson, *supra* note 22, at 147–48; I. Brant, James Madison: Father of the Constitution, 1787–1800, at 324 (1950); 10 The Papers of Alexander Hamilton 302–04 (H. Syrett ed. 1961).

51. *United States v. Gerlach Livestock Co.,* 339 U.S. 725, 738 (1950); *Helvering v. Davis*, 301 U.S. 619, 640 (1937); *United States v. Butler*, 297 U.S. 1, 65–66 (1936). *See supra* note 43 and accompanying text.

52. *Miami Herald Publishing Co. v. Tornillo*, 418 U.S. 241 (1974).

53. *Red Lion Broadcasting Co. v. FCC*, 395 U.S. 367 (1969).

54. *Wyman v. James*, 400 U.S. 309 (1971).

55. *First National Bank of Boston v. Bellotti*, 435 U.S. 765 (1978).

56. 405 U.S. 538, 552 (1972).

57. *Id.*

58. In preparing this paper, I found the following works stimulating: B. Ackerman, Private Property and the Constitution (1977); G. Dietze, In Defense of Property (1971); R Schlatter, Private Property: The History of an Idea (1951); B. Siegan, Economic Liberties and the Court (1980); McCloskey, *Economic Due Process and the Supreme Court,* 1962 Sup. Ct. Rev. 34, Monaghan, *Of 'Liberty' and 'Property,'* 62 Cornell L. Rev., 405 (1977); Oakes, *Property Rights in Constitutional Analysis Today,* 56 Wash. L. Rev. 583 (1981); Van Alstyne, *Cracks in the 'New Property',* 62 Cornell L. Rev. 445 (1977), and *The Recrudescence of Property Rights As the Foremost Principle of Court Liberties: The First Decade of the Burger Court,* 43 Law & Contemp. Probs. 66 (1980).

3

The Right Is Wrong on Rights

In 1987 the Senate rejected the nomination of Robert Bork by the largest vote in history against a nominee for the Supreme Court, although he was preeminently qualified. His constitutional opinions, which accounted for the nomination, brought his defeat. Bork provoked intense opposition because he was perceived as a conservative judicial activist who had made himself a symbol of opposition to liberal activism. He remains the nation's foremost theoretician of a constitutional jurisprudence of originalism or original meaning: "All that counts is how the words used in the Constitution would have been understood at the time" the Constitution was ratified (p. 144).

This book solidifies Bork's position as an intellectual role-model for scores of federal judges appointed by President Reagan. The book also elaborately defends Bork's views and explains his defeat by "left-liberal" pressure groups that, he alleges, politicized the judicial process. The title of the book, *The Tempting of America*, refers to "the temptation of results without regard to democratic legitimacy" (p. 2).

In his first section, Bork selectively surveys the history of judicial activism. He depicts an increasing politicization and leftward movement of the Court from liberty-oriented doctrines to equality-oriented ones. Judicial activism began with the first decision on constitutional law. It reached an ugly climax in the years following the Civil War, when the Court savaged congressional civil rights laws and betrayed the Fourteenth Amendment's promise of equal citizenship. Bork omits this bleak chapter of our judicial history, conserving his space to lambast the Warren Court for its activism in the cause of equality.

In the middle part of the book, Bork criticizes theorists, left and right, who support judicial activism—that is, deciding on a basis other than Bork's concept of original understanding or intent. Finally, he narrates the story of his own conformation ordeal. He places the rejection of his nomination in the context of a "war" for control of the legal culture and even for America's soul. The book will confirm the beliefs of Bork's liberal opponents and conservative supporters. Unfortunately, Bork, who inhabits a Manichaean universe, does not address himself to moderates who endorse judicial restraint without embracing his brand of originalism.

Bork claims that "liberal elites" seek to destroy the idea of the rule of law and make the philosophy of originalism a disqualification for judicial office. That claim conflicts with the confirmation of William Rehnquist as chief justice and the unanimous conformations of Antonin Scalia and Anthony Kennedy, who share many of Bork's views. Moreover, Bork initially had the support of moderates and some liberals. When Senator Edward Kennedy demagogically distorted Bork's record to inspire a fear of him, I wrote to congratulate Bork on his nomination and to wish him well. I thought he should be judged on the basis of his judicial record and believed that his opinions would not be predictable.

Before the final vote on Bork's nomination, however, several studies of his opinions strongly indicated a systematic hostility to feminists, blacks, gays, and labor. Bork angrily disputes these accusations. He takes none of the blame for his defeat, alleging that the hearings, including his five days of testimony, changed "no one's mind." In fact he lost several initially indecisive senators including Southern Democrats and members of his own party. He waffled on numerous issues, causing some to declare that they did not understand him and others to speak of his "confirmation conversion."

I had occasion to write to Bork again in mid-1989. Having heard about his book-in-progress, I advised that he should connect his judicial philosophy with the classic tradition of judicial self-restraint associated with James Bradley Thayer, Oliver Wendell Holmes, Louis Brandeis, and Felix Frankfurter. I thought he should show that judicial self-restraint was the overwhelmingly dominant view of liberals for the first half of this century. Henry S. Commager's *Majority Rule and Minority Rights* (1943) pretty well summed up that viewpoint. It was, I wrote:

a principled viewpoint but I would suppose that it became popular among liberals as a way of protesting judicial activism of the conservative sort, the only sort known in our judicial history until the Warren Court. When liberal activism developed, most liberals began to modify their views, as did Commanger. I remember warning him that endorsing activism was wrong as a matter of proper judicial philosophy and as a matter of political strategy. Someday, I warned, the conservatives would regain control of the Supreme Court and write decisions that liberals would deplore. Conservatives today, for the most part, say they oppose judicial activism. My colleague Harry Jaffa believes that a time may come when the government may limit the size of families, require abortions, and encourage euthanasia. He warns his fellow conservatives not to oppose judicial activism or the reading of natural rights into the Ninth Amendment, for both will be needed in the future. He and I disagree; I prefer judicial self-restraint. I think that your view of the matter took a wrong step when seeking to graft originalism onto that view [of judicial self-restraint].

Bork declined the advice, and his book, I think, is the worse for it by making originalism the only correct basis for decision. Originalism has the merit of giving the impression that the faith and opinions of the founding fathers are the basis of decision, rather than judicial subjectivity. The trouble with constitutional camouflage, however, is that its wearer may think his personal views are invisible, even that a reference to *The Federalist* or to Joseph Story's *Commentaries on the Constitution* (1833) makes his own views objective.

Bork is big on objectivity. He dismisses my book, *Original Intent and the Framers' Constitution* (1988), because I argued that the opinions of the Framers were subjective and because I demolished a view that no moderately sophisticated originalist holds. In fact, I give Bork more space and serious consideration than any other originalist; he refers to none of my arguments against his views nor does he answer them. The unsophisticated originalism that Bork claims is my target is, he says, "the subjective intent of the Framers" rather than "the objective meaning that constitutional language had when it was adopted" (p. 218). Bork finds that meaning in the public understanding in 1789 of the words used in the Constitution; that understanding, he states, can be ascertained by examining convention debates, public discussions, and newspapers. The great bulk of my book, unlike Bork's, is based on such sources. I do not know, though, why ratifier opinion or public opinion is more objective than the opinion of the Framers. Bork declares that "what the ratifiers understood themselves to be enacting must be taken to be what the public of that time would have understood the words to mean" (p. 144). True enough, but their understanding, when not elusive, doesn't determine the outcome of real cases, and in cases of doubt, the text they ratified, not their understanding of what it meant, matters most.

Story, whom Bork selectively uses, made the definitive rejection of ratifier intent in a passage unknown to Bork or ignored by him. Said Story in his *Commentaries*:[1]

> In different states and in different conventions, different and very opposite objections are known to have prevailed; and might well be presumed to prevail. Opposite interpretations, and different explanations of different provisions, may well be presumed to have been presented in different bodies, to remove local objections, or to win local favor. And there can be no certainty, either that the different state conventions in ratifying the constitution, gave the same uniform interpretation to its language, or that, even in a single state convention, the same reasoning prevailed with a majority, much less with the whole of the supporters of it. [I: 388–89]

Story continued by observing that the terms of a document may have differently impressed different people. Some drew conclusions that others repudiated. Some thought about it cursorily and others profoundly. Some may have understood its terms too strictly, others too broadly. Story added that not even the members of the Philadelphia Convention understood the Constitution in the same way. "Every member," he wrote, "necessarily judged for himself" (p. 389). And in the state conventions, the well-known "diversity of construction" given by different people "in different conventions" required an emphasis on the point that no such thing as a unified "Framer" or ratifier intent existed. The result is that we must always bear foremost in mind a crucial fact: "Nothing but the text itself was adopted by the whole people" (p. 384).

In response to the argument by Jefferson that we should conform as much as possible to ratifier intent, Story retorted:

> Now, who does not see the utter looseness, and incoherence of this canon. How are we to know, what was thought of particular clauses of the constitution at the time of its adoption? In many cases no printed debates give any account of any construction; and where any is given, different people held different doctrines. Whose is to prevail? Besides; of all the state conventions, the debates of five only are preserved, and these very imperfectly. What is to be done, as to the other eight states? . . . What is to be done, as to the eleven new states, which have come into the Union under constructions, which have been established, against what some persons may deem the meaning of the framers of it? [I: 390–91]

Story also raised the question whether the views of the authors of

The Federalist are to be followed—and they conflicted with each other and also changed their minds—or the differing views by others expressed at the time. If we are also to consider the opinions of the voters, as well the Framers, he asked, "can we know those opinions?" And how are we to gather what Jefferson called the "probable meaning" of statesmen and others who left conjectures from scattered documents, private papers, and table talk? And when probable meanings turn out to be understood differently by different people, "what interpretation is to be followed? These, and many questions of the same sort, might be asked. "It is obvious," Story concluded, again, "that there can be no security to the people in any constitution of government, if they are not to judge of it by the fair meaning of the words of the text . . . " (I:391). Yet, when Bork speaks of originalism as the only correct basis of judicial decision, he means ratifier intent, and he thinks Story is an authority for it.

Bork persistently uses his sources in a selective way, oversimplifying, misrepresenting, and contradicting himself. He is both for and against judicial tests of reasonableness. He claims to favor original understanding but nowhere criticizes opinions that depart from it if he does not object to them, as in cases involving executive agreements, nonunanimous juries, verdicts by juries of less than twelve members, immunity grants that compel one to be a witness against oneself, exceptions to the warrant requirement of the Fourth Amendment, and cases involving departures form the word "all" in the Sixth Amendment. As a matter of fact, Bork seems not to oppose judicial activism when matters on the conservative agenda are at issue, and he takes for granted that judicial review is a constitutional power.

Consider the following statement on the interpretation of the Constitution:

> . . . it must be construed now as it was understood at the time of its adoption. It is not only the same in words, but the same in meaning . . . and as long as it continues to exist in its present form, it speaks not only in the same words, but with the same meaning and intent with which it spoke when it came from the hands of its framers, and was voted on and adopted by the people of the United States. Any other rule of construction would abrogate the judicial character of this court, and make it the mere reflex of the popular opinion or passion of the day. This court was not created by the Constitution for such purposes.

Those words, a classic statement of judicial originalism, are Roger Taney's in *Dred Scott,* an opinion pronounced by Bork to be the worst before *Roe v. Wade.* He seems not to know that *Dred Scott* is an unri-valed specimen of the judicial philosophy that he espouses. He dis-cusses Taney's opinion only in terms of substantive due process of law (which Bork claims to hate), a matter occupying only a couple of lines in a fifty-five page opinion; and, in fact, only three Justices passingly relied on substantive due process. Far more significant is a matter that Bork ignores: the Court's reliance on a theory of dual citizenship, state and national, as a basis for denying that Scott could maintain a diversity of citizenship suit in a United States court; he could not because under the law of the state in which he resided he was a slave.

Bork does not understand the *Slaughterhouse Cases* either. Know-ing nothing about Jacobus tenBroek's *Antislavery Origins of the Four-teenth Amendment* (1951), Howard Jay Graham's *Everyman's Consti-tution: Historical essays on the Fourteenth Amendment* (1968), Wil-liam Wiecek's *Sources of Antislavery Constitutionalism in America* (1977), or Michael K. Curtis's *No State Shall Abridge: The Fourteenth Amendment and the Bill of Rights* (1968), basic works on the origins of the Fourteenth Amendment, Bork admits that its privileges and immunities clause mystifies him. He understands that in the *Slaughter-house Cases* the Court butchered the clause, but he ignores the fact that by so doing the Court foredoomed civil rights legislation. He also ignores the theory of dual citizenship by which the Court consigned the fate of the freedman to the white supremacists in Southern states. Bork passes off one of the most egregious specimens of judicial activ-ism as a "victory for judicial moderation" (p. 39).

Representing himself as a constitutional purist or minimalist, Bork professes to rely exclusively on originalism as a way of understanding the Constitution. He can dismiss decades of constitutional doctrine by observing that the Constitution makes no reference to the right or the power claimed in some case. He is, of course, literally correct, but seems not to understand that the Constitution exists to define and limit government authority, not to define and limit individual rights. He states: "There being nothing in the Constitution about maximum hours laws, minimum wage laws, contraception, or abortion, the Court should have simply said that and left the legislative decision where it was" (p. 225). His jurisprudence seems to sustain government powers over rights. If applied consistently Bork's originalism would also cripple the gov-ernment, because the power to enact wages and hours law is not mentioned by the Constitution either. Bork is not consistent, however. His originalism means "that entire ranges of problems and issues are placed off-limits for judges. Courts will say of particular controversies that no provision reaches the issues presented, and the controversies are not therefore for judges to resolve. The statute or executive action will be allowed to stand" (p. 163). When he wants to he capably finds that adapting the Constitution to today's world, in order to prevent its provisions from becoming meaningless, is a judicial function. I am not clear, however, where an originalist finds that proposition in the Constitution, in ratifier intent, or in the public understanding of 1789. The doctrine that the Court should expound the law rather than do justice is tolerable in Holmsian thought, from which it derives. When Bork employs it, one understands that most Americans prefer the motto inscribed over the Court's portals: "Equal Justice Under the Law."

Bork's distempered book fails as a defense of originalist jurisprudence, because originalism rests on the views of the framers and ratifiers, and Bork, as a historian, is functionally illiterate. Moreover, the historical sources are simply inadequate to provide a viable constitutional jurisprudence that will decide actual cases. But, Bork wants from history just a premise or principle to apply to constitutional issues. He acknowledges, however, that history yields various and conflicting premises and that able and sincere originalist judges who apply the same premises can reach differing results. His acknowledgement means that originalism leaves room for considerable subjectivity. Even when judges reach the same results by different reasoning, the results rather than the reasoning, principles, or precedents, seem determinative.

Bork himself has employed discrepant premises and reached discrepant results at various times. In a 1968 *Fortune* article, for example, he favored "legitimate activism" and found a warrant for it in the Ninth Amendment, which says that the enumeration of rights should not be construed to deny or disparage other rights. To Bork that meant that the Bill of Rights "is an incomplete, open-ended document, and that the work of completion is, at least in major part, a task for the Supreme Court." The amendment extended the range of individual freedoms "far beyond the text of the Constitution." From that amendment and enumerated rights judges should properly draw "new natural rights."[2] Today that is all anathema to Bork. When the grand theorist of originalism is inconsistent, as he often is, or changes his mind, the theory—which is supposed to yield impersonal results free from judicial subjectivity—loses credibility. What originalists attribute to the wisdom of the founders turns out to be their own wisdom dressed in eighteenth-century ruffles.

As for the Ninth Amendment, Bork thinks it means only that rights already held by the people under state law would remain with the people. Even by that view of the amendment, it protects significant rights against national violation and, after the incorporation doctrine, against state violation. Moreover, the unenumerated rights held by the people include natural rights. From Virginia to California state declarations of rights protect inherent rights that cannot be divested by government, including a right to enjoy life and liberty, with the means of acquiring property and pursuing and obtaining happiness. Bork no longer wants judges to construe natural rights, leaving them a constitutional cadaver. If the public believed in judicial review at the time of the Constitution's adoption, it was for the purposing of enforcing rights, natural or civil, against government infringement.

Bork's 1989 wisdom shrivels most old rights and regards new ones as "preposterous." He equates federalism and states rights, arguing that if a state discriminates on grounds of race or religion, the injured parties are free to emigrate. "In this sense, federalism is the constitutional guarantee most protective of the individual's freedom to make his own choices" (p. 53). Similarly, Bork formerly believed that an act of Congress outlawing racial discrimination in hotels and theaters and restaurants would infringe on the rights of white-supremacist business owners. Today he repudiates that position, but I doubt that he would have voted to sustain the constitutional authority of Congress to enact the statute.

Any right not mentioned in the Constitution doesn't have constitutional existence, according to Bork—not a right to privacy, to have an abortion, to travel, to practice contraception, to free associate, or any right that is not enumerated. ("Liberty," it seems, is not an enumeration.) When Bork opposes a right as having no constitutional warrant, he ridicules it by showing it as an absolute. Thus a right to procreate, if it existed, would require conjugal visitors for prisoners, and the right to privacy would mean a right to engage in prostitution, to sexually abuse children, and to use addictive drugs. Yet Bork is wonderfully inconsistent. Although the Fourth Amendment protects "papers" and not "words" against unreasonable searches, and although the founders knew about eavesdropping and did not protect against it, Bork derives a right against electronic eavesdropping. Here, he says, judges must understand rights in the context of changing circumstances, rather than allow them to become meaningless. He refuses, however, to acknowledge that the free press clause or the equal protection clause has a similar capacity for adaptation to a changed world—or even that they mean what they say. Their language is general. "The equal protection of the laws" contains no limitation to any particular group of beneficiaries, and the clause immediately follows the Fourteenth Amendment's general declaration of citizenship. The word "race" is not in the amendment. Yet Bork still regards the guarantee of equal protection as restricted to a historical intent to forbid racial discrimination. On this view, equal protection offers nothing to women, aliens, homosexuals, or the aged. Time and again his analyses end in his ipse dixit.

So, Bork argues, the Constitution means what it says when it says what he means. Sometimes the literal words should govern; sometimes the words should be taken to embody a larger general principle; sometimes original purpose should triumph over the words. As Bork says, an honest judge "know that he often intuits a conclusion" and then finds supporting reasons (p. 71). That proposition is undeniable, and this book is Exhibit A.

Notes

1. Joseph Story, Commentaries on the Constitution of the United States, 3 vols. (1833, 1st ed.).
2. Robert H. Bork, "The Supreme Court Needs a New Philosophy," Fortune 78 (December 1968): 170.

4

On the Origins of the Free Press Clause

I. Introduction

In 1806 the United States commenced common law prosecutions of six Connecticut citizens for seditious libel against President Thomas Jefferson.[1] According to the indictments, two of the defendants had committed the crime in the course of preaching sermons and the others in newspaper print. The infamous Sedition Act of 1798 having expired, and Federalist party control of Connecticut stymieing state punishment, the government prosecuted the cases in the belief that the federal courts possessed jurisdiction over the common law crime of seditious libel.[2] Eventually, political considerations also forced Jefferson's administration to reverse itself on the issue of a federal common law of crimes and to drop the prosecutions except for those against Barzillai Hudson and George Goodwin, the editors of a Federalist newspaper in Hartford. Prior to trial, their case was appealed to the Supreme Court for a decision on the question of whether the federal courts possessed jurisdiction over nonstatutory criminal offenses. Somehow a decision was deferred until Republican appointees dominated the Supreme Court, which finally ruled in 1812 against the existence of a federal common law of crimes.[3] The case was decided without argument by counsel and without reasoned consideration by a divided Court which did not note the fact of division.[4] It was decided against several circuit court precedents established by members of the Supreme Court who had been important Framers of the Constitution or closely associated with the Framers.[5] Although the bizarre prosecutions of 1806 came to nothing, they did not bespeak a broad Jeffersonian conception of the scope of political opinions or a fixed belief that the first amendment conflicted with the law of seditious libel.

In 1806 Thomas Paine, the foremost pamphleteer in the English language, a friend of the radicals in England and France as well as those in America, and a condemned seditionist, published an essay on "Liberty of the Press" in a New York newspaper.[6] He began by criticizing the "licentiousness" of Federalist editors and noted that nothing was more common than "the continual cry of the *Liberty of the Press.*"[7] Undertaking to define the term because it was being used "without being understood,"[8] Paine drew from English history a Blackstonian conclusion[9] that the abolition of previous censorship had made the press only as free as speech had always been. He ended:

> A man does not ask liberty beforehand to say something he has a mind to say, but he becomes answerable afterwards for the atrocities he may utter.
>
> In like manner, if a man makes the press utter atrocious things he becomes as answerable for them as if he had uttered them by word of mouth. Mr. Jefferson has said in his inaugural speech, that *'error of opinion might be tolerated, when reason was left free to combat it.'* This is sound philosophy in cases of error. But there is a difference between error and licentiousness.
>
> Some lawyers in defending their clients . . . have often given their opinion of what they defined the liberty of the press to be. One said it was this, another said it was that, and so on, according to the case they were pleading. Now these men ought to have known that the term *liberty of the press* arose from a FACT, the abolition of the office of Imprimateur [*sic*], and that opinion has nothing to do with the case. The term refers to the fact of printing *free from prior restraint,* and not at all to the matter printed, whether good or bad. The public at large—or in case of prosecution, a jury of the country—Will be judges of the matter.[10]

Paine's views in this respect represented those of the Framers of the Constitution and the first amendment.[11]

The Framers had a genius for studied imprecision. They deliberately phrased the Constitution in generalized terms and without a lexicographical guide; they outlined an instrument that would serve future generations. Like Martin Chuzzlewit's grandnephew who had no more than "the first idea and sketchy notions of a face,"[12] the Constitution, including the Bill of Rights, purposely was made to embody first ideas and sketchy notions. Men trained in the common law, such as the Framers, avoided detailed codes, which become obsolete with a change in the particular circumstances for which they were adopted, and instead tended to formulate expansive and comprehensive principles. The principles—not the Framers' understanding and applications of them—were meant to endure.

The first amendment's injunction, that there shall be no law abridging the freedom of speech or press, was boldly stated if narrowly understood. The bold statement, not the narrow understanding, was written into the fundamental law.[13] There is no evidence to warrant the belief, nor is there valid cause or need to believe, that the Framers possessed the ultimate wisdom and best insights on the meaning of freedom of expression. But what the first amendment said is far more important than what its Framers meant. It is enough that they gave constitutional recognition to the principle of freedom of speech and press in unqualified and undefined terms.

But it is not enough for David A. Anderson.[14] He craves the comfort of knowing that a patriotic lineage, the fatherhood of the Framers, buttresses his civic convictions about the Constitution. Although the Framers' wisdom may well have passed out-of-date, Anderson needs the past's original intentions to anchor present preferences. He finds "solace," he tells us,[15] in knowing that whatever those original intentions may have been, the Supreme Court will not at this late date exempt states and federal courts from the first amendment. He is alarmed, however, by the thought that those intentions are "not irrelevant" with respect to future cases on the free press clause.[16] "If Levy's interpretation is correct, then history provides no support whatsoever for the rights now being asserted in the name of freedom of the press. . . . "[17] And, he adds, if my interpretation is correct, the Supreme Court has misread history or has given it short shrift in various opinions of which he approves.[18] Accordingly, Anderson succumbs to the impulse to recreate the past. He must make it coincide with our rhetorical traditions of freedom and yield a message that will edify the judicial mind. Thus, some touching up here and there on behalf of a good cause seems in order. This Article examines Anderson's contentions and the methodology he uses to conform the origins of the free press clause to his views.

II. Anderson's Views

Anderson's rewriting of the past is based upon his view that the law of seditious libel was invalid by the time of the American Revolution. He writes that the doctrine had become "impotent,"[19] and that there was "principled opposition" to seditious libel on the part of the public.[20] He states that the power of the legislature to punish for breach of parliamentary privilege had become ineffective by the time of the Revolution.[21] While admitting that what the Framers meant by "freedom of the press" is uncertain,[22] he argues that full protection of the press was intended,[23] that the "Congress shall not" formulation of the first amendment was to have "no significance whatsoever,"[24] and that the Framers did not believe in a federal common law of crimes.[25] Each of these contentions will be examined below.

A. Whether the Law of Seditious Libel Was Impotent

Anderson believes that as a result of popular opposition, the law of seditious libel had become "impotent" by the time of the American Revolution.[26] He states this under the section headed "The Meaning of Freedom of the Press in 1789," therefore implying that because the law of seditious libel had lost its teeth, freedom of the press could not entail a criminal responsibility for publications of a seditious character, at least not for criticism of government. "If," asks Anderson, "the Framers expected the press to operate as an effective check on government, how could they have tolerated the law of seditious libel, which made criticism of government a crime?"[27] Anderson's mistake is in thinking that criticism of the government was a crime.[28] It was not—not even in England, where, presumably, Anderson would concede that the law of seditious libel had not become impotent.

1. *Seditious Libel in England.* The common law did not stigmatize or condemn criticism of the government as criminal. The inherent vagueness of the crime of seditious libel made satisfactory definition of it difficult. The definition of the crime could take into account the malicious or criminal intent of the accused, or the bad tendency or falsity of his remarks. Seditious libel always had been an accordionlike concept, expandable or contractable at the whim of judges.

Judged by actual prosecutions, the crime consisted of defaming, condemning, or ridiculing the government—its form, constitution, officers, laws, conduct, or policies—to the jeopardy of the public peace. In effect, any malicious criticism which could be construed as having the tendency to lower the government in the public's esteem, to hold it up to contempt or hatred, or to disturb the peace was seditious libel and exposed the speaker or writer to criminal prosecution. Words damaging to the government that tended, however remotely, to cause a breach of the peace, constituted seditious libel according to the courts.

But such reasoning explained nothing because *every* crime theoretically breached the king's peace. Thus, criticism of the government that went too far, not the tendency of the words to breach the peace, distinguished the crime of seditious libel, although loose judicial language sometimes suggested otherwise. Loose language invariably characterized the crime, because the government always alleged that the defendant spoke or wrote wickedly, falsely, scandalously, scurrilously, and seditiously, or some combination thereof. Theoretically, one might say or print what he pleased, but he was responsible to the common law for malicious utterances that tended towards contempt, ridicule, hatred, scorn, or disrepute of other persons, religion, government, or morality.

Blackstone, the oracle of the common law to the American Framers, summarized the law of crown libels in 1769:

> [W]here blasphemous, immoral, treasonable, schismatical, seditious, or scandalous libels are punished by the English law . . . the *liberty of the press,* properly understood, is by no means infringed or violated. The liberty of the press is indeed essential to the nature of a free state; but this consists in laying no *previous* restraints upon publications, and not in freedom from censure for criminal matter when published. Every freeman has an undoubted right to lay what sentiments he pleases before the public; to forbid this is to destroy the freedom of the press; but if he publishes what is improper, mischievous, or illegal, he must take the consequences of his own temerity. . . . But to punish (as the law does at present) any dangerous or offensive writings, which, when published, shall on a fair and impartial trial[29] be adjudged of a pernicious tendency, is necessary for the preservation of peace and good order, of government and religion, the only solid foundations of civil liberty. Thus the will of individuals is still left free; the abuse only of that free will is the object of legal punishment. Neither is any restraint hereby laid upon freedom of thought or inquiry: liberty of private sentiment is still left; the disseminating or making public of bad sentiments, destructive of the ends of society, is the crime which society corrects.[30]

Thus, men trained in the common law believed that the press most effectively could discharge its function as a check on government if it did not indulge in malicious offensiveness which discredited it.

Some harmless animadversions did result in prosecutions, but the law's potential suppressiveness notwithstanding, the English press hardly could have been freer in practice than it was. Newspapers and tracts spewed forth vitriolic aspersions on public men and measures and commented unrestrainedly on all sorts of matters of public concern. Without a constitutional guarantee of freedom of the press and despite occasional prosecutions that were meant to be exemplary, the

English press fearlessly and vigorously criticized as it pleased. English libertarian theory stayed far ahead of its American counterpart throughout the eighteenth century, and not until the 1760's did the press in America become as free as the press had been in England since the end of the licensing system in 1694. The fact that seditious libel was a crime did not make criticism of the government illegal or even risky.

Partisanship and polemics so characterized the English press that as early as 1712 a writer, possibly Joseph Addison, signing himself as "Tory Author" and taking for granted the right to criticize the government, sought to define the bounds of that right. He approvingly quoted an unnamed Whig who said, "There never was a good Government that stood in fear of Freedom of Speech, which is the natural Liberty of Mankind; nor was ever any Administration afraid of Satyr [satire] but such as deserv'd it."[31] Private persons should have the right to criticize the government, but there must be reasonable restraints. Freedom of speech, as well as of press, should be confined to the limits set by truthfulness, good taste, due submission, and innocency of malice. Tory Author favored "Legal Liberty," the right to speak, write, or print "whatever is not against Law." He stated:

> I believe all we mean by Restraining the Press, is to hinder the Printing of any Seditious, Schismatical, Heretical or Antimonarchical Pamphlets. We do not intend to destroy Printing itself or to abridge any one Set of Men of the Liberties of *Englishmen;* That is, of Writing and Printing what the Law allows; what may be consistent with our Loyalty to the Q—n, and our Love to the Publick Peace; what is not against Morals or Good Manners. And surely there may be a Restraint put upon such Things without striking at the Press itself.[32]

Thus, Tory Author believed that freedom of expression had a broad scope and a high value when kept under the reasonable restraints of the common law, without which true liberty would degenerate to licentiousness.

The right to criticize the government was an eighteenth-century cliche and not seriously disputed. At the close of the century, James Madison noted that in England, where the common law threatened those who used the press in a manner offensive to the government, punishment was "occasional," yet everyone knew that "the freedom exercised by the press, and protected by public opinion far exceeds the limits prescribed by the ordinary rules of law." The English press, Madison declared, criticized the government "with peculiar freedom."[33]

2. *Seditious Libel In America.* Had the common law of seditious libel become impotent in America by the time of the Revolution? In the period between the Declaration of Independence and the ratification of the first amendment (1776–1791), America had its first opportunity to develop a legal system and a society in which all men were free to express their opinions, however unpopular, on any subject, short of direct and immediate incitement to crime. But no American state took the opportunity to abandon or seriously to limit the oppressive common law of seditious libel.

On the contrary, ten of the thirteen original states, all but Rhode Island, Connecticut, and South Carolina, expressly adopted the common law system after separating from England. Virginia, for example, did so by statute in 1776: "[T]he common law of England . . . shall be the rule of decision, and shall be considered as in full force, until the same shall be altered by the legislative power of this colony."[34] Six states did so by their constitutions. New Jersey, for example, provided in its constitution of 1776 that "the common law of England, as well as so much of the statute law, as have been heretofore practiced in this Colony, shall remain in force, until they shall be altered by a future law. . . . "[35] No state statute abolished or altered the common law of criminal defamation in general, or seditious libel in particular, and no state court ruled that the free press clause of its state constitution rendered void the prosecution of a libel. Every state with a free press clause in its constitution provided that England's common law before the Revolution was to operate unless inconsistent with or repugnant to some other constitutional or statutory provision.[36] In New York and the three other states which did not protect freedom of the press, there is no basis for implying that the idea that a republican form of government may be criminally libeled by the opinions of its citizens was to be discarded.[37] As for the nine states that constitutionally protected freedom of the press, one may argue that the law of criminal utterances was inconsistent with or repugnant to a free press guarantee; but such an argument must be based on inferences from later libertarian premises and would lack the support of evidence from the 1776–1791 period. The evidence supports the opposing view, as in the two Carolinas, whose constitutions banned seditious utterances.[38]

Anderson professes reluctance to "believe that the press clauses that were included in nine state constitutions were intended to do nothing more than preserve the English common law."[39] He assumes a far greater degree of rationality and purposefulness in the writing of the press clause than actually existed.[40] He also assumes that a free press clause made a significant difference, although the presses in states without free press clauses functioned as freely as those in states with such clauses—and in England, the home of Blackstone and Mansfield, the press behaved as if the common law did not exist and was as free in practice as its American counterparts. If to repudiate the Blackstone-Mansfield view of the common law's restrictions on political expression was a revolutionary objective, the Americans of the revolutionary period strangely did not say so. No state asserted in any way that the law of seditious libel was incompatible with a constitutional guarantee of freedom of the press or with a republican form of government.

a. *Whiting.* If the law of seditious libel had become impotent or if a free press clause in a state constitution superseded the common law of libels, how do we explain the conviction of Dr. William Whiting? In 1787 a jury convicted him before the Supreme Judicial Court of Massachusetts sitting in Great Barrington, the scene of Whiting's crime. No ordinary libeler, Whiting was Chief Justice of the Court of Common Pleas of Berkshire County. In 1786, shortly before the fall term of his court, he had written an article, signed "Gracchus," censuring the government for unjust laws and recommending that a virtuous people who lacked redress of grievances should "disturb the government."[41] Whiting did not publish the article but read it to insurgents who supported Shays' rebellion. Whiting was dismissed from his judicial post, convicted of writing a seditious libel, and received a sentence of imprisonment for seven months, a one hundred pound fine, and sureties for good behavior for five years. Governor James Bowdoin and his Council denied a petition for a pardon but remitted the prison sentence. No one claimed that the free press clause of the state constitution stood in the way of a prosecution for seditious libel.[42]

b. *Freeman.* In 1791 Edmund Freeman, a newspaper editor, for having grossly libeled the private life of a member of the Massachusetts legislature, was criminally prosecuted on the theory that his words tended to breach the public peace of the Commonwealth. The prosecutor, Attorney-General James Sullivan, later the Jeffersonian governor of the state, maintained that the constitutional guarantee of a free press meant only the absence of a licensing act. He quoted Blackstone at interminable length to prove the point and urged that licentiousness must be distinguished from liberty. The defendant's attorneys did not disagree but denied that Freeman had licentiously breached the peace and sought to prove the accuracy of his publication.[43]

Three judges of the state's high court presided at the trial. Chief Justice Francis Dana charged the jury in full accordance with prosecutor Sullivan's argument on the definition of liberty of the press, although Dana informed the jury that he sympathized with the defense of truth even as he noted that he reserved a ruling on the question.[44] The jury's verdict was not guilty, but as the historian of *The Development of Freedom of the Press in Massachusetts* concluded:

> [A] judicial construction of liberty of the press in the state had been announced, differing in no wise from the opinions of Chief Justice Hutchinson in 1768 or of the Superior Court of Judicature in 1724. In effect it was affirmed that the constitutional provision of 1780 was merely declaratory of the law as it had existed for nearly sixty years, with an added prohibition of any possible reestablishment of censorship.[45]

Eight years later, in 1799, Massachusetts convicted an editor of the Boston *Independent Chronicle* for seditious libel.[46]

c. *Oswald.* Politics, not a free press clause, saved Eleazar Oswald of the Philadelphia *Independent Gazetteer* when he challenged the Pennsylvania Supreme Court in 1782.[47] Oswald's newspaper spoke for the state's party that backed the nationalist cause in Congress and sought modification of the state's majoritarian constitution of 1776. The party's leadership, which included James Wilson, John Dickinson, and Robert Morris, contributed to the *Independent Gazetteer* under pen names, but "the public generally knew who the authors were."[48] Nothing in Oswald's credo for a free press prepared readers for his slashing journalism.[49] In his first issue, in which he attempted a "just Definition of the Liberty of the Press," he sounded respectful of the law. "Some contend for an unbounded liberty," he wrote, but not he. An unbounded liberty would turn the freedom of the press "to the worst Purposes, and occasion much more Evil than Good." He did, however, support everyone's right to communicate his sentiments "if delivered with Decency, and under reasonable Regulations."[50]

Less than six months after Oswald's first issue, the sheriff arrested him on a warrant from Chief Justice Thomas McKean of the state supreme court. When Oswald accused the court of bias and severity, McKean charged him with having published a "seditious, scandalous, and infamous LIBEL" on the court's administration of justice.[51] Released on bail, Oswald showed his contempt by reprinting the offensive article, by lampooning Judge George Bryan as "that excrescence,"[52] and by damning McKean as another bloody Jefferies.[53] The court rearrested him and raised his bail to one thousand pounds. Oswald wrote to a friend that the chief justice of Pennsylvania had attacked the freedom of the press and that he, Oswald, was "to have a public Trial . . . as a *Libeller*. The infamous English doctrine of Libels being introduced by the more infamous Judges and Lawyers, in an American court."[54] Because Oswald must have heard of precedents such as Zenger's case or McDougall's,[55] his meaning seems unfathomable, but one or two of his contributors repudiated the very concept of seditious libel.[56] So heroic and unprecedented an accomplishment makes Oswald's case memorable.

McKean could order Oswald's arrest but could not try him without an indictment by a grand jury. Although he tried twice, he could not wrest an indictment from that body.[57] Oswald believed that the grand jury thereby rejected "the Doctrine of Libels," but as Judge George Bryan said, writing as "Adrian," witnesses before the grand jury testified that the printer had been misinformed and the grand jury inferred that his mistake involved no guilt. Bryan, the probable author of Pennsylvania's free press clause, believed that Oswald had seditiously libeled the court.[58] McKean and the grand jury went public with their dispute, dealing mainly with the question of whether the grand jury could interview witnesses not previously approved by the court. It is of interest that Oswald, his lawyer, and the foreman of the grand jury were seen conversing privately in a tavern. Moreover, among the witnesses whom the grand jury interviewed without McKean's approval were major political figures including James Wilson, the lawyer for one of the defendants to whom Oswald had extended his sympathy when he slammed the court for its bias and severity.[59] Oswald's party thus outmaneuvered the court in influencing the grand jury.

The Oswald case shows the Pennsylvania Supreme Court's belief that the constitutional guarantee of a free press was compatible with the doctrine of seditious libel, although two writers and probably others disagreed. The emergence of a sweeping libertarian opinion in Pennsylvania was especially significant and precocious, but infertile. No one anywhere in the nation repeated the thought until the Sedition Act controversy.

Within six years McKean convicted Oswald in *Respublica v. Oswald*.[60] A grand jury more compliant than that of 1782 indicted the editor for a criminal libel. Oswald defended himself in his *Independent Gazetteer*. Alluding to "prejudices . . . against me on the bench,"[61] he appealed to his jury for a fair trial. More out of hope than accuracy, he added, "The doctrine of libels being a doctrine incompatible with law and liberty, and at once destructive of the privileges of a free country in the communication of our thoughts, has not hitherto gained any footing in *Pennsylvania*."[62] He supposed that his fellow citizens would not allow the freedom of the press to be violated "upon any refined pretence . . . which oppressive ingenuity or courtly study can invent."[63]

McKean ordered Oswald's arrest, promptly tried him without a jury, and convicted him for his seditious contempt of the court. The chief justice ruled that "there is nothing in the constitution of this state, respecting the liberty of the press, that has not been authorized by the constitution of that kingdom [England] for near a century past."[64] He also observed that although every man might publish his opinions, the peace and dignity of society required an inquiry into a writer's motives so as to distinguish between publications "which are meant for use and reformation, and with an eye solely to the public good, and those which are intended merely to delude and defame. To the latter description, it is impossible that any good government should afford protection and impunity."[65] Oswald's crime, McKean believed, consisted of his willful attempt to prejudice his jury and corrupt the administration of justice.[66] Oswald received a sentence of one month in prison and a ten pound fine.

Oswald then requested the Pennsylvania Assembly to prefer impeachment charges against McKean and his associates for procedural irregularities and for violating the liberty of the press. William Lewis, who had prosecuted Oswald, defended the judges before the Assembly in a speech endorsing Blackstone's definition of a free press. Lewis concluded that the "dawn of true freedom" had arisen in England with the expiration of the licensing system.[67] Oswald received considerable support for his accusation of procedural irregularities, but no one endorsed his repudiation of the law of criminal libels, although William Findley noted that every person had a right to state his opinion on "public proceedings," and he warned of the danger of allowing judges to punish contempts against themselves. The Assembly resolved that Oswald's charges were groundless.[68] In 1797 McKean, the Jeffersonian chief justice, again ruled that the state's free press clause was merely declaratory of the common law.[69]

d. *The Pennsylvania Constitution.* Pennsylvania adopted a new state constitution in 1790, shortly after it ratified the first amendment.[70] James Wilson drafted the new constitution, the speech and press clause of which explicitly made citizens criminally liable for abuse of that freedom. The new clause, preceding Fox's Libel Act[71] by two years, allowed the jury to decide whether the accused's statement was libelous as a matter of law; it also preceded Lord Campbell's Act of 1843[72] by making truth a defense in a prosecution for criminal libel.[73] Pennsylvania's constitution of 1790 was the first to embody these Zengerian reforms, which unquestionably liberalized the law of libel.

Anderson distorts the 1790 free press clause with a mistaken remark that the state constitution of 1790 was " 'exceedingly reactionary.' "[74] He does not understand that James Alexander, Cato, Father of Candor, and other libertarians whom he approvingly quotes advocated the very reforms that the free press clause of 1790 guaranteed. Anderson later observes that the Federalists of 1789, who framed the first amendment, "were a very different group" from the Federalists of 1798, who adopted the Sedition Act.[75] But the Pennsylvania Federalists of 1790—Wilson, Dickinson, Morris, and company—were among the Framers of the Constitution, who were the Federalists of 1789.

B. Whether Parliamentary Privilege Had Become Ineffective

The power of the legislature to punish for breach of parliamentary privilege had not become ineffective by the time of the Revolution, contrary to Anderson.[76] It remained a vital power, usable when the occasion warranted, as the Keteltas case demonstrated. In 1796 William Keteltas published blistering criticisms of the New York Assembly in the newspapers. The Assembly, smarting from his censure, which it took to be seditious, summoned him to appear before its bar. Keteltas admitted authorship of the offensive articles. The Assembly promptly and without debate found him guilty of a breach of parliamentary privilege. When Keteltas refused to humble himself by admitting his wrong and asking pardon, the Assembly immediately ordered him jailed.[77]

The case presented a perfect opportunity for a libertarian argument in defense of Keteltas. Representative John Bird, a Republican member of the Assembly, raised the issue in the right terms: "[S]hall we attempt to prevent citizens from *thinking,* from giving their *opinion* on the acts of the legislature? *Shall we stop the freedom of the press?*"[78]

Bird spoke in vain; his questions were ignored. Although Keteltas became a popular hero among the Jeffersonian faithful in New York, and his case became a *cause celebre,* freedom of the press and the right of a citizen to criticize the government played no part in the extensive arguments on Keteltas' behalf. Not even Keteltas himself, an experienced politician and lawyer, spoke to the issue, although while in prison he published five articles protesting the "unconstitutional, tyrannical, and illegal" proceedings of the Assembly.[79] He based his defense on the narrow argument that he had not breached any of the privileges of the house and that the house could not lawfully deprive any citizen of his liberty without benefit of grand jury proceedings and trial by jury.

An anonymous supporter of Keteltas signing himself "Camillus Junius," possibly Brockholst Livingston, acknowledged that verbal insults to the house "ought not to pass unpunished."[80] The proper remedy, he said, was a jury trial that protected the rights of the accused:

> The Courts of criminal jurisdiction are open to prosecutions, which the Attorney General may commence by information or indictment. A libel tending to asperse or vilify the house of Assembly or any of its members, may be as severely punished in the Supreme Court, as a libel against government. This, then, . . . is the remedy they should appeal to. . . .[81]

Keteltas, freed on a writ of habeas corpus as soon as the legislature ended its session, brought an unsuccessful suit for false imprisonment against the speaker of the house. The Assembly supported its speaker by a vote of 88 to 1, and the court ruled against Keteltas.[82] Four years later the Senate of the United States found that a printer's allegedly seditious publication constituted a "high breach of privileges."[83]

Anderson confuses the facts about parliamentary privilege cases, which he knows about only from *Legacy of Suppression.* The Massachusetts House did not release Daniel Fowle because public opinion opposed the legislative power to imprison for seditiousness; it released him because public opinion, according to Fowle, demanded merciful consideration for his sick wife. More important, Fowle never referred to liberty of the press or to any aspect of free discussion.[84] Likewise, Anderson wholly misreads the Alexander McDougall case of New York, 1770–1771, a case that strongly illustrated the power of the legislature to do as it pleased with citizens who published offensive remarks.[85] George Clinton, one of McDougall's few supporters in the legislature, remarked that the legislature could throw him out the window if it pleased.[86] Although public opinion probably supported McDougall, Anderson alleges that it did so because it opposed the legislative power to punish for seditious contempts. There is no basis for that allegation.[87] The cases of Pride in Virginia,[88] Husband in North Carolina,[89] Powell in South Carolina,[90] McDougall in New York, and Rome in Rhode Island[91] prove that the power to punish for breach of parliamentary privilege was still effective on the eve of the Revolution.

C. Whether Principled Opposition Existed to the Law of Seditious Libel

Political resistance to royal authority underlay the public opposition in Massachusetts to indictments of patriot writers. Anderson, however, sees "principled opposition to seditious libel" on the part of the public, which, he alleges, was "hostile to the use of seditious libel by its own elected representatives in the Assembly."[92] Such an assertion cannot be taken seriously.

If a grand jury refused to indict, Anderson sees principled opposition to the law of seditious libel, not an insufficiency of evidence, or popular support for a local factional leader, or a grand jury intimidated by patriot mobs. If a trial jury refused to convict, Anderson sees principled hostility to the law of seditious libel, not a reasonable doubt of guilt or a belief that truth should be a defense to a charge of libel. If a legislature jailed a seditious libeler, Anderson sees his release, when the legislature is no longer in session and without further authority to hold the libeler in prison, as principled opposition and a victory for public opinion.[93]

Anderson, who is supposedly proving that by the time of the Revolution public opinion had rendered the legislative power to imprison for seditious insults ineffective, hedges his bets by concluding that anything that happened before 1776 does not really count (unless he wants to use it).[94] It does not count, we belatedly learn, because state constitutional provisions protecting freedom of the press did not yet exist. But the evidence before 1776 must count because the significant issue is what the concept of freedom of the press meant to Americans. In the absence of evidence to the contrary, the conceptual meaning of freedom of the press did not change in 1776 from its earlier meaning at the time of Fowle's case in 1754 or McDougall's in 1770–1771. If the pre-1776 evidence is not relevant, Anderson should not produce the testimony of the colonial period from *Cato's Letters,* Zenger's defense, James Alexander, Father of Candor, and the Quebec declaration.[95]

1. *The Massachusetts Radicals.* As for the supposed opposition to the doctrine of seditious libel by the Massachusetts radicals during the controversy with England, one of their leaders, John Adams, defiantly urged in the columns of the *Boston Gazette* in 1765 that its editors should fearlessly publish "with the utmost freedom, whatever can be warranted by the laws of your country"[96]—no rejection of the doctrine of seditious libel. The same newspaper, the mouthpiece of the radicals, told its readers in 1767, "Political liberty consists in a freedom of speech and action, so far as the laws of a community will permit, and no farther: all beyond is criminal, and tends to the destruction of Liberty itself."[97] Joseph Warren and Samuel Adams toasted a grand jury for vindicating the freedom of the press—not because the jury rejected the doctrine of seditious libel, but because it rejected "the absurd doctrine, *the more true, the more libellous.'*[98] In his *Novanglus* letters, John Adams in 1774 censured "the scandalous license of the tory presses,"[99] and though he differed with Governor Thomas Hutchinson on what words constituted abuse of the press, he and Hutchinson agreed on the fundamental principle that abuse of the press, as each understood it, existed apart from true liberty of the press.[100] By early 1776 Adams proposed that making adherence to the independence movement the legal test of loyalty would have the beneficial result of stopping "unfriendly" newspapers, and then "[t]he presses will produce no more seditious or traitorous speculations. Slanders upon public men and measures will be lessened."[101] Adams did not disagree with Blackstone about the criminality of seditious libel, but only as to the particular words that constituted the crime. Twenty-two years later President Adams acted consistently when he signed the Sedition Act and urged prosecutions under it.

2. *The Quebec Declaration.* The Quebec declaration of the Continental Congress in 1774 made a strong statement about the functions of a free press, as Anderson points out three times,[102] but he neglects to inform readers that the Quebec declaration endorsed only the diffusion of "liberal" sentiments on the administration of government. The Committee of Inspection for Newport, Rhode Island, which included

the censorship and intimidation of printers among its duties, demonstrated the American understanding of the Quebec declaration by invoking it as justification for boycotting printers who diffused illiberal or "wrong sentiments respecting the measures now carrying on for the recovery and establishment of our rights."[103] In 1776 Congress urged that the states enact legislation to prevent people from being "deceived and drawn into erroneous opinion."[104] The Quebec declaration at its time was propaganda, and Anderson himself uses it as propaganda.

3. *Oswald's Case.* When I wrote *Legacy of Suppression* I discovered not a single instance of anyone prior to the ratification of the first amendment advocating that the law of seditious libel conflicted with free government or with political liberty. *Legacy of Suppression* produced a generation of critics, but only one, Dwight L. Teeter, discovered that such libertarian advocacy existed before 1791. When Oswald's case agitated Pennsylvania in 1782, according to Teeter, several newspaper articles, all signed with pen names, showed that their authors rejected the law of seditious libel.[105] Teeter broke new ground, although he made mistakes and exaggerated the extent of his discovery. Only two writers, one signing himself "Junius Wilkes" and the other "Candid," took the position ascribed to them by Teeter.[106] Chief Justice McKean, not "Junius Wilkes" or "Candid," authoritatively described the law of Pennsylvania on the meaning of freedom of the press in 1782. McKean did so again in Blackstonian terms in 1788, on the occasion of the second Oswald case,[107] and still again in 1799, when Pennsylvania prosecuted William Cobbett.[108] When McKean imprisoned Oswald in 1788 for his seditious contempt, and the printer again declared that the chief justice had violated his freedom of the press, the Philadelphia newspapers printed no articles supporting Oswald on that point. The pseudononymous views of "Junius Wilkes" and "Candid" had fallen on barren ground. Not later referred to or repeated in substance or in name, they were as dead as yesterday's newspaper; they surely did not represent a significant sector of public opinion.

4. *Cato.* Anderson also declares that *Cato's Letters,* the influential essays that originally appeared in the *London Journal* in 1720, "objected to seditious libel."[109] Anderson mistakenly believes that because Cato advocated truth as a defense and a rule providing that any ambiguity in a publication should be construed as revealing an innocent intent, Cato "repudiated the existing common law of seditious libel."[110] But elsewhere in his article Anderson accurately recognizes that truth

as a defense scarcely modified Blackstonian principles.[111] The Sedition Act of 1798 required a showing of malicious intent and allowed the defense of truth, yet was Blackstonian at its core. Zengerian principles and the law of seditious libel harmonized.

Moreover, for all his criticisms of the enforcement of that law, Cato declared that he did not wish to be misunderstood as arguing for the uncontrolled liberty of men to calumniate each other or the government. As to "Libels against Government, like all others, they are always base and unlawful,"[112] especially when untrue, and should be punished as an abuse of liberty so long as England's "very good Laws" were "prudently and honestly executed, which I really believe they have for the most part been since the Revolution."[113] In a related essay, Cato reinforced the thought, saying, "I do agree, when the natural and genuine Meaning and Purport of Words and Expressions in libellous Writings carry a criminal Intention, that the Writer ought not to escape Punishment by Subterfuge or Evasion. . . . "[114] Cato did not condemn the doctrine of seditious libel, did not call it a Star Chamber doctrine, which it was, and did not advocate an overt acts test or immunity for political opinions.[115]

5. *Cushing and Adams.* Anderson also contends that the opinion of Chief Justice William Cushing of Massachusetts, expressed in a letter to John Adams in 1789, suggests "that the American view of freedom of the press was not Blackstone's."[116] That is false. Anderson quotes Cushing as saying that the free press clause of the Massachusetts Constitution "must exclude *subsequent* restraints, as much as *previous restraints,*"[117] a quotation that is out of context and deceiving. If Anderson read the entire Cushing-Adams correspondence, which I made available in two books,[118] and if he read five pages of my commentary on that text, he knows that Cushing meant to exclude from subsequent punishment only defendants who could prove the truth of their alleged libels. Cushing also said, "When the press is made the vehicle of falsehood and scandal, let the authors be punished with becoming rigour."[119] In connection with the Cushing-Adams correspondence, Anderson concedes that truth as a defense constituted "only a minor (and generally ineffectual) modification of Blackstonian principles."[120] That concession contradicts his view that Cushing repudiated subsequent restraint or represented a dissenting tradition that repudiated Blackstonianism.

Although he knows that Adams and Cushing both supported the

Sedition Act of 1798, Anderson adds that both nevertheless recognized the inadequacy of Blackstonianism. Apparently, a point requires emphasis: The Sedition Act embodied Zengerian reforms, and in that sense, it was the epitome of everything eighteenth-century libertarians had fought for. They had advocated that a defendant charged with seditious libel should have the opportunity of proving the truth of his statements and that if the jury believed him, he should be acquitted. The Sedition Act guaranteed truth as a defense and the jury's power to return a general verdict. The statute also accepted the crux of the Blackstonian concept of criminal responsibility for publishing seditious libel. Thus, the acceptance of Zenger meant the acceptance of Blackstone. The Zenger defense had not rejected the crime of seditious libel.

The frail protection offered to freedom of the press by the Cushing-Adams proposals of 1789 manifested itself when only one Sedition Act jury returned a verdict of acquittal.[121] The Sedition Act juries, like Cushing and Adams, shared a belief in the predominant doctrine that opinions can criminally assault government. To be sure, those opinions had to be malicious and false, but the law of seditious libel, even modified, implied an extremely narrow concept of freedom of the press.

A final observation must be made about the Cushing-Adams correspondence: It is not a dependable revelation of the intention underlying constitutional guarantees of freedom of the press or speech. Cushing and Adams were proposing, not disposing. They were not representing the constitutional law of Massachusetts as of 1789 or for many years thereafter.[122] As Cushing's bewilderment about the meaning of the state's free press clause[123] showed and as his comment that the questions he raised had never been decided[124] also showed, he clearly did not expose the general understanding of that clause's meaning in the minds of the 1780 convention that framed it. Cushing had been at that convention; Adams actually had written the first draft. Adams agreed in 1789 that it "would be" better to construe the clause as Cushing suggested, namely that "truth of fact" should be a defense to a charge of criminal libel. The two were discussing an "innovation," the word Adams used, exactly as Madison had, to describe the defense of truth.[125]

6. *Madison.* Madison is Anderson's last and "most important dissenter" on his list of those who supposedly repudiated the concept of seditious libel.[126] Indeed Madison did, as I explained at length in

Legacy of Suppression, but he did not do so until 1799, after the Sedition Act had radicalized his thinking and produced a new libertarian system of thought.[127] Madison's views of 1799 were ad hoc in nature, not reflections of a position that he had held in 1789. If his statements in his great *Virginia Report* of 1799–1800 can be admitted as evidence of prior belief, so can the later beliefs of other Framers and their allies, such as John Adams, William Cushing, Samuel Chase, Oliver Ellsworth, James Iredell, Alexander Hamilton, John Marshall, William Paterson, and many others who believed not only in a Blackstonian understanding of the freedom of the press but even in the constitutionality of the Sedition Act of 1798.

Anderson's treatment of Madison's views might not warrant further consideration because at one point he completely agrees with me: "[I]t is true that he [Madison] never articulated a 'libertarian' theory of freedom of the press until the Sedition Act controversy."[128] But Anderson also states that Madison asserted in his 1799–1800 *Report* "not only that the press clause superseded the common law, but that it was so understood in the First Congress."[129] Anderson then adds that if my view is to be accepted, "We must believe that Madison in 1799 misrepresented (or misunderstood) his own views of ten years earlier,"[130] and in a footnote says, "Levy never explains why Madison, in 1799, would misstate his own views of 1789."[131] I have never explained because Madison did not misstate or misrepresent his earlier views. Anderson misunderstands him. Anderson's authority for Madison's earlier views, which are supposed to be similar to his views of 1799, is my abridgment of Madison's *Virginia Report*. Anderson does not quote from the *Report* to prove his point, because he cannot prove it. Madison wrote as follows:

> To these observations, one fact will be added, which demonstrates that the common law cannot be admitted as the *universal* expositor of American terms, which may be the same with those contained in that law. The freedom of conscience, and of religion, are found in the same instruments which assert the freedom of the press. It will never be admitted, that the meaning of the former, in the common law of England, is to limit their meaning in the United States.[132]

I do not read that passage to be a declaration that the First Congress understood the press clause to supersede the common law. On the contrary, Madison is saying that the religious liberty clause should not be construed in common law terms. Neither in the passage quoted nor in any other does Madison refer to the understanding of the free press clause by the First Congress. Earlier in the *Report,* when Madison discusses the common law meaning of freedom of the press, he does not even imply that the First Congress had a different understanding, because nowhere in the *Report* does he mention what the First Congress understood the free press clause or the concept of freedom of the press to mean. In addition to misreading Madison's *Report,* Anderson uncritically accepts Vincent Blasi's assertion that in 1789, when recommending the proposition that became the first amendment, Madison had outlined his theory of liberty upon which his later *Report* was based.[133] But Madison's great speech introducing the proposals that became the Bill of Rights did not in any way bear out the contention that his views of 1799 on the free press clause were like those of 1789. All of Blasi's quotations and paraphrases from Madison come from the *Report* of 1799–1800.[134] Blasi produces no proof of his assertion by comparing what Madison said in 1789 with what he said ten years later. Until that proof is produced, Blasi and Anderson will convince only those who assume the infallibility of their words. Madison did not even discuss or explain his free press proposal in 1789. The issue is not whether in 1789 Madison believed that Congress had no power to legislate on the press; it is, rather, the meaning of the concept of freedom of the press, of seditious libel, and of the continuing validity of the common law—Madison addressed none of these in 1789.

D. What the Framers Meant by "Freedom of the Press"

I have taken the view that the Framers must have understood the concept of the freedom of the press in the conventional Blackstonian sense, because any novel understanding would have required some explanation.[135] Neither the legislative history[136] nor the debate on the ratification of the Constitution revealed a novel understanding of freedom of the press, a fact that Anderson does not contest. However, he states that my reasoning is "dubious" because the "Bill of Rights contained numerous provisions that had no established common law meanings—the establishment clause, the free exercise clause, and the due process clause, to name the most obvious. Yet there is no record of any debate about the meaning of these either."[137] What seems obvious is that Anderson is confused. The term "due process of law" had an established common law meaning that derived from English history going back to 1354.[138] The unique American experience with establishments of religion and religious liberty had produced a general understanding of the meaning of establishments and free exercise. America never had an establishment of religion in the European sense of a national church or a formal union between a nation state and a single church, with that church alone enjoying financial support and special privileges denied to all other churches.[139] By 1789 America understood the term "establishment of religion" to mean government aid to religion, whether on an impartial or preferential basis.[140]

Experience also supplied a widespread understanding of the meaning of the free exercise clause, namely that people could believe what they wanted about religion and that, within reason, the state ought not to command what conscience prohibits nor prohibit what conscience commands. The term "free exercise" of religion had an American history going back to the Maryland Toleration Act of 1649.[141] Given the American experience with religious liberty and establishments of religion, no one could have believed that the first amendment incorporated the common law meaning or any meaning other than that dictated by experience.

By contrast, the free press clause, like the due process clause, had only an established common law meaning: freedom to speak, write, and publish as one pleased, subject to subsequent punishment for being too offensive. If the first amendment's free press clause comprehended another meaning, what could it have been? Two other meanings were possible, one deriving from the Zenger case and the other from a repudiation of seditious libel's core concept that government can be criminally assaulted by words alone.

The compatibility of the Zenger defense and the common law is clear from the Pennsylvania press clause of 1790. Notwithstanding its recognition of truth as a defense to a charge of libel and its recognition of the power of a jury to decide the criminality of a publication, Anderson properly interprets the Pennsylvania clause as Blackstonian because it stipulated the responsibility of anyone abusing the liberty of the press.[142] Thus, even if the principles of the Zenger defense had received widespread acceptance at the time of the framing of the first amendment, the free press clause still incorporated a Blackstonian meaning. In 1789, however, those principles of 1735 were still controversial and were not yet established.

In 1788, for example, when urging Madison to add a bill of rights to the proposed Constitution, Jefferson stated, "A declaration that the federal government will never restrain the presses from printing any thing they please, will not take away the liability of the printers for false facts printed."[143] The phrasing shows Jefferson's belief that a free press guarantee did not foreclose subsequent punishment for abuse of the press; Jefferson accepted the crux of Blackstone on criminal libels. Madison, who construed Jefferson's recommendation in its most favorable light, observed in reply, "The Exemption of the press from liability in every case for *true facts is* also an innovation and as such ought to be well considered."[144] The remark shows that after half of a century the principle of the Zenger defense was still an "innovation." On consideration, Madison did not add the truth-as-a-defense principle to the amendment that he proposed to Congress. Jefferson thought that Madison's free press proposal was too broad and urged its alteration to exclude freedom to publish "false facts . . . affecting the peace of the confederacy with foreign nations."[145] In a political dispute such as that triggered by Jay's Treaty, Jefferson's proposal, if adopted, could have had suppressive effects.

As for the repudiation of the law of seditious libel, an intention to supersede the doctrine does not emerge from the legislative history of the free press clause. Furthermore, at a time when truth as a defense, a mere modification of the common law, was still an innovation, the constitutional guarantee of freedom of the press hardly could have meant that the common law on seditious libel had been superseded, as Anderson contends. A free press clause without the law of seditious libel would have emancipated all political opinions. If Madison had been bent on revolutionizing the common law of seditious libel, he hardly would have written privately that he was engaged in "the nauseous project of amendments" whose main objective was "to kill the opposition every where,"[146] and he would not have told the House that "if we confine ourselves to an enumeration of simple acknowledged principles, the ratification will meet with but little difficulty. Amendments of a doubtful nature will have a tendency to prejudice the whole system. . . ."[147]

E. What the Framers Meant by "Congress Shall Make No Law"

In 1789 when Madison proposed a free press clause to Congress, he neglected to use language recommended by the Virginia ratifying convention that the freedom of the press "cannot be cancelled, abridged, restrained, or modified, by any authority of the United States."[148] Compared to the formulation of the finished amendment, "Congress shall make no law," Virginia's more comprehensive version would have applied to the President and federal judiciary, making impossible a federal common law of seditious libel or other abridgments by the executive or the courts. But Anderson diminishes the importance of the Virginia phrase "by any authority of the United States" and adds that the final specification of Congress was meaningless.[149]

Anderson rightly observes that Madison proposed a free press clause similar to the one urged by the Virginia ratifying convention in its recommended bill of rights. The phrase "by any authority of the United States," Anderson writes, "appeared only in the 'form of ratification' by which the convention officially assented to the original Constitution," and that "form of ratification" was drafted by a committee different from that which drafted the proposed bill of rights.[150] However, Madison was a member of both committees, and, even had he not been, the preface to the form of ratification scarcely can be dismissed. The Virginia convention surely attached considerable importance to its formal ratification statement that any power not granted to the United States could not be exercised by any authority of the United States, and that the two rights that Madison later called the "choicest"[151]—the liberty of conscience and freedom of the press—could not be abridged by any authority of the United States. Anderson clearly goes too far when he declares that the reference to Congress in the final draft of the first amendment "had no significance whatsoever," meaning that the Framers understood "Congress" as equivalent to the federal government.[152] That interpretation is unlikely. By deliberately specifying Congress, the Framers must have meant not to specify the United States. They had constructed a government of three branches and knew the difference between the government of the United States and its legislative branch. Anderson also is capable of appreciating clear language when he wants to—he observes, for example, that if Congress had meant the free press clause to have a common law meaning, it could have specifically said so, as it did in the seventh amendment.[153] By the same logic Congress could have said "the federal government" if that is what it meant. In any case the first amendment's language must take precedence over its Framers' possible misunderstanding of that language. We should not be too hasty to conclude that the Framers did not mean what they said or that they said one thing and meant something very different.

Anderson concludes his point with an extraordinary concession—that even if the specification of Congress "was purposeful, its apparent purpose would have been merely to make clear that the amendment imposed no limitation on the states."[154] On the contrary, that purpose would have been equally fulfilled if the amendment had specified the government of the United States or any authority of the United States. The specification of Congress, rather, made clear that Congress had no power to abridge the freedom of the press, thereby satisfying the public demand for that restriction on the powers of Congress. Specifying Congress "to make clear that the amendment imposed no limitation on the states" seems to be an indirect way to reserve power to the states. I agree, however, that a primary purpose of the first amendment was to reserve to the states an exclusive authority to *legislate* in the field of speech and press. Anderson calls that remark of mine "Levy's states' rights argument"[155] and exposes it to some scorn.[156] Yet he makes the same point: The amendment specified Congress "merely to make clear that the amendment imposed no limitation on the states."[157]

F. Whether the Framers Believed in a Federal Common Law of Crimes

James Wilson of Pennsylvania, who was second only to Madison in influencing the shape of the Constitution and second to none as a master of law, had opinions on freedom of the press that Anderson finds unpalatable. He therefore degrades Wilson's significance. After quoting a few lines from Wilson, beginning with the word "if," Anderson explains that Wilson was speaking hypothetically about a procedure that would be employed in the event that Congress passed a sedition act. Anderson claims that the statement he quotes from Wilson indicates nothing about a federal common law of crimes, contrary to my contention.[158]

But Wilson was not speaking hypothetically, no more than any Framer did in Philadelphia in 1787 or during the ratification controversy, when explaining how he expected the new national government would operate.[159] Wilson was answering antiratificationist critics who had denounced his widely reported Statehouse Yard speech for ratification and against the need for a bill of rights.[160] That speech had provoked many Anti-Federalist replies. "A Democratic Federalist" answered that the federal courts probably would prosecute those who libeled the United States. If the judicial power of the United States extended "to ALL CASES, in *law* and *equity,* arising under this [C]onstitution," then, the writer argued, "the tribunal of the United States may claim a right to the cognizance of all offenses against the *general government,* and *libels* will not probably be excluded."[161] The Zenger case, he recalled, proved that men in high power disliked liberty of the press.[162]

A pamphlet by "A Federalist Republican" also answered Wilson. Without speaking to the issue of libel prosecutions, the writer contended that the press faced real danger from Congress' delegated power to tax; stamp duties could "as effectually abolish the freedom of the press as any express declaration."[163] Another Pennsylvania Anti-Federalist, probably William Findley, warned in an essay for Oswald's newspaper:

> The Liberty of the Press is not secured, and the powers of Congress are fully adequate to its destruction, as they are to have the trial of *libels,* or *pretended libels* against the United States, and may by a cursed abominable Stamp Act (as the *Bowdoin Administration* has done in Massachusetts) preclude you effectually from all means of information. Mr. W[ilson] has given you no answer to these arguments.[164]

At the Pennsylvania ratifying convention, John Smilie, who like William Findley was an Anti-Federalist leader, advocated that a bill of rights be appended to the Constitution. "Suppose," declared Smilie, "Congress to pass an act for the punishment of libels and restrain the liberty of the press, for they are warranted to do this. What security would a printer have, tried in one of their courts?"[165] On the next day, December 1, 1787, Robert Whitehall, another Anti-Federalist leader, declared that Congress could "destroy the liberty of the press." Under the copyright clause, he observed, Congress could secure to authors "the right of their writings. Under this, they may license the press, *no doubt;* and under licensing the press, they may suppress it."[166] Once again Smilie added that "Congress have a power to restrain libels."[167]

James Wilson's speech of December 1 at the ratifying convention directly answered his critics. After reasserting that the new government had "no power whatsoever" concerning the press and that "no law in pursuance of the Constitution can possibly be enacted to destroy that liberty," he declared:

I presume it was not in the view of the honorable gentleman to say that there is no such thing as a libel or that the writers of such ought not to be punished. The idea of the liberty of the press is not carried so far as this is any country—*what is meant by liberty of the press, is that there should be no antecedent restraint upon it;* but that every author is responsible when he attacks the security or welfare of the government or the safety, character, and property of the individual. With regard to attacks upon the public, the mode of proceeding is by a prosecution. . . . Now, sir, if this libel is to be tried, it must be tried where the offense was committed; for under this Constitution, as declared in the second section of the third Article, the trial must be held in the state; therefore on this occasion it must be tried where it was published, if the indictment is for publishing; and it must be tried likewise by a jury of that state.[168]

If Congress had no power to legislate on the press and yet a libel against the United States was punishable in a federal court in the state where the publication was made, Wilson assumed the existence of a federal common law of crimes; he assumed, that is, that the federal courts possessed jurisdiction over nonstatutory crimes against the United States. His point was that although libels were subject to federal prosecution, the defendant would not be worse off than a defendant prosecuted in a state court for libeling the state. Wilson went further by contending that the federal defendant would be no worse off even if "the general government . . . had the power to make laws on this subject," which he denied. No Anti-Federalist disagreed with Wilson on the key point, however. They did not accept Wilson's contention that Congress lacked power to abridge the press, but they did not contest his claim that the federal courts could prosecute libels against the United States—and no one said that a free press guarantee would operate to prevent such prosecutions.

At his first opportunity, Justice Wilson, on circuit duty, presided over the trial of a person charged with commission of a nonstatutory crime. All members of the Supreme Court during its first decade believed in the existence of a federal common law of crimes.[169] In Henfield's case, members of Washington's cabinet, including Hamilton and Jefferson, supported the prosecution and John Marshall later noted with regret that a jury acquitted Henfield after he had been indicted, in part, "at common law, for disturbing the peace of the United States."[170]

Anderson's treatment of the matter of a federal common law of crimes is odd. He concedes the facts but adds that because the Supreme Court repudiated a federal common law of crimes "at its earliest opportunity, early judicial assumptions to the contrary cannot be considered authoritative on the issue of the Framers' intent."[171] However, the Supreme Court's decision of 1812 is worthless as a revelation of the Framers' intent, especially since the Court decided the case without arguments and without reasoned judgment, and the Justices were divided. Chief Justice John Marshall and Justices Story and Washington were the probable dissenters, although we know for certain only that Story dissented.[172] Moreover, those "early judicial assumptions" were held by important Framers including James Wilson, William Paterson, Oliver Ellsworth, and close associates such as John Jay and James Iredell, all of whom spoke more authoritatively about the Framers' intent than did the majority Justices in 1812.

III. Anderson's Methodology

Having discussed Anderson's views concerning the free press clause,[173] this Article now will examine the methodology by which Anderson reaches his conclusions. This methodology includes his general critique of "the Levy thesis"[174] and his use of historical evidence.[175]

A. Anderson's Critique of the "Levy Thesis"

As I read Anderson, a significant part of his article consists either of criticizing propositions that I have advanced and later accepting them despite the criticisms, or of exploding propositions that he attributes to me but which I did not make. An example of the first device, discussed above,[176] is his acceptance of the first amendment as a states' rights amendment—that is, one reserving to the states a power to legislate on the subject of the press. Another example is Anderson's treatment of my statement that to the Federalists, "the national government, *even in the absence of the First Amendment,* could not make speech or press a legitimate subject of restrictive legislation. The amendment itself was superfluous."[177] Anderson has fun with that statement as he asserts that "Levy concedes that his reading makes the press clause meaningless. . . ."[178] I concede nothing of the kind. Anderson himself twice quotes a statement by me concerning one purpose of the amendment that makes it considerably more than meaningless: The amendment "was intended to prohibit any Congressional regulation of the press, whether by means of a licensing act, a tax act, or a sedition act."[179] Anderson notes another purpose that I ascribed to the amendment: "[t]o quiet public apprehension [by offering] an added security that Congress would be limited to the exercise of its delegated powers."[180] Anderson calls that a "sop." Yet Madison thought that sop indispensable to persuade a hesitant public to support the new government with confidence that it would respect its limitations.[181] Still another purpose of the amendment is reiterated by Anderson throughout his article, the one he calls the "structural role of press freedom" as a bulwark of liberty or a check on government.[182] Anderson's many proofs that that was a purpose of the amendment, or, at least, a meaning of freedom of the press, all derive directly from *Legacy of Suppression.* To be sure, he cites primary sources such as *Cato's Letters,* Congress' Quebec declaration, and Virginia's Declaration of Rights, but all that material appears in *Legacy.*[183] Anderson does not quote properly another appropriate source, Blackstone. As readers will note from my quotation from Blackstone above,[184] he also supported the structural role of press freedom. Interestingly, Anderson's version of Blackstone is as follows: "The liberty of the press . . . consists in laying no previous restraints upon publications, and not in freedom from censure for criminal matter when published."[185] Anderson's ellipsis marks delete these words from Blackstone: "The liberty of the press is indeed essential to the nature of a free state . . . "—the crux of the structural role of press freedom. It was Blackstonian as well as Catonian. Yet when the same point suits Anderson's purpose he adopts it: "The one point upon which the Framers did make their intention clear was that Congress had no legitimate power to pass *any* law respecting the press."[186] That concession contradicts several pages of Anderson's criticism of my work.[187]

A proposition that Anderson attributes to me and then lambasts is that the first amendment was the source of reserved state power over the press.[188] Anderson correctly says that the Framers inferred the power "from the limited nature of the federal government's power over the press."[189] I said this in *Legacy of Suppression.*[190] But Anderson declares, "Without the states' rights purpose, the Levy interpretation ascribes to the press clause no legal effect at all."[191] Elsewhere, however, he accurately remarks that I regard the clause primarily as an added limitation on the powers of Congress, preventing it from enacting a sedition act.[192] That limitation gives the clause some legal effect.

Anderson also states that I fail to see the free press clause as a general guarantee of freedom of the press.[193] I do indeed fail to see that. The amendment is a general denial to Congress of a power to legislate. It is not a positive recognition of a right held by all to freedom of the press. The Bill of Rights is a bill of restraints upon government. The theory underlying the Bill of Rights—indeed, the Constitution—is that the people reserve all rights not ceded to government. The theory is not that the Constitution must affirmatively recognize a right before it can be said to exist. We have become too accustomed to the assumption that the only rights we have are those that the government has been expressly denied the power to violate. In our constitutional system of government, we are free because the government is not; the government is not free because of the limitations imposed upon it by the Constitution, including the Bill of Rights. We are free not because the Constitution enumerates rights positively, but because it limits government and protects some rights negatively.

When Anderson dissects the "Levy thesis," he finds that it consists of three tenets. The first is that, to the Framers, freedom of the press meant "nothing more than freedom from prior restraint."[194] The fatuousness of that proposition is mine, not Anderson's. Freedom of the press at the time of the first amendment's framing meant no prior restraints, but that is hardly all that it meant. My mistake appeared not in *Legacy of Suppression* but in my introduction to a collection of primary sources on the first amendment, where I declared that freedom of the press meant "merely" no prior restraints.[195] One word, "merely," provides Anderson with a target that he justifiably strikes at again and again. What he calls my second tenet is that the Framers meant Congress to be wholly powerless over the press.[196] As I noted earlier,[197] Anderson himself embraces that proposition quite explicitly.[198] The third tenet, Anderson states, is that "the real purpose of the press clause was to reserve to the states exclusive power to regulate the press."[199] My word was "primary"[200] rather than "real," and I did not say that the first amendment was "the source" of the reservation of state power,[201] but no matter; Anderson should have criticized the statement because the amendment has many purposes, only one of which was to reserve regulatory power to the states. Despite his criticism, however, he finally embraces that proposition also, as noted earlier,[202] when he stated that the apparent purpose of the specification of Congress was "to make clear that the amendment imposed no limitation on the states."

B. Anderson's Use of Historical Evidence

Apart from Anderson's misrepresentation of my work, his use of historical evidence is irresponsible and a major weakness of his article. Even when he sounds plausible and cites appropriate authorities, he misleads; the reader, unless familiar with those authorities, cannot know that they do not sustain Anderson's interpretation or that he misstates the facts.

I have chosen for illustration the following paragraph from Anderson's section "Interpreting the Legislative History," because he thinks that section is important, because he presents the paragraph as the most important of his conclusions about the legislative history of the first amendment, and because he is frankly interpretative. He writes:

> Fourth (and most important), freedom of the press was viewed not merely as a desirable civil liberty, but as a matter integral to the structure of the new government. The press clause was the product of revolutionary ferment. There were no guarantees of press freedom in colonial charters and little agitation to add them. The demand for legal protection of the press was contemporaneous with the demand for independence and self-government. The rhetoric often came from the pens of Englishmen, such as John Wilkes, "Cato," and "Father of Candor," but the realities that made the rhetoric relevant were the confrontations of American printers like John Peter Zenger and Eleazer Oswald with royal governors and other local representatives of the crown.[203]

Very little in that paragraph conforms with historical fact. The quoted paragraph has five sentences; the five paragraphs in the following discussion correspond to those sentences.

First: From Cato to Blackstone, the view of the press as integral to liberty was English. Freedom of the press, therefore, was as integral to government in England as in America; nothing was unique or special about the structural role of the press to "the new government." Except for advocating truth as a defense, English libertarians before 1763 recommended no substantive change in the common law of seditious libel. Accordingly, the structural role of the press harmonized with common law.

Second: Although the press clause, like every clause, first appeared in American constitutions that were written during the American Revolution, freedom of the press was not a product of revolutionary ferment any more than was freedom of religion or trial by jury. The British did not attack the colonists' freedom of the press, and the colonists did not list British violations of freedom of the press in any of their numerous documents of protest. The revolutionary controversy did produce some rights—for example, the American concept of unreasonable searches and seizures was in part a product of revolutionary ferment against the British use of writs of assistance. But the American press could not have been freer than it was in fact from the Stamp Act controversy to the battle of Lexington.

Third: So what? Colonial charters contained no guarantees of a score of rights, and there was no agitation, not a "little" agitation, to add them. Charters could not be added to. Anderson does not understand the nature and function of those charters.

Fourth: No demand at all existed for the legal protection of the press, and Anderson cites none. The first free press clause, in the Virginia Declaration of Rights, was the product of George Mason, the great planter and amateur political theorist, who composed alone and without being confronted by demands. Mason wrote on the premise that separation from England had thrust Virginians back into a state of nature from which they might emerge by entering into a new social compact, reserving to the people their fundamental rights. Political theory, not demands for legal protection of the press, produced the first press clause. Furthermore, the demand for independence had nothing to do with a demand for a press clause. Rather, independence was the occasion of the first written constitutions, nine of which included press clauses. The second press clause appeared in Pennsylvania's Constitution of 1776, the only constitution that also guaranteed freedom of speech. The convention that adopted that clause on freedom of speech and press, according to Dwight A. Teeter, also passed a sedition law punishing verbal opposition to the war and providing that two justices of the peace might imprison for the war's duration anyone whom they found to be "dangerous."[204] The other states tended to copy or improvise from the Virginia or Pennsylvania press clauses and acted out of imitativeness and a conscious carrying out of the social contract theory, rather than out of responsiveness to demands for a press clause.

Fifth: John Wilkes supplied no rhetoric for freedom of the press; he held orthodox opinions on the subject. In all of his work, nothing suggests disagreement with the common law of seditious libel. He declared that the expression of opinion should not give any public offense to any establishment or individual. "The crime," he declared, "commences from thence, and the magistrate has a right to interpose or even to punish outrageous and indecent attacks on what any community has decreed to be sacred; not only the rules of good breeding, but the laws of society are then infringed."[205] Father of Candor suggested wider bounds for freedom of the press, but unlike Cato he was not admired or quoted in America. No American of the 1776–1791 period emulated Father of Candor in rejecting the bad tendency test of political opinions and applying in its place the overt acts test.[206] On the other hand, Father of Candor also regarded wilfully false opinions against a just administration as seditious. The defense of the press upon which he most relied derived from the Zenger case.[207] Zenger himself, whom Anderson invokes in mythic opposition to royal tyranny, represented a popular cause. No grand jury would indict him. He had the support of the popular assembly. Had he attacked the assembly, he would have been a forgotten victim of the legislature's power to punish critics for breach of parliamentary privilege. Anderson uses Zenger's name to rely on conventional images rather than historical facts. He ignores that the royal judges posed no real threat to the colonial press, a point he himself makes elsewhere,[208] and neglects to notice that in *Legacy* I said, "The notoriety of the Zenger trial derives in part because it was so isolated a phenomenon."[209] I also demonstrated that, in New York in particular, the popular assemblies kept printers submissive.[210] Moreover, the Zenger case stands for the proposition that the jury should decide the criminality of an utterance and that truth should be a defense to a charge of criminal libel. Those propositions were not clarion calls of the American Revolution, were still "innovative" to Madison in 1788 and to John Adams in 1789, and were not accepted in American law until 1790 by the "reactionary" Pennsylvania Constitution and the Sedition Act of 1798. As for Eleazer Oswald, he never had a confrontation with a royal governor or his representatives. Oswald's nemesis was a revolutionary leader and signer of the Declaration of Independence, Thomas McKean.

V. New Directions

Legacy of Suppression is far more reliable than the introduction to the anthology upon which Anderson directed most of his ammunition, but not even the original book is acceptable to me now. That book bears a title, and a thesis implied by that title, that I no longer accept as valid. The forthcoming *Emergence of a Free Press,* a revision and substantial expansion of the original, more accurately expresses my view of the additional evidence that I have sifted. Anderson concludes his article by suggesting that the Framers understood both the relationship of a free press to free government and the need for protecting the press's freedom.[211] That proposition is timid and tautological. Anyone who has read American newspapers from 1776 to 1791, when the first press clauses in the state constitutions and the first amendment were framed, would realize that the American press, like the British, was astonishingly scurrilous. Politically, it was beyond the capacity of the law of criminal libels to control. I would conclude that by the time of the framing of the first amendment, those who wrote it, being practical politicians, must have intended to protect the press with which they were familiar. They could not have done otherwise.

Notes

1. L. Levy, Jefferson and Civil Liberties 61–66 (1963).
2. J. Smith, Freedom's Fetters 188–220 (1956) discusses federal common law prosecutions for seditious libel prior to the Sedition Act of 1798. None of the prosecutions reached the trial stage.
3. *United States v. Hudson and Goodwin*, 11 U.S. (7 Cranch) 32, 34 (1812).
4. That the Court divided is known from Justice Story's dissent in a circuit decision of the next year, *United States v. Coolidge*, 1 Gallison 488, 494–95 (1st Cir. 1813), and from the later statement of Justice Johnson in United States v. Coolidge, 14 U.S. (1 Wheat.) 415, 416 (1816). 2 W. Crosskey, Politics and the Constitution 782 (1953) stated that Chief Justice Marshall and Justice Washington dissented without noting that fact for the record. Crosskey offered no proof; however, one may surmise those justices' views tentatively from their being Federalists of the founding generation who believed in the existence of a federal common law of crimes and from Marshall's approving depiction of the 1793 prosecution of Gideon Henfield in 5 J. Marshall, The Life of Washington 40–42 (Citizens' Guild ed. 1926).
5. Among the Supreme Court justices who accepted jurisdiction of common law crimes while on circuit duty were John Jay, James Wilson, Oliver Ellsworth, William Paterson, James Iredell, and Samuel Chase. In *United States v. Worrall*, 2 U.S. (2 Dall.) 384, 391 (1798), Chase rejected the existence of a federal common law of crimes, but in United States v. Sylvester (1799), an unreported case in manuscript, Final Record of the United States Circuit Courts of Massachusetts, 1790–1799, at 303, 305 (1800), Chase changed his mind when presiding over a common law prosecution for counterfeiting which ended in a conviction. For further cases, see Levy, *supra* note 1, at 201 n.72; for an excellent discussion of the subject, see Presser, *A Tale of Two Judges,* 73 Nw. U.L. Rev. 26, 46–72 (1978).
6. The American Citizen (N.Y.), Oct. 20, 1806, *reprinted in* 10 The Life and Works of Thomas Paine 287 (W. Van der Weyde ed. 1925) [hereinafter cited as Paine].
7. *Id.* at 288.
8. *Id.*

9. For Sir William Blackstone's views on freedom of the press, see *infra* note 30 and accompanying text.
10. 10 Paine, *supra* note 6, at 289–90 (emphasis in original).
11. A major theme of L. Levy, Legacy of Suppression (1960) is that freedom of the press during the period of the framing (1787–1791) meant exemption from prior restraint but responsibility, under the criminal law, for abuse of the liberty to publish whatever one pleased.
12. C. Dickens, Martin Chuzzlewit 76 (National Library ed. 1930).
13. The Framers addressed the future, not the past. Their insistence that they were merely expressing a common understanding reflected an Anglo-American habit of going forward while facing backwards: Rights that should exist are established on the fictitious pretense that they have ever existed, and arguments are concocted to give the fiction the appearance of both reality and legality.
14. Anderson, *The Origin of the Press Clause,* 30 UCLA L. Rev. 455 (1983).
15. *Id.* at 496.
16. *Id.*
17. *Id.*
18. *Id.* at 506 n.288. Apparently, I would have been to blame if the Court had decided those cases according to my "reading" of history, but I get no credit when it produces "good" results. When Anderson quotes from *New York Times Co. v. Sullivan,* 376 U.S. 254, 276 (1964), *see* Anderson, *supra* note 14, at 521 n.372, ellipsis marks appear where the Court cited *Legacy of Suppression* as authority for the proposition that the verdict of history proves the unconstitutionality of the Sedition Act of 1798. Personally, I do not believe that historians influence appellate judges, who use scholarship as a garnish to provide the appearance of objectivity and respectability.
19. Anderson, *supra* note 14, at 510; *see infra* notes 26–75 and accompanying text.
20. Anderson, *supra* note 14, at 512; *see infra* notes 92–134 and accompanying text.
21. Anderson, *supra* note 14, at 513–14; *see infra* notes 76–91 and accompanying text.
22. Anderson, *supra* note 14, at 486–87.
23. *Id.* at 488; *see infra* notes 135–47 and accompanying text.
24. Anderson, *supra* note 14, at 501; *see infra* notes 148–57 and accompanying text.
25. Anderson, *supra* note 14, at 503; *see infra* notes 158–72 and accompanying text.
26. Anderson, *supra* note 14, at 510.
27. *Id.* at 493.
28. *Id.* at 509, 514.
29. Blackstone's endorsement of a "fair and impartial" trial was meaningless to the libertarians of the time, because he explicitly repudiated one of their two major gauges of fairness, the right of the defendant to prove the truth of his alleged libel. Moreover, Blackstone ignored the other libertarian gauge of fairness at a time when it was the principal issue of contention: the right of the jury rather than of the judge to decide the criminality of the alleged libel. For a discussion of that issue, see Levy, *supra* note 11, at 151–63.
30. 4 W. Blackstone, Commentaries *151–52 (1769), *reprinted in* L. Levy, Freedom of the Press from Zenger to Jefferson 104–05 (1966) (emphasis in original).
31. Thoughts of a Tory Author 13 (London 1712).
32. *Id.* at 1–2 (emphasis in original).
33. 4 J. Madison, Letters and Writings 544 (1865) (Richmond 1850).
34. 9 The Statutes at Large; Being a Collection of All the Laws of Virginia from the First Session of the Legislature, in the Year 1619 127 (W. Hening ed. 1823).
35. N.J. Const. of 1776, art. XXII, *reprinted in* 5 The Federal and State Constitu-

tions, Colonial Charters, and Other Organic Laws 2598 (F. Thorpe ed. 1909) [hereinafter cited as Thorpe]. For the constitutional provisions of the other five states, see Del. Const. of 1776, *reprinted in* 1 Thorpe, at 567; Md. Const. of 1776, art. III, *reprinted in* 3 Thorpe, at 1686–87; N.Y. Const. of 1777, art. XXXV, *reprinted in* 5 Thorpe, at 2635; Mass. Const. of 1780, art. VI, *reprinted in* 3 Thorpe, at 1910, N.H. Const. of 1784, *reprinted in* 4 Thorpe, at 2469.

36. Hall, *The Common Law: An Account of Its Reception in the United States,* 4 Vand. L. Rev. 791, 797–800 (1951) and 1 R. Powell, The Law of Real Property §§ 48–63 (1981) survey the reception state by state.

37. The lack of protection given to freedom of the press in New York is interesting because New York had been the home of Zenger's case forty years earlier. John Peter Zenger was prosecuted for seditious libel in 1735 by New York as a result of his aspersions on Governor William Cosby in the *New York Weekly Journal,* which Zenger printed. At his trial Zenger's counsel, Andrew Hamilton, offered to prove that the words charged as libelous were true and argued that truth should be a defense against a charge of libel. He further argued that the jury should render a general verdict of guilty or not guilty—deciding whether the words were libelous as a matter of law—rather than render a special verdict on the factual issue of whether the defendant printed the words charged and leave to the court the question of whether the words constituted libel as a matter of law. The jury, ignoring the court's instructions, acquitted Zenger. *See generally* J. Alexander, A Brief Narrative of the Case and Trial of John Peter Zenger (Katz ed. 1972). In effect, New York repudiated the principles of the Zenger defense when the state constitution of 1777 expressly adopted the common law as of the date of the outbreak of the war with England. *See* N.Y. Const. of 1777, art. XXXV, *reprinted in* 5 Thorpe, *supra* note 35, at 2635–36.

38. N.C. Const. of 1776, art. XXXIV, *reprinted in* 5 Thorpe, *supra* note 35, at 2793; S.C. Const. of 1778, art. XXXVIII, *reprinted in* 6 Thorpe, *supra* note 35, at 3257.

39. Anderson, *supra* note 14, at 534.

40. Americans executed the task of writing their revolutionary constitutions and declarations of rights in a seemingly haphazard fashion. Inexplicably, of the eleven original states that framed constitutions (Rhode Island and Connecticut simply retained their charters with references to Britain deleted), two passed over freedom of the press; four ignored the right of a defendant to be represented by counsel in a criminal case; six failed to protect the right against unreasonable searches and seizures; six omitted a provision against compulsory self-incrimination; incredibly, six neglected the right to the writ of habeas corpus; six, again, took no notice of a right to indictment by grand jury, and eight made no provision against bills of attainder. *See also* Dumbauld, *State Precedents for the Bill of Rights,* 7 J. Pub. L. 323 (1958), especially Appendix A, "Table of Topics in State Bills of Rights," at 343–44.

41. Riley, *Dr. William Whiting and Shays' Rebellion,* 66 Proc. Am. Antiquarian Soc. 119, 124 (1956).

42. *See generally id.* For Whiting's essay and letters, see *id.* at 131–66. Anderson, *supra* note 14, at 513 n.324, refers to a statement by Congressman John Nicholas, Feb. 25, 1799, which asserted that the law of libels was "a dead letter" because of the state free press clauses and that he knew of "no use of the law to punish seditious libels." Nicholas was wrong, as is shown by the Whiting case, and the Oswald and Keteltas cases described below. *See infra* notes 47–69, 76–83 and accompanying text.

43. The case is reported in the Boston *Independent Chronicle.* The indictment, the

allegedly libelous publication, and Sullivan's introductory address are reprinted in Independent Chronicle (Boston), Feb. 24, 1791. The arguments of defense counsel appear at *id.*, Mar. 3, 1791, and Mar. 10, 1791.

44. Sullivan's closing argument is at *id.*, Mar. 17, 1791, and Dana's charge is at *id.*, Mar. 24, 1791. The trial testimony was not reproduced.

45. C. Duniway, The Development of Freedom of the Press in Massachusetts 143 (1906).

46. Levy, *supra* note 11, at 209–12 (case of T. Adams and A. Adams).

47. *See generally* Teeter, *The Printer and the Chief Justice: Seditious Libel in 1782–83*, 45 Journalism Q. 235 (1968).

48. R. Brunhouse, The Counter-Revolution in Pennsylvania, 1776–1790, at 5 (1942).

49. On Oswald, see J. Wheeler, The Maryland Press, 1777–1790, at 19–36 (1938).

50. Independent Gazetteer (Philadelphia), Apr. 23, 1782. That was the conventional way of acknowledging the common law's restraints. In Teeter, *Decent Animadversions: Notes Toward a History of Free Press Theory, reprinted in* Newsletters to Newspapers 237–45 (D. Bond & W. McLeod eds. 1977), Teeter omitted Oswald's rejection of an "unbounded Liberty," leaving the misleading impression that Oswald supported it.

51. Independent Gazetteer, Oct. 15, 1782.

52. *Id.;* see *id.*, Jan. 11, 1783, for Oswald's later account.

53. *See* Teeter, *supra* note 47, at 238.

54. Letter from Oswald to General John Lamb (Nov. 26, 1782) *(quoted in* Teeter, *supra* note 47, at 239). Teeter thought that Oswald's remark showed "disgust with seditious libel" and that "Wilkes" in Independent Gazetteer, Oct. 19, 1782, showed the same disgust. Teeter, *supra* note 47, at 239. Oswald did not use the term or anything like it, nor did "Wilkes," who merely believed that the state constitution vested a right to comment on public proceedings, including the conduct of courts.

55. On *McDougall's Case*, see *infra* notes 85–86 and accompanying text.

56. "Junius Wilkes" in Independent Gazetteer, Nov. 9, 1782; "Candid," in *id.*, Dec. 14, 1782. Teeter, *supra* note 47, at 240 purported to describe "Candid's" views but confused him with "Koster." "Impartial" in Freeman's Journal (Philadelphia), Jan. 1, 1783, mentions Pennsylvania criminal libel prosecutions contradicting Oswald's remark that the doctrine of libels was being introduced in his case.

57. *See* Independent Gazetteer, Dec. 31, 1782; Jan. 1, 1783; Jan. 11, 1783; Jan. 18, 1783; see also Extracts From the Diary of Jacob Hiltzheimer, 1765–1798, at 52–54 (J. Parsons ed. 1893) for remarks by a member of the grand jury; Pennsylvania Gazette (Philadelphia), Jan. 8, 1783, for the grand jury's apologia.

58. Freeman's Journal, Jan. 15, 1783, and Jan. 29, 1783 (Bryan as "Adrian").

59. Pennsylvania Gazette, Jan. 29, 1783, for McKean writing as "Jurisperitus." "Aristides," id., Jan. 22, 1783, like Oswald, Independent Gazetteer, Jan. 11, 1783, believed that the grand jury rejected the doctrine of libels. Teeter, *supra* note 47, at 242, makes Aristides reject the law of seditious libel, which Aristides indirectly had mentioned as "the doctrine of criminal libels," while mistakenly observing in passing that Pennsylvania's courts had not received that doctrine.

60. 1 U.S. (1 Dall.) 319 (Pa. 1788).

61. 1 U.S. (1 Dall.) at 320 (quoting Independent Gazetteer, July 1, 1788).

62. *Id.*

63. *Id.*

64. 1 U.S. (1 Dall.) at 322.

65. *Id.* at 325.

66. *Id.* at 326.

67. *Id.* at 331 n.*.

68. The record of the impeachment proceedings appears *id.* at 330–37 n.*. The *Independent Gazetteer* published many articles on Oswald's behalf but not on the free press or criminal libel issue. No Junius Wilkes came forward, as in 1782. The focus in 1788 fell on the procedural irregularities: With no grand jury indictment or jury trial, Oswald was convicted by a judge who had a stake in the outcome of the case.

69. Trial of William Cobbett, *reprinted in* State Trials of the United States During the Administration of Washington and Adams 324–32 (F. Wharton ed. 1849) [hereinafter cited as Wharton].

70. Pa. Const. of 1790, *reprinted in* 5 Thorpe, *supra* note 35, at 3092–103.

71. 32 Geo. 3, ch. 60 (1792).

72. 6 & 7 Vict., ch. 96 (1843).

73. 2 J. Stephen, A History of the Criminal Law of England 343–84 (1883). Previously, the law of criminal libel allowed the jury to decide only whether the accused had in fact made the statement alleged, leaving to the judge the right to decide as a matter of law whether the statement was libelous. Furthermore, truth was not a defense because the greater the truth, the greater the provocation and therefore the greater the libel.

74. Anderson, *supra* note 14, at 490 n.211 (quoting J. Selsam, The Pennsylvania Constitution of 1776, at 259 (1971)).

75. *Id.* at 518. The Sedition Act of 1798 also recognized truth as a defense and the power of the jury to return a general verdict. Until 1798 libertarians relied completely on the Zenger defense, which did not repudiate the crime of seditious libel.

76. *Id.* at 513–14, relying on Teeter, A Legacy of Suppression: Philadelphia Newspapers and Congress During the War for Independence, 1775–1783 (unpublished dissertation, University of Wisconsin, 1966) [hereinafter cited as Teeter, Legacy of Suppression], shows that the Philadelphia newspapers freely attacked the Continental Congress and public measures and officials of Pennsylvania. Anderson fails to add Teeter's explanation of the reason that newspapers enjoyed a practical "immunity" from prosecution. The Continental Congress had no power to punish its critics, and, as for attacks on government in state politics, "Powerful men or men with powerful friends wrote for the newspapers. Political power helped to shield the printers from punishment." Teeter, *Press Freedom and the Public Printing: Pennsylvania, 1775–83*, 45 Journalism Q. 445, 448–49 (1968); *see also id.* at 449 n.28 (Congress).

77. For the best discussion of the Keteltas case, see A. Young, The Democratic Republicans of New York 480–93 (1967). *See also* Journal of the Votes and Proceedings of the General Assembly of New York, 19th Sess. (March 8, 1796); Greenleaf's New York Journal and Patriotic Register (N.Y.), Mar. 11, 1796 [hereinafter cited as New York Journal].

78. New York Journal, Mar. 11, 1796 (emphasis in original).

79. The Argus, or Greenleaf's New Daily Advertiser (N.Y.), Apr. 4, 1796; Apr. 5, 1796; Apr. 7, 1796; Apr. 8, 1796; Apr. 12, 1796 [hereinafter cited as The Argus].

80. The Argus, Mar. 15, 1796, *reprinted in* Levy, *supra* note 30, at 165.

81. *Id.*

82. The Time Piece (N.Y.), Dec. 22, 1797.

83. Smith, *supra* note 2, at 294 (case of William Duane).

84. Levy, *supra* note 11, at 39–41. *Cf.* Anderson, *supra* note 14, at 511–12.
85. *See* Levy, *supra* note 11, at 78–85.
86. New York General Assembly, Journal of Votes and Proceedings of the General Assembly of the Colony of New York, 1769–1771, at 8 (Albany 1820).
87. *See* Levy, *supra* note 11, at 78–83.
88. Journals of the House of Burgesses of Virginia, 1766–1769, at 91, 97, 98–99, 100, 110, 120–21, 125 (J. Kennedy ed. 1906).
89. *See* Levy, *supra* note 11, at 75–76. Anderson, *supra* note 14, at 511, reports only that grand juries would not indict Husband, but not that the House expelled him from membership and held him in jail.
90. *See* Levy, *supra* note 11, at 76–78. Anderson, *supra* note 14, at 511 n.318, reports that the Assembly challenged the Council's authority to punish for breach of parliamentary privilege but not that the Assembly used Powell's case to advance its own in an intramural struggle with the Council. Each house protested against the other. The Assembly denied that the Council was a parliamentary body thus to augment its own powers, not to protect freedom of the press.
91. *See* L. Levy, Origins of the Fifth Amendment 413 (1968).
92. Anderson, *supra* note 14, at 512.
93. *Id.* at 510–13.
94. *See id.* at 512–13.
95. *Id.* at 463–64, 488–89, 491–92, 509–12, 523–28.
96. Boston Gazette (Boston), August 1765, *reprinted in* 3 The Works of John Adams 447–64 (C.F. Adams 2d ed. 1865) (1st ed. Boston 1850) [hereinafter cited as Adams].
97. Boston Gazette, March 9, 1767, *reprinted in* Levy, *supra* note 30, at 95.
98. J. Quincy, Reports of Cases Argued and Adjudged in the Superior Court of Judicature of the Province of Massachusetts Bay, Between 1761 and 1772, at 278 (reissued 1969) (1st ed. Boston 1865) [hereinafter cited as Reports of Cases] (emphasis in original).
99. 4 Adams, *supra* note 96, at 32.
100. For Hutchinson's views, which were like Blackstone's, see Reports of Cases, *supra* note 98, at 244–45, 263, *discussed in* Levy, *supra* note 11, at 67–70.
101. Letter to J. Winthrop, June 23, 1776, *reprinted in* 9 Adams, *supra* note 96, at 409.
102. Anderson, *supra* note 14, at 463–64, 490–91, 523–24.
103. Levy, *supra* note 11, at 177 (quoting 2 American Archives Consisting of a Collection of Authentic Records 12–13 (P. Force ed. 4th ser. 1839)).
104. Levy, *supra* note 11, at 181 (quoting 4 Journals of the Continental Congress 18 (W. Ford ed. 1906)).
105. Teeter, *supra* note 47, at 239–41.
106. *See supra* notes 54–57 for some of Teeter's errors. He attributed to "Koster" the views of "Candid," a genuine radical. "Koster," "Aristides," and "Wilkes" did not repudiate the doctrine of seditious libel. Nor did Francis Bailey, the editor of Philadelphia's *Freeman's Journal.* Teeter mistakenly believed that the principles of the Zenger defense—truth as a defense to the charge of libel and the right of the jury to decide the criminality of the words—repudiated the doctrine of seditious libel. He also believed that the free press clause of the Pennsylvania Constitution of 1776 was incompatible with Blackstonianism, and therefore alleged that Bailey contradicted himself because he invoked the free press clause's protection of an unrestrained press yet endorsed the law of seditious libel. *See* Teeter, *supra* note 50, at 241. Bailey had no quarrel with that law, as shown by his credo in *Freeman's Journal,* June 13, 1782. Anderson, relying on Teeter for

far more than Teeter proves, cautiously says that Bailey did not repudiate the law of seditious libel "altogether." Anderson, *supra* note 14, at 527. Bailey did not repudiate it at all. Without the support of Teeter, or, rather, supported only by "Junius Wilkes" and "Candid," whom Anderson did not read except in Teeter, a substantial section of Anderson's argument dies.

107. *See supra* text accompanying notes 60–69.
108. Trial of Cobbett, *reprinted in* Wharton, *supra* note 69, at 323.
109. That is, to the *law* of seditious libel. Anderson, *supra* note 14, at 526. "Cato" was John Trenchard and Thomas (not William) Gordon, joint authors of Cato's Letters: Or, Essays on Liberty, Civil and Religious (6th ed. 1755) [hereinafter cited as Cato's Letters].
110. Anderson, *supra* note 14, at 526.
111. *Id.* at 528–29 n.414.
112. 1 Cato's Letters, *supra* note 109, at 250 ("Reflections upon Libelling").
113. 3 *id.* at 299 ("Discourse upon Libels").
114. *Id* at 302–03 ("Second Discourse upon Libels").
115. Anderson mauls my treatment of Cato, which he finds "perplexing." Anderson, *supra* note 14, at 525 n.395. 1 myself was perplexed by his presentation of it until I compared what he says I said with what I actually said, and discovered that his presentation was inaccurate. Anderson says, "Levy implies that Cato approved of libel prosecutions under some circumstances, yet he recognizes that Cato's approval of good libel laws 'prudently and honestly executed' was merely a 'genuflection toward the law— keeping Cato on the safe side.'" *Id.* This is what I said: "But it was abundantly clear, notwithstanding this genuflection toward the law—keeping Cato on the safe side—that he thought the law of criminal libel was neither good nor prudently executed, indeed that it was quite dangerous to public liberty and good government." Levy, *supra* note 11, at 119. Also, Anderson concludes, "Levy dismisses Cato as a 'flashing star. . . . '" Anderson, *supra* note 14, at 527. I hardly think that I *dismiss* Cato, whose work I feature as the leading libertarian statement on freedom of the press in the eighteenth century on either side of the Atlantic, until the Sedition Act forced Americans to repudiate the law of seditious libel. *Legacy is* devoted to Cato. *See* Levy, *supra* note 11, at 115–21. Levy, *supra* note 30, at 10–24, reprints Cato on freedom of the press and libel law as presented to Americans by Zenger's press. The copy of *Cato's Letters* used by Anderson and wrongly dated 1791 rather than 1971—the first reprint of the work since 1755—was produced under my general editorship. Cato is a favorite of mine, and my saying that he was far ahead of his time is no dismissal. It was I who said Cato was "adored, quoted, and plagiarized" in America. Levy, *supra* note 30, at xxvi. This is important because Anderson says I disparage Cato's importance in America and dismiss him because he was English. On the overt acts test, see *infra* note 206.
116. Anderson, *supra* note 14, at 528.
117. *Id.* (quoting letter from William Cushing to John Adams (Feb. 18, 1789), *reprinted* in Levy, *supra* note 30, at 150 (emphasis Cushing's)).
118. Levy, *supra* note 11, at 193–96; Levy, *supra* note 30, at 147–53.
119. Levy, *supra* note 11, at 194–95.
120. Anderson, *supra* note 14, at 529 n.414.
121. Smith, *supra* note 2, at 185.
122. *See* Levy, *supra* note 11, at 212 n.72. *Commonwealth v. Blanding*, 20 Mass. (3 Pick.) 304, 313 (1825), still interpreted freedom of the press in Blackstonian terms.

123. *See* Levy, *supra* note 11, at 193–95.
124. Levy, *supra* note 30, at 149.
125. *See infra* text accompanying note 144.
126. Anderson, *supra* note 14, at 529.
127. Levy, *supra* note 11, at 273–82.
128. Anderson, *supra* note 14, at 531.
129. *Id.*
130. *Id.* at 535.
131. *Id.* at 535 n.446.
132. J. Madison, Virginia Report of 1799–1800, *reprinted in* Levy, *supra* note 30, at 216–17.
133. Blasi states:
     In attempting to assess the original understanding of the First Amendment, it is important that Madison articulated as early as 1789 the theory of liberty on which he based his Virginia Report of 1799–1800. This fact casts some doubt on the thesis advanced by Professor Levy that a libertarian theory of freedom of speech was not accepted at the time the First Amendment was adopted and only emerged 10 years later as a result of the political jockeying over the Alien and Sedition Acts of 1798.
     Blasi, *The Checking Value in First Amendment Theory,* Am. B. Found. Research J. 521, 535–36 n.60 (1977).
134. *Id.* at nn.58–66 and accompanying text constitutes the questionable material. Although none of Blasi's Madison sources is from 1789, the reader cannot know that fact from Blasi's footnotes, which do not identify the document from which Blasi is quoting. Anderson, *supra* note 14, at 510 n.308, attributes a statement by Madison to 1789, but the source which Anderson cites in that note clearly shows that the date was 1800.
135. *See* Levy, *supra* note 11, at 225.
136. Anderson relies heavily on the legislative history of the first amendment's free press clause. A quarter of his article describes that legislative history, which he alleges casts doubt on "the Levy interpretation." Anderson, *supra* note 14, at 494. He also declares that the legislative history has been ignored because it is inconsistent with the conclusions of my work. *Id.* at 534. That is an equally unsupportable judgment. The legislative history of the clause is consistent with my interpretation; if the two had conflicted, someone during the past quarter of a century eagerly would have exposed the conflict. We now have only Anderson's ipse dixit that the conflict exists, not proof that it does.
     I did not ignore the legislative history, nor did my predecessors. Francis N. Thorpe and David Matteson had reviewed it when tracing the framing of the Bill of Rights, and Milton Konvitz had focused on the framing of the first amendment. 2 F. Thorpe, The Constitutional History of the United States 199—263 (1901); Matteson, *The Organization of the Government under the Constitution,* in S. Bloom, History of the Formation of the Union under the Constitution 294–328 (1943); M. Konvitz, Fundamental Liberties of a Free People 345–61 (1957). Anderson used no sources that I and the others had not used; he has not discovered anything. In fact he has grossly inflated the importance of the legislative history of the free press clause. Having reviewed it for 22 pages—more fully, to be sure, than anyone previously—he concludes, "The legislative history of the press clause is, of course, inconclusive . . . because the Framers simply did not articulate what they meant by 'freedom of the press,'" and "there is no record whatever of the meanings ascribed to the amendment by the ratifying legislatures."

Anderson, *supra* note 14, at 486. Therefore, any doubt cast on my view is based on Anderson's presuppositions, not on the legislative history. On one matter concerning the legislative history I concede a point to Anderson. When the free press clause was before the Senate, a motion was made and defeated to protect freedom of the press "in as ample a manner as hath at any time been secured by the common law." In *Legacy* I remarked that we do not know whether the Senate defeated that motion "on the ground that it was too narrow, too broad, or simply unnecessary." Levy, *supra* note 11, at 224. Anderson argues that it could not have been too broad. I agree, but not for his reason, that there were broader views "in the air." Anderson, *supra* note 14, at 500. I have breathed the air deeply and detect only the aroma of "Junius Wilkes" and "Candid." *See supra* notes 56, 108–09. We do not know why the proposer of the motion in the Senate said "in as ample a manner as hath at any time been secured by the common law" instead of "as secured by the common law." He may have had Zengerian principles in mind. He may have identified the common law, as so many Americans did, with a system of law that protected personal liberties and restrained government. His motion need not be read in narrow Blackstonian terms, which is why I guessed that the Senate could have defeated it because it was too broad; but the chances are greater that the motion was defeated because the Senate believed that it was too narrow or unnecessary.

137. Anderson, *supra* note 14, at 486 n.192.
138. *See* R. Mott, Due Process of Law 1–24 (1926); *see generally* Jurow, *Untimely Thoughts: A Reconsideration of the Origins of the Due Process of Law,* 19 Am. J. Legal Hist. 265 (1975).
139. In the five southern colonies the Church of England had been legally established, but no state church existed in the other colonies. Five (Rhode Island, Pennsylvania, Delaware, New Jersey, and New York) never had any kind of establishment, and the remaining three (Massachusetts, Connecticut, and New Hampshire) had uniquely American dual establishments by the 1730's. After the Revolution the only establishments of religion in the United States were multiple establishments, which were unknown to England or Europe: the public support of several different churches or of all with preference to none. Six states (Massachusetts, Connecticut, New Hampshire, Maryland, South Carolina, and Georgia) allowed multiple establishments, and no establishment existed in the other seven states.
140. *See generally* L. Levy, *No Establishment of Religion: The Original Understanding,* in Judgments: Essays on American Constitutional History 169 (1972).
141. *See generally* S. Cobb, The Rise of Religious Liberty in America (1902). On the Maryland Toleration Act, see Documents in American History 31–32 (H. Commager ed. 1949).
142. Anderson, *supra* note 14, at 488, 490 n.211.
143. Letter to Madison, July 31, 1788, *reprinted in* 13 Papers of Thomas Jefferson 442 (J. Boyd ed. 1950).
144. 6 *id.* at 316 (remarks on Jefferson's draft of a constitution for Virginia, *ca.* Oct. 15, 1788) (emphasis in original).
145. 15 *id.* at 367 (to Madison, Aug. 28, 1789).
146. Letter to R. Peters, Aug. 19, 1789, *reprinted in* 12 The Papers of James Madison 346–47 (R. Rutland ed. 1979) [hereinafter cited as Papers of Madison].
147. *Id.* at 340 (Aug. 15, 1789).
148. 3 J. Elliot, The Debates in the Several State Conventions on the Adoption of the Federal Constitution 656 (2d ed. Philadelphia 1901) (1st ed. Philadelphia 1836)

[hereinafter cited as Elliot, Debates].

149. Anderson, *supra* note 14, at 501, 502–03.
150. *Id.* at 502.
151. Speech of June 8, 1789, in Congress, *reprinted in* 12 Papers of Madison, *supra* note 146, at 203.
152. Anderson, *supra* note 14, at 501.
153. *Id.* at 499. What the Framers of the seventh amendment meant by their explicit reference to the common law is not clear. We do not know whether they intended the common law of England, as Justice Story asserted in *United States v. Wonson*, 28 F. Cas. 745 (C.C.D. Mass. 1812) (No. 16,750), or the common law of the individual states in which cases were to be tried by federal courts. Whatever was meant, the reference to common law was intended to appease public opinion, which demanded a guarantee of jury trial in civil as well as in criminal cases. *See* Wolfram, *The Constitutional History of the Seventh Amendment,* 57 Minn. L. Rev. 639, 653–730 (1973).
154. Anderson, *supra* note 14, at 501.
155. *Id.* at 508.
156. For example, he says that the argument requires that the amendment be read as "Congress shall make no law abridging *the power of the states to abridge* the freedom of speech, or of the press." *Id.* at 507 (emphasis Anderson's).
157. *Id.* at 501.
158. *Id.* at 504. Anderson adds that I emphasized Wilson's statement because he was an influential Framer and "the only one to express himself on the meaning of freedom of the press." *Id.* at 504 n.285. Anderson then doubts that Wilson was a spokesman for those who framed the first amendment because he was not a member of the First Congress, which adopted it. But I did not connect Wilson in any way with the framing of the first amendment. I counted him as a major witness on the meaning of the concept of a free press, but I did not assert that he was the only Framer who explained the meaning of the term "freedom of the press," because he was not. Hugh Williamson of North Carolina, another signer of the Constitution, declared in a 1788 essay that when the licensing system expired in England, "the press became perfectly free." Remarks on the New Plan of Government (1788), *reprinted in* Essays on the Constitution 394–408 (P. Ford ed. 1892). George Nicholas of Virginia and James Iredell of North Carolina, close associates of the Framers, similarly construed freedom of the press to mean no prior restraints. *See* 3 Elliot, Debates, *supra* note 148, at 247 (2d ed. rev. 1941); Answers to Mr. Mason's Objections to the New Constitution (1788), *reprinted in* Pamphlets on the Constitution 333–70 (P. Ford ed. 1888) [hereinafter cited as Pamphlets]. Anti-Federalists, contrary to Anderson, *supra* note 14, at 497, did not have more expansive views than the Framers or the Federalists in the First Congress who backed the first amendment. Melancthon Smith of New York and Richard Henry Lee of Virginia believed that England had a free press because the licensing system no longer existed. *See* An Address to the People of the State of New York (1788), *reprinted in* Pamphlets, *supra,* at 87–115; Observations . . . In a Number of Letters from the Federal Farmer, Letter IV (1787), *reprinted in* 2 The Complete Anti-Federalist 245–51 (H. Storing ed. 1981) [hereinafter cited as Anti-Federalist]. Lee's praise of England, which equated no prior restraints with freedom of the press, appeared in the most widely circulated of all Anti-Federalist tracts, *Letters from the Federal Farmer.* Anti-Federalists sought to sabotage or defeat the Bill of Rights after Madison urged it in the First Congress. *See* Levy, *supra* note 11, at 226–33.
159. Even if Wilson were speaking hypothetically, he could no more be dismissed for

that reason than could the essays by Hamilton, Madison, and Jay in *The Federalist*. But, rather than speaking hypothetically, Wilson was discussing a procedure that would be followed if Congress exercised a power that he insisted it did not have.

160. 2 The Documentary History of the Ratification of the Constitution 167 (M. Jensen ed. 1976) [hereinafter cited as Documentary History].

161. Pennsylvania Herald (Philadelphia), Oct. 17, 1787, *reprinted in* 2 Documentary History, *supra* note 160, at 193–98 (emphasis in original).

162. *Id.*

163. A Review of the Constitution . . . By a Federal Republican (1787), *reprinted in* 3 Anti-Federalist, *supra* note 158, at 81.

164. Independent Gazetteer, Nov. 6, 1787, *reprinted in* 3 Anti-Federalist, *supra* note 158, at 93 (emphasis in original).

165. 2 Documentary History, *supra* note 160, at 441.

166. 2 *id.* at 454. Whitehall professed to believe that the fear of prior restraint as well as of subsequent punishment was still real. He advocated a free press clause to prevent censorship in advance of publication. Blackstone too had defined freedom of the press as the absence of prior restraints.

167. *Id.*

168. *Id.* at 455 (emphasis added).

169. Trial of Gideon Henfield (1793), *reprinted in* Wharton, *supra* note 69, at 49–89; *see also supra* note 5. Justice Samuel Chase initially disagreed but changed his mind. *See supra* note 5.

170. 5 J. Marshall, *supra* note 4, at 41.

171. Anderson, *supra* note 14, at 503.

172. *See supra* note 4.

173. *See supra* notes 19–172 and accompanying text.

174. Anderson, *supra* note 14, at 494–509; *see infra* notes 176–202 and accompanying text.

175. *See infra* notes 203–10 and accompanying text.

176. *See supra* notes 154–57 and accompanying text.

177. Anderson, *supra* note 14, at 505–06 (quoting Levy, *supra* note 30, at lvii (emphasis in original)).

178. Anderson, *supra* note 14, at 505.

179. *Id.* at 496, 498–99 (quoting Levy, *supra* note 30, at lvi).

180. Anderson, *supra* note 14, at 506 (quoting Levy, *supra* note 30, at lvii)

181. *See* 12 Papers of Madison, *supra* note 146, at 347 (Madison to Peters, Aug. 19, 1789) and Madison's great speech to Congress on June 8, 1789, recommending the amendments that became the Bill of Rights. In the speech he made the point at least seven times. *See id.* at 197–209.

182. Anderson, *supra* note 14, at 488–94.

183. *See, e.g.,* Levy, *supra* note 11, at 15–20, 176–77.

184. See *supra* note 30 and accompanying text.

185. Anderson, *supra* note 14, at 495 n.244.

186. Anderson, *supra* note 14, at 522; see also *id.* at 536 for another statement of the same point: The Framers "had denied that the federal government had any power to control the press, even in the absence of a first amendment."

187. *Id.* at 500–06.

188. *Id.* at 507.

189. *Id.*

190. Levy, *supra* note 11, at 225–26.

191. Anderson, *supra* note 14, at 508.

192. *Id.* at 496, 499.
193. *Id.* at 496.
194. *Id.* at 498.
195. Levy, *supra* note 30, at lv. Anderson, *supra* note 14, at 498 n.253, says that he relied primarily on the 1966 introduction to my anthology "as the most mature statement of Levy's position," but the introduction was merely an abridged version of *Legacy* with qualifications and subtleties as well as supporting evidence eliminated.
196. Anderson, *supra* note 14, at 498–99.
197. *See supra* notes 177–87 and accompanying text.
198. Anderson, *supra* note 14, at 522.
199. *Id.* at 499.
200. Levy, *supra* note 30, at lix.
201. *See id.*
202. *See supra* notes 154–57 and accompanying text.
203. Anderson, *supra* note 14, at 488–89.
204. Teeter, Legacy of Suppression, *supra* note 76, at 79–80.
205. J. Wilkes, English Liberty 132 (London 1769), *quoted in* Levy *supra* note 11, at 147–48.
206. The overt acts test is a test to determine the permissible scope of freedom of expression. According to that test, opinions should be immune from criminal punishment, and only illegal conduct or criminal acts should be penalized. The test originated in the seventeenth century in suggestive remarks by Roger Williams, William Walwyn, and Baruch Spinoza, primarily to promote the cause of religious liberty. To the same end, the Reverend Philip Furneaux developed the test fully in the next century and Thomas Jefferson adopted it. *See* Levy, *supra* note 11, at 90–91, 95, 154–57, 166–68, 188–89. Such libertarians advocated the test as an alternative to the prevailing bad tendency test, according to which the expression of an opinion was punishable if it tended to stir animosity to the established religion of a state or to the government, its officers, or measures. Thus, the preamble to Jefferson's Virginia Statute of Religious Freedom declared that allowing the civil magistrate to restrain the profession of opinions "on the supposition of their ill tendency . . . at once destroys all religious liberty." The government's rightful purposes, Jefferson continued, were served if its officers did not interfere until "principles break out into overt acts against peace and good order." 2 Papers of Thomas Jefferson, *supra* note 143, at 546. The overt acts test, therefore, sharply distinguished words from deeds, and, in Furneaux's words, was based on the proposition that the "penal laws should be directed against *overt acts only* . . . and not against *principles,* or the *tendency* of principles." P. Furneaux, *Letters to . . . Blackstone,* in The Palladium of Conscience 34 (Letter III) (facsimile ed. 1974) (1st ed. Philadelphia 1773) (emphasis in original).
207. *See* Levy, *supra* note 11, at 149–54.
208. Anderson, *supra* note 14, at 510.
209. Levy, *supra* note 11, at 19.
210. *Id.* at 44–49, 78–85.
211. Anderson, *supra* note 14, at 537.

5

The *Legacy* Reexamined

In my book, *Legacy of Suppression,*[1] I challenged the conventional wisdom[2] about the intent underlying the press clause of the first amendment. I argued that historical evidence showed that while the clause was meant to restrain the federal Congress absolutely, it was not intended to restrain the states or the federal courts. I further argued that even if the amendment had a broader reach, the "freedom of the press" it originally protected was freedom from licensing, censorship, and other forms of prior restraint. It did not protect the press from subsequent punishment for its publications. Specifically, it was not meant to eliminate the law of seditious libel.

I remain convinced that the revolutionary generation did not seek to wipe out the core idea of seditious libel, that the government may be criminally assaulted by mere words, that the legislatures were more suppressive than the courts, that the freedom of political expression remained quite narrow until 1798 (except for a few aberrant statements), that English libertarian theory usually stayed in the vanguard of American theory, that the Bill of Rights in its immediate history was in large measure a lucky political accident, and that the first amendment was as much an expression of federalism as of libertarianism. I still contend that tarring and feathering a Tory editor because of his opinions shows a rather restricted meaning and scope of the freedom of the press. Indeed, one may ask whether there was free speech during the Revolutionary era if only the speech of freedom was free.

But *Legacy of Suppression* is scarcely beyond criticism. The most common fault found by knowledgeable reviewers was that it paid insufficient attention to press practices.[3] Those critics were right. In researching *Legacy,* I scanned hundreds of issues of colonial, revolutionary, and early national newspapers looking for discussions of freedom of the press. The discussions I found reflected only stunted understandings, but I was oblivious to the fact that after the enactment of the Stamp Act, in 1765, American newspapers *practiced* freedom of the press. Their pages screamed out scathing denunciations of public men and measures.

The legal definition of seditious libel remained what it had been from the time of Hawkins[4] to Mansfield[5]—malicious, scandalous falsehoods of a political nature that tended to breach the peace, instill revulsion or contempt in the people, or lower the citizenry's esteem for its rulers. But the scope of actual political discourse had widened so greatly that seditious libel was reduced to a narrow category of verbal offenses against the government, its officials, and its policies. Prosecutions were infrequent and the press was habitually scurrilous.

State governments realized that prosecutions might fail or backfire because critics often represented strong factions or influential citizens. Moreover, (except in a time of crisis, such as Shay's Rebellion) the populace tended to distrust an administration that sought to imprison its critics. Indeed, the press could not have endured as calumnious and hostile as it was without public support. For the most part, people understood that scummy journalism unavoidably accompanied the benefits to be gained from a free press. They also seemed to understand that critics vented unfavorable opinions in order to excite a justifiable contempt for the government and that to prosecute those critics would be to immunize from criticism public officials who probably deserved to be disliked or distrusted. That was the teaching of *Cato's Letters*[6] and the Zenger case.[7] The actual freedom of the press had slight relationship to the legal conception of freedom of the press as a cluster of constraints.

In short, the law threatened repression, but the press conducted itself as if the law scarcely existed.[8] The American experience with a free press was as broad as the theoretical inheritance was narrow. The obvious conclusion from this, which I failed to draw in *Legacy*—and which none of my critics drew—is that the framers of the press clauses of the first state constitutions and of the first amendment could only have meant to protect the press as they knew it. In other words, they constitutionally guaranteed the *practice* of freedom of the press. They did not adopt its legal definition as found in Blackstone or in the views of the libertarian theorists. By freedom of the press, the framers meant a right to engage in rasping, corrosive, and offensive discussions on all topics of public interest. A narrow understanding of the common law definition had become unsuitable for a republican nation. Although libertarian theory had not caught up with press practice, that practice established a foundation for the new libertarianism that would emerge after the Sedition Act.

I do not gracefully accept my acknowledgment that the press of the new nation functioned as if the law of criminal libel hardly mattered. My principal thesis—that neither the American Revolution nor the framers of the first amendment intended to abolish the common law of seditious libel—remains unchanged. The argument that freedom of political expression existed as a fact and therefore undermines the thesis of *Legacy of Suppression* is an odd one in some respects, on all fours with the proposition that the existence of so many heretics during the reign of Bloody Mary proves there was a great deal of freedom of religion, despite the fires at Smithfield. I am interested, to use an analogy, in the concept of crime, and therefore do not find crime-rate statistics to be helpful. In our own time, obscenity is illegal, although we live in a society saturated by it and witness few prosecutions. So too the rarity of prosecutions for seditious libel and the existence of an unfettered press do not illumine the scope and meaning of freedom of the press or the law on freedom of the press.

Nonetheless, the failure of *Legacy* to discuss press practices and their implications is a serious one. Accordingly, I have prepared a new version of the book that so substantially alters its viewpoint on the actual condition of the press that I have abandoned the original title as partly misleading. The revised edition will be entitled *The Emergence of Free Press.*[9]

There are some criticisms of *Legacy,* however, that I cannot accept. I take particular issue with a recent article by Professor William Mayton.[10] Mayton finds an intent to reject the doctrine of seditious libel in both the Constitution's structure of federalism and limited powers and in its restrictions regarding the punishment of treason. In support of this thesis, he claims that 18th century political theory suggests "a legacy of idealism" rather than a "legacy of suppression." Mayton's understanding of both the Constitution's structure and the political theory underlying the document is flawed.[11] In the first part of this comment, I discuss (and thoroughly disagree with) Mayton's structural arguments; in the second part, I criticize his intellectual history.

I. Mayton's New Understanding

A. *Federalism and Delegated Powers*

The Antifederalists urged the states not to ratify the Constitution in part because it lacked a bill of rights. The members of the Constitutional Convention had omitted a bill of rights because they believed that it would be superfluous. As I wrote in *Legacy:*

> The Federalists who expressed themselves on the subject unanimously concurred in stating that Congress, or the "general government," had no power whatever to legislate in a manner violative of personal liberties, no power, for example, to legislate on matters respecting speech or press unless to protect literary property by enacting copyright laws. A bill of rights, as Hamilton argued, would be a bill of restraints on national powers, but "why declare that things shall not be done which there is no power to do? Why, for instance, should it be said that the liberty of the press shall not be restrained, when no power is given by which restrictions may be imposed." The Framers intended a federal system of government to exercise only such powers as were specifically enumerated or were necessary and proper to carry out those enumerated. It followed that the power to punish for criminal libels was denied to the United States in the minds of the Framers. They had vested no such power and intended that none be exercised or abused. In other words, the Framers believed that even without an express limitation such as that later imposed by the First Amendment, Congress was bereft of authority to restrict freedom of speech or press in any manner.[12]

Although this is elementary and traditional lore, Mayton gives the impression that I am ignorant of it, that he has discovered it, and that from it he derives "a new understanding of the original guarantee of the liberty of expression."[13] By the original guarantee he does not mean the first amendment. Indeed, he lambasts me (*Legacy "is* wrong"[14]) for thinking that the first amendment has some significance;[15] he contends that the rights-oriented theory of liberty of expression inspired by the first amendment obscures the original structural protection of speech. According to Mayton, "limitations and dispersals of government power in the original, unamended Constitution, . . . extended a strong guarantee of liberty of expression."[16] Others may not find such a strong guarantee in an inference from structure and silence, however. Notwithstanding the remarks from *Legacy* quoted above, Mayton alleges that I excluded or treated as insignificant those structural protections.[17] His new understanding has two prongs. The original guarantee, he first asserts, "was made possible by federalism, by an allocation to the states rather than to the federal government of an authority to suppress speech harmful to person and property."[18] Second, the "Constitution's treason clause is an explicit manifestation of this original guarantee."[19]

Mayton's "new understanding" is neither new nor original. Even his interpretation of the treason clause is borrowed from Willard Hurst.[20] The passage from *Legacy* cited above shows that Mayton's new understanding originated in 1787. The framers argued that the Constitution contained various protections of liberty, including a right to trial by jury in criminal cases, a narrow definition of treason, a ban on titles of nobility, free speech for legislators, a guarantee that the citizens of each state should have the same privileges and immunities of citizens in other states, a ban on religious tests for office, a guarantee of the writ of habeas corpus, prohibitions on bills of attainder and *ex post facto* laws, and a guarantee that each state have a republican form of government. The framers also declared that still other provisions of the Constitution—for example, the election of public officials, the representative system, the separation of powers among the three branches of government, and the requirement that revenue and appropriation measures originate in the House of Representatives—had a libertarian character. Accordingly, the framers maintained, as Hamilton stated in *The Federalist* #84, "that the Constitution is itself, in every rational sense, and to every useful purposes, a Bill of Rights."[21]

If the framers were right in 1787, Mayton, though derivative, is also right; the first amendment, indeed, the entire Bill of Rights, need not have been added to the Constitution, and it "contributed to a misinterpretation of the original scheme" of constitutional protections.[22] By this reasoning, the unamended Constitution extended strong protections against infringements of religious liberty, the right to counsel, and due process of law. It also strongly protected citizens against unreasonable searches and seizures, compulsory self-incrimination, and cruel and unusual punishments. In fact, it extended strong protection to every right mentioned in the Bill of Rights.

The American people of 1787 understood, however, that they were entitled to an explicit reservation of their rights against government, that a bill of rights is a bill of restraints upon government, and that people may be free only if the government is not. They understood a point that escapes Mayton: If the crime of treason required a tight, written definition, other rights required explicit definitions too. Those who demanded a bill of rights had the better argument if only because of the Framers' obvious inconsistencies. The Constitution explicitly protected some rights, but not others. Moreover, a strong argument could be made that everything not reserved had been delegated to the national government by implication. As James Wilson declared:

> A bill of rights annexed to a constitution is an enumeration of the powers reserved. If we attempt an enumeration, everything that is not enumerated is presumed to be given. The consequence is, that an imperfect enumeration would throw all implied powers into the scale of the government and the rights of the people would be rendered incomplete.[23]

That theory causes the argument from structuralism to self-destruct. Moreover, as proponents of a bill of rights contended, delegated powers, especially when implemented by the necessary and proper clause, might be exercised in a way to abridge reserved rights. It was James Madison and not some Antifederalist demagogue who—in a speech that is a running refutation of Mayton's structuralism argument—urged Congress to recommend amendments that would protect "the great rights of mankind," and declared that Congress might employ general warrants in the enforcement of its tax measures.[24] And Antifederalists, answering *The Federalist* #84 and Wilson's State House Yard speech,[25] warned that Congress might abridge the freedom of the press by taxing the press or, in the absence of a restraint upon Congress, by enacting a sedition act.[26]

B. The Treason Clause

Mayton argues that the Framers intended the treason clause to prevent seditious libel prosecutions by protecting dissident speech in two ways: First, by requiring an overt act, the clause prevents speech alone from constituting treason. Second, by eliminating a historical English category of treasonous offenses—"compassing or imaging the king's death"—it prohibits punishment of speech as "constructive treason."[27] Mayton relies for his proof "on the processes of drafting and ratifying the original Constitution" and asserts that "[t]hese processes were such as to force a break with the historical practices of both seditious libel and constructive treason."[28] But Mayton offers little historical evidence to prove his points about the treason clause, perhaps because such evidence does not exist. Moreover, even if he were correct about the history, and speech could not be punished as treason, that would not prevent the prosecution of speech as some other crime.

Nothing in the records of the Constitutional Convention bears out Mayton's historical thesis, so it is not surprising that he offers no proof as to the drafting of the treason clause. As for ratification, he has one pertinent but slight piece of evidence. In North Carolina, Richard Dobbs Spaight observed that under the treason clause complaints or writings alone could not constitute treason.[29] This is the only evidence purporting to prove that the Framers intended the treason clause to prohibit prosecutions for seditious libel. Mayton attempts to bolster his argument by referring to statements by James Wilson, James Madison, James Iredell, and George Nicholas.[30] None of these statements, however, construed the treason clause as a protection of free speech or even referred to free speech.[31] Mayton also relies upon the work of Willard Hurst, who concluded that the treason clause was meant to be a free speech provision. But despite Hurst's illustrious reputation, he asserted the proposition without proving it. Hurst referred only to the ratification debates in North Carolina and Virginia, showed only Spaight making the nexus between free speech and the treason clause, and conceded that even in 1798, when the constitutionality of the Sedition Act was at issue, only John Taylor in the Virginia Assembly relied on the treason clause to oppose the Sedition Act. Neither the Jeffersonians in the Congress, nor Madison and Jefferson in the Virginia and Kentucky Resolutions, nor Madison in his attack on the Sedition Act in his *Report* of 1799–1800 suggested that the treason clause prohibited sedition laws.[32] Yet Mayton confidently declares: "The recorded discussion of the treason clause shows a common understanding of the clause as a free speech provision."[33]

Describing the treason clause as a free speech protection is not baseless, if one really believes that there is a possibility of Congress designating dissident speech as treason. In the seventeenth century some dissident speech could be punished under the rubric of "compassing or imaging the king's death," a branch of constructive treason. Because the treason clause embraces only overt acts, it prevents dissident speech from being construed as treason. Mayton makes this point by focusing on the overt acts provision of the treason clause, although he might just as well have focused on the clause's definition of treason: levying war against the United States or adhering to its Enemies, giving them Aid and Comfort.[34] Mayton's agenda, however, requires that he lay a basis for his claim that speech, as contrasted with overt acts, should be constitutionally immune from prosecution.

But the treason clause does not prevent the prosecution of dissident speech or press, because the government can charge an offense other than treason.[35] Mayton approvingly quotes *Legacy* for the assertion that "[u]tterances once held to be treasonable became wholly assimilated within the concept of seditious libel" by the early eighteenth century.[36] This assimilation mooted the issue of dissident speech being treason. In any case, the clause prevents the government from prosecuting dissident speech as treason, but not from prosecuting dissident speech. The treason clause did not prevent the Sedition Act and was not the basis for a constitutional attack on that act. Nor did the clause prevent prosecutions for constructive treason having nothing to do with dissident speech. John Adams and Thomas Jefferson drafted a model treason act in 1776, but the two also drafted the first American articles of war, which punished by courts-martial any "traitorous or disrespectful words" against the authority of the United States or of a state in which the offender might be quartered.[37] The latter document remained in effect until 1806, when Jefferson was President. At one point a staunch Jeffersonian in Congress denounced the provision against "traitorous" words as a second sedition law. Congress responded by substituting "contemptuous" for "traitorous" but extended the offense to include criticisms of the President.[38] An authoritative historian of military law, asserting that the right to use "contemptuous" words against the President and Congress "is of the essence of civil liberties of a citizen," has compared this provision to the Sedition Act.[39] Nonetheless, the article proscribing contemptuous and disrespectful words against the government or the President shows that the treason clause did not protect dissident speech. The primary function of the treason clause is to prevent treason convictions for overt acts that fall short of levying war or adhering to the nation's enemies. Given the Constitution's definition of treason, any overt *acts* not squaring with that definition would constitute constructive treason; Mayton conveys the inaccurate impression that constructive treason referred only to dissident speech. If the treason clause ended constructive treason, as he asserts, the reason is that the courts have thwarted the government's promiscuous interpretations of the Constitution's definition of treason.[40]

Mayton wrongly concludes that eliminating the old treason of compassing the death of the king denied to Congress the power to suppress speech by devising constructive treasons.[41] The crime of compassing the king's death "continued [in England] through the ratification of the United States Constitution."[42] Mayton mentions trials in England in 1794 and concludes that the framers "specifically" blocked such suppression of political dissent by enacting the treason clause.[43] But Mayton's chronology is wrong, his cause-and-effect analysis is wrong, and he has no proof for his thesis about the purpose of the treason clause other than the remark by Spaight. The crime of compassing the king's death had effectively died out in England long before the framing of the Constitution. The most recent case involving a prosecution for compassing the king's death occured in 1663.[44] Mayton cites none more recent [45]

In any case, compassing the king's death could not possibly have been a crime in republican America. The United States dropped that category of treason, not as a result of the treason clause having as its object the protection of dissident speech, but as a result of the Declaration of Independence. Denying the authority of the Crown and laying a legal foundation for prosecutions of dissident Tory speech[46] added to the reasons for dropping that category of treason.

Mayton seems to place his emphasis on constructive treason and compassing the king's death because he wants to justify his assertion that the overt act test is the proper test for prosecutions of speech. He attempts to demonstrate the existence of a consensus that an overt acts requirement foreclosed the possibility that dissident speech could be prosecuted under the treason clause. But the historical record is not as conclusive as Mayton portrays it. The Statute of Treasons of 1352 included the crime of compassing the king's death but required an "overt act." This fact leads Mayton to state: "Speech, in and of itself, was not however, generally thought to constitute treason or 'an overt act'. . . . "[47] But that was no longer true by the time of Henry VIII, when, as Mayton notes, treason statutes were enacted "without the overt act requirement and aimed at dissident speech."[48] Forgetting this, Mayton then constructs an eccentric history of the rise of seditious libel, casting the Star Chamber as the villain, and tells us that seditious libel was created as a new crime that "did not fall under the English Statute of Treasons and thereby evaded the overt act limitation."[49] *Twyn's Case* in 1663, which Mayton describes, and *Sidney's Case* in 1683,[50] which he doesn't mention, proved that speech and writings had become overt acts for which a person could be prosecuted under the law of treason. *Pine's Case* of 1629 is Mayton's authority for the rule that speaking disrespectful words about the king was not treason.[51] The rule of *Sidney's Case,* however, is that the deliberate act of writing the words, even if unpublished, is an overt act proving the treason.[52]

Nonetheless, Mayton relies on the overt acts test to prove that the unamended Constitution structurally extinguished the power of the United States to punish the crime of seditious libel. A close reading of his sources shows that they do not prove what he claims they do. For example, he says that James Wilson "described seditious libel" as an unwarranted attempt by the Star Chamber to wrest libel law to the purpose of the ministers.[53] Neither in the passage cited nor anywhere else did Wilson refer to seditious libel. Wilson made no reference to words against government or government officials or to anything else that might be described as "seditious libel." He referred only to the fact that the "malicious defamation of any person" was a common law crime.[54] Mayton does not distinguish between criminal libel, based on malicious defamation of a person, and seditious libel, based on malicious defamation of the government, its measures, or its officers.

Mayton's structuralism argument, based on the principle of federalism and the treason clause, is an artificial construct based on inferences that enable one to prove whatever one pleases by abstract logic. If appropriate historical evidence does not matter, we could embellish the structuralism argument almost at will.

Mayton's structuralism thesis sets forth the treason clause as a free speech guarantee that established an overt acts test for determining the criminality of words, thus overturning the doctrine of seditious libel. That thesis is as valid and convincing as would be structuralism arguments spun out of the guarantee clause,[55] the legislators' free speech clause,[56] and the privileges and immunities clause.[57] The value of those arguments from the standpoint of logic may be considerable (which I doubt); but as revelations of the original meaning of the free press, they are worthless, absent historical proofs from 1791 and earlier.

II. A Legacy of Idealism?

Mayton's section on "a legacy of idealism"[58] purports to dismiss about 150 pages of intensive analysis of eighteenth century thought on freedom of the press that I presented in *Legacy of Suppression,* even while drawing on—and distorting—that analysis. The eighteenth century political philosophy to which the framers of the Constitution were heirs did not, as Mayton claims,[59] reject the doctrine of seditious libel. Such a rejection did not occur until the 1790s, after the framing of the Constitution.[60] Nor was the overt acts test—to determine when the government has infringed "a forbidden zone of speech"—"establish[ed]" in the eighteenth century.[61] "Establish" conveys a sense of permanency not mere advocacy or suggestion; in neither law nor theory did the overt acts requirement become established as a test for the criminality of political speech either in the eighteenth century or afterwards. By the close of that century it was still a rarely endorsed or advocated principle.[62]

Mayton states that in the eighteenth century, "notions about the incompatibility of democratic government with the suppression of political speech were strong and well known."[63] He documents this, however, not with evidence from 1735 or 1776 or 1787, but from Madison's *Report* of 1799–1800 and some remarks by Sir James Fitzjames Stephen.[64] Mayton does not seem to recognize that Madison frequently changed his mind regarding freedom of the press. In 1788 he switched from opposing to supporting a bill of rights,[65] and in early 1799 he favored state prosecutions for criminal libel, but by the close of that year favored only private damage suits.[66] Given Madison's record of switching, and absent proof that in 1789 he held the views expressed later, Mayton's reliance on Madison's later views as revelations of his earlier ones is anachronistic. Mayton's reliance on the writings of James Fitzjames Stephen is also misguided. Stephen did not examine eighteenth century political philosophy and was not summarizing an eighteenth century viewpoint; he was presenting his own liberal Victorian viewpoint. Stephen's chapter on seditious libel, which summarized only case law and treatise writers, does not mention a single instance of the repudiation of the doctrine of seditious libel. In fact, Stephen concluded his section on seditious libel in the eighteenth century with a discussion of Fox's Libel Act of 1792, which allowed English juries to decide whether the words used by a defendant constituted seditious libel.[67]

Mayton offers not a fig leaf of evidence to cover his naked assertion that eighteenth century thought rejected the doctrine of seditious libel. He quotes no sources from before 1794 that say anything that amounts to a rejection of that doctrine. *Legacy* quoted many people rejecting the doctrine, both in England and America, after the adoption of the first amendment, but not before.

Mayton declares: "Levy discredits a significant portion of the liberal philosophy of [the eighteenth century] because it defended 'religious rather than political speech.'"[68] I did not discredit that philosophy. I extolled it, at length. The phrase to which Mayton refers appears in a passage in which I simply mentioned a fact, namely that the Reverends Philip Furneaux, Ebenezer Ratcliffe, and Alexander Kippis were "advocates of the overt-acts test, but none of them had taken a stand on the problem of seditious libel. They had defended religious rather than political speech."[69] I began a five page discussion of Furneaux, a dissenting minister, by noting that he published a volume in 1770 criticizing Blackstone's exposition of the laws of toleration, stating:

> The crime of blasphemous libel was analogous to that of seditious libel, the main difference being that the sanctions of the law were thought necessary to protect the good reputation of God or religion instead of the government. While Furneaux never addressed himself to the problem of political speech, the principles which he supported were as applicable to the law of seditious libel as to the libels on religion. It was Furneaux who advocated the ultralibertarian thesis that the expression of opinions, religious opinions to be sure, should be entirely free. He flatly rejected the bad-tendency test of words, proposing in its place punishment of overts only.
>
> Furneaux was not the first to advocate this view. His predecessors as noted earlier, had been Walwyn, Spinoza, Montesquieu, and Father of Candor. In their cases, however, the principle of punishing deeds instead of words had been incidentally mentioned in the midst of a body of doctrine to which it was foreign. They had acknowledged the principle, to their vast credit, but left it unused as if it were a round hole into which the square pegs of their thought would not fit. By contrast, Furneaux built his whole structure around that principle, thereby avoiding the inconsistencies and exceptions to it that his precursors had made foundational. Furneaux alone smashed through the heavy crust of conventional limitations on expression in which other libertarians had acquiesced.[70]

Thus, far from discrediting the liberal philosophy of the eighteenth century, I paid it admiring attention in *Legacy*.

Mayton begins his discourse on eighteenth century political philosophy with a description of Spinoza's theory of free speech.[71] Mayton neglects to discuss the significant exceptions that Spinoza made to his principle that words should not be punished. The state, Spinoza wrote, has the "right to treat as enemies all men whose opinions do not, on all subjects, entirely coincide with its own," although, properly, it should punish only politically injurious speech—the equivalent of a sedition act. All "opinions would be seditious ... which by their very nature nullify the compact by which the right of free action was ceded."[72] Encouraging the people to disagree with their rulers, counseling civil disobedience, advocating the enactment of laws by unconstituted authority, or teaching against the keeping of contracts were, for Spinoza, exceptions to his rule that only overt acts, rather than mere words, should be punishable.[73] Even Spinoza, for all his tolerance, drew the line at seditious utterances, which he construed as tantamount to seditious acts.

According to Mayton, John Trenchard and Thomas Gordon (writing in the 1720s as "Cato"), and James Alexander "objected to laws against speech because of their indeterminancy."[74] But Mayton offers no proof to support this; and he cannot, because it is false. He also alleges that Cato argued that government could not legitimately wield a power over public speech.[75] In fact, Cato argued that it could.

Cato declared that he did not wish to be misunderstood as arguing for the uncontrolled liberty of men to calumniate each other or the government. He stated: "Libels against the Government ... are always base and unlawful," especially when untrue, and should be punished as an abuse of liberty so long as England's "very good laws" were "prudently and honestly executed, which I really believe they have for the most part been since the Revolution."[76] In a related essay, Cato reinforced the thought by saying, "I do agree, when the natural and genuine Meaning and Purport of Words and Expressions in libellous Writings carry a criminal Intention, that the Writer ought not to escape Punishment by Subterfuge or Evasion. ... "[77] Perhaps, as I pointed out in *Legacy,* these are mere genuflections that served to keep Cato on the safe side of the existing law. Cato believed that the law of criminal libel was neither good nor prudently executed, indeed, that it proved quite dangerous to public liberty and good government. He disapproved of prosecutions for libel except in extreme cases and even then only under a law which did not penalize criticism whose validity was demonstrable. But he would not have violated the law even if he had said outright that seditious libel was a Star Chamber doctrine that should be abandoned. So it is unlikely that his statements favoring punishment of seditious libel were insincere.

Alexander, the editor of the *New York Weekly Journal,* wrote the articles for which John Peter Zenger, the paper's printer, was indicted for seditious libel. I praised Alexander as the greatest American libertarian theorist of the colonial period;[78] he masterminded Zenger's defense, and after being disbarred by Chief Justice James DeLancey, secured the legal services of Andrew Hamilton, whom he briefed. Alexander also wrote the report of the case that made it live in our history.[79] The Zenger defense did not rely on a repudiation of the law of seditious libel, at least not of its core concept that the government can be criminally assaulted by words alone. Rather, the defense relied on an appeal to the members of the jury that they should decide whether the publications were libelous, and should acquit Zenger if they believed the publications to have been true. Neither Alexander nor Hamilton rejected the doctrine of seditious libel. In 1733 Alexander wrote that anyone who spoke "irreverently and disrespectfully of Magistrates . . . was and is, always will be, criminal. . . . "[80] A year later, Alexander commented: "[Some printers] abused the press with impunity, and I cannot understand how any honest man can see anything, especially a thing essential to the preservation of the Constitution, abused with great satisfaction." He conceded that "abuses that dissolve society and sap the Foundation of Government are not to be sheltered under the Umbrage of the Liberty of the Press."[81] The Hamilton-Alexander trial argument granted that "nothing ought to excuse a man who raises a false charge or accusation, even against a private person, and that no manner of allowance ought to be made to him who does so against a public magistrate."[82] Hamilton never conducted a frontal assault on the concept of seditious libel. He praised criticism of a "bad administration" or an "arbitrary government," but did not defend the lawfulness of criticism of a good or just government.[83] So too, Alexander conceded in his 1737 essay on freedom of speech that "to infuse into the minds of the people an ill opinion of a just administration, is a crime that deserves no mercy. . . . "[84]

Another of Mayton's witnesses is Ben Franklin. Mayton states that Franklin did not even support state prosecutions for seditious libel, because he favored only state laws providing civil remedies for defamation.[85] In the essay by Franklin that Mayton discusses, however, Franklin did not mention defamation of the government except to say in passing that those guilty of it should be tarred and feathered.[86] During a lifetime in politics and publishing, Franklin never criticized the doctrine of seditious libel. On the contrary, he actively supported the prosecution of William Smith and William Moore in 1758 by championing their "kangaroo" trial—by the assembly—for breach of parliamentary privilege in the form of seditious libel.[87] Franklin never endorsed or advocated the view that a republican government and the law of seditious libel are incompatible. If, as Mayton said, Franklin's essay of 1789 disapproved of anything approximating seditious libel laws, Federalist advocates of the Sedition Act would not have quoted Franklin as if he supported their view.[88] Jeffersonians, incidentally, did not dispute the point. At the Pennsylvania ratifying convention, James Wilson, a great Framer, declared "that there is given to the general government no power whatsoever concerning [the press]. . . . "[89] Mayton relies on this quote,[90] but then quickly moves on. Wilson, however, did not stop at that point. In reply to Antifederalist charges that federal judges might proceed under federal statutes punishing libels, Wilson continued:

> I presume it was not in the view of the honorable gentleman to say that there is no such thing as libel or that the writers of such ought not to be punished. The idea of the liberty of the press is not carried so far as this in any country—*what is meant by liberty of the press is that there should be no antecedent restraint upon it;* but that every author is responsible when he attacks the security or welfare of the *government,* or the safety, character and property of the individual.
>
> With regard to attacks upon the public, the mode of proceeding is by a prosecution. . . . [91]

Wilson's statement leaves no doubt that he believed the law of seditious libel to be in force, because he spoke of the legal responsibility of writers who attacked the security or welfare of the government, and he added that for such attacks the remedy was prosecution. He believed that the federal courts had jurisdiction over seditious libel, because in the same statement he referred to Article III of the Constitution, which describes the judicial power of the United States.[92] No one at the Pennsylvania convention denied Wilson's exposition of the law.[93]

Mayton declares accurately that James Iredell of North Carolina denied that Congress could legislate on the press except to make copyright law.[94] Mayton does not state, however, that in the same paragraph of the same essay Iredell praised England as a place "where the press is as free as ourselves."[95] And, despite his approving quotation from a 1799 circuit court opinion on the treason clause by Justice Iredell, Mayton does not disclose that in the same opinion Iredell expounded a Blackstonian view of the free press clause of the first amendment.[96] According to Mayton, Iredell's view that Congress or the general government had no power over the press represented a "consensus" that "included those opposed to the Constitution."[97] The remark is obtuse because most Antifederalists warned that were the Constitution ratified, Congress would suppress the press. Mayton does not understand that the reason Wilson and the Federalists reiterated that Congress had no power over the press is that they were refuting an Antifederalist charge; nor does Mayton understand that the first amendment was added to the Constitution to allay the public's fear, aroused by that charge, that Congress would and could harm a free press. The elementary fact is that Antifederalists and Federalists shared no consensus about the power of the United States.

In a different sense Mayton is right. Richard Henry Lee, a major Antifederalist leader, and James Iredell represented a consensus in the sense that both believed that the meaning of a free press clause should be sought in England. England was Lee's model, for he believed that the common law adequately protected freedom of the press. In England, he declared in his "Federal Farmer"—the most widely read and influential Antifederalist tract—the people had obtained the Magna Carta, the power of taxation, the 1689 Bill of Rights, "and, as an everlasting security and bulwark of their liberties, they fixed . . . the freedom of the press."[98] That is, in 1694, Parliament allowed the expiration of the laws requiring the prior restraint of the press, and the press had been free ever since. That was the Blackstonian view, the basis of the consensus.

Mayton relies quite heavily on the Statute of Religious Freedom,[99] enacted by Virginia in 1785, because it explicitly embodied the overt acts test.[100] But neither Jefferson, the author of the bill, nor Madison, who secured its passage, nor Virginia, the state that enacted it, applied the overt acts test to political opinions. The test applied to religious opinions only.

Jefferson had first proposed a religious liberty provision in 1776, when drafting a constitution for Virginia. The first two drafts of his 1776 religious liberty clause suggest the narrowness of his thinking on the scope of *political* expression. The initial draft, after declaring that no person should be compelled to frequent or maintain any religious service or institution, added, "but seditious behavior [is] to be pun[ish]able by civil magistrate[s] acc[or]d[in]g to the laws already made or hereafter to be made."[101] On reconsideration, he bracketed but did not delete this phrase. In his second draft, Jefferson again revealed his impulse to punish politically unacceptable opinions: *"But [the lib-*

erty of religious opinion] shall not be held to justify seditious preaching or conversation against the authority of the civil government."[102] Again, on reconsideration Jefferson bracketed the quoted words. He apparently groped for a way to insure the unfettered right to propagate religious opinion without relinquishing the power of the state to curb dangerous political expression and without permitting freedom for seditious opinions under the guise of religious expression. In the end Jefferson omitted the restrictive clause from the third and final draft, possibly because he recognized that the task at hand was to guarantee religious liberty rather than to acknowledge the unquestioned power of the state to prosecute seditious libels. The right to religious liberty, moreover, was the one above all others to which he was most deeply devoted, and he was willing to take risks to insure it.

Significantly, Jefferson never applied the overt acts test to political opinions. Although his own religious faith was deeply held, he felt quite indifferent about that of others. In his *Notes on the State of Virginia,* which he began in 1780, Jefferson remarked that whether his neighbor said that there were twenty gods or none, "neither picks my pocket nor breaks my leg."[103] But political opinions could pick his pocket or break his leg: He worried about permitting religiously founded opinions "against the civil government"; he supported political test oaths; he denied civil rights to nonjurors; and he was ready to imprison carriers of "traitorous opinions" in times of crisis.[104] In 1783, when proposing a new constitution for Virginia, Jefferson exempted the press from prior restraints but provided for prosecution in cases of false publication.[105] In 1788, when urging Madison to support a bill of rights to the new federal Constitution, Jefferson made the same recommendation.[106] Madison construed this recommendation in its most favorable light, observing: "The Exemption of the press from liability in every case for *true facts* is . . . an innovation and as such ought to be well considered."[107] Yet, after such consideration, Madison did not add the truth-as-a-defense principle to the amendment on the press which he offered when proposing a federal bill of rights to Congress.[108] Yet Madison's phrasing appeared too broad for Jefferson, who stated that he would be pleased if the press provision were altered to exclude freedom to publish "false facts . . . affecting the peace of the confederacy with foreign nations."[109] Such a clause would have great suppressive possibilities in the context of a foreign policy controversy like Jay's treaty, the Louisiana Purchase, or the Embargo Acts.

Jefferson's threshold of tolerance for hateful political ideas was less than generous, and he intended his great statute to protect only beliefs about religion. "The declaration that religious faith shall go unpunished," he wrote in 1788, "does not give impunity to criminal acts dictated by religious error."[110]

Finally, Mayton distorts my thesis that a new libertarianism emerged after the passage of the Sedition Act, alleging, without evidence, that it already existed prior to 1789.[111] The new libertarianism rejected the principles of the Zenger defense,[112] which had epitomized the liberalism of the eighteenth century on the issue of freedom of the press. The new libertarianism finally realized that those principles insufficiently protected the press, because the Sedition Act, its infamous reputation notwithstanding, incorporated Zengerian principles. Mayton, however, presents the Sedition Act as embodying for the first time the principles of Blackstonianism,[113] as if no one previously had supported subsequent punishment for licentious or malicious misuse of the freedom of the press. On one brief comment by Spaight, Mayton erects a thesis about the treason clause being a free speech provision. In the process, he ignores dozens of comments by theorists, legalists, printers, and constitutionmakers acknowledging that freedom of the press meant only no prior restraints, or that freedom of the press did not immunize seditious libel. In the sense that Blackstonianism implied that seditious libel was a crime, the Sedition Act embraced Blackstonianism and the new libertarianism repudiated it. What was new about the new libertarianism was the outright rejection of the very concept of seditious libel. The new libertarianism asserted that free republican government and the crime of seditious libel were incompatible even at a state level.[114] It repudiated the old distinction between licentiousness and liberty, abandoned the requirement of proving malice as being of little use to a defendant in a political trial, assaulted the claim of truth-as-a-defense on the ground that the truthfulness of political opinions could not be proved, and perhaps most significantly, discarded reliance on the jury as a defense against prosecutorial and judicial bias. The new libertarianism relied on the overt acts test; although the test was not new, invocation of it in cases of political opinion was.[115]

III. Conclusion

The new libertarianism was truly new and transformingly radical; it advanced a novel understanding and theory of the freedom of the press. In 1964 the Supreme Court relied on the emergence of the new libertarianism to buttress one of its most important free press decisions, *New York Times Co. v. Sullivan*.[116] Before this case, the Court, speaking through Justice Black, had assumed that either the American Revolution or the First Amendment had meant "to get rid of the English common law on liberty of speech and press" and that "there are no contrary implications in any part of the history of the period in which the First Amendment was framed and adopted."[117] This remark by Black followed his quotation from Madison's *Virginia Report of 1799–1800*, which asserted the unconstitutionality of the Sedition Act, a statute that might be thought to constitute a "contrary implication." The Court's version of history changed remarkably after the publication of *Legacy of Suppression*. In the Court's revised view, what counted in giving the First Amendment content was not its framers' understanding but *subsequent* public opinion—the new libertarianism: "The central meaning" of the amendment undermined the Sedition Act and broadened the theory of a free press because "the attack upon its validity has carried the day in the court of history."[118] A *Legacy of Suppression* had indeed become *The Emergence of a Free Press*.

Notes

1. L. Levy, Legacy of Suppression: Freedom of Speech and Press in Early American History (1960).
2. *See, e.g, Abrams v. United States*, 250 U.S. 616, 630–31 (1919) (Holmes, J., dissenting); Z. Chafee, Jr., Free Speech in the United States 20–21 (1941).
3. *See, e.g.* Jensen, Book Review, 75 Harv L. Rev. 456 (1961) (reviewing L. Levy, *supra* note 1). Jensen correctly notes that citing prosecutions gives no idea of what day-to-day journalism was like, and refers to the example of Pennsylvania, where the newspapers after Independence contained "vast amounts of some of the bitterest, most dishonest (and seditious) writing in American political history. Despite the law there was freedom of expression in fact *Id.* at 457. *See also* Anderson, *The Origins of the Press Clause,* 30 U.C.L.A. L. Rev. 455, 494–509 (1983); Levy, *On the Origins of the Free Press,*— U.C.L.A. L. Rev.—(1985) (forthcoming).
4. 1 W. Hawkins, A Treatise of the Pleas of the Crown 544–45 (8th ed. London 1824).
5. Rex v. Almon, A.D 1770, in 20 A Complete Collection of State Trials 803 (T.B. Howell ed. London 1816) [hereinafter cited as State Trials.].

6. J. Trenchard & T. Gordon, Cato's Letters; or Essays on Liberty, Civil and Religious, and Other Important Subjects 96–103, 246–54 (3d. ed. London 1733).

7. J. Alexander, A Brief Narrative of the Case and Trial of John Peter Zenger (S. Katz 2d ed. 1972).

8. This was as true of England as of the United States. In 1799 Madison observed that in England, despite the common law on the press and "the occasional punishment of those who use it with a freedom offensive to the government," all knew that "the freedom exercised by the press, and protected by the public opinion, far exceeds the limits prescribed by the ordinary rules of law." The English press, said Madison, criticized the Ministry "with peculiar freedom," and during elections for the House of Commons, the calumnies of the press raged. J. Madison, The Virginia Report of 1799–1800, Touching the Alien and Sedition Laws 221 (Richmond 1850). Despite the law, the English press was so robust, partisan, and controversial that vituperation of public men and measures jarred the senses. The American press enjoyed at least as much freedom.

9. L. Levy, Emergence of a Free Press (1985). The new edition is reviewed in this issue. *See* Rabban, Book Review, 37 Stan. L. Rev. 795 (1985).

10. Mayton, *Seditious Libel and the Lost Guarantee of a Freedom of Expression,* 84 Colum. L. Rev. 91 (1984).

11. Mayton in fact does not even understand the conclusions I drew in *Legacy of Suppression.* He says that *Legacy* concluded that the first amendment "was intended to absorb th[e] practice [of seditious libel]." *Id.* at 92. I did not depict the amendment as "absorbing" (whatever that means) anything except a narrow concept of freedom of the press. I sought instead to show that while the Framers did not understand freedom of the press (not speech) to mean a right to engage in seditious libel with impunity, neither did they intend that Congress have the power to enact measures against seditious libel or the press in any way.

12. Levy, *supra* note 1, at 225–26 (footnotes omitted). *See also* 2 M. Farrand, The Records of the Federal Convention of 1787, at 617–18 (1911).

13. Mayton, *supra* note 10, at 94.

14. *Id.* at 93 (emphasis in original).

15. *Id.*

16. *Id.* at 94.

17. *Id.*

18. *Id.*

19. *Id.*

20. J.W. Hurst, The Law of Treason in the United States (1971).

21. The Federalist No. 84, at 600 (A. Hamilton) (H. Dawson ed. 1864).

22. Mayton, *supra* note 10, at 93.

23. 2 The Documentary History of the Ratification of the Constitution 388 (M. Jensen ed. 1976) [hereinafter cited as Documentary History].

24. 12 The Papers of James Madison 205–06 (C. Hobson & R. Rutland eds. 1979).

25. *See* 2 Documentary History, *supra* note 23, at 167–74.

26. *Id.* at 310–11, 441; 13 Documentary History, *supra* note 23, at 479, 535–37. *See also* 1 The Complete Anti-Federalist 97 (H. Storing ed. 1981); 2 The Complete Anti-Federalist, *supra,* at 146, 177, 193–94, 329–30; 3 The Complete Anti-Federalist, *supra,* at 20, 81; 6 The Complete Anti-Federalist, *supra,* at 8–11, 145.

27. Mayton, *supra* note 10, at 115.

28. *Id.* at 95.

29. *Id.* at 116 (quoting 4 The Debates in the Several State Conventions on the Adoption of the Federal Constitution 209 (J. Elliot ed. 1866 & photo. reprint

1941) [hereinafter cited as State Convention Debates].

30. Mayton, *supra* note 10, at 115 n.134, 116 nn.137 & 139.

31. Wilson, who came far closer to addressing the issue of speech than did the others, merely said that the law of treason "should be determinate." 2 The Works of James Wilson 663 (R. McCloskey ed. 1967). To Mayton that becomes a remark "relating to the indeterminacy of laws against speech." Mayton, *supra* note 10, at 115.

32. J.W. Hurst, *supra* note 20, at 137–38, 154–59, 181–83.

33. Mayton, *supra* note 10, at 116.

34. U.S. Const. art. III, § 3.

35. For example, under the Espionage Act of 1917 the United States prosecuted about 2000 people for saying the war was unchristian or for criticizing the Red Cross. *See* Z. Chafee, Jr. *supra* note 2, at 51 (1948).

36. Mayton, *supra* note 10, at 102 n.63. *Cf* Hamburger, *The Development of the Law of Seditious Libel,* 37 Stan. L. Rev. 661 (1985).

37. L. Levy, Jefferson and Civil Liberties: The Darker Side 26 (1963). *See also* J.W. Hurst, *supra* note 20, at 83–84.

38. L. Levy, *supra* note 37, at 26–27.

39. Wiener, *Courts-Martial and the Bill of Rights: The Original Practice II,* 72 Harv. L. Rev. 266, 268 (1958).

40. Thomas Jefferson was primarily responsible for providing models for the treason clause, but he also devised and supported legislation directed against a traitor in thought, but not in deed, as well as against acts opposed to Independence but less than treason. J.W. Hurst, *supra* note 20, at 83–90, 117; L. Levy, *supra* note 37, at 28. When Jefferson was President he demanded treason prosecutions for Aaron Burr and his confederates, and also for the armed violators of his Embargo laws. In these instances the federal courts denounced the efforts of his administration to revive the discredited crime of constructive treason by prosecuting overt acts short of the constitutional definition. L. Levy, *supra* note 37, at 70–80, 130–33.

41. Mayton, *supra* note 10, at 102.

42. *Id.* at 101–02.

43. *Id.* at 102.

44. *Rex v. Twyn,* 15 Charles II A.D. 1663, in 6 State Trials, *supra* note 5, at 513.

45. The prosecutions of Thomas Hardy, *Rex v. Hardy,* 35 George III A.D. 1794, in 24 State Trials, *supra* note 5, at 199, and John Horne Tooke, *Rex v. Horne Tooke,* 35 George III A.D. 1794, in 25 State Trials, *supra* note 5, at 1, for advocating universal suffrage and annual elections in 1794 were intended to punish critics of Parliament, not the Crown, although the indictments used the old formula of compassing. After the cases ended in acquittals, Parliament revived the crime of constructive treason in order to have a statutory foundation for subsequent prosecutions. 2 T.E. May, The Constitutional History of England Since the Accession of George Third 164–69 (1863). Obviously, neither the prosecutions of 1794 nor the Parliamentary acts of 1795 could possibly have influenced the writing of the treason clause in 1789, although they did influence the adoption of the Sedition Act of 1798.

46. Despite a congressional act of 1776 defining treason similarly to the way that the treason clause was to define it in 1787, "the concept of treasonable adherence to the enemy," wrote Hurst, "was certainly given an extremely sweeping application in the [state] legislation which imposed penalties ranging from heavy fines or jail sentences to the death sentence and complete forfeiture of property

for the mere utterance of opinions denying the independent authority of the new states and asserting the continued sovereignty of the King." J.W. Hurst, *supra,* note 20, at 100.

47. Mayton, *supra* note 10, at 99.
48. *Id.* at 100.
49. *Id.* at 105.
50. Rex v. Sidney, 35 Charles II A.D. 1683, in 9 State Trials, *supra* note 5, at 818.
51. Mayton, *supra* note 10, at 105.
52. 4 W. Blackstone, Commentaries *80–81.
53. Mayton, *supra* note 10, at 103.
54. 2 The Works of James Wilson, *supra* note 31, at 650. Mayton also mistakenly alleges that Wilson condemned "the public offense of seditious libel." Mayton, *supra* note 10, at 113 n.122. Wilson did not condemn the doctrine of seditious libel. He attacked only the failure of the common law to provide Zengerian principles. Wilson, in fact, favored prosecuting perpetrators of seditious libel. *See* text accompanying note 91 *infra.*
55. "The United States shall guarantee to every State in this Union a Republican Form of Government. . . . " U.S. Const. art. IV, § 4. It is possible to deduce from this clause that the United States has no power over seditious libels. In a republican form of government, the treasonous crime of compassing the king's death cannot exist, there being no king. The purpose of defining compassing the king's death as a crime was to suppress dissident speech. In a republican government, therefore, dissident speech cannot be suppressed. Moreover, in a republican government, the people are the masters of the government, rather than its servants. As James Madison himself argued in 1794, "[i]f we advert to the nature of Republican Government, we shall find that the censorial power is in the people over the Government, and not in the Government over the people. Freedom of the Press from Zenger to Jefferson lxvii (L. Levy ed. 1966) (quoting 2 Annals of Cong. 934 (1794)). The crime of seditious libel, although suited to England, conflicts with the genius of government in America. Consequently, it can be argued, American constitutionmakers eliminated that crime when constitutionally protecting freedom of the press.
56. Such reasoning supposedly proves, too, that article I, section 6, guaranteeing freedom of debate for members of Congress, by necessary implication guarantees freedom of speech for anyone qualified to vote. If free speech is necessary for congressmen, it is even more necessary for their sovereigns, the people whom they represent. The electorate must pass judgment on the proceedings of Congress and insure that the government operates for the benefit of the governed. The people cannot fulfill their electoral duties if they are denied access to any viewpoint. Accordingly, their agents in Congress are powerless to abridge freedom of political expression. So reasoned opponents of the Sedition Act. *See, e.g.,* Hortensius, An Essay on the Liberty of the Press (Philadelphia 1799), *reprinted in* G. Hay, Two Essays on the Liberty of the Press (1970); J. Thomson, An Enquiry, Concerning the Liberty, and Licentiousness of the Press, and the Uncontrollable Nature of the Human Mind 20–22 (New York 1801 & photo. reprint 1970).
57. The privileges and immunities clause of article IV, section 2, could be used to support the same conclusion. In 1787, citizens of many states counted freedom of the press among their privileges and immunities, and the citizens of Pennsylvania also enjoyed a free speech guarantee in their state constitution of 1776. Under article IV, section 2, citizens of every other state were logically entitled

to the privileges and immunities of Pennsylvania. Accordingly, the privileges and immunities clause extended to all citizens of the nation unfettered freedom of political discourse—a freedom incompatible with the doctrine of seditious libel.

58. Mayton, *supra* note 10, at 108–114.

59. *Id.* at 109 n.98.

60. Two pieces denouncing the doctrine of seditious libel were published in response to Pennsylvania's prosecution of Eleazar Oswald in 1782. *See Junius Wilkes,* Independent Gazetteer, Nov. 9, 1782 (Philadelphia); *Candid,* Independent Gazetteer, Dec. 14, 1782. No one remembered or repeated the exceptional and precocious arguments made by these anonymous writers, nor did anyone else attack the validity of sedition laws until the Sedition Act controversy in 1798.

61. Mayton, *supra* note 10, at 109.

62. In *Legacy,* I traced the origins and development of the overt acts requirement in detail. *See* L. Levy, *supra* note 1, at 90–91, 94, 153–57, 164–65, 172, 188–89, 251–52, 254–55. Mayton mistakenly remarks that "an overt act requirement was made a part of the text of the Constitution." Mayton, *supra* note 10, at 109. The treason clause was no doubt the "establishment" he was talking about. That remark occurs not in his discussion of the treason clause, where it would be accurate, but in the context of his claim that in the eighteenth century the doctrine of seditious libel was rejected and the power of government to punish speech that might be injurious to government was condemned. Mayton conflated two different overt acts tests, the one in the Constitution referring to acts that proved the levying of war or adherence to the country's enemies, and the other relating to free speech, which is not in the Constitution at all, not even as amended.

63. Mayton, *supra* note 10, at 109. Mayton does not confront the abundant evidence discussed in *Legacy of Suppression* that would tarnish his view. He does not discuss, for example, the statement made in 1753 by William Livingston, a protege of James Alexander and a future framer of the Constitution, that when a printer "prostitutes his Art by the Publication of any Thing injurious to his Country, it is criminal. . . . It is high Treason against the State." L. Levy, *supra* note 1, at 142 (quoting The Independent Reflector, Aug. 30, 1753, *quoted in* 1 The Journals of Hugh Gaine, Printer 12–13 (P. Ford ed. 1902)). Similarly, he does not mention that the *Boston Gazette,* the mouthpiece of John and Sam Adams, declared on March 9, 1767: "Political Liberty consists in a freedom of speech and action, so far as the laws of a community permit, and no farther: all beyond is criminal, and tends to the destruction of Liberty itself." Boston Gazette, Mar. 9, 1767, at 4, col. 1. Consider also that Massachusetts and Pennsylvania prosecuted seditious libels prior to and after 1791, notwithstanding free press guarantees. For the Massachusetts cases, see C. Duniway, The Development of Freedom of the Press in Massachusetts 146 (1906) (discussing the conviction of J.S. Lillie); Riley, *Dr. Willam Whiting and Shay's Rebellion,* in 6 Proceedings of the American Antiquarian Society 119 (1956) (discussing the prosecution of William Whiting, Chief Justice of the Court of Common Pleas of Berkshire County); Independence Chronicle, May 11, 1799 (discussing the prosecution of Edward Freeman); Independence Chronicle, Apr. 29, 1799; Independence Chronicle, Mar. 7, 1799; Independence Chronicle, Mar. 4, 1799; Independence Chronicle, Feb. 14, 1799. For a Pennsylvania case, see Republica v. Oswald, I U.S. (1 Dall.) 319 (1788) (prosecution of Eleazar Oswald); Teeter, *The Printer and the Chief Justice: Seditious Libel in 1782–83,* 45 Journalism Q. 235 (1968); *see also*

Republica v. Dennie, 4 Yeates (Pa.) 267 (1805) (ending in an acquittal, but not bespeaking a repudiation of the common law or a broad understanding of freedom of the press). For state constitutional provisions proscribing seditious utterances, see note 110 *infra.*

64. Mayton, *supra* note 10, at 127 n.185.

65. *Compare* Madison's speech of June 12, 1788, in 11 The Papers of James Madison, *supra* note 24, at 130–31 *with* his letter of October 15, 1788, *id.* at 287–91. When Madison framed the Bill of Rights, he wrote privately that he was engaged in "the nauseous project of amendments" whose chief purpose was "to kill the opposition everywhere." 12 The Papers of James Madison, *supra* note 24, at 346–53. This comment does not sound like that of someone intent on revolutionizing the common law of seditious libel. Nor does his statement before the House that when one defined abstractions such as freedom of the press, enumeration of simple acknowledged propositions would speed ratification, whereas questionable amendments might be harmful." *Id.* at 339–40. Given the novelty of the proposition that an irreconcilable conflict existed between political liberty and seditious libel, no one in 1789 could have regarded the proposition as a "simple acknowledged" proposition. Even the Zengerian proposition that truth should be a defense against a charge of seditious libel was not widely accepted in 1789. The only simple acknowledged principle about freedom of the press in 1789 remained Blackstonian in character: One had freedom to publish whatever he pleased subject to criminal liability for abusing that freedom.

66. *Compare* Madison's "Address" of January 4, 1799, in 6 Writings of James Madison 333–34 (G. Hunt ed. 1910) *with* his Virginia Report of 1799–1800, J. Madison, *supra* note 8, at 224.

67. 2 J.F. Stephen, History of the Criminal Law in England Ch. 14 (1883).

68. Mayton, *supra* note 10, at 109 n.98. Mayton claims that religious and political speech cannot be separated. *Id.* It is true that these two forms of speech are interrelated. *See* L. Levy, *supra* note 1, at 7. In many instances religious and political speech can be separated, however, especially in the absence of an alleged establishment of religion. Jefferson often distinguished the two forms of speech. *See* texts accompanying notes 101–102, 110 *infra.*

69. L. Levy, *supra* note 1, at 172. For a discussion of the three men, see *id.* at 164–70.

70. *Id.* at 164–65.

71. It is unclear why Mayton places Spinoza (1632–77) in the eighteenth century.

72. B. de Spinoza, *Theologico-Political Treatise,* in 1 The Chief Works of Benedict de Spinoza 1, 260 (R.H.M. Elwes trans. 1891 & photo. reprint 1951).

73. He wrote that if a man "accuses the authorities of injustice, and stirs up the people against them, or if he seditiously strives to abrogate the law without their consent, he is a mere agitator and rebel." *Id.* at 259. Spinoza added that a person "who holds that the supreme power has no rights over him, or that promises ought not to be kept, or that everyone should live as he pleases . . . is seditious, not so much from his actual opinions and judgment, as from the deeds which they involve, for he who maintains such theories abrogates the contract which tacitly, or openly, he made with his rulers." *Id.* at 260.

74. Mayton, *supra* note 10, at 112.

75. *Id.*

76. J. Trenchard & T. Gordon, *supra* note 6, at 250.

77. *Id.* at 302–03. For my discussion of Cato in *Legacy of Suppression,* see L. Levy, *supra* note 1, at 115–21.

78. L. Levy, *supra* note 1, at 129, 136–37.

79. J. Alexander, *supra* note 7. Mayton cites this work to establish his legacy of idealism." *See* Mayton, *supra* note 10, at 112 nn.118 & 120.
80. N.Y. Weekly J., Nov. 19, 1733.
81. N.Y. Weekly J., Nov. 4, 1734.
82. J. Alexander, *supra* note 7, at 84.
83. *Id.* at 65, 84, 88, 99.
84. Pennsylvania Gazette, Dec. 1, 1737 (Philadelphia).
85. Mayton, *supra* note 10, at 114.
86. 10 The Writings of Benjamin Franklin 40 (A. Smyth ed. 1907), *quoted in* L. Levy, *supra* note 1, at 187.
87. For a description of the Smith and Moore case, see G. Dargo, Roots of the Republic 118–26 (1974); L Levy, *supra* note 1, at 53–61. For examples of Franklin's support of a legislative prosecution for seditious libel, see 8 The Papers of Benjamin Franklin 28 10, 87–88 (L. Labaree ed. 1982).
88. *See* 2 Annals of Cong. 2102, 2169–70 (1798).
89. 2 Documentary History, *supra* note 23, at 455.
90. Mayton, *supra* note 10, at 118.
91. 2 Documentary History, *supra* note 23, at 455.
92. *Id.*
93. Contrary to Mayton's assertions, *see* Mayton, *supra* note 10, at 125 n.180, Wilson was not being hypothetical. He was answering Robert Whitehill and John Smilie, the Antifederalist leader, who had asserted that the Congress might define and the federal courts might try libels against the United States. 2 Documentary History, *supra* note 23, at 441, 454. Wilson was no more hypothetical than any other speaker and writer during the ratification controversy, including the authors of *The Federalist.* All were arguing about how the United States government would operate if the proposed Constitution were ratified.
94. Mayton, *supra* note 10, at 118.
95. Iredell, *Observations,* in Pamphlets on the Constitution of the United States 361 (Ford ed. 1888). *See* text accompanying note 98 *infra.*
96. *See* F. Wharton, State Trials of the United States During the Administration of Washington and Adams 478–79 (Philadelphia 1849), *quoted in* L. Levy, *supra* note 1, at 242–43.
97. Mayton, *supra* note 10, at 118.
98. 2 The Complete Anti-Federalist, *supra* note 26, at 271.
99. *See* Mayton, *supra* note 10, at 112–13.
100. 12 The Statutes at Large Being a Collection of All Laws of Virginia: From the First Session of the Legislature in the Year 1619, ch. XXXIV, at 84–86 (W. Hening ed. Richmond 1823).
101. 1 Papers of Thomas Jefferson 344 (J. Boyd ed. 1950). For copies of the three drafts of the Constitution composed by Jefferson in May and June of 1776, see *id.* at 337–64.
102. *Id.* at 353 (emphasis in original).
103. T. Jefferson, Notes on the State of Virginia 159 (W. Peden ed. 1955).
104. *See* L Levy, *supra* note 40, at 25–41.
105. *See* 6 Papers of Thomas Jefferson, *supra* note 101, at 304.
106. *Id.* at 316.
107. Madison's original proposal of June 8, 1789 was: "The people shall not be deprived or abridged of their right to speak, to write, or to publish their sentiments; and the freedom of the press, as one of the great bulwarks of liberty, shall be inviolable." 1 Annals of Cong. 451.

108. *Id.*
109. 15 Papers of Thomas Jefferson, *supra* note 101, at 367.
110. 13 Papers of Thomas Jefferson, *supra* note 101, at 442–43. For a general discussion of Jefferson and freedom of political opinions, see L Levy, *supra* note 37, at 42–69. What Jefferson meant may be seen in the constitutions of two states that provided that the free exercise of religion could not justify libeling their government. North Carolina's article of religious liberty contained the qualification: "Provided, that nothing herein contained shall be construed to exempt preachers of treasonable or *seditious discourses,* from legal trial and punishment." N.C. Const. art. XXIV (1776), *reprinted in* 5 The Federal and State Constitutions, Colonial Charters, and Other Organic Laws 2793 (F. Thorpe ed. 1909) [hereinafter cited as Constitutions] (emphasis added). If preachers were not exempt from the law of seditious libel, others were not either. Similarly, a clause in South Carolina's constitution stated: "No person whatsoever shall speak anything in their religious assembly irreverently or *seditiously* of the government of this State." S.C. Const. art. XXXVIII (1778), *reprinted in* 6 Constitutions *supra,* at 3257 (emphasis added). If seditious speech was prohibited in church, by implication, it was prohibited elsewhere. The religious freedom provisions in the first constitutions of New York, N.Y. Const. art. XXXVIII (1777), *reprinted in* 5 Constitutions, *supra,* at 2637; New Hampshire, N.H. Const. art. V (1784), *reprinted in* 4 Constitutions, *supra,* at 2454; Massachusetts, Mass. Const. art. II (1780), *reprinted in* 3 Constitutions, *supra,* at 1889 Georgia, G.A. Const. art. LVI (1777), *reprinted in* 2 Constitutions, *supra,* at 784 and Maryland, MD. Const. art. XXXIII (1776), *reprinted in* 3 Constitutions, *supra,* at 1689, contained qualifying clauses that were similar to, though less explicit than those of the Carolinas. This provision, for example, provided that no one "under colour of religion . . . shall disturb the good order, peace or safety of the State, or shall infringe the laws of morality. . . . " At common law, an utterance tending to disturb the peace of the state was seditious. New York, New Hampshire, Massachusetts. and Georgia used similar language, prohibiting exercises of religion repugnant to the public peace or safety.
111. *See* Mayton, *supra* note 10, at 125–26.
112. *See* notes 80–83 *supra* and accompanying text.
113. *See* Mayton, *supra* note 10, at 125–26.
114. Mayton seems to believe that a state constitutional guarantee of freedom of the press imposed no limits on the state police power. *See* id. at 94, 130–31.
115. For a discussion of the new libertarianism, see L. Levy, *supra* note 1, at 249–97.
116. 376 U.S. 254 (1964). Justice William Brennan declared for the Court: "If neither factual error nor defamatory content suffices to remove the constitutional shield from criticism of official conduct, the combination of the two elements is no less adequate. This is the lesson to be drawn from the great controversy over the Sedition Act of 1798, 1 Stat. 586, which first crystallized a national awareness of the central meaning of the First Amendment. See Levy, *Legacy of Suppression* (1960) at 258 *et seq.* "
117. *Bridges v. California,* 314 U.S. 252, 264–65 (1941).
118. *New York Times Co. v. Sullivan,* 376 U.S. 254, 276 (1961).

6

Flag Desecration

The word "desecration" has religious overtones. It means defiling the sacred. Flag burning is the secular equivalent of the offense of blasphemy, a verbal crime signifying an attack, by ridicule or rejection, against God, the Bible, Jesus Christ, Christianity, or religion itself. Flag burning is comparable to a verbal attack on the United States. Burning the nation's symbol signifies contempt and hatred by the flag burner of the things he or she believes the flag stands for, such as colonialism, imperialism, capitalism, exploitation, racism, or militarism. To the overwhelming majority of Americans, however, the flag embodies in a mystical and emotional way the loyalty and love they feel for the United States. With few exceptions we venerate the flag because it symbolizes both our unity and diversity; our commitment to freedom, equality, and justice; and perhaps above all, our constitutional system and its protection of individual rights.

Like blasphemy, therefore, flag burning tests the outermost limits of tolerance even in a free society. Burning the flag is a most offensive outrage that stretches to the breaking point the capacity of a nation to indulge dissidents. But that same form of desecration is not only an act of vandalism; it is symbolic expression that claims the protection of the free speech clause of the First Amendment. Therein lies the problem and the paradox: should the flag represent a nation whose people have a right to burn its revered symbol?

Imprisoning flag burners would not mean that book burning and thought control are next. We know how to distinguish vandalism from radical advocacy; we would not regard urinating on the Jefferson Memorial or spray painting graffiti on the Washington Monument as a form of constitutionally protected free speech. Special reasons exist for protecting the flag from the splenetic conduct of extremists. A society should be entitled to safeguard its most fundamental values, but dissenters have a right to express verbal opposition to everything we hold dear. Yet, nothing is solved by saying that it is better to live in a country where people are free to burn the flag if they wish, rather than in a country where they want to burn it but cannot. We know the difference between suppressing a particularly offensive mode of conduct and a particularly offensive message. The problem is, however, that the particular mode of conduct may be the vehicle for communicating that offensive message. To suppress the message by suppressing the conduct involves governmental abridgment of a First Amendment freedom. So the Supreme Court held in *Texas v. Johnson* in 1989.

In 1984 in Dallas, Gregory Johnson, a member of the Revolutionary Communist Youth Brigade, a Maoist society, publicly burned a stolen American flag to protest the renomination of Ronald Reagan as the Republican candidate. While the flag burned, the protesters, including Maoists, chanted, "America, the red, white, and blue, we spit on you." That the flag burning communicated an unmistakable political message was contested by no one. The police arrested Johnson not for his message but for his manner of delivering it; he had violated a Texas statute that prohibited the desecration of a venerated object by acts that seriously offended onlookers.

State appellate courts reversed Johnson's conviction on ground that his conduct constituted constitutionally protected symbolic speech. Given its context—the Republican convention; Reagan's foreign policy; the protestors' demonstrations, marches, speeches, and slogans—Johnson's burning the flag was clearly speech of the sort contemplated by the First Amendment. The Texas courts also rejected the state's contention that the conviction could be justified as a means of preventing breach of the public peace. In fact, the state admitted that no breach of the peace occurred as a result of the flag desecration. The Supreme Court, 5–4, affirmed the judgment of the Texas Court of Criminal Appeals.

Justice William J. Brennan, spokesman for the majority, showed his political savvy by emphasizing that the courts of the Lone Star State, where red-blooded John Wayne patriotism flourishes, recognized "that the right to differ is the centerpiece of our First Amendment freedoms." Government cannot mandate a feeling of unity or "carve out a symbol of unity and prescribe a set of approved messages to be associated with that symbol." Brennan added that although the First Amendment literally forbids the abridgment of only "speech," the Court had labeled as speech a variety of conduct that communicated opinions, including the wearing of black arm bands to protest war, a sit-in by blacks to protest racial segregation, picketing, and the display of a red flag. Indeed the state conceded that Johnson's conduct was politically expressive. The question was whether that expression could be constitutionally proscribed, like the use of fighting words calculated to provoke a breach of peace. Apart from the fact that no breach occurred here, Brennan reminded, a prime function of free speech is to invite dispute. The "fighting words" doctrine had no relevance in this case because the message communicated by flag burning did not personally insult anyone in particular.

Whether the state could justify the conviction as a means of preserving the flag as a symbol of nationhood and national unity depended on the communicative impact of the mode of expression. Brennan insisted that the restriction on flag desecration was "content-based." Johnson's political expression, he declared, was restricted because of the content of the message that he conveyed. This point is important and unpersuasive. As Chief Justice William H. Rehnquist for the dissenters said, burning the flag was no essential part of the exposition of ideas, for Johnson was free to make any verbal denunciation of the flag that he wished. He led a march through the streets of Dallas, conducted a rally on the front steps of the city hall, shouted his slogans, and was not arrested for any of this. Only when he burned the flag was he arrested. Texas did not punish him because it or his hearers opposed his message, only because he conveyed it by burning the flag.

Brennan replied that by punishing flag burning the state prohibited expressive conduct. "If there is a bedrock principle underlying the First Amendment," he wrote, "it is that the Government may not prohibit the expression of an idea simply because society finds the idea itself offensive or disagreeable." By making an exception for the flag, Texas sought to immunize the ideas for which it stands. Whatever it stands for should not be insulated against protest. In the context of this case, the act of flag burning constituted a means of political protest. Compulsion is not a constitutionally accepted method of achieving national unity.

Brennan believed that the flag's deservedly cherished place as a symbol would be "strengthened, not weakened, by our holding today. Our decision is a reaffirmation of the principles of freedom and inclusiveness that the flag best reflects, and of the conviction that our toleration of criticism such as Johnson's is a sign and source of our strength." This was the Court's strongest point.

Texas v. Johnson provided Court watchers with the pleasure of seeing judicial objectivity at work, for the Court did not divide in a predictable way. The majority included Justices Antonin Scalia and Anthony M. Kennedy, Reagan-appointed conservatives, whereas the dissenters included Justice John Paul Stevens, a liberal moderate. Stevens wrote his own dissent. He believed, oddly, that public desecration of the flag "will tarnish its value." He also thought that the Texas statute that the Court struck down did not compel any conduct or profession of respect for any idea or symbol. The case had nothing to do with disagreeable ideas, he said; it involved offensive conduct that diminishes the value of the national symbol. Texas prosecuted Johnson because of the method he used to express dissatisfaction with national policies. Prosecuting him no more violated the First Amendment than prosecuting someone for spray painting a message of protest on the Lincoln Memorial.

Rehnquist's dissent was suffused with emotional theatrics about the flag and patriotism. His point was that the flag was special, as two hundred years of history showed. Even if flag burning is expressive conduct, he reasoned, it is not an absolute. But he thought it not to be expressive conduct. Flag burning was no essential part of any exposition of ideas, he claimed, but rather was "the equivalent of an inarticulate grunt" meant to antagonize others. By the same reasoning, however, one might say that flag flying is also a grunt of patriotism. That does not alter the point that flag burning is malicious conduct—vandalism rather than speech.

Zealous politicians, eager to capitalize on their love for the flag and opposition to those who burned it, sought to gain political advantage from the Court's opinion. President George Bush, a war hero, had helped spur a paroxysm of patriotism in 1988 by assaulting his opponent for having vetoed a bill that would have compelled teachers to lead their students in a Pledge of Allegiance every day. Bush, having made a photo opportunity of visiting a flag factory in 1988, made another after the decision in *Texas v Johnson,* by holding a ceremony in the White House rose garden. Accepting a replica of the Iwo Jima

Memorial, depicting the marines hoisting the flag on a bloody wartime site, Bush condemned flag burning as a danger to "the fabric of our country" and demanded a constitutional amendment outlawing desecration of the flag.

Cynical observers shouted "cheap politics" and criticized the President and his supporters for trying to cover up problems concerning the savings and loan scandals, the deterioration of the nation's schools, the ballooning national debt, the urban underclass, and the army of homeless beggars in American cities. Bush's opponents declared that he sought to desecrate the Constitution by indulging in escapist politics and seeking the first revision of the Bill of Rights in two centuries. Many conservatives in Congress agreed that tampering with the Bill of Rights was not the way to treat the problem of flag burning. Democrats, who felt obligated to "do something" at the risk of being branded unpatriotic, offered the Flag Protection Act of 1989, and so headed off the amendment movement. The new act of Congress provided that whoever knowingly mutilates, defaces, physically defiles, or burns the flag shall be fined or imprisoned for a year, or both.

Members of the "lunatic left" promptly defied the act of Congress by burning the flag on the Capitol steps for the benefit of the TV cameras. Shawn Eichman and company got the publicity they wanted and were arrested. They quickly filed motions to dismiss, on grounds that the act of Congress was unconstitutional; that is, the flag they burned symbolized their freedom to burn it. The government asked the Supreme Court to reconsider its holding in *Texas v. Johnson* by holding that flag burning is a mode of expression, like fighting words, that does not enjoy complete protection of the First Amendment.

The Court, by the same 5–4 split, refused to alter its opinion. Brennan, again the majority spokesman, acknowledged that the government may create national symbols and encourage their respectful treatment, but concluded that it went too far with the Flag Protection Act "by criminally proscribing expressive conduct because of its likely communicative impact." Desecrating the flag was deeply offensive to many people, like virulent racial and religious epithets, vulgar repudiations of conscription, and scurrilous caricatures, all of which came within the First Amendment's protection, notwithstanding their offensiveness.

The government sought to distinguish the Flag Protection Act from the state statute involved in *Johnson,* on the theory that the act of Congress did not target expressive conduct on the basis of the content of its message. The government merely claimed its authority to protect the physical integrity of the flag as the symbol of our nation and its ideals. Brennan replied that destruction of the flag could in no way affect those ideals or the symbol itself. The invalidity of the statute derived from the fact that its criminal penalties applied to those whose treatment of the flag communicated a message. Thus, *United States v. Eichman,* resulting in the voiding of the act of Congress, was a replay of *Johnson.*

Stevens, for the dissenters, recapitulated his previous contentions. He believed that the majority opinion concluded at the point where analysis of the issue ought to begin. No one, he declared, disagreed with the proposition that the government cannot constitutionally punish offensive ideas. But, he argued, certain methods of expression, such as flag burning, might be proscribed if the purpose of the proscription did not relate to the suppression of ideas individuals sought to express, if that proscription did not interfere with the individual's freedom to express those ideas by other means, and if on balance the government's interest in the proscription outweighed the individual's choice of the means of expressing themselves. Stevens expatiated on the flag as a symbol and insisted that the government should protect its symbolic value without regard to the specific content of the flag burner's speech. Moreover, Eichman and the other dissidents were completely free to express their ideas by means other than flag burning. Stevens apparently missed the point that Eichman had a right to choose his own means of communicating his political protest. What disturbed Stevens most was the belief that flag burners actually have damaged the symbolic value of the flag. And he added the following in a veiled allusion to the shenanigans of would-be amenders of the Constitution: "Moreover, the integrity of the symbol has been compromised by those leaders who seem to advocate compulsory worship of the flag even by individuals whom it offends, or who seem to manipulate the symbol of national purpose into a pretext for partisan disputes about meaner ends."

Every nation in the world has a flag, and many of them, including some democracies, have laws against desecrating their flag. No other nation has our Bill of Rights. The year 1991 marked the 200th anniversary of its ratification. It requires no limiting amendment. The American people understand that they are not threatened by flag burners, and the American people prefer the First Amendment undiluted. They understand that imprisoning a few extremists is not what patriotism is about. Forced patriotism is not American. Flag burning is all wrong, but a lot of wrongheaded speech is protected by the Constitution. When the nation celebrated the bicentennial of the Bill of Rights, it celebrated a wonderfully terse, eloquent, and effective summation of individual freedoms. Time has not shown a need to add "except for flag burners." That exception, as the Court majority realized, might show that the nation is so lacking in faith in itself that it permits the Johnsons and Eichmans to diminish the flag's meaning. They are best treated, as Brennan urged, by saluting the flag that they burn or by ignoring them contemptuously.

Bibliography

Greenawalt, Kent 1990 O'er the Land of the Free Flag Burning as Speech. *UCLA Law Review* 37:925–947.

Kmiec, Douglas W. 1990 In the Aftermath of *Johnson* and *Eichman. Brigham Young University Law Review* 1990:577–638.

7

The Incorporation Doctrine

According to the incorporation doctrine the Fourteenth Amendment incorporates or absorbs the Bill of Rights, making its guarantees applicable to the states. Whether the Bill of Rights applied to the states, restricting their powers as it did those of the national government, was a question that arose in connection with the framing and ratification of the Fourteenth Amendment. Before 1868 nothing in the Constitution of the United States prevented a state from imprisoning religious heretics or political dissenters, or from abolishing trial by jury, or from torturing suspects to extort confessions of guilt. The Bill of Rights limited only the United States, not the states. James Madison, who framed the amendments that became the Bill of Rights, had included one providing that "no State shall violate the equal rights of conscience, of the freedom of the press, or the trial by jury in criminal cases." The Senate defeated that proposal. History, therefore, was on the side of the Supreme Court when it unanimously decided in *Barron v. Baltimore* (1833) that "the fifth amendment must be understood as restraining the power of the general government, not as applicable to the States," and said that the other amendments composing the Bill of Rights were equally inapplicable to the States.

Thus, a double standard existed in the nation. The Bill of Rights commanded the national government to refrain from enacting certain laws and to respect certain procedures, but it left the states free to do as they wished in relation to the same matters. State constitutions and common law practices, rather than the Constitution of the United States, were the sources of restraints on the states with respect to the subjects of the Bill of Rights.

Whether the Fourteenth Amendment was intended to alter this situation is a matter on which the historical record is complex, confusing, and probably inconclusive. Even if history spoke with a loud, clear, and decisive voice, however, it ought not necessarily control judgment on the question whether the Supreme Court should interpret the amendment as incorporating the Bill of Rights. Whatever the framers of the Fourteenth intended, they did not possess ultimate wisdom as to the meaning of their words for subsequent generations. Moreover, the privileges and immunities, due process, and equal protection clauses of section 1 of the amendment are written in language that blocks fixed meanings. Its text must be read as revelations of general purposes that were to be achieved or as expressions of imperishable principles that are comprehensive in character. The principles and purposes, not their framers' original technical understanding, are what was intended to endure. We cannot avoid the influence of history but are not constitutionally obligated to obey history which is merely a guide. The task of constitutional interpretation is one of statecraft: to read the text in the light of changing needs in accordance with the noblest ideals of a democratic society.

The Court has, in fact, proved to be adept at reading into the Constitution the policy values that meet its approval, and its freedom to do so is virtually legislative in scope. Regrettably in its first Fourteenth Amendment decision, in the *Slaughterhouse Cases* (1873), the Court unnecessarily emasculated the privileges and immunities clause by ruling that it protected only the privileges and immunities of national citizenship but not the privileges and immunities of state citizenship, which included "nearly every civil right for the establishment and protection of which organized government is instituted." Among the rights deriving from state, not national, citizenship were those referred to by the Bill of Rights as well as other fundamental rights. Justice Stephen J. Field, dissenting, rightly said that the majority's interpretation had rendered the clause "a vain and idle enactment, which accomplished nothing. . . . " The privileges and immunities clause was central to the incorporation issue because to the extent that any of the framers of the amendment intended incorporation, they relied principally on that clause. Notwithstanding the amendment, *Barron v. Baltimore* remained controlling law. The Court simply opposed the revolution in the federal system which the amendment's text suggested. The privileges and immunities of national citizenship after *Slaughterhouse* were those that Congress or the Court could have protected, under the supremacy clause, with or without the new amendment.

In *Hurtado v. California* (1884) the Court initiated a long line of decisions that eroded the traditional procedures associated with due process of law. *Hurtado* was not an incorporation case, because the question it posed was not whether the Fourteenth Amendment incorporated the clause of the Fifth guaranteeing indictment by grand jury but whether the concept of due process necessarily required indictment in a capital case. In cases arising after *Hurtado*, counsel argued that even if the concept of due process did not mean indictment, or freedom from cruel and unusual punishment, or trial by a twelve-member jury, or the right against self-incrimination, the provisions of the Bill of Rights applied to the states through the Fourteenth Amendment; that is, the amendment incorporated them either by the privileges and immunities clause, or by the due process clause's protection of "liberty." In *O'Neil v. Vermont* (1892), that argument was accepted for the first time by three Justices, dissenting; however, only one of them, John Marshall Harlan, steadfastly adhered to it in *Maxwell v. Dow* (1900) and *Twining v. New Jersey* (1908), when all other Justices rejected it. Harlan, dissenting in *Patterson v. Colorado* (1907), stated "that the privilege of free speech and a free press belong to every citizen of the United States, constitute essential parts of every man's liberty, and are protected against violation by that clause of the Fourteenth Amendment forbidding a state to deprive any person of his liberty without due process of law." The Court casually adopted that view in obiter dictum in *Gitlow v. New York* (1925).

Before *Gitlow* the Court had done a good deal of property-minded, not liberty-minded, incorporating. As early as *Hepburn v. Griswold* (1870), it had read the protection of the contract clause into the Fifth Amendment's due process clause as a limitation on the powers of Congress, a viewpoint repeated in the *Sinking Fund Cases* (1879). The Court in 1894 had incorporated the Fifth's just compensation clause into the Fourteenth's due process clause and in 1897 it had incorporated the same clause into the Fourteenth's equal protection clause. In the same decade the Court had accepted substantive due process, incorporating within the Fourteenth a variety of doctrines that secured property, particularly corporate property, against "unreasonable" rate regulations and reformist labor legislation. By 1915, however, procedural due process for persons accused of crime had so shriveled in meaning that Justice Oliver Wendell Holmes, dissenting, was forced to say that "mob law does not become due process of law by securing the assent of a terrorized jury."

The word "liberty" in the due process clause had absorbed all First Amendment guarantees by the time of the decision in *Everson v. Board of Education* (1947). Incorporation developed much more slowly in the field of criminal justice. *Powell v. Alabama* (1932) applied to the states the Sixth Amendment's right to counsel in capital cases, as a "necessary requisite of due process of law." The Court reached a watershed, however, in *Palko v. Connecticut* (1937), where it refused to incorporate the ban on double jeopardy. Justice Benjamin N. Cardozo sought to provide a "rationalizing principle" to explain the selective or piecemeal incorporation process. He repudiated the notion that the Fourteenth Amendment embraced the entire Bill of Rights, because the rights it guaranteed fell into two categories. Some were of such a nature that liberty and justice could not exist if they were sacrificed. These had been brought "within the Fourteenth Amendment by a process of absorption" because they were "of the very essence of a scheme of ordered liberty." In short, they were "fundamental," like the concept of due process. Other rights, however, were not essential to a "fair and enlightened system of justice." First Amendment rights were "the indispensable condition" of nearly every other form of freedom, but jury trials, indictments, immunity against compulsory self-incrimination, and double jeopardy "might be lost, and justice still be done."

The difficulty with *Palko's* rationalizing scheme was that it was subjective. It offered no principle explaining why some rights were fundamental or essential to ordered liberty and others were not; it measured all rights against some abstract or idealized system, rather than the Anglo-American accusatory system of criminal justice. Selective incorporation also completely lacked historical justification. And it was logically flawed. The Court read the substantive content of the First Amendment into the "liberty" of the due process clause, but that clause permitted the abridgment of liberty with due process of law. On the other hand, selective incorporation, as contrasted with total incorporation, allowed the Court to decide constitutional issues as they arose on a case-by-case basis, and allowed, too, the exclusion from the incorporation doctrine of some rights whose incorporation would wreak havoc in state systems of justice. Grand jury indictment for all felonies and trials by twelve-member juries in civil suits involving more than twenty dollars are among Bill of Rights guarantees that would have that result, if incorporated.

In *Adamson v. California* (1947) a 5–4 Court rejected the total incorporation theory advanced by the dissenters led by Justice Hugo L. Black. Black lambasted the majority's due process standards as grossly subjective; he argued that only the Justices' personal idiosyncrasies could give content to "canons of decency" and "fundamental justice." Black believed that both history and objectivity required resort to the "specifics" of the Bill of Rights. Justices Frank Murphy and Wiley Rutledge would have gone further. They accepted total incorporation but observed that due process might require invalidating some state practices "despite the absence of a specific provision in the Bill of Rights." Justice Felix Frankfurter, replying to Black, denied the subjectivity charge and turned it against the dissenters. Murphy's total-incorporation-"plus" was subjective; total incorporation impractically fastened the entire Bill of Rights, with impedimenta, on the states along with the accretions each right had gathered in the United States courts. Selective incorporation on the basis of individual Justices' preferences meant "a merely subjective test" in determining which rights were in and which were out.

Frankfurter also made a logical point long familiar in constitutional jurisprudence. The due process clause of the Fourteenth, which was the vehicle for incorporation, having been copied from the identical clause of the Fifth, could not mean one thing in the latter and something very different in the former. The Fifth itself included a variety of clauses. To incorporate them into the Fourteenth would mean that those clauses of the Fifth and in the remainder of the Bill of Rights were redundant, or the due process clause, if signifying all the rest, was meaningless or superfluous. The answer to Frankfurter and to those still holding his view is historical, not logical. The history of due process shows that it did mean trial by jury and a cluster of traditional rights of accused persons that the Bill of Rights separately specified. Its framers were in many respects careless draftsmen. They enumerated particular rights associated with due process and then added the due process clause partly for political reasons and partly as a rhetorical flourish—a reinforced guarantee and a genuflection toward traditional usage going back to medieval reenactments of Magna Carta.

Numerous cases of the 1950s showed that the majority's reliance on the concept of due process rather than the "specifics" of the Bill of Rights made for unpredictable and unconvincing results. For that reason the Court resumed selective incorporation in the 1960s, beginning with *Mapp v. Ohio* (1961) and ending with *Benton v. Maryland* (1969). The Warren Court's "revolution in criminal justice" applied against the states the rights of the Fourth through Eighth Amendments, excepting only indictment, twelve-member civil juries, and bail. *In re Winship* (1970) even held that proof of crime beyond a reasonable doubt, though not a specific provision of the Bill of Rights, was essential to due process, and various decisions have suggested the Court's readiness to extend to the states the Eighth Amendment's provision against excessive bail.

The specifics of the Bill of Rights, however, have proved to offer only an illusion of objectivity, because its most important clauses, including all that have been incorporated, are inherently ambiguous. Indeed, the only truly specific clauses are the ones that have not been incorporated—indictment by grand jury and civil trials by twelve-member juries. The "specific" injunctions of the Bill of Rights do not exclude exceptions, nor are they self-defining. What is "an establishment of religion" and what, given libels, pornography, and perjury, is "the freedom of speech" or "of the press"? These freedoms cannot be abridged, but what is an abridgment? Freedom of religion may not be prohibited; may freedom of religion be abridged by a regulation short of prohibition? What is an "unreasonable" search, "probable" cause, or "excessive" bail? What punishment is "cruel and unusual"? Is it really true that a person cannot be compelled to be a witness against himself in a criminal case and that the Sixth Amendment extends to "all" criminal prosecutions? What is a "criminal prosecution," a "speedy trial," or an "impartial" jury? Ambiguity cannot be strictly construed. Neutral principles and specifics turn out to be subjective or provoke subjectivity. Moreover, applying to the states the federal standard does not always turn out as expected. After *Duncan v. Louisiana* (1968) extended the trial by jury clause of the Sixth Amendment to the states, the Court decided that a criminal jury of less than twelve (but not less than six) would not violate the Fourteenth Amendment, nor would a non-unanimous jury decision. Examples can be multiplied to show that the incorporation doctrine has scarcely diminished the need for judgment and that judgment tends to be personal in character.

On the whole, however, the Court has abolished the double standard by nationalizing the Bill of Rights. The results have been mixed. More than ever justice tends to travel on leaden feet. Swift and certain punishment has always been about as effective a deterrent to crime as our criminal justice system can provide, and the prolongation of the criminal process from arrest to final appeal, which is one result of the incorporation doctrine, adds to the congestion of prosecutorial caseloads and court dockets. However, the fundamental problem is the staggering rise in the number of crimes committed, not the decisions of the Court. Even when the police used truncheons to beat suspects into confessions and searched and seized almost at will, they did not reduce the crime rate. In the long run a democratic society is probably hurt more by lawless conduct on the part of law-enforcement agencies than by the impediments of the incorporation doctrine. In the First Amendment field, the incorporation doctrine has few critics, however vigorously particular First Amendment decisions may be criticized.

Bibliography

Abraham, Henry J. 1977 *Freedom and the Court,* 3rd ed. Pages 33–105. New York: Oxford University Press.

Cortner, Richard C. 1981 *The Supreme Court and the Second Bill of Rights: The Fourteenth Amendment and the Nationalization of Civil Liberties.* Madison University of Wisconsin Press.

Friendly, Henry J. 1967 *Benchmarks.* Pages 235–265. Chicago: University of Chicago Press.

Henkin, Louis 1963 "Selective Incorporation" in the Fourteenth Amendment. *Yale Law Journal* 73:74–88.

North, Arthur A. 1966 *The Supreme Court: Judicial Process and Judicial Politics.* Pages 65–133. New York Appleton-Century-Crofts.

8

Incorporation and the Wall

Establishment clause cases rarely concern acts of the national government. The usual case involves an act of a state, and the usual decision restricts religion in the public schools or government aid to sectarian schools. The First Amendment, as incorporated within the Fourteenth Amendment, operates as a ban against state action, and nonpreferentialists hate that fact. They hate the incorporation doctrine. The incorporation doctrine is that the Fourteenth Amendment's due process clause incorporates within its protection of "liberty" most of the provisions of the Bill of Rights, thereby imposing on the states the same limitations imposed by the Bill of Rights on the United States. In the absence of the incorporation doctrine, nothing in the United States Constitution would prevent a state from outlawing an unpopular religious sect, establishing a particular church, storming into private homes without a warrant, imprisoning people who speak their minds in unpopular ways, or taxing local newspapers too critical of the state government. The due process clause of the Fourteenth Amendment, which has been the basis of the incorporation doctrine, states that no state shall deprive any person of life, liberty, or property without due process of law.

Because the United States has no constitutional power to make laws that directly benefit religion and because under the incorporation doctrine the Fourteenth Amendment imposes upon the states the same limitations as the First Amendment places on the United States, the states have no constitutional power to aid religion directly either. Therefore, nonpreferentialists break a lance against reading the First Amendment's establishment clause into the Fourteenth as a limitation on the states. If the Fourteenth Amendment did not incorporate the First Amendment, the states would be free from the restraints of the United States Constitution and would be able to enact any measure concerning religion, subject only to such limitations as might exist in the individual state constitutions. Some nonpreferentialists and accommodationists therefore advocate the overruling of the incorporation doctrine. In its absence, the establishment clause, said a nonpreferentialist judge, would "not bar the States from establishing a religion."[1]

To expect the Supreme Court to turn back the clock by scrapping the entire incorporation doctrine is so unrealistic as not to warrant consideration. Attorney General Edwin Meese, Professor James McClellan, and other reactionaries indulge their emotions when denouncing the Court for six decades of decisions based on a doctrine that has "shaky" foundations or for pursuing its "revolutionary course" in making the First Amendment applicable to the states in the cases beginning with *Gitlow v. New York*[2] in 1925 and in "arbitrarily" assuming religious liberty and freedom from establishments of religion to be within the liberty of the Fourteenth Amendment's due process clause.[3] But such extravagance of language persuades no one who remembers that the revolutionists were led not by Chief Justice Earl Warren but by Justice Edward T. Sanford, joined by fellow conservatives on the Supreme Court, including Justices James C. McReynolds, George Sutherland, Pierce Butler, Joseph McKenna, Willis Vandevanter, and William Howard Taft, among others; and the *Gitlow* Court was unanimous as to the incorporation doctrine. In 1940 the *Cantwell* Court, which incorporated the free exercise clause and, by obiter dictum, the establishment clause, spoke unanimously through Owen Roberts, one-time nemesis of the New Deal.[4] And, in 1947 the *Everson* Court too was unanimous on the incorporation issue.[5] Attorney General Meese, Professors McClellan and Robert L. Cord, and others, complain that incorporation began belatedly in 1925 with *Gitlow* and the free speech clause of the First Amendment.[6] In fact, as early as the late nineteenth century the Court used the incorporation doctrine to protect property rights; in 1894 the Court read the equal protection clause of the Fourteenth Amendment to include or incorporate the eminent domain or takings clause of the Fifth Amendment in order to strike down rate regulation,[7] and then in 1897 the Court crammed the eminent domain clause into the Fourteenth's due process clause to achieve the same end.[8] The incorporation doctrine has a history so fixed that over-throwing it is as likely as bagging snarks on the roof of the Court's building. Of all the amendments constituting the Bill of Rights, the First Amendment is the least likely to be thrown out of its nesting place within the word "liberty" of the Fourteenth. The Hughes Court unanimously awarded the First Amendment the laurels of uttermost fundamentality: no freedoms are more precious or more basic than those protected by the First Amendment.[9]

Even so, eminent constitutional scholars including Edward S. Corwin and Robert G. McCloskey, among others, have suggested that a principled distinction can be made between the establishment clause and the other clauses of the First Amendment, allowing the disincorporation of the establishment clause. Their point is that the clause does not protect an individual freedom; it does not provide a right to do something. Government may violate one's personal right to speak freely or worship as he pleases if he pleases, but government cannot violate one's right not to be subject to an establishment of religion. Advocates of this view state it as if it were self-evidently true. As McCloskey said, "It requires a semantic leap to translate 'liberty' into 'disestablishment' when by definition the forbidden establishment need involve no restriction of the liberty of any individual."[10] By what definition? The semantic leap covers about a millimeter of space: freedom from an establishment, even a nonpreferential one, is an indispensable attribute of liberty. That was the principal theme of Madison's Remonstrance and a theme of the Virginia Statute of Religious Freedom. An establishment, Madison argued, "violated the free exercise of religion" and would "subvert public liberty."[11]

The belief that freedom from an establishment of religion is indispensable was not just the product of rationalists who cared little about revealed religion. From the religious founders of Rhode Island, Roger Williams and John Clarke, to the leading American Baptists a century and a half later, such as Isaac Backus and John Leland, evangelicals who profoundly cared about the purity of Christian faith had warned against the corrupting embrace of government, and they had advocated separation in order to *defend* religion. To them the integrity of religion and of religious liberty depended on the promptings of private conscience unsullied by the assistance of government. Madison's Remonstrance bore the influence of his Orange County neighbor, the great Baptist preacher John Leland, as well as that of the deistic Jefferson, who cared more about the purity of public liberty.

The aggressive personal liberties of the First Amendment, we are also told, must be exercised to be enjoyed, and therefore they seem to be distinguishable from disestablishment as a form of liberty. Freedom *of* religion, from this viewpoint, is unlike freedom *from* disestablishment. But that is only a partial truth, because freedom of religion and the freedoms of speech, press, and assembly are also freedoms from government ("Congress shall make no law . . . "). They are freedoms from government impositions and measures that create a suffocating civic environment within which the possibility of exercising and enjoying personal freedoms has been diminished. Freedom from seditious libel laws, from taxes on knowledge, from prosecutions for blasphemy, from censorship, and from disabilities arising because of one's associations or religion are similar in nature to freedom from establishments in the sense that the First Amendment creates immunities that form a wall behind which freedom can flourish. What Zechariah Chafee, one of the leading civil libertarians of the twentieth century, called "the most important human right in the Constitution" is a "freedom from" or an immunity: the right to the writ of habeas corpus or freedom from arbitrary arrest.[12] Numerous rights deemed fundamental by the Supreme Court are immunities that cannot be exercised by individuals. No one can affirmatively exercise a negative right, such as the right to be free from compulsory self-incrimination or to be free from cruel and unusual punishments. These are, nevertheless, personal rights; only specific individuals can be denied freedom from compulsory self-incrimination or from cruel and unusual punishment.

There is another and equally important dimension to all rights, however personal, and that is the social or civic dimension. By imposing restraints upon government, they make it possible for the body politic to be free for private and voluntary judgments by all members. Public as well as private liberty is the beneficiary. Taxes spent for religion violate the right to support religion voluntarily and privately. Religious exercises in the public schools are intimidating or humiliating to those who must voluntarily decline to participate. Such assistance to religion therefore damages public liberty. As Madison said, an establishment of religion "violates equality by subjecting some to peculiar burdens." The fruits of such an establishment, he argued, include "bigotry and persecution" and "will destroy that moderation and harmony which the forbearance of our laws to intermeddle with Religion has produced among its several sects."[13] Public liberty and personal civil liberty require an exemption from government-sponsored programs that spur bigotry.

Although Madison thought that taxes for the religion of one's choice (a general assessment bill aiding all Christian sects) differed only in degree, not in principle, from the Inquisition, Professor Robert McCloskey thought otherwise. He believed that no useful purpose is served to talk as if the evil of modern establishments, as the Supreme Court understands them, is comparable to that of persecutions or pogroms. The state-church involvements that the Court considers, he wrote, include "nudging of moppets in the direction of religion instruction classes, a modest amount of classroom praying and Bible reading." That, he added, "is not the stuff from which crusades and martyrs are made."[14] That judgment has little historical merit and probably no psychological merit. McCloskey himself admitted that it is wrong to contend "that such involvements are not noxious at all."[15] He mentioned both the coercion of children and the harmful effect upon the political process. "It is arguable," he wrote with some equanimity, "that religion has a special propensity to stir emotions and breed animosities when it becomes a subject of political controversy" and, one should add, when it becomes a subject of educational controversy too.

McCloskey might not have spoken so lightly about nudging moppets had he remembered the history of religion in our public schools. In the nineteenth century, Catholic children were flogged for refusing to participate in Protestant services—just a "modest amount" of classroom prayer and reading from the King James Version of the Bible. In Philadelphia in 1842 a Roman Catholic bishop asked that the Catholic children be allowed to use their own version of the Bible and be excused from other religious instruction in the public schools. The result was "two years of bitterness and mob violence, the burning of two Catholic churches and a seminary, and finally three days of rioting in which thirteen people were killed and fifty wounded—in the City of Brotherly Love."[16]

Of course, McCloskey was right: we are not talking about church-state involvements that threaten pogroms or inquisitions. Justice Lewis F. Powell correctly observed: "At this point in the 20th century we are quite far removed from the dangers that prompted the Framers to include the Establishment Clause in the Bill of Rights. . . . The risk . . . even of deep political division along religious lines . . . is remote."[17] Indeed, we have progressed so much that the fallout from a released time program, which at least has the virtue of keeping religion out of the public schools, is merely some virulent anti-Semitism, evidenced by Jewish children being called "Christ killer" and "dirty Jew."[18] In sum, reading freedom from disestablishment into the meaning of the "liberty" protected against state infringement by the Fourteenth Amendment makes the same sense and stands on the same principle as reading the free exercise clause into "liberty.

Those who expect a conservative Supreme Court, likely to become more conservative as older liberal Justices are replaced, to overrule the incorporation doctrine with respect to the establishment clause underestimate the political shrewdness of the Court. It does not matter whether liberal or conservative activists dominate the Supreme Court. The precipitous repudiation of entrenched doctrines would appear too obviously the result of subjective choices. Wherever possible the Court has avoided a dramatic overruling of its precedents, and it is likely to continue to do so. In the art of judging, a proper regard for appearances counts. The Court must seem to appreciate the values of coherence, stability, and continuity with the past. Judges, especially conservative ones, prefer to avoid sudden shifts in constitutional law. Any person who reaches the highest court is sophisticated enough to appreciate the strategic and political values of achieving desired results by indirection. Overruling is a device of last resort, employed only when other alternatives are unavailable or unavailing. The Court will not overrule the incorporation doctrine; it will not turn back the clock. But, it is quite likely to reinterpret precedents, distinguishing away some, blunting others, and making new law without the appearance of overruling or disrespecting the past. The Court will nourish the impression that it is for standing pat. It merely refuses to endorse further expansion of rights but faithfully hews to fundamental doctrines.

In a 1985 case the Supreme Court had to reconsider the incorporation doctrine, because a federal district judge in Alabama expressly repudiated it in a bizarre opinion holding that the establishment clause did not bar states from establishing a religion. The Supreme Court, however, serenely continued to employ the doctrine after treating the lower court opinion with something close to the contemptuous disdain it deserved. Not even the reactionary Justice Rehnquist, a loose cannon on the Supreme Court, aimed at the incorporation doctrine. He utterly misconstrued the establishment clause in an interpretation not accepted by any other member of the Court and he grossly distorted history, but he embraced the doctrine, even if reluctantly, when he declared: "Given the 'incorporation' of the Establishment Clause as against the States via the Fourteenth Amendment in *Everson,* States are prohibited as well [as the United States] from establishing a religion or discriminating between sects."[19]

Perhaps the chief reason that the incorporation doctrine will continue undiminished in vitality is that no need exists to overthrow it in order to achieve the results that promote religious interests. One scholar got his history all wrong when he declared that the framers of the First Amendment did not mean to prevent the United States from giving nonpreferential aid to religion if the aid is incidental to the performance of a delegated power, but he stumbled on a truth about the politics of constitutional law. Power that is illegitimately exercised under one constitutional rubric may be valid under another.[20]

Although Congress has no constitutional authority to legislate on religion as such or make it the beneficiary of legislation or other government action, the blunt fact is that regardless of what the Framers intended and regardless of the absence of a power to legislate on religion, the United States does possess constitutional powers to benefit or burden religion as an indirect result of the exercise of delegated powers. For example, the First Congress, in the course of debating the amendments that became the Bill of Rights, recommended a day of national thanksgiving and prayer, and it also reenacted the Northwest Ordinance. Passed in 1787 by the Congress of Confederation, the Northwest Ordinance included a clause providing that schools and the means of education should be encouraged because religion, like morality and knowledge, is "necessary to good government and the happiness of mankind. And without doubt, religion (Protestantism) constituted an important part of the curriculum at that time. Significantly, however, Congress in 1789 did not reenact the provision of 1787 by which one lot in each township was to be set aside "perpetually for the purposes of religion."[21] "The vast majority of Americans, as Thomas Curry wrote, "assumed that theirs was a Christian, i.e. Protestant country, and they automatically expected that government would uphold the commonly agreed on Protestant ethos and morality. In many instances, they had not come to grips with the implications their belief in the powerlessness of government in religious matters held for a society in which the values, customs and forms of Protestant Christianity thoroughly permeated civil and political life."[22] When the Congress that adopted the First Amendment promoted religion in the Northwest Ordinance or by urging a national day of prayer, it acted unconstitutionally—by later standards. Usually, however, some plausible pretext can be found for the constitutionality of government action. For example, Congress could constitutionally have benefited religion indirectly in the reenactment of the Northwest Ordinance by virtue of an express power to make "needful rules" for the governance of the territories. In a real case the Supreme Court would have a difficult task to explain why territories could not be governed without official encouragement of religion. Few real cases exist, however, and the Court rarely troubles to think seriously about the delegated powers that might be exercised legitimately in a manner benefiting religion. What are those powers?

Under the power to "make rules for the government and regulation" of the armed forces, Congress provided for military and naval chaplains and paid them from public taxes. Under the power to govern its own proceedings, both chambers of Congress have provided for legislative chaplains. Under the power to punish violators of federal laws by imprisonment Congress has built prisons and provided chaplains for the inmates. Congress may close government buildings on the sabbath and on religious holidays, because it controls federal property. Under the power to coin money Congress has placed a theistic motto on United States coins and currency. Under the power to levy taxes, Congress has made exemptions for churches and clergymen. Under the power to raise armies and therefore the power to lay down the terms for conscription, Congress has exempted conscientious objectors and clergymen. By the exercise of the treaty power the government has made treaties with the Indians and has implemented those treaties by appropriations for religion, ostensibly for the purpose of civilizing, Christianizing, and pacifying the Indians. The examples can be extended. However, the Supreme Court does not bother to explain much when it sustains some "accommodation" to religion.

The same authority that can incidentally benefit religion by the exercise of legitimate powers may also injure religion. A power to help is also a power to hinder or harm. Congress could draft conscientious objectors or tax church property for example. That it does not do so is a matter of politics not the result of constitutional power. Those who clamor for additional government support of religion should beware of the risks to religion from government entanglements. Those damaging risks are possible, if not likely.[23]

From a constitutional standpoint, however, government can go too far in implementing a spirit of "benevolent neutrality," to use a phrase of Chief Justice Warren Burger,[24] by serving religious needs. Benign "accommodation" is one thing; an implicit alliance with religion or state encouragement or sponsorship of it is another, although the Supreme Court has not distinguished the two in any consistent manner. Congress cannot constitutionally spend tax monies for the erection or maintenance of houses of worship, although it can tax almost as it pleases and spend almost as it pleases for "the common defense and general welfare." Nor can government financially assist a private sectarian school that is integrally a part of the religious mission of the denomination operating that school. The limits on the employment of authorized powers include the proscription against establishments of religion.

The establishment clause is over two centuries old. At the time the First Amendment was framed, government and religion were much closer than they are today, but nothing was clearer than the fact that financial aid to religion or religious establishments constituted an establishment of religion. The establishment clause should be far broader in meaning now than it was when adopted, because the nation is far more religiously pluralistic and is growing ever more so. Then, for all practical purposes religion meant Christianity and Christianity meant Protestantism. But Roman Catholics now compose the largest denomination in the nation, and about 6,000,000 American citizens are Jews. In addition, there are several scores of sects and substantial numbers of adherents to religions that were unknown in 1789, including Mormons, Christian Scientists, Pentecostalists, Jehovah's Witnesses, members of the Unification Church and Hare Krishnas. The number of Muslims, Buddhists, Confuscianists, Hindus, Sikhs, and Taoists is increasing.

We should not want the ban on establishments of religion to mean only what it meant in 1789 or only what its framers intended. Oliver Wendell Holmes said, "historical continuity with the past is not a duty, it is only a necessity."[25] That delphic statement can be construed to mean that we cannot escape history because it has shaped us and guides our policies, but we are not obliged to remain static. Two hundred years of expanding the meaning of democracy should have some constitutional impact. We are not bound by the wisdom of the Framers; we are bound only to consider whether the purposes they had in mind still merit political respect and constitutional obedience. History can only be a guide, not a controlling factor. If we followed the framers of the Constitution blindly, we would be duplicating the method of the *Dred Scott* decision by freezing the meaning of words at the time they became part of the Constitution. Holmes wisely declared that courts—and he might have added scholars—are apt to err by sticking too closely to the words of law when those words "import a policy that goes beyond them."[26] The significance of words, he taught, is vital, not formal, and is to be gathered not simply by taking dictionary definitions "but by considering their origin and the line of their growth."[27]

The broad purpose of the establishment clause should not be the only thing kept in mind. A little common sense helps too in the constitutional politics of its interpretation, and that common sense should come from public interest lawyers and counsel representing defense organizations as well as from courts. Those who profess to be broad separationists ought to understand that popular government will continue to aid religion and show respect for it, and that not every accommodation with religion, deriving from incidental assistance, is necessarily unconstitutional. Indeed, separationists ought to understand that even if they profoundly believe that a practice is unconstitutional, wisdom sometimes dictates against pressing a suit. Trying to insure that the wall of separation is really impregnable might be futile and dangerously counterproductive. Indeed, the cracks in the wall might be more numerous than at present without seriously harming it or the values that it protects. A moment of silence in the public school for meditation or prayer, posting the Ten Commandments on the school bulletin board, or even saying a bland interdenominational prayer would not really make much difference, if they were not omens that the cause of religion would be still further promoted by government. Accommodationists seem insatiable and use every exception as precedents for still more exceptions. The moral majority does not compromise. Consequently passionate separationists who see every exception as a disaster, tend to run around, like Chicken Little, screaming, "The wall is falling, the wall is falling." It really is not and will not, so long as it leaks just a little at the seams. If it did not leak a little, it might generate enough pressure to break it. There is a legal maxim *Lex non curat de minimis,* which means that the law does not concern itself with trifles. The *de minimis* concept has some value, as Madison understood, although the American Civil Liberties Union has not always understood. Suits brought by the ACLU to have courts hold unconstitutional every cooperative relationship between government and religion can damage the cause of separation by making it look over-rigid and ridiculous. One of the principal arguments of separationists against certain practices that breach the wall of separation, particularly in the field of education, is that those practices are divisive and stimulate conflict among people of differing faiths. Some silly suits, such as those seeking to have declared unconstitutional the words "under God" in the pledge of allegiance or in the money motto "In God We Trust," have the same deleterious effects. Separationists who cannot appreciate the principle of *de minimis* ought to appreciate a different motto—"Let sleeping dogmas lie."

The *de minimis* principle, of course, has two sides. People who are eager to have Nativity scenes displayed at Christmas in publicly owned places tend to say *"de minimis."* Their insensitivities are about on a par with that of the Supreme Court when it decided that the city of Pawtucket's creche was as nonsectarian as the accompanying figures of Santa Claus and Rudolph the Red-Nosed Reindeer. *De minimis* can doubtlessly be made to cover practices damaging to the salutary benefits of separation between government and religion. Protestants used to say *de minimis* when Roman Catholics objected to the use of the King James Bible in the public schools. In 1854, for example, a Maine court upheld the expulsion of a Catholic child for refusing to read that Bible, even though the court acknowledged that the law regarded every religion as having equal rights. However, added the court, "reading the Bible is no more an interference with religious belief, than would reading the mythology of Greece and Rome be regarded as interfering with religious belief or an affirmance of the pagan creeds."[28] Whether a practice seems *de minimis* may depend on the perspective from which it is seen. What is trifling to the majority may be threatening and offensive, even persecuting, to a minority.

Accommodationists and nonpreferentialists also go too far and can be equally insensitive to the rights of others in the overaggressive pursuit of their own interests. Like separationists, they too press suits to have the fundamental law enshrine their beliefs. In *Board of Trustees v. McCleary,* a case left unresolved by the Supreme Court's 4-to-4 tie vote in 1985, the issue was whether citizens can force the public display of a Christmas creche on public land contrary to the decision of the town of Scarsdale, New York.[29] The tie vote left standing a federal Court of Appeals decision against Scarsdale on the ground that the town had denied free speech in a public forum. If nude dancing, flag burning, and Nazi marches are symbolic speech worthy of constitutional protection, so too is a nativity scene at Christmas time in a public park. But a creche on public property during a religious holiday and without Santa and his cohorts is a sacred symbol that has a religious, not a secular, purpose. Nude dancing, flag burning, and marches by Nazis, being without religious significance, cannot possibly violate the establishment clause. The status of a public park as a public forum cannot justify its unconstitutional use. But the Court of Appeals, relying on the Supreme Court's offensive creche precedent of 1983, found no infringement of establishment clause values.[30] Zealots who suddenly demand the right to spread their prayer rugs in the midst of traffic, when churches and homes are available, should tempt the Court to remind us about the virtues of limits even on devotional exercises, not to mention those virtues adhering to local option, which some conservative judges claim on occasion to respect.

Strategists in the opposing camps see every nonpreferential aid to religion as a precedent that might warrant still further aid. The nonpreferentialists, who too often are really preferentialists seeking their cut of the pie or who care as little for minorities as a former majority cared about them, eagerly claim that every existing aid proves the invalidity of an overbroad principle of separation. But exceptions to the principle do not impair its enduring value. If history teaches anything, Madison touched truth when he declared that "religion and government will both exist in greater purity, the less they are mixed together."[31] Fortunately, the opposing forces in our system have courts to resort to rather than bats and bricks, but the losing side in any case tends to react like Bret Harte's M'liss. Upon being told that the sun had obeyed Joshua's command to stand still in the heavens, she slammed her astronomy book shut with the defiant assertion, "It's a damned lie. I don't believe it."[32] The Court rarely convinces those who think it wrong, perhaps because no establishment clause question can be dissected so precisely that it has only one side and because religion is a subject that is overladen with emotion. Religion goes to the core of human existence.

Americans ought to bear in mind that forbearance is sometimes better than disputation or litigation. They should realize that a faulty political compromise may be better than judicial dictation, which does not satisfy the loser and can corrupt the spirit of the victor. We profess to respect majority rule and minority rights, but when the minority wins, the majority claims that the minority rules, and when the majority wins, the minority feels oppressed. Circumventing the courts, demonstrating the civility due one another, and reaching a deal might not be a bad idea. In his old age, Jefferson wisely observed: "A Government [or society] held together by the bands of reason only, requires much compromise of opinion; that things even salutary should not be crammed down the throats of dissenting brethren, especially when they may be put into a form to be willingly swallowed, and that a good deal of indulgence is necessary to strengthen habits of harmony and fraternity."[33] Such a homily has meant so little to us that we now are where we are. We are common victims of our own Supreme Court, which thinks a publicly sponsored creche is secular and therefore not an establishment of religion,[34] but thinks too that it saw a forbidden establishment in a state police power measure aimed at keeping boisterous patrons of a tavern from disturbing a church.[35]

The principles of forbearance, mutual compromise, and indulgence might be well served by court decisions that keep religious exercises completely out of public schools and conspicuous public places, but that open the doors wide to public support of everything secular in the private sectarian schools and to secular measures that aid those schools. The Court possesses the craft and authority to reach any result it wants, and it ought to relieve the burden of so-called double taxation on those who pay to send their children to private school. Private sectarian schools fulfill the goals of education at much savings to the public. So too the Court should keep the public schools free from sectarianism to fulfill their mission as the common meeting ground of the citizens of a pluralistic democracy.

The words of the establishment clause are not empty vessels into which judges may pour nearly anything they wish. Some Justices of the Supreme Court, however, in candid moments have confessed that they believe otherwise. In 1948 Justice Robert Jackson wrote of the difficulty of separating the secular from the religious: "It is idle to pretend that this task is one for which we can find in the Constitution one word to help us as judges to decide where the secular ends and the sectarian begins in education. Nor can we find guidance in any other legal source. It is a matter on which we can find no law but our own presuppositions."[36] Similarly Justice Byron White later declared:

> No one contends that he can discern from the sparse language of the Establishment Clause that a State is forbidden to aid religion in any manner or, if it does not mean that, what kind of or how much aid is permissible. And one cannot seriously believe that the history of the First Amendment furnishes unequivocal answers to many of the fundamental issues of church-state relations. In the end, the courts have fashioned answers to these questions as best they can, the language of the Constitution and its history having left them a wide range of choice among many alternatives. But decision has been unavoidable; and in choosing, the courts necessarily have carved out what they deemed to be the most desirable national policy governing various aspects of church-state relationships.[37]

Whether Jackson and White were right about the guidance available from the Constitution or from history, the reality is that the Court exercises a freedom almost legislative in character, bringing us close to the intolerable, a Humpty Dumpty Court. Humpty Dumpty told Alice scornfully that when he used a word it meant just what he chose it to mean, neither more nor less. "The question is," said Alice, "whether you can make words mean so many different things." "The question is," said Humpty Dumpty, "which is to be master—that's all."[38] In our system of government the Supreme Court tends to be master on domestic issues. But the judges of the highest tribunal are supposed to enforce constitutional limitations, not make national policy or determine what policy is desirable for the nation.

The establishment clause may not be self-defining, but it embodies a policy which time has proved to be best. Despite continuing complaints about the wall of separation between government and religion, that is the policy embodied by the establishment clause. The Constitution erected that wall. If the fact that it is the policy of the Constitution does not satisfy, history helps validate it. A page of history is supposed to be worth a volume of logic, so let us consider a page from Tocqueville. Slightly more than half a century after Independence he wrote that "the religious atmosphere of the country was the first thing that struck me on my arrival in the United States." He expressed "astonishment" because in Europe religion and freedom marched in "opposite directions." Questioning the "faithful of all communions," including clergymen, especially Roman Catholic priests, he found that "they all agreed with each other except about details; all thought that the main reason for the quiet sway of religion over their country was the *complete separation of church and state*. I have no hesitation in stating that throughout my stay in America I met nobody, lay or cleric, who did not agree about that."[39]

Because the domains of religion and government remain separated, religion in the United States, like religious liberty, thrives mightily, far more than it did 200 years ago when the vast majority of Americans were religiously unaffiliated. In a famous letter to the Baptist Association of Danbury, Connecticut, President Jefferson spoke of the "wall of separation." After declaring that religion belonged "solely between man and his God," Jefferson added: "I contemplate with sovereign reverence that act of the whole American people which declared that their legislature should 'make no law respecting an establishment of religion, or prohibiting the free exercise thereof,' thus building a wall of separation between church and state."[40] The usual interpretation of Jefferson's Danbury Baptist letter by those who seek to weaken its force is either to minimize it or to argue that he was here concerned only with the rights of conscience, and that these would "never be endangered by treating all religions *equally* in regard to support" by the government.[41] Neither interpretation is valid.

The rights-of-conscience argument ignores the fact that Jefferson quoted the establishment clause in the very sentence in which he spoke of a wall of separation, indicating that he was concerned with more than protection of the free exercise of religion. In any case, Jefferson most assuredly did believe that government support of all religions violated the rights of conscience. His Statute of Religious Freedom expressly asserts that "even forcing him [any man] to support this or that teacher of his own religious persuasion, is depriving him of the comfortable liberty of giving his contributions . . . [No] man shall be compelled to frequent or support any religious worship, place, or ministry whatsoever. . . . "[42]

The second technique of robbing the Danbury letter of its clear intent to oppose any government support of religion belittles it as a "little address of courtesy" containing a figure of speech . . . a metaphor."[43] Or, as Edward S. Corwin suggested, the letter was scarcely "deliberate" or "carefully considered"; it was rather "not improbably motivated by an impish desire to heave a brick at the Congregationalist-Federalist hierarchy of Connecticut. . . . "[44] Jefferson, however, had powerful convictions on the subject of establishment and religious freedom, and he approached discussion of it with great solemnity. Indeed, on the occasion of writing this letter he was so concerned with the necessity of expressing himself with deliberation and precision that he went out of his way to get the approval of the attorney-general of the United States. Sending him the letter before dispatching it to Danbury, Jefferson asked his advice as to its contents and explained:

> Adverse to receive addresses, yet unable to prevent them, I have generally endeavored to turn them to some account, by making them the occasion, by way of answer, so sowing useful truths and principles among the people, which might germinate and become rooted among their political tenets. The Baptist address, now enclosed, admits of a condemnation of the alliance between Church and State, under the authority of the Constitution. It furnished an occasion, too, which I have long wished to find, of saying why I do not proclaim fast and thanksgiving days, as my predecessors did."[45]

On the matter of proclaiming fast and thanksgiving days, President Jefferson departed from the precedents of Washington and Adams, and went further even than Madison, by utterly refusing on any occasion to recommend or designate a day for worship, citing as a reason, among others, the clause against establishments of religion.[46] However, even Jefferson was not wholly consistent when it came to an establishment of religion. He used the treaty power to make an Indian treaty that provided federal monies to serve the religious needs of a tribe, and he approved of legislation, under the power to regulate Indian affairs, that underwrote missionary expenses to "propagate the Gospel among the Heathen."[47] But contrary to Attorney General Edwin Meese, what the government could do under the Constitution as to Indians, it cannot constitutionally do, by treaty or statute, as to American citizens. Congress did not extend American citizenship to all American Indians until 1924.[48] The Fourteenth Amendment which granted citizenship to anyone born or naturalized in the United States did not apply to Indians, who had an anomalous status as members of domestic, dependent nations, neither citizens nor aliens.

Jefferson cared deeply about the rights of conscience, but he cared too for the government's freedom from religion. However, Roger Williams, who cared even more deeply about religion, had spoken of the "wall of separation" more than a century and a half before Jefferson. In 1644 Williams wrote that the wall existed to preserve the integrity of religion by walling out corrupting influences:

> First, the faithful labors of many witnesses of Jesus Christ, extant to the world, abundantly proving that the church of the Jews under the Old Testament in the type and the church of the Christians under the New Testament in the antitype

were both separate from the world; and that when they have opened a gap in the hedge or *wall of separation* between the garden of the church and the wilderness of the world, God hath ever broke down the wall itself, removed the candlestick, and made His garden a wilderness, as at this day. And that therefore if He will ever please to restore His garden and paradise again, it must of necessity be walled in peculiarly unto Himself from the world; and that all that shall be saved out of the world are to be transplanted out of the wilderness of the world, and added unto His church or garden.[49]

Thus, the wall of separation had the allegiance of a most profound Christian impulse as well as a secular one. To Christian fundamentalists of the Framers' time the wall of separation derived from the biblical injunction that Christ's kingdom is not of this world. The wall of separation ensures the government's freedom from religion and the individual's freedom of religion. The second probably cannot flourish without the first.

Separation has other bountiful results. Government and religion in America are mutually independent of each other, much as Jefferson and Madison hoped they would be. Government maintains a benign neutrality toward religion without promoting or serving religion's interests in any significant way except, perhaps, for the policy of tax exemption. To be sure, government's involvement with religion takes many forms. The joint chiefs of staff supposedly begin their meetings with prayer, as do our legislatures. The incantation, "God save the United States and this honorable Court" and the motto "In God We Trust" and its relatives are of trifling significance in the sense that they have little genuine religious content. Caesar exploits, secularizes, and trivializes, but leaves organized religion alone. Free of government influence, organized religion in turn does not use government for religious ends. Thus, history has made the wall of separation real. The wall is not just a metaphor. It has constitutional existence. Even Chief Justice Burger has approvingly referred to Jefferson's "concept" of a wall as a "useful signpost" to emphasize separateness.[50] Despite its detractors and despite its leaks, cracks, and its archways, the wall ranks as one of the mightiest monuments of constitutional government in this nation. Robert Frost notwithstanding, something there is that loves a wall.

Notes

1. *Jaffree v. James*, 554 F. Supp. 1130, 1132 (SD Ala. 1983); *Wallace v. Jaffree*, 105 S. Ct. 2479, 2485 (1985).

2. 268 U.S. 652 (1952). In *Gitlow,* the Court ruled that the word "liberty" of the Fourteenth Amendment incorporated the First Amendment's protection of freedom of speech, with the result that a state could not abridge freedom of speech any more than the United States could.
3. Meese, "ABA Washington Speech" of July 9, 1985, 18 pp., at pp. 13–14; typescript supplied by the Department of Justice. Reported in the *Los Angeles Times,* July 10, 1985, Part I, pp. 1 and 6, and *New York Times,* "Meese and His Candor," by Stuart Taylor, Jr. See also James McClellan, "The Making and Unmaking of the Establishment Clause," in Patrick B. McGuigan and Randall R. Rader, eds. *A Blueprint for Judicial Reform* (Washington, D.C., 1981), p. 296.
4. *Cantwell v. Connecticut,* 310 U.S. 296 (1940).
5. 330 U.S. 1 (1947).
6. Robert L. Cord, *Separation of Church and State: Historical Fact and Current Fiction* (New York, 1982), p. 99; Meese, ABA Speech, 1985, p. 12; McClellan, "The Making and Unmaking," p. 316.
7. *Reagan v. Farmers' Loan & Trust Co.,* 154 U.S. 362, 399 (1894).
8. In *Chicago, Burlington & Quincy RR. v. Chicago,* 166 U.S. 226 (1897), the Court read the Fifth Amendment's eminent domain clause into the due process clause of the Fourteenth Amendment. The Court officially dates the incorporation doctrine with this 1897 case. See *Hawaii Housing Authority v. Midkiff,* 104 S. Ct. 2321, 2331 note 7 (1984). See also *Smyth v. Ames,* 169 U.S. 466 (1898). In *United Rys. v. West,* 280 U.S. 234 (1930), the Court struck down as *confiscatory* a government fixed rate schedule that allowed a profit of 6.26 percent. Protecting First Amendment freedoms from state abridgment seems no more revolutionary or arbitrary than protecting property rights.
9. *Palko v. Connecticut,* 302 U.S. 319 (1937).
10. Robert G. McCloskey, "Principles, Powers, and Values: The Establishment Clause and the Supreme Court," in *1964 Religion and the Public Order,* ed. Donald A. Giannella (Chicago, 1965), p. 11. See also Edward S. Corwin, *A Constitution of Powers in a Secular State* (Charlottesville, Va., 1951), pp. 113–16.
11. *Madison Papers,* VIII, pp. 300, 304.
12. Zechariah Chafee, *How Human Rights Got into the Constitution* (Boston, 1952), p. 51. Article I, section 9, protects the "Privilege of the Writ" from being suspended except when the public safety requires suspension. Parsing that provision of the Constitution the way nonpreferentialists analyze the establishment clause would reduce the "Privilege" to a nullity.
13. *Madison Papers,* VIII, pp. 300, 301, 302.
14. McCloskey, "Principles, Powers, and Values," p. 25.
15. Ibid.
16. James O'Neill, *Religion and Education under the Constitution,* (New York, 1949) pp. 26–27. See also Ray Allen Billington, *The Protestant Crusade* (New York, 1938), pp. 142–65, 220–37, and Leo Pfeffer, *Church, State, and Freedom* (Boston, 1967, rev. ed.), pp. 416–44.
17. *Wolman v. Walter,* 433 U.S. 229, 263 (1977).
18. Affidavit of Leah Cunn in trial proceedings of *Zorach v. Clausen,* 343 U.S. 306 (1952), the second released time case, quoted in Pfeffer, *Church, State, and Freedom,* p. 417. I know from personal experience something about the divisive and prejudicial effects that result from religious exercises in the public schools. In 1935–36, I went to school in DeKalb, Ill., which had, in McCloskey's words, "a modest amount of praying and Bible reading" plus some christological celebration of Christmas; my refusal to participate stigmatized me and unleashed latent anti-

Semitism. I learned to associate religion in the public schools with my gym teacher's motto for coaching softball, "No kikes on our team," and with getting beaten up regularly because I was "the Jew bastard" and "Christ killer" who refused to pray in school.

19. *Wallace v. Jaffree*, 105 S. Ct. 2479, 2520 (1985). The federal judge in *Jaffree v. Board of School Commissioners*, 553 Fed. Supp. 1104 (S.D. Ala., 1983), was W. Brevard Hand of the district court in Mobile, who relied on the unreliable, the works of James McClellan and Robert L. Cord, previously cited. Attorney General Edwin Meese also advocated the repudiation of the incorporation doctrine. See his "ABA Speech," 1985, pp. 12–14. Meese believes that the establishment clause bans merely a "national church," and he does not even consider the words "no law respecting."

20. Michael Malbin, *Religion and Politics: The Intentions of the Authors of the First Amendment* (Washington, D.C., 1978), pp. 14, 16–17. In *Gibbons v. Ogden*, 9 Wheaton 1 (1824), the Court denied that the states possessed a concurrent power over interstate commerce and held void a state act that conflicted with a federal coastal licensing act. However, in *Willson v. Blackbird Creek Marsh Co.*, 2 Peters 245 (1829), the Court held that a state exercising its police power might dam up a navigable stream, shutting out a vessel licensed under the same federal statute. Congress could not outlaw compulsory racial segregation in public accommodations under its Thirteenth or Fourteenth Amendment powers, but could effectuate the same purpose in the exercise of its interstate commerce power. Compare *Civil Rights Cases*, 109 U.S. 3 (1883), with *Heart of Atlanta Motel v. U.S.*, 379 U.S. 241 (1964).

21. *Journals of the Continental Congress,* ed. Worthington C. Ford et al. (Washington, D.C., 1904–1937), XXXIII, pp. 399–400.

22. Thomas Curry, *The First Freedoms* (New York, 1986), p. 219.

23. See the forebodings of Dean M. Kelley, "Confronting the Danger of the Moment," in Jay Mechling, ed., *State and Public Policy* (Washington, D.C., 1978), pp. 13–14, 16–18. On the same point, see also William Bentley Ball, "Mediating Structures and Constitutional Liberty," in ibid., pp.49–59. See also Ball's "Religious Liberty: New Issues and Past Decisions," in Patrick B. McGuigan and R. R. Rader, eds., *A Blueprint for Judicial Reform* (Washington, D.C.; 1981), pp. 327–49. Ball writes from the standpoint of an accommodationist or nonpreferentialist; Kelley is a Christian separationist whose intellectual ancestors designed the establishment clause.

24. *Walz v. Tax Commission*, 397 U.S. 664, 676–77 (1970).

25. Oliver Wendell Holmes, *Collected Legal Papers,* ed. Harold Laski (New York, 1920), p. 191.

26. *Olmstead v. U.S.*, 277 U.S. 438, 469 (1928).

27. *Gompers v. U.S.*, 233 U.S. 604, 610 (1914).

28. *Donahoe v. Richards,* 38 Maine 379, 399 (1854).

29. *Board of Trustees of Scarsdale v. McCreary*, 105 S. Ct. 1859 (1985).

30. *McCreary v. Stone*, 739 F. 2d 716 (C.A. 2 1984). On nude dancing, see *Schad v. Mt. Ephraim*, 452 U.S. 61 (1981); on flag burning, *Street v. New York*, 394 U.S. 576 (1969).

31. Letter to E. Livingston, July 10, 1822, in *The Writings of James Madison,* ed. Gaillard Hunt (New York, 1900–1910, 9 vols.), IX, p. 100.

32. Bret Harte, "M'Liss" (1873), in *The Luck of Roaring Camp and Other Tales* (New York, 1892), p. 171.

33. Letter to E. Livingston, April 4, 1824, in *The Writings of Thomas Jefferson,* ed.

Albert E. Bergh (Washington, D.C., 1907, 20 vols.), XVI, p. 25.

34. *Lynch v. Donnelly*, 104 S. Ct., 1355 (1984).

35. *Larkin v. Grendel's Den*, 103 S. Ct., 505 (1983).

36. *McCollum v. Board of Education*, 333 U.S. 203, 237–38 (1948).

37. *Committee for Public Education v.* Nyquist, 413 U.S. 756, 820 (1973), dissenting opinion.

38. Lewis Carroll, *Through the Looking Class,* chap. 6.

39. Alexis de Tocqueville, *Democracy in America,* ed. J. P. Mayers and Max Lerner, trans. George Lawrence (New York, 1969), pp. 271–72. Emphasis added.

40. Letter of January 1, 1802, in *Writings of Thomas Jefferson,* XVI, pp. 281–82.

41. O'Neill, *Religion and Education,* p. 81.

42. *Jefferson Papers,* II, 545.

43. O'Neill, *Religion and Education,* pp. 83, 81–82.

44. Edward S. Corwin, "The Supreme Court as National School Board," *Law and Contemporary Problems,* XIV (Winter 1949), p. 14.

45. *Works of Thomas Jefferson,* ed. P. L. Ford (New York, 1892–1899, 10 vols.), IX, pp. 346–47.

46. See Anson Phelps Stokes, *Church and State in the United States* (New York, 1950, 3 vols.), I, pp. 490–91 and 335–36.

47. Cord, *Separation of Church and State,* pp. 261–64, 268–70, reprints the documents. Cord, pp. 57–80, grossly exaggerates the significance of federal aid to religion among Indians as if it somehow justified aid to religion among citizens. Aid to Indians, under either the treaty power or the power to regulate Indian affairs, is not worth two cents as a precedent for anything else.

48. Edwin Meese III, "Address before the Christian Legal Society," San Diego, California, September 29, 1985, pp. 9–10. Department of Justice transcript.

49. Roger Williams, *A Letter of Mr. John Cottons* (1643), in *The Complete Writings of Roger Williams* (New York, 1963, Russell & Russell ed.), I, p. 392. I have followed the modernized version of Perry Miller, *Roger Williams: His Contribution to the American Tradition* (New York, 1962), p. 98. Emphasis added.

50. Larkin v. Grendel's Den, 103 S. Ct. 505, 510 (1982).

9

The Fourth Amendment:
Search and Seizure

Before the American Revolution, the right to be secure against unreasonable searches and seizures had slight existence. British policies assaulted the privacy of dwellings and places of business, particularly when royal revenues were at stake. The right to be taxed only by the consent of representatives of one's choice was the great right whose violation helped cause the Revolution. British attempts to enforce tax measures by general searches also occasioned deeply felt resentments that damaged relations between England and the American colonies, and provoked anxious concerns that later sought expression in the Fourth Amendment. That amendment repudiates general warrants by recognizing a "right of the people to be secured in their persons, houses, papers, and effects, against unreasonable searches and seizures." Any warrant that is vague about the persons, places, or things to be searched violates the specificity required by the command of the amendment that warrants shall issue only "upon probable cause, supported by oath or affirmation, and particularly describing the place to be searched, and the persons or things to be seized."

The Fourth Amendment would not have been possible but for British legal theory, which Britons of North America inherited and cherished as their own. The Fourth Amendment emerged not only from the American Revolution; it was a constitutional embodiment of the extraordinary coupling of Magna Carta to the appealing fiction that a man's home is his castle. That is, the amendment resulted from embellishments on the insistence, which was rhetorically compelling, though historically without foundation, that government cannot encroach on the private premises of the individual subject. What mattered was not what Magna Carta actually said but what people thought it said or, rather, what it had come to mean. What also mattered was the inspiring imagery that swelled the sense of freedom in the ordinary subject. William Pitt expressed it best in a speech in Parliament in 1763, when he declaimed: "The poorest man may, in his cottage, bid defiance to all the forces of the Crown. It may be frail; its roof may shake; the wind may blow through it; the storm may enter; the rain may enter, but the King of England may not enter; all his force dares not cross the threshold of the ruined tenement."[1] The assertion that "a man's house is his castle" goes back at least to the early sixteenth century, and it was repeated with such frequency that it became a cliché.[2]

The first person to link the privacy of one's home to a right secured by Magna Carta seems to have been Robert Beale, clerk of the Privy Council, in 1589. Beale asked rhetorically what had happened to chapter 39 of the great charter when agents of a prerogative court, acting under its warrant, could "enter into mens houses, break up their chests and chambers" and carry off as evidence whatever they pleased.[3] That Beale's statement was historically unsound is unimportant compared to the fact that he took a feudal document, which protected the barons, and converted it into a constitution for everyone. Creative glosses like Beale's would make Magna Carta a talismanic symbol of freedom, subjecting all authority, including the royal prerogative, to the rule of law. Construing chapter 39 to be a ban on general warrants helped make a myth that would transform American thinking about privacy rights against government.

One of the most strategically significant places for the belief that a legal writ authorizing a legitimate search must be specific as to persons and places was Sir Edward Coke's *Institutes of the Laws of England.*[4] From the Puritans of Massachusetts Bay, who studied Coke, to Jefferson, who admiringly said of him that "a sounder Whig never wrote" nor one more learned "in the orthodox doctrines of British liberties," Americans regarded Coke as the foremost authority on English law.[5] Coke's authority legitimated the belief that Magna Carta outlawed general warrants based on mere surmise.

Sir Matthew Hale, another seventeenth-century legal luminary, more systematically analyzed the problem of search and seizure in his book, *History of Pleas of the Crown.*[6] Hale criticized warrants that failed to name the persons sought for crime or the places to be searched for evidence of theft. He even laid a basis for the concept of probable cause by maintaining that the person seeking a warrant should be examined judicially under oath so that the magistrate could determine whether he had grounds for his suspicions. Hale also asserted that an officer who made an illegal search and arrest was liable to a civil suit for false arrest.[7]

Beale, Coke, and Hale did not stand alone. They invented a rhetorical tradition against general searches, which Sergeant William Hawkins and Sir William Blackstone continued.[8] But the rhetoric was empty; the tradition had almost no practical effect. Beale's views leaked out through officially licensed publications that sought to refute him, but he did not dare publish his manuscript.[9] Coke's own report of *Semayne's Case* of 1604 refuted the accuracy of the propositions that he advanced in his *Institutes*, for in that case the court had held that although a man's house is his castle, his privacy did not extend to his guests or to "cases where the King is a party."[10] Coke's own experience shows best that the maxim represented only the frailest aspiration, not the law in cases involving the crown. In 1634, when Coke lay dying, the Privy Council's agents searched his home and law chambers for seditious papers and seized not only the manuscripts of his voluminous legal writings but also his personal valuables, including his money, keys, jewelry, will, and a poem addressed to his children.[11] Hale's book did not even get published until sixty years after his death. Pitt spoke in a losing cause; Parliament enacted the excise bill whose passage he so eloquently opposed as dangerous to the liberty of the subject. Blackstone made only a passing remark against general searches; his target, rather, was the general arrest warrant.

In fact, English law was honeycombed with parliamentary enactments that relied on warrantless general searches and on general warrants for their enforcement, including hue and cry methods, sumptuary legislation, and measures aimed at punishing theft, at governing crafts and guilds, bankruptcy, and military recruitment, as well as measures preventing illegal imports, manufactures, poaching, counterfeiting, unlicensed printing, seditious, heretical, or lewd publications, and nonpayment of taxes. Taxes extended to hearths and stoves, to estates, to intoxicating drinks, to a variety of consumer goods such as salt, candles, soap, glass and paper, and to foreign goods. The king's customs office and his exchequer depended on both the general warrant and warrantless searches as ordinary means of collecting royal revenues, and Parliament passed dozens of pieces of legislation to provide the taxes and authorize general searches.[12] Promiscuously broad warrants allowed officers to search wherever they wanted and to seize whatever they wanted, with few exceptions. An eighteenth-century collection of warrants contains 108 authorized by secretaries of state or by the King's Bench for the period 1700–1763, all but two of which were general warrants.[13] The frequency in the use of general warrants substantially increased as time went by.[14]

General searches completely pervaded colonial law as well as Great Britain's. Colonial legislation on search and seizure either copied Britain's or derived from it; until 1750, all handbooks for justices of the peace, who issued warrants, contained or described only general warrants. William Cuddihy asserts that a "colonial epidemic of general searches" existed, indeed, that until the 1760s "a man's house was even less of a legal castle in America than in England," because the Americans, when adapting English models, ignored exceptions.[15] As a result, warrants in America tended to give their enforcers every discretion. The Fourth Amendment would not emerge from colonial precedents; rather, it would repudiate them; or, as Cuddihy states, "The ideas comprising the Fourth Amendment reversed rather than formalized colonial precedents. Reasonable search and seizure in colonial America closely approximated whatever the searcher thought reasonable."[16]

Officers or their informants merely reported that an infraction of the law had occurred or that they had a suspicion, not that a particular person was suspected or that a particular place contained evidence of a crime; on the basis of such an assertion, a magistrate issued a warrant. Neither custom, judicial precedent, nor statutory law provided that he should interrogate the seeker of the warrant to determine the credibility of the suspicion or of his informant. The magistrate made no independent determination of his own whether a basis existed for the warrant other than the assertion that a crime had occurred or that a basis existed for some suspicion. Magistrates had an obligation to provide the warrant, rather than deny one or limit one to a particular person or place that was suspected. Probable cause in a modern sense did not exist; not even a reasonable basis for suspicion existed. Although an officer seeking a warrant more than likely would designate a particular person or place if known to him in advance, he need not do so to get a warrant.

Colonial documents contain no suggestion of a right against general warrants. Recommendations for them were common in the manuals that had been published in the colonies before 1763 for the use of justices of the peace. American legal writers even relied on the great authority of Coke and Hale as proof that an officer could forcibly enter a person's house.[17]

In 1756, however, the province of Massachusetts enacted extraordinary legislation that reversed the tide of practice by abandoning general warrants in favor of warrants founded on some elements of particularity. The legislation of 1756 marked a watershed in Massachusetts law, indeed in Anglo-American law. As Cuddihy states, beginning in 1756 "Massachusetts invented the statutory prototypes of the Fourth Amendment."[18] The new legislation resulted mainly from a vehement public clamor against provincial legislation of 1754. The excise act of that year authorized tax collectors to interrogate any subject, under oath, on the amount of rum, wine, and other spirits he had consumed in his private premises in the past year and taxed it by the gallon. Pamphleteers condemned the measure in hyperbolic language. John Lovell, a Boston schoolmaster whose pupils had included John Hancock and Samuel Adams, called it "the most pernicious attack upon *English Liberty* that was ever attempted," and the minister of the Brattle Church imagined that he saw a revival of the Inquisition, requiring people to incriminate themselves. One pamphlet, *The Monster of Monsters* (the excise act), so savagely attacked the legislature that it condemned the tract as a seditious libel, and imprisoned its seller and the suspected author.[19] That author warned of the danger of the tax collector having power to break chains, doors, locks, and bolts, and invade bedchambers and winecellars.[20] In the torrent of tracts against the excise, it was described as a violation of Magna Carta, of the sanctity of one's home as his castle, and of natural rights.

The provincial impost laws, which employed general warrants for enforcement, provoked such animosity that mobs threatened impost officers who tried to collect duties on uncustomed imports—foreign goods on which the duties had not been paid. The hostility to general searches further intensified as the result of two other practices. In 1755 the royal governor of Massachusetts issued ex officio writs of assistance, a type of general warrant that became enormously controversial. And, since 1745, British impressment gangs, operating under a general warrant provided by the governor, had been invading private premises as well as taverns and inns seeking to kidnap able-bodied men for service in the royal navy [21]

Enforcement of the excise and impost acts by general searches, the introduction into the province of writs of assistance, and the general warrants for impressment gangs produced a hullabaloo that the enactments of 1756 sought to allay. The excise and impost acts of that year required an element of probable cause only in the sense that the informant had the obligation to swear on oath that he knew that an infraction of the law had occurred in the place specified. The justices of the peace, who issued the warrants, had no discretion to deny a petition for one; magistrates made no independent judgment whether adequate grounds for the issuance of the warrant existed. But, the informant had to swear that he had "just cause" for his sworn statement. The officer conducted his search during the daytime, only in the designated location, and could seize only things or objects regulated by the statute that he enforced by his search and seizure. The statutes of 1756 also authorized warrants of arrest for named individuals.[22] "The British, in short," Cuddihy states, "introduced writs of assistance into Massachusetts just as the colony itself was rejecting the legal assumptions on which they were based."[23]

The writ of assistance was a type of general warrant deriving its name from the fact that a crown official possessed the legal authority to command the assistance of a peace officer and the assistance, if necessary, of all nearby subjects, in his execution of the writ. Parliament authorized writs of assistance by an act of 1662 that empowered the Court of Exchequer to issue a writ to a customs official who, with the assistance of a constable, could enter "any House, shop, Cellar, Warehouse or Room or other Place, and in Case of Resistance to break open Doors, Chests, Trunks and other packages, there to seize" any uncustomed goods.[24] The writ, once issued, lasted for the life of the sovereign, and therefore constituted a long-term hunting license for customs officers on the lookout for smugglers and articles imported in violation of the customs laws. In 1696 Parliament extended the act of 1662 to the colonies, but because the Court of Exchequer did not operate in America, no way existed to enforce it. Massachusetts, however, had extended the jurisdiction of its own high court to include the jurisdiction of the Court of Exchequer, thus opening the possibility of enforcement in that colony and in New Hampshire, which copied Massachusetts.[25]

When George II died, the high court of Massachusetts, presided over by Chief Justice Thomas Hutchinson, heard *Paxton's Case,* a petition by a customs officer for a new writ of assistance.[26] James Otis Jr. appeared, he said, on behalf of the inhabitants of Boston to oppose issuance of the writ. Any fastidious legal historian must acknowledge that Otis's argument compounded mistakes and misinterpretations. In effect, he reconstructed the fragmentary evidence buttressing the rhetorical tradition against general searches, and he advocated that any warrant other than a specific one violated the British constitution. That Otis distorted history is pedantic; he was making history. By an old British technique, which Coke himself had practiced, Otis sought the creation of new rights while asserting strenuously that they had existed nearly from time immemorial. His speech electrified young John Adams, who was present in the courtroom and took notes. As an old man, fifty-six years later, he declared, "Otis was a flame of Fire! . . . Then and there was the first scene of the first Act of Opposition to the arbitrary Claims of Great Britain. Then and there the child Independance [sic] was born." On the night before the Declaration of Independence, Adams asserted that he consider "the Argument concerning Writs of Assistance . . . as the Commencement of the Controversy, between Great Britain and America."[27] Adams's reaction to Otis's speech is so important because a straight line of progression runs from Otis's argument in 1761 to Adams's framing of Article XIV of the Massachusetts Declaration of Rights of 1780 to Madison's introduction of the proposal that became the Fourth Amendment.[28]

We have Adams's brief notes of Otis's speech made at the time of the speech and the fuller version made by Adams not long after. The fuller version takes about twenty minutes to read by comparison with the original which took Otis four to five hours to deliver.[29] He denounced the writ of assistance as an instrument of "slavery," of "villainy," of "arbitrary power, the most destructive of English liberty and [of] the fundamental principles of the constitution. . . . " The writ reminded him of the kind of power that had cost one English king his head and another his throne. The only legal writ, Otis asserted, was a "special warrant directed to specific officers, and to search certain houses, &c. especially set forth in the writ may be granted . . . upon oath made . . . by the person, who asks [for the warrant], that he suspects such goods to be concealed in those very places he desires to search."[30] In the recent past, Otis alleged, only special warrants existed, authorizing search of particularly named houses, and they were issued only after the complainant had taken an oath to support his suspicion; "special warrants only are legal," he concluded. He condemned writs of assistance because they were perpetual, universal (addressed to every officer and subject in the realm), and allowed anyone to conduct a search in violation of the essential principle of English liberty that a peaceable man's house is his castle. A writ that allowed a customs officer to enter private homes when he pleased, on bare suspicion, and even to break locks to enter, was void. An act of Parliament authorizing such writs was void because it violated the British constitution, and courts should not issue an unconstitutional writ.[31]

Otis lost his case. The writs issued, but Americans found a cause and a constitutional argument. In 1762 the Massachusetts legislature passed a bill that would have required all writs to be as specific as the warrants used by provincial officers to enforce the excise and impost acts, but the royal governor vetoed the bill. Thereafter, crowds frequently prevented enforcement or "rescued" goods seized by customs agents. In a 1766 case a Boston merchant, believing that in "whig Boston Whig furies made Whig law," used force to barricade his home, as a crowd gathered. Officers prudently decided that calling on bystanders to assist as a *posse comitatus* might result in a loss of life— their own—and abandoned efforts to enforce the writ. After a rescue in Falmouth (Portland), Maine, the governor conceded that public opposition had effectively paralyzed the use of writs to conduct searches and seizures. Britain's Attorney General William DeGrey decided that the act of Parliament that authorized the writ allowed them to issue only from the Court of Exchequer, whose writ did not run in America.[32] In London, far more than DeGrey's technical opinion damaged the principle of general warrants.

John Wilkes's studied insult of the king's speech in 1763, in the forty-fifth number of his journal *North Britain,* provoked massive retaliation by the government. One of the secretaries of state issued general search warrants for the arrest of everyone connected with *North Britain* #45. Crown agents enforcing the warrants had unfettered discretion to search, seize, and arrest anyone as they pleased. They ransacked printer's shops and houses, and arrested forty-nine persons including Wilkes, a member of Parliament, his printer, publisher, and booksellers. The officers seized his private papers for incriminating evidence after a thorough search; thousands of pages and scores of books belonging to persons associated with him were also seized. The House of Commons voted that *North Britain* #45 was a seditious libel and expelled Wilkes, and he was eventually convicted and jailed. The government found, however, that it had mounted a tiger; no one since the time of John Lilburne, more than a century earlier, had proved to be such a resourceful and pugnacious antagonist. Wilkes had quickly filed suits for trespass against everyone, from flunky to minister, connected with the warrant that had resulted in his undoing; others who had suffered searches and arrest filed similar suits. A legal donnybrook ensued. On the one hand, the government, based on about two hundred informations, had engaged in mass arrests and searches, and on the other, the victims filed a couple of dozen suits for trespass and false imprisonment. The Wilkes case became the subject of sensational controversies, angry tracts, and confusing trials. Wilkes would emerge from his prosecution a popular idol, the personification of constitutional liberty to Englishmen on both sides of the Atlantic. Although he focused mainly on the dangers of general warrants and the seizures of private papers, some of his supporters also championed freedom of the press and the right against self-incrimination.[33]

In the colonies, "Wilkes and Liberty" became a slogan that patriot leaders exploited in the service of American causes. In New York, for example, Alexander McDougall, a leader of the Sons of Liberty who had censured a bill to provision the king's troops, posed as an American Wilkes and turned his imprisonment into a theatrical triumph, as had Wilkes, while his supporters used the number 45, the seditious issue of *North Britain,* as a symbol of their cause. On the forty-fifth day of the year, for example, forty-five Liberty Boys dined on forty-five pounds of beef from a forty-five-month-old bull, drank forty-five toasts to liberty—liberty of the press, liberty from general warrants, liberty from compulsory self-accusation, liberty from seizure of private papers—and after dinner marched to the jail to salute McDougall with forty-five cheers. On another festive liberty day, forty-five songs were sung to him by forty-five virgins, every one of whom, according to some damned Tory, was forty-five years old.[34] The Fourth Amendment, as well as the First and the Fifth, owes something to the Wilkes cases. Unlike *Paxton's Case,* the Wilkes cases filled the columns of American newspapers from Boston to Charleston.

The first of these cases, *Huckle v. Money,* established the doctrine, traceable at least to Hale, that crown officers are liable to damage suits for trespass and false imprisonment resulting from unlawful search. Chief Justice Charles Pratt said, when charging the jury: "To enter a man's house by virtue of a nameless warrant, in order to procure evidence, is worse than the Spanish Inquisition, a law under which no Englishman would wish to live an hour." The jury awarded 300 pounds in damages, an excessive sum for the deprivation of a journeyman printer's liberty for six hours, but on appeal Pratt ruled that the small injury done to one of low rank meant nothing compared to the "great point of the law touching the liberty of the subject" invaded by a magistrate of the king in an exercise of arbitrary power "violating Magna Carta, and attempting to destroy the liberty of the kingdom, by insisting on the legality of this general warrant. . . . "[35] In *Wilkes v. Wood* (1763), Pratt presided over a similar trial and engaged in similar rhetoric ("totally subversive of the liberty of the subject"); the jury awarded damages of 1,000 pounds to Wilkes, who later got an award of 4,000 pounds against the secretary of state who had issued the warrant.[36] In fact, the government paid a total of about 100,000 pounds in costs and judgments.[37]

In one of the Wilkes cases, the government appealed to England's highest criminal court, the King's Bench, and Lord Mansfield, the chief justice, agreed that the warrants in the Wilkes cases were illegal. Although the common law, he observed, authorized arrests without warrant and Parliament had often authorized searches and arrests on the basis of general warrants, in this case no circumstance existed justifying warrantless searches or arrests, and no act of Parliament was involved. Accordingly, a secretarial warrant, based on executive authority, leaving discretion to the endorsing officer, "is not fit." Mansfield thought that the "magistrate ought to judge; and should give certain directions to the officer"—a foundation for what later emerged as probable cause.[38]

The victories of the Wilkesites encouraged other victims of secretarial warrants in seditious libel cases to bring suits for damages. The most important of those cases, *Entick v. Carrington* (1765), resulted in an opinion by Chief Justice Pratt, now Lord Camden, which the Supreme Court of the United States would describe as "one of the landmarks of English liberty."[39] Victory for the government, Camden declared, would open the secret cabinets of every subject whenever the secretary of state suspected someone of seditious libel. The law required no one to incriminate himself for that would be "cruel and unjust" to the innocent and guilty alike, "and it should seem, that search for evidence is disallowed upon the same principle." Camden held that neither arrests nor general warrants could issue on executive discretion, and he implied that evidence seized on the authority of such a warrant could not be used without violating the right against self-incrimination. Similarly, the Supreme Court in 1886 ruled that the Fourth and Fifth Amendments have an "intimate relation" and "throw great light on each other."[40]

In 1764 and 1765 the House of Commons irresolutely debated whether general warrants should be regarded as illegal, and in 1766 it repeated the debate. The upshot was the passage of three resolutions, not statutes, that revealed a victory for the narrow position of Mansfield rather than the broader one of Camden. The Commons condemned general warrants in all cases involving arrests but condemned general warrants for searches only in cases where the warrants issued from the executive branch in connection with the crime of seditious libel. Secretarial search warrants in treason cases remained legal. The resolutions of 1766 left in place the elaborate system of warrantless searches when authorized by Parliament, and of general searches when undergirded by statutory authority. The House of Lords rejected a proposal from the Commons that would have restricted general search warrants to cases of treason and felony. Thus, the reforms resulting from the judicial decisions and parliamentary resolves of 1763 to 1766 conformed to the prime directive of England's law of search and seizure: even promiscuously general searches did not violate the liberty of the subject or infringe the maxim about a man's home so long as Parliament had laid down the law.[41]

On the other hand, the Wilkes cases and the parliamentary debates unleashed a lot of rhetoric that went far beyond the reality of actual judicial holdings and legislative resolves. Americans were practiced in making a highly selective use of authorities and other sources that suited their needs. They could even turn Blackstone, that spokesman for parliamentary supremacy, into an advocate of constitutional restraints. In Britain, Englishmen often spoke thunderously but thrashed about with a frail stick; in America they threw the stick away, contenting themselves with the thunder. They found a lot of it in Pitt, Camden, Wilkes, and in "Father of Candor," all of whom they knew well. Father of Candor was the author of a little book of 1764, "on libels, warrants, and the seizure of papers," which had gone through seven editions by 1771. He condemned general warrants as "excruciating torture,"[42] and he urged that search warrants should be specific as to persons, places, and things, and should be sworn on oath.[43] That was the sort of thing Americans could exploit when confronted by Parliament's determination to impose writs of assistance on the colonies.

Twenty years after the Townshend Acts of 1767, James Madison, speaking in the First Congress on the occasion of recommending the amendments to the Constitution that became the Bill of Rights, recalled that the legislative power constituted a great danger to liberty; in Britain, he noted, "they have gone no farther than to raise a barrier against the power of the Crown; the power of the Legislature is left altogether indefinite."[44] Notwithstanding grandiose rhetoric against general warrants, Parliament in 1767 superseded its act of 1696, which had extended writs of assistance to America without providing a mechanism for granting them under the seal of the Court of Exchequer. The Townshend Acts of 1767 provided that the highest court in each colony possessed authority to issue writs of assistance to customs officers to search where they pleased for prohibited or uncustomed goods and to seize them.

The Townshend Acts, therefore, expanded the controversy over writs of assistance to all of the thirteen colonies. What had been a local controversy, centering mainly on Boston, spread continent-wide. Only the two colonies, Massachusetts and New Hampshire, that had previously experienced the writs, continued to issue them, although the mobs "liberated" seized goods as often as not. Elsewhere the provincial high courts stalled, compromised, or declined the writ. The New York court issued the writ but deviated from the exact language authorized by Parliament, with the result that the customs officers refused to execute the deviant writ and sought one in the correct form. It was not forthcoming; indeed, applications kept getting lost or mislaid. In 1773, five years after the first application, the New York court held that "it did not appear to them that such Writs according to the form now produced are warranted by law and therefore they could not grant the motion."[45]

Something like that happened in several colonies. In Connecticut, Chief Justice Jonathan Trumbull and Judge Roger Sherman refused to be rushed into making a decision on the application for a writ. Trumbull remarked privately that he and his associates were not clear "the thing was in itself constitutional."[46] Chief Justice William Allen of Pennsylvania was more forthcoming. In 1768 he declared that he had no legal authority to issue the writ. Customs officials sent Allen's statement to Attorney General William DeGrey in London for his opinion. He thought that Allen would see the error of his ways if confronted by a copy of the writ, a copy of the act of Parliament, and a copy of the opinion of England's attorney general.[47] On a new application for the writ backed by English legal artillery, Allen replied that he would grant "particular [not general] writs whenever they are applied for on oath." The customs agent must swear he knew or had reason to believe that prohibited or uncustomed goods were located in a particular place. Allen's groping toward a concept of probable cause as well as specific warrants became clearer as customs officials vainly persisted to engage his cooperation.[48]

In South Carolina a judge, explaining his court's refusal to issue the writ, stated that it "trenched too severely and unnecessarily upon the safety of the subject secured by Magna Charta." After five years of persistence, however, the customs officials got a writ of assistance in South Carolina.[49] In Georgia, where the judges declined to issue the writ, they said they would authorize a search warrant for a specific occasion if supported by an affidavit.[50]

Virginia issued writs of assistance in 1769 but undermined the process by annexing a degree of specificity obnoxious to the customs office. Its agent had to swear an oath in support of his suspicion and could obtain a writ only for a special occasion and for a limited duration of time. The Virginia judges alleged that the writ sought by the customs office under the Townshend Act was "unconstitutional" because it allowed the officer "to act under it according to his own arbitrary discretion." The customs office appealed to England for support against the Virginia court. Attorney General DeGrey had to acknowledge that he knew of "no direct and effective means" to compel a provincial court to award a writ of assistance. He asserted that judges might be impeached for contumacious refusal to execute an act of Parliament, but he did not know how to proceed in such a case. He preferred to believe that Virginia's judges had acted out of a mistaken understanding of the law. Virginia's court, however, remained contumacious.[51]

Between 1761 and 1776 a glacial drift in American legal opinion can be discerned toward increased reliance on specific warrants. Law books, including manuals of the justices of the peace, began to recommend specific warrants in some cases; most, however, relied on general warrants, as did American judges in actual practice. American rhetoric and reality diverged. John Dickinson's *Letters of a Pennsylvania Farmer,* which circulated in every colony, censured general warrants and repeated the cliché about a man's home being his castle; but Dickinson did not recommend specific warrants in their place or condemn any warrantless searches. Americans never spoke of a right to privacy as such, although they understood the concept, and like their British counterparts expressed outrage over the possibility that customs agents might "break the rights of domicil," "ransack houses," and "enter private cabinets" or "secret repositories."[52] The best known of such remarks, which received considerable publicity in the colonies, was that of the Boston Town Meeting of 1772, which complained:

> Thus our houses and even our bed chambers, are exposed to be ransacked, our boxes chests & trunks broke open ravaged and plundered by wretches, whom no prudent man would venture to employ even as menial servants; whenever they are pleased to say they suspect there are in the house wares &c for which the dutys have not been paid. Flagrant instances of the wanton exercise of this power, have frequently happened in this and other sea port Towns. *By* this we are cut off from that domestick security which renders the lives of the most unhappy in some measure agreeable. Those Officers may under colour of law and the cloak of a general warrant break thro' the sacred rights of the Domicil, ransack mens houses, destroy their securities, carry off their property, and with little danger to themselves commit the most horred murders.[53]

In all the American rhetoric, only one writer seems to have urged special warrants in place of warrantless searches and general warrants. Some writers revealed that their objection lay against a parliamentary empowerment, rather than one by their own assemblies.[54] General searches continued in the colonies as the prevailing standard, not the specific warrants used in Massachusetts. Nevertheless, some colonies became more familiar with specific warrants and even used them in various kinds of cases. Cuddihy states:

> The failure of colonial legislatures and courts to abandon general searches for domestic consumption locates the "American Revolution Against Writs of Assistance" in clearer perspective. Appeals to Magna Carta notwithstanding, the typical searches actually authorized by judges and legislators in the colonies had remained as general as those in the writs of assistance rejected by local judiciaries and intellectuals. Damning such searches under British auspices was one thing; renouncing them oneself was another matter. In Connecticut, where judicial resistance to those writs was most extreme in 1769, the local code of that year included an impost enforced by search warrants strongly resembling the writs. The same conclusion applied equally to Pennsylvania. Had Allen, Trumbull, or any of the

Connecticut newspaper essayists wished to attack general searches on principle alone, they need have looked no further than Pennsylvania and Connecticut, for local session laws and judicial search warrants had read like writs of assistance throughout the histories of those colonies. Only when those searches loomed from a foreign quarter and threatened political autonomy was the civil libertarian threat posed by them announced.[55]

In sum, one need only add that Otis's extraordinary forensic effort of 1761 on behalf of specific warrants, which a Boston newspaper printed in 1773, bore scarce fruit elsewhere, at least not until well after the Revolution.

The Declaration of Independence, however, spurred the definition of American ideals. Although that document, which itemized the king's perfidies, failed to say anything about search and seizure or even about general warrants, it inspired the making of the first state constitutions. In the midst of war, Americans engaged in the most important, creative, and dynamic constitutional achievements in history, among them the first written constitutions and the first bills of rights against all branches of government. Their provisions on search and seizure are significant because they distilled the best American thinking on the subject, constituted benchmarks to show the standard by which practise should be measured, and provided models for the Fourth Amendment.

Virginia, the oldest, largest, and most influential of the new states, anticipated the Declaration of Independence by adopting a Declaration of Rights on June 12, 1776, and completed its constitution before the month ended. Article 10 of the Declaration of Rights provided: "That general warrants, whereby any officer or messenger may be commanded to search suspected places without evidence of a fact committed, or to seize any person or persons not named, or whose offence is not particularly described and supported by evidence, are grievous and oppressive, and ought not to be granted."[56] Obviously this provision is a substantial step in the direction of specific warrants. Its force is weakened by the wishy-washy climax: certain warrants are grievous, not illegal, and "ought" not be granted, but the language imposes no prohibition against them. The concept of probable cause is stunted with respect to searches but considerably broader with respect to arrests. The search may be conducted, presumably under warrant, if the fact of a crime has been established, though no need exists to show a connection between the crime and the place to be searched, and there is no reference to a need for specificity with respect to the things to be seized. Moreover, the warrant need not be based on a sworn statement. Probable cause must be shown for the criminal involvement of the persons to be arrested; far more than mere suspicion is required for an arrest.

As the first search and seizure provision in any American constitution, Virginia's had egregious deficiencies as well as pioneering attainments. That the attainments might have been better still is evident from the fact that in a committee draft of May 27, the property to be seized had to be "particularly described." We do not know why that clause was omitted in the final draft.[57] We do know that the provision could have been far worse or altogether nonexistent. George Mason, who provided the original draft of the Declaration of Rights had omitted a search and seizure provision and Thomas Jefferson's draft of a state constitution omitted one, too.[58] Edmund Randolph may have been right in recalling that his state's search and seizure provision "was dictated by the remembrance of the seizure of Wilkes's paper under a warrant from a Secretary of State,"[59] but Virginia went well beyond a condemnation of general warrants issued under executive authority.

In August 1776 Pennsylvania adopted its extraordinary constitution preceded by a Declaration of Rights influenced by Virginia yet original in major respects. Its tenth article provided:

> That the people have a right to hold themselves, their houses, papers, and possessions free from search and seizure, and therefore warrants without oaths or affirmations first made, affording a sufficient foundation for them, and whereby any officer or messenger may be commanded or required to search suspected places, or to seize any person or persons, his or their property, not particularly described, are contrary to that right, and ought not to be granted.[60]

That provision is memorable because it recognizes a right of the people in affirmative terms rather than merely declaring against general warrants or grievous searches. And, the right of the people is broad, promiscuously so; there is no such thing as an absolute right to be free from search and seizure. The provision meant, rather, that searches and seizures made without specific warrants "ought"—that weak word again—not to be granted. Even that proposition had to be subject to exceptions, because no evidence suggests that Pennsylvania intended to depart from common law exceptions to the need for a warrant if a peace officer was in hot pursuit of a felon or had reason to believe that the felon might escape if the officer called time out to obtain a warrant. Exigent circumstances of various kinds always allowed warrantless arrests and even warrantless searches and seizures of evidence of crime, of weapons, or of contraband. The Pennsylvania provision had the virtue of including a requirement for specificity with respect to the things seized when a warrant was attainable. It was also the first to require that the warrant be available only if the informant swore or affirmed that he had "sufficient foundation" for specific information about the person, place, or things described. Probable cause, attested to on oath, derives partly from Pennsylvania's contribution to the constitutional law of search and seizure.

Delaware's Declaration of Rights of 1776 derived its search and seizure provision partly from Maryland and partly from Pennsylvania, though the Delaware variant was truncated; it omitted the clause recognizing the right of the people. It also omitted a requirement for specificity respecting the property to be seized under a warrant, yet deplored as grievous any warrant for the seizure of property not based on a sworn statement. Delaware's contribution consisted, rather, in the fact that its provision was the first to declare "illegal" any warrants not meeting the constitutional requirement of specificity.[61] In this respect, the Delaware provision was based on a draft of the Maryland Declaration of Rights, not yet adopted.[62] The texts of the search and seizure provisions of these two states were nearly the same. As Delaware copied Maryland, North Carolina copied Virginia, and Vermont copied Pennsylvania.[63]

Similarly, New Hampshire in 1784 would copy Massachusetts, which did not adopt its Declaration of Rights and Constitution until 1780. As a source of the Fourth Amendment, the Massachusetts provision on search and seizure was the most important of all the state models, because it was the one that the Fourth Amendment most resembles. The Massachusetts provision was the work of John Adams, the witness to and recorder of Otis's monumental speech in Paxton's Case about twenty years earlier. Through Adams and Article 14 of the Massachusetts Declaration of Rights, Otis's influence at last bore triumphant fruits. Article 14 declared:

> Every subject has a right to be secure from all unreasonable searches, and seizures of his person, his houses, his papers, and all his possessions. All warrants, therefore, are contrary to this right, if the cause or foundation of them be not previously supported by oath or affirmation; and if the order in the warrant to the civil officer, to make search in suspected places, to arrest one or more suspected persons, or to seize their property, be not accompanied with a special designation of the persons

or objects of search, arrest, or seizure and no warrant ought to be issued but in cases and with the formalities, prescribed by the laws.[64]

The detail of the provision is striking. No other right received such particularity in the Massachusetts constitution, and, like the provision of Pennsylvania, which Adams borrowed, it is a "right" that is protected. The right is to be secure against "unreasonable search, and seizures," the first use of the phrase that would become the prime principle of the Fourth Amendment. The warrant must be based on sworn statement providing "cause or foundation" for the warrant, but the provision omits, amazingly, a requirement that the search, arrest, or seizure occur within specifically designated premises.[65]

The war years were the worst possible for testing whether American practices matched American ideals or constitutional provisions. Search and seizure was a method of fighting the enemy and those suspected of adhering to his cause. Perhaps the grossest violation of a constitutional provision occurred in Pennsylvania in 1777. Three years earlier Congress had complained about customs officials breaking and entering without authority. In 1777, though, Congress urged Pennsylvania's executive council to search the homes of Philadelphians, mostly Quakers, whose loyalty to the American cause was suspect. Congress wanted to disarm such persons and to seize their political papers. Pennsylvania's executive council authorized a search of the homes of anyone who had not taken an oath of allegiance to the United States. The searches of at least six Quaker homes were conducted cruelly and violently, and all sorts of books, papers, and records were confiscated; over forty people were arrested and deported without trial, let alone conviction, to Virginia, where they were detained until the next year.[66] Nothing that the British had done equaled the violation of privacy rights inflicted by Pennsylvania on its "Virginia Exiles," in defiance of the state constitution and a writ of habeas corpus by the state chief justice, but with the support of Congress.

American adherence to professed principles stands up far better and is more fairly tested after the shooting stopped. Between 1782 and the ratification of the Constitution, five states—Maryland, New York, North and South Carolina, and Georgia employed general searches. The southern states conventionally employed warrantless searches without restriction against slaves, especially to detect vagrants and fugitives. But all five states used general warrants to enforce their impost laws. Although Maryland's constitution banned general warrants, Maryland used them to enforce excise laws and laws regulating bakers. Such laws, however, derived from past experience. More significant, perhaps, is the fact that the laws of Massachusetts kept faith with its commitment to specific warrants. Moreover, Rhode Island, which had no constitution, and New Jersey, which had one but did not include a search and seizure clause, enacted legislation that required the use of specific warrants. In the remaining states, general warrants continued to be used, but specific warrants were becoming more common, especially in cases of theft. In Virginia, the trend toward specificity was pronounced, if belated.[67]

In Connecticut, which, like Rhode Island, had no constitution, the state supreme court delivered an opinion of major consequence that voided a general warrant directed against every person and place suspected by the victim of a theft. The state chief justice ruled that a justice of peace, in granting a warrant, had an obligation "to limit the search to such particular place or places, as he, from the circumstances, shall judge there is reason to suspect," and he must limit the arrests under the warrant to those persons found with the stolen goods. The warrant before the court, the chief justice concluded, "is clearly illegal," because not specific. The case, *Frisbie v. Butler* (1787), shows that probable cause as determined independently by a magistrate was not an unknown concept.[68]

The failure of the Framers to include in the Constitution a bill of rights exposed it to the withering criticism of those who opposed ratification for any reason. Ten days after the Convention adjourned, Richard Henry Lee of Virginia, a member of Congress, sought to wreck the ratification process by moving that Congress adopt a bill of rights. Acting out of a genuine fear of the proposed national government, Lee had troubled to frame his own bill of rights rather than simply urging the famous one of his own state. He omitted numerous liberties of importance, but included a search and seizure clause of significance: " . . . the Citizens shall not be exposed to unreasonable searches, seizures of their papers, houses, persons, or property." Lee had constructed the clause from the Massachusetts Constitution of 1780. It was the broadest on the subject.

Lee's colleague from Virginia, James Madison, led the fight against Lee's motion. Madison observed that the Articles of Confederation required that all thirteen state legislatures would have to approve the Lee proposals if endorsed by Congress. That would cause confusion because of the Convention's rule that ratification by nine state conventions would put the Constitution into operation.[69] Lee's motion lost, but he did not quit. He wrote his *Federal Farmer* letters, the best of the Anti-Federalist tracts.[70]

In an early letter, Lee discoursed on the rights omitted from the proposed Constitution. The second one he mentioned was the right against unreasonable warrants, those not founded on oath or on cause for searching and seizing papers, property, and persons.[71] In another letter he included the term "effects," which would become part of the Fourth Amendment.[72] In his final word on the subject, he urged a constitutional provision "that all persons shall have a right to be secure from all unreasonable searches and seizures of their persons, houses, papers, or possessions; and that all warrants shall be deemed contrary to this right, if the foundation of them be not previously supported by oath, and there be not in them a special designation of persons or objects of search, arrest, or seizure."[73]

Other Anti-Federalists also popularized the demand for a provision on searches and seizures, and some used significant language. "Centinel" employed an extract from the Pennsylvania constitution The "Dissent" of the Pennsylvania convention's Anti-Federalists, which also circulated throughout the country in newspapers and pamphlet form, used a truncated form of the same provision. "Brutus," another whose writings were reprinted almost everywhere, used his own formulation against warrants that were not specific.[74] Anti-Federalists who addressed the issue usually opposed general warrants in purple language, either reflecting fear or calculated to inspire it. Newspapers in the four largest states reprinted the rant of "A Son of Liberty," who depicted federal officers dragging people off to prison after brutal searches and confiscations that shocked "the most delicate part of our families."[75] No one could compete with the florid fears expressed by that first-rate demagogue, Patrick Henry.[76]

Virginia's convention ratified the Constitution with recommendations for amendments to be considered by the First Congress. Among them was a detailed provision on the right of every free person "to be secure from all unreasonable searches and seizures; the provision also required sworn warrants to be based on "legal and sufficient cause." The Virginia recommendation of 1788 of unknown authorship, was moved by George Wythe on behalf of a powerful bipartisan committee which included James Madison.[77] The committee blended the precedents of the Pennsylvania and Massachusetts state constitutions and the recommendations of Richard Henry Lee. Virginia was the first state to ratify with a search and seizure recommendation. North Carolina copied it in her recommended amendments; New York and Rhode Island did so also, with slight changes.[78]

Without a single supporter when he began his fight in the House for amendments safeguarding personal liberties, Madison struggled to overcome apathy and opposition from members of his own party as well as the Anti-Federalists. He meant to win over the great body of people who withheld their support of the new government in the sincere belief that the Constitution should secure them against the abuse of powers by the United States. And he meant to isolate the leaders of the opposition by depriving them of their supporters. But Madison could have achieved his goals and redeemed his campaign pledge by taking the least troublesome route. On the issue of search and seizure, for example, he might have shown up the Anti-Federalists by proposing that the United States would not enforce its laws by searches and seizures that violated the laws of the states, most of which still allowed general warrants. That would have put the burden on the states to bring about reforms securing the rights of citizens against unreasonable searches and seizures. Or, Madison might have simply proposed that the United States would not employ general warrants.[79] Or, he might have recommended the weak formulation of his own state's constitution, with its omission of specificity for the things to be seized, its failure to require a sworn statement, and its flabby assertion that "grievous" warrants "ought" not to be granted. Even Virginia's excellent 1788 recommendation for a search and seizure provision to be added to the federal Constitution employed the same "ought."

If Madison had chosen a formulation narrower than the one he offered, only the citizens of Massachusetts could consistently have criticized him. Facing a variety of minimal options, any of which would have been politically adequate, Madison chose the maximum protection conceivable at the time. He recommended:

> The rights of the people to be secured in their persons, their houses, and their other property, from all unreasonable searches and seizures, shall not be violated by warrants issued without probable cause, supported by oath or affirmation, or not particularly describing the places to be searched, or the persons or things to be seized.[80]

No one previously had proposed the imperative voice, "shall not be violated," rather than the wishful "ought not," which allowed for exceptions. "Probable cause" was also a significant contribution, or became so; it required more than mere suspicion or even reasonable suspicion, as had its antecedents such as "just cause" and "sufficient foundation." Above all, Madison used the positive assertion drawn from Pennsylvania and Massachusetts that the people have rights against "unreasonable searches and seizures"—John Adams's formulation for the Massachusetts constitution.

A House Committee of Eleven, composed of one member from each state, deleted the crucial phrase that establishes the general principle of the Fourth: no "unreasonable searches and seizures." Specificity in warrants is the lesser half of the amendment, because it provides the standard of reasonableness only when a search or seizure is conducted with a warrant. But the standard of reasonableness must also apply to warrantless searches according to the Fourth Amendment. The committee version initially declared that the "rights of the people to be secured in their persons, houses, papers, and effects, shall not be violated by warrants issuing without probable cause, supported by oath or affirmation, and not particularly describing the places to be searched, and the persons or things to be seized."[81] During the debate by the House acting as the Committee of the Whole, Elbridge Gerry of Massachusetts moved the restoration of "unreasonable seizures and searches." Oddly, he said he did so on the presumption that a "mistake" had been made in the wording of the clause, which he corrected by changing "rights" to "right" and "secured" to "secure." The effect was to provide security or, as we might say, privacy to the people; Gerry's motion changed the meaning from a protection of the right to a protection of individuals in their persons, homes, papers, and effects. The Committee of the Whole adopted his motion but defeated others that were also important.[82] According to the House Journal, the defeated motions of August 17 were reported as agreed upon by the Committee of the Whole. Thus, the provision recommended to the House, in the articles arranged by a special committee of three, read:

> The right of the people to be secure in their persons, houses, papers, and effects, against unreasonable searches and seizures, shall not be violated; and no warrants shall issue, but upon probable cause, supported by oath or affirmation, and particularly describing the place to be searched, and the persons or things to be seized.[83]

The changes that seem to have been sneaked in did more than eliminate a double negative. The entire provision was split into two parts separated by a semicolon. The first part fixed the right of the people and laid down the standard against unreasonable searches and seizures. The second part required probable cause for the issue of a specific warrant. No other changes were made except in the number of the article. Its text remained the same as adopted by the House and accepted by the Senate. Thus, Otis and Adams finally had a belated but cardinal impact on the making of the Fourth Amendment, even though Madison was immediately influenced by Lee and Virginia's recommendation. Lee, whom Virginia's legislature had elected to the United States Senate instead of Madison, bitterly complained to Patrick Henry that the idea of recommending amendments to the Constitution turned out to be political suicide; the Bill of Rights made impossible the amendments most desired by the Anti-Federalists limiting national powers concerning taxes, treaties, and commerce.[84]

When Madison had first recommended to the House that it consider amendments to the Constitution, some Anti-Federalists thought the House should not neglect the more important business of passing a law for the collection of duties. That law, which passed seven weeks before the amendments were adopted for state consideration, contained a clause on search and seizure. It allowed collectors and naval officers to enter and search any ships suspected of having uncustomed goods and to seize such goods. That is, Congress authorized general searches for the search and seizure of ships—warrantless, general searches. By contrast, if an officer suspected the concealment of uncustomed goods in a building on land, he must apply for a specific warrant before a magistrate and under oath state the cause of his suspicion, and he "shall . . . be entitled to a warrant to enter such house, store, or any place (in the day time only)" and to conduct the search for and seizure of uncustomed goods.[85] Thus, the statute enacted before the framing of the Fourth Amendment required magistrates to issue the warrant on the basis of the officer's suspicion, not on the magistrate's independent judgment of the question of whether probable cause existed.

Allowing the officer who executed a warrant to determine its specificity put the fox in charge of the chicken coop. The magistrate in effect accepted the officer's sworn statement that he was acting in good faith. That is difficult to reconcile with the fact that the good faith execution of a general warrant by a customs officer in the years before the Revolution did not, to American whigs, validate the warrant or the seizures under it.

The adoption of the Fourth Amendment changed the situation drastically. In March 1791, before the amendment had been formally ratified but after approval by nine state legislatures, Congress enacted a tax on liquor, whether imported or distilled in the United States. The statute reflected the meaning of the Fourth Amendment. Unlike the collections act of 1789, the act of 1791 explicitly empowered magistrates to decide for themselves whether an officer had probable cause. Any judge with jurisdiction might issue a 'special warrant' for the detection of fraudulently concealed spirits, but the warrant was lawful only "upon reasonable cause of suspicion, to be made out to the satisfaction of such judge or justice of the peace" and sworn under oath. That became the basis in federal law for the determination of probable cause.[86]

The amendment constituted a swift liberalization of the law of search and seizure. Its language was the broadest known at the time. It provided no remedy, however, for an illegal search or seizure, or for the introduction in evidence of illegally seized items. It contained principles that were as vague as they might be comprehensive; "probable" and "unreasonable," even if judicially determined, remained uncertain in meaning, and Congress made no provision for the liability, civil or criminal, of federal officers who violated the amendment. Moreover, no exclusionary rule existed. Consequently, the right of privacy created by the amendment, while better secured by the fundamental law in comparison to previous practices and standards, depended on congressional and judicial adherence to the spirit of the amendment. In effect, the meaning of the right to privacy depended then, as now, upon the interpretation of the "probable cause" that justified a specific warrant and, above all, on the reasonableness of searches and seizures.

Notes

1. Quoted in Nelson B. Lasson, *The History and Development of the Fourth Amendment to the United States Constitution* (Baltimore: Johns Hopkins University Press, 1937), pp. 49–50. Variations of the statement exist, and its date is not certain. 1766 is the commonly used date. The earliest report of the statement, according to William Cuddihy, is from a tract of 1783. Cuddihy, "The Fourth Amendment: Origins and Original Meaning," Ph. D. dissertation, Claremont Graduate School, manuscript-in-progress, citing William Godwin, *The History . . . of William Pitt* (London, 1783), pp. 152–53. Cuddihy believes that Pitt made the statement in

connection with an excise act of 1763, not on a question involving general warrants. Cuddihy is the best authority on the origins of the Fourth Amendment. However, I have minimized citations to his work, which is still being radically revised and lacks a fixed pagination, especially if I can cite a printed source instead. This note is by way of acknowledging my debt to him even when I cite others. I am responsible, however, for interpretations that I put on the data.

2. Cuddihy, "The Fourth Amendment," introduction, citing a 1505 opinion of Chief Justice John Fineux in a King's Bench case reported in the Year Books.

3. Leonard W. Levy, *Origins of the Fifth Amendment* (New York: Oxford University Press, 1968), pp. 170–71, 466.

4. Sir Edward Coke, *Institutes of the Laws of England* (London, 1628–1644, 4 vols.), IV, pp. 176–77.

5. Francis R. Aumann, *The Changing American Legal System* (Columbus: Ohio State University Press, 1940), pp. 46–47, and Charles Warren, *A History of the American Bar* (Boston: Little, Brown, 1911), p. 174.

6. Sir Matthew Hale, *History of Pleas of the Crown,* ed. Solom Emlyn (London, 2 vols., 1st ed., 1736), I, pp. 577–83; II, pp. 107–11, 149–52.

7. See Lasson, *History of the Fourth,* pp. 35–36, for discussion of Hale.

8. Serjeant William Hawkins, *A Treatise of the Pleas of the Crown* (London, 1724, 2nd ed., 2 vols.), II, pp. 81–82, and William Blackstone, *Commentaries on the Laws of England* (Oxford, 1766–1769, 4 vols.), I, pp. 288, 308. Blackstone, we are told, wrote boldly . . . against discretionary search and seizure." William Cuddihy and B. Carmon Hardy, A Man's House Was Not His Castle: Origins of the Fourth Amendment," *William and Mary Quarterly,* 3rd ser., 38 (July 1980):385. The entire comment by Blackstone on search and seizure, in vol. I, p. 308, is: "the rigour and arbitrary proceedings of excise-laws seem hardly compatible with the temper of a free nation. For the frauds that might be committed in this branch of the revenue, unless a strict watch is kept, make it necessary, wherever it is established, to give the officers a power of entering and searching the houses of such as deal in excisable commodities, at any hour of the day, and, in many cases, of the night likewise."

9. Levy, *Origins,* p. 171.

10. 5 Coke Reports 91a, 91b, 93a, 78 English Reports 194–95, 198.

11. Lasson, *History of the Fourth,* pp. 31–32, and Catherine Drinker Bowen, *The Lion and the Throne: The Life and Times of Sir Edward Coke* (Boston: Little, Brown, 1956), pp. 533–34.

12. Cuddihy, "The Fourth Amendment," chaps. 1–4, discusses search and seizure in Great Britain prior to 1763.

13. Philip Carteret Webb, ed., *Copies of Warrants Taken from the Records Office Books of the Kings Bench at Westminster; The Original Office Books of the Secretaries of State* . . . (London, 1763), pp. 10–72.

14. Cuddihy and Hardy, "A Man's House," p. 382.

15. Cuddihy, "The Fourth Amendment," chap. 7 on American colonies to 1761. Cuddihy and Hardy, "A Man's House," p. 388.

16. Cuddihy, "Fourth Amendment," chap. 7.

17. Ibid.

18. Ibid., chap. 10.

19. Levy, *Origins,* pp. 386–87. See Paul S. Boyer, "Borrowed Rhetoric: The Massachusetts Excise Controversy of 1754," *William and Mary Quarterly,* 3rd ser., 21 (1964):328–51.

20. M. H. Smith, *The Writs of Assistance Case* (Berkeley: University of California,

1978), pp. 113–14.

21. Cuddihy and Hardy, "A Man's House," pp. 396–97. Cuddihy informs me that the governors of most colonies with major ports denied the royal navy's request for impressment warrants, and that in New York, naval officers conducted warrantless searches in defiance of the governor, with the result that they were imprisoned.

22. Act of Feb. 28, 1756, chap. 31, sect. 24, *Acts and Resolves . . . of the Province of Massachusetts Bay* (Boston, 1869–1922, 21 vols.), III, p. 109. Ibid., III, pp. 936–37, for the impost act of April 20, 1756.

23. Cuddihy and Hardy, "A Man's House," p. 397.

24. 13 & 14 Car. 2, chap. 11, sect. 5, as quoted by the crown attorney Jeremiah Gridley in Paxton's Case, reported in L. Kinvin Wroth and Hiller B. Zobel, eds., *Legal Papers of John Adams* (Cambridge, Mass.: Harvard University Press, 1965, 3 vols.), II, p. 131; Smith, *Writs of Assistance Case,* pp. 17–50, contains a detailed account of the originating legislation. On the writs, see also the documents and annotations by Justice Horace Gray, Jr., in Josiah Quincy, Jr., ed., *Reports of Cases Argued and Adjudged in the Superior Court of Judicature of the Massachusetts Bay Between 1761 and 1772* (Boston, 1865), Appendix I, pp. 395–540.

25. Wroth and Zobel, *Legal Papers of Adams,* II, p. 132.

26. Smith, *Writs of Assistance Case,* is a massive study of Paxton's Case.

27. Both statements by Adams quoted in Wroth and Zobel, *Legal Papers of Adams,* II, p. 107.

28. For the Massachusetts Declaration, see Bernard Schwartz, ed., *The Bill of Rights: A Documentary History* (New York: Chelsea House, 1971, 2 vols.), I, p. 342, sect. XIV. Madison's proposal in his speech of June 8, 1789, in the First Congress is in ibid., II, p. 1027.

29. Wroth and Zobel, *Legal Papers of Adams,* reprinted both versions of the speech, II, pp. 125–29, 139–44, with elaborate annotations. The longer version was first published by the *Massachusetts Spy* (Boston), April 29, 1773, p. 3. In John Kukla, ed., *The Bill of Rights: A Lively Heritage* (Richmond: Virginia State Library, 1978), pp. 8597, William Cuddihy, "From General to Specific Search Warrants," at p. 93, alleges that Otis "cited Sir Edward Coke's exaggeration of Magna Carta, incorrectly asserted that Coke required all search warrants to be specific, and appealed to 'higher law'." Cuddihy cites Wroth and Zobel as his source for Otis's remarks, but that source does not show any reference by Otis to Coke's use of Magna Carta to condemn general warrants or to any reliance by Otis on Coke as an authority for specific warrants. Quincy, ed., *Reports of Cases,* pp. 51–57, includes a fourteen-line extract from Otis, in which Otis's claim that a writ of assistance is illegal is backed by these citations: "1 Inst. 464. 29M." Vol. I of Coke's *Institutes* is on feudal tenures. "29M," a reference to the famous judgment-of-peers or by-law-of-the-land clause, seems to support the point. However, Gray's discussion of Otis's quotations from Coke on Magna Carta, cap. XXIX," in Quincy's *Reports,* pp. 483–85, has nothing to do with search and seizure.

30. Wroth and Zobel, *Legal Papers of Adams,* II, p. 141; I have not followed the capitalization of the original.

31. Ibid., p. 144. Curiously, in the briefer version of the speech, Otis relied more fully on Coke's decision in Dr. Bonham's Case, 8 Coke's Reports 113b, 118a (C.P. 1610), and more clearly asked the court to hold the act unconstitutional, Wroth and Zobel, *Legal Papers of Adams,* II, pp. 127–28.

32. Smith, *Writs of Assistance Case,* pp. 442–47, 542–43; Quincy, ed., *Reports of Cases,* pp. 437–38, 446, 495–99; John Phillip Reid, *In Rebellious Spirit* (University Park: Pennsylvania State University Press, 1979), pp. 1–35.

33. See Robert R. Rea, *The English Press in Politics, 1760–1774* (Lincoln: University of Nebraska press, 1963), pp. 40–85; Raymond Postgate, *That Devil Wilkes* (New York: Vanguard Press, 1929); George Nobbe, *The North Briton: A Study in Political Propaganda* (New York: Columbia University Press, 1939), chap. 16; and George Rude, *Wilkes and Liberty* (Oxford: Oxford University Press, 1962).

34. Leonard W. Levy, *Emergence of a Free Press* (New York: Oxford University Press, 1985), p. 79. For the fallout of the Wilkes cases in America, see Patricia Bonomi, *A Factious People: Politics and Society in Colonial New York* (New York: Columbia University Press, 1971), pp. 267–76; Pauline Maier, *From Resistance to Revolution* (New York: Knopf, 1972), pp. 162–77; Jack P. Greene, Bridge to Revolution: The Wilkes Fund Controversy in South Carolina 1769–1775," *Journal of Southern History* 27 (1963):19–52.

35. *Huckle v. Money*, 95 Eng. Rep. 768 (C.P. 1763), in Philip B. Kurland and Ralph Lerner, eds., *The Founders' Constitution* (Chicago: University of Chicago Press, 1987, 5 vols.), V, p. 230.

36. 98 Eng. Rep. 489 (C.P. 1763), in ibid., pp. 230–31.

37. Thomas Erskine May, *Constitutional History of England Since the Accession of George III* (New York, 1880, 2 vols.), p. 249. May is the source for the earlier statement that the government filed 200 informations in these cases; ibid., II, p. 112.

38. *Money v. Leach*, 97 Eng. Rep. 1075 (K.B. 1765), in Kurland and Lerner, eds. *Founders Constitution,* V, p. 235.

39. *Boyd v. United States*, 116 U.S. 616, 626 (1886), citing *Entick v. Carrington*, 95 Eng. Rep. 807 (K. B.), most easily available in Kurland and Lerner, eds., *Founders' Constitution,* V, pp. 233–35.

40. 19 Howell's *State Trials* at pp. 1038, 1041, 1063, 1073. *Boyd v. United States*, 116 U.S. 616, 633 (1886).

41. My generalizations are based on the discussion in the dissertation by Cuddihy, "The Fourth Amendment," which cites contemporary sources and recommends as the best summary of the accounts [Robert Bisset], *History of the Reign of George III* (London, 1782–1783, 2 vols.), I, pp. 182–88, and John Adolphus, *History of England* (London, 1802, 3 vols.), I, pp. 152–54, 191–92, and 235–36.

42. Father of Candor, *An Enquiry Into the Doctrine Lately Propagated Concerning Libels, Warrants, and the Seizure of Papers* (London, 1764, reprinted by Da Capo Press of New York, 1970), p. 55.

43. Ibid., pp. 55–56.

44. Speech by Madison, June 8, 1789, in Schwartz, ed., *Bill of Rights,* II, p. 1028.

45. Oliver Dickerson, "Writs of Assistance as a Cause of the American Revolution," in Richard B. Morris, ed., *Era of the American Revolution* (New York: Columbia University Press, 1939), pp. 54–58.

46. Cuddihy, "Fourth Amendment," citing a manuscript letter. Dickerson, "Writs of Assistance," pp. 52–54.

47. Quincy, ed., *Reports,* pp. 453–54, for De Grey's opinion, dated Aug. 20, 1768.

48. Dickerson, "Writs of Assistance," pp. 59–60.

49. Cuddihy, "Fourth Amendment, citing William Henry Drayton, *A Letter from Freeman of South-Carolina* (Charles Town, 1774), pp. 19–20; Dickerson, "Writs of Assistance," p. 67.

50. Dickerson, "Writs of Assistance," p. 66.

51. Ibid., pp. 68–71.

52. Cuddihy, "Fourth Amendment," collects many of such statements from newspapers and tracts of the time.

53. "The Rights of the Colonies," 1772, in Schwartz, ed., *Bill of Rights,* I, p. 206.
54. William Henry Drayton, cited above, n. 49, seems to have been the exception.
55. Cuddihy, "Fourth Amendment," chap. 15 on "Writs of Assistance."
56. Schwartz, ed., *Bill of Rights,* I, p. 235.
57. Ibid., p. 238, Article 12.
58. Ibid., pp. 232, 243–46.
59. Ibid., p. 248.
60. Ibid., p. 265.
61. Ibid., p. 278, Article 17.
62. Ibid., pp. 279, 283, Article 23.
63. Ibid., pp. 287, 323.
64. Ibid., p. 342.
65. For New Hampshire, see ibid., p. 377, Article 19.
66. Isaac Sharpless, *A History of Quaker Government in Pennsylvania* (Philadelphia, 1900, 2 vols.), II, pp. 151–68.
67. Cuddihy, "Fourth Amendment," chap. 17, which covers the states in the 1780s.
68. 1 Kirby (Conn.) 231–35 (1787), excerpted in Kurland and Lerner, eds., *Founders' Constitution,* V, p. 237.
69. Lee's Proposed Amendments, Sept. 27, 1787, in Merrill Jensen, ed., *The Documentary History of the Ratification of the Constitution. Constitutional Documents and Records, 1776–1787* (Madison: State Historical Society of Wisconsin, 1976), I, pp. 325–40; the quotation from Lee is at p. 338.
70. *Observations . . . in a Number of Letters from the Federal Farmer* (New York, 1787), a tract that sold several thousand copies in a few months. Reprinted in Herbert J. Storing, ed., *The Complete Anti-Federalist* (Chicago: University of Chicago Press, 1981, 7 vols.), II, pp. 214–357. Lee's authorship is not certain, but the author's remarks on search and seizure accord with Lee's motion in Congress and with his letter of Dec. 22, 1787, in ibid., V, p. 117.
71. Ibid., II, p. 249, Letter IV, Oct. 12, 1787.
72. Ibid., II, p. 262, Letter VI, Dec. 25, 1787.
73. Ibid., II, Letter XVI, Jan. 20, 1788.
74. Ibid., II, pp. 136 and 153 for Centinel (Samuel Bryan of Pennsylvania); ibid., III, p. 151, for the Pennsylvania minority; and ibid., II, p. 375, for Brutus (Robert Yates of New York).
75. Ibid., VI, p. 35. See also John DeWitt, in ibid., IV, p. 33, and Mercy Otis Warren, in ibid., p. 279.
76. Jonathan Elliot, ed., *The Debates in the Several State Conventions* (Philadelphia, 1836–1845, 5 vols.), III, pp. 58, 412, 448–49, and 588, for Henry's oratory on the despoliations of hearth and home by tyrannical federal agents unrestricted by a requirement of specific warrants.
77. Lee was not a member of the Virginia convention. Mason, a member of the Wythe committee, had omitted from his draft of the Virginia Declaration of Rights a search and seizure provision. The Wythe committee ignored the weak provision in their own state's constitution. See Robert A. Rutland, ed., *The Papers of George Mason* (Chapel Hill: University of North Carolina Press, 1979, 3 vols.), III, note on p. 1071.
78. Charles Tansill, ed., *Documents Illustrative of the Formation of the Union of the American States* (Washington, D. C.: Government Printing Office, 1927), pp. 1030, 1036, 1046, and 1054. The recommendations of North Carolina and Rhode Island were made too late to be of influence; Congress had already recommended the Bill of Rights.

79. In his speech of June 8, 1789, urging amendments, Madison took note of the fact that one argument against the Constitution was that the government, under the necessary and proper clause, might enforce the collection of its revenue laws by issuing general warrants. Schwartz, ed., *Bill of Rights*, II, pp. 1030–31.

80. Ibid., p. 1027.

81. Ibid., p. 1061, and p. 1112, Aug. 17.

82. Ibid., p. 1112, Aug. 17. Cuddihy, relying on newspaper accounts rather than on Thomas Lloyd's *Congressional Register*, which is the source of the debates of the First Congress in *Annals of Congress*, declares that Egbert Benson of New York, not Gerry, made the motion to reintroduce the standard of no unreasonable searches and seizures.

83. Schwartz, ed., *Bill of Rights, p.* 1123.

84. Lee to Henry, Sept. 14, 1789, in William Wirt Henry, *Patrick Henry* (New York, 1891, 3 vols.), III, p. 399.

85. Statutes at Large, 1st Cong., sess. I, chap. 5, sec. 24, July 31, 1789, An Act to Regulate the Collection of Duties, vol. I, p. 43.

86. Statutes at Large, 1st Cong., sess. III, chap. XV, sec. 32, March 3, 1791, vol. I, p. 207.

10

The Exclusionary Rule

When the police obtain evidence by violating the Bill of Rights, the victim of their misconduct may lack any effective legal remedy. Yet some enforcement mechanism is necessary if several important constitutional guarantees are to be a reality and not merely expressions of hope. The Supreme Court responded to this concern by developing a series of rules that have come to be known in the aggregate as the exclusionary rule. In typical application, the rule is that evidence obtained in violation of a person's constitutional rights cannot be used against that person in his or her trial for a criminal offense. The rule is most frequently applied to exclude evidence produced by searches or seizures made in violation of the Fourth Amendment. However, a coerced confession obtained in violation of the defendant's Fifth Amendment right against self-incrimination, or a statement taken from the defendant in violation of his Sixth Amendment's guarantee of the right to counsel, would also be inadmissible at his trial.

The term "exclusionary rule" is of modern origin, but even at common law a coerced confession was excluded or inadmissible as evidence, because its involuntariness cast serious doubt on its reliability. No one today seriously argues that this long-standing rule of evidence should be abandoned. Other aspects of the exclusionary rule, however, have been the source of major controversy among members of the judiciary, professional commentators, law enforcement officials, and the public.

The controversy did not become intense until the era of the Warren Court. But as far back as *Weeks v. United States* (1914) the Supreme Court had unanimously held that evidence seized in violation of the

177

Fourth Amendment was inadmissible in a *federal* criminal prosecution. However, even after the Court had held in *Wolf v. Colorado* (1949) that the Fourth Amendment's guarantee against unreasonable searches and seizures was applicable to the states, the Court had continued until 1961 to resist the argument that the exclusionary rule should also be extended to *state* prosecutions. In that year, in *Mapp v. Ohio*, the Warren Court held that the Fourteenth Amendment did, indeed, impose on the states the exclusionary rule derived from the Fourth Amendment. Subsequent decisions broadened the Sixth Amendment guarantee of the right to counsel to govern the procedures for police interrogation and for the use of lineups; each of these developments was accompanied by an extension of the exclusionary rule to state-court proceedings. Since the "fruit of the poisonous tree" doctrine requires the exclusion not only of evidence immediately obtained by these various forms of constitutional violation but also of other evidence derived from the initial violations, the exclusionary rule in its modern form results in the suppression of many items of evidence of unquestioned reliability and the acquittal of many persons who are guilty.

The primary purpose of the exclusionary rule, as the Supreme Court said in *Elkins v. United States* (1960), "is to deter—to compel respect for the constitutional guaranty in the only effectively available way—by removing the incentive to disregard it." Yet this deterrent function is only part of the exclusionary rule's justification. A court that allows the government to profit from unconstitutional police action sullies the judicial process itself, by becoming an accomplice in an unlawful course of conduct. When the Court first applied the rule in *Mapp* to state-court prosecutions, it said:

> There are those who say, as did Justice (then Judge) [Benjamin N.] Cardozo, that under our constitutional exclusionary doctrine "the criminal is to go free because the constable has blundered." . . . In some cases this will undoubtedly be the result. But, . . . "there is another consideration—the imperative of judicial integrity." . . . The criminal goes free, if he must, but it is the law that sets him free. Nothing can destroy a government more quickly than its failure to observe its own laws, or worse, its disregard of the charter of its own existence. As Mr. Justice Louis D. Brandeis, dissenting, said: . . . "Our government is the potent, the omnipresent teacher. For good or for ill, it teaches the whole people by its example. . . . If the government becomes a lawbreaker, it breeds contempt for law."

The evidence seized in an illegal search—a knife, a packet of heroin, counterfeit plates—is as trustworthy and material as if the search had been lawful. The rule's critics argue that to protect the privacy of the search victim by letting a guilty person escape responsibility for his crime is illogical. It would make more sense, they say, to use the evidence (as do the courts in Great Britain, for example) and provide civil or criminal remedies against the errant police officers. If the rule's purpose is to deter police lawlessness, the critics argue, the rule misses the point: prosecutors, not police officers, feel the immediate effects of the rule. If the rule is designed to maintain respect for the courts, they ask how the public can be expected to respect a system that frees criminals by suppressing trustworthy evidence of their guilt.

How many criminals do go free when the constable blunders? Inadequate studies provide no clear-cut answer, except that opponents of the exclusionary rule grossly exaggerate the number of felons it sets loose, and they tend to dramatize the worst cases. In California, whose supreme court has created the most stringent exclusionary rule in the nation, a study by the National Institute of Justice showed that .78 percent of all accused felons are not prosecuted because of search and seizure problems, and of those released, nearly three-fourths were involved in drug-related cases. The effect of the exclusionary rule is slight in cases involving violent crimes. When the charge is murder, rape, assault, or robbery, prosecutors decide not to proceed in one out of every 2,500 cases. Studies of felony court records in other states reach similar conclusions. Only 0.4 percent of all cases that federal prosecutors decide not to prosecute are rejected because of search problems. At the trial level, motions to suppress illegally seized evidence are rarely granted in cases of violent crime. If the exclusionary rule were abolished, the conviction rate in all felony cases would increase by less than half of one percent. Translated into absolute figures, however, thousands of accused felons are released nationally as a result of the exclusionary rule, most of them in drug and weapons possession cases. Street crime does not flourish, though, because of the exclusionary rule, even though it does protect criminals, as do all constitutional rights. They also protect society and help keep us free.

The rule's effectiveness in deterring illegal searches is hotly debated. The critics point out that some ninety percent of criminal prosecutions do not go to trial but are disposed of by pleas of "guilty." (The figure varies from state to state, and according to the nature of the crime.) Without a trial, there is no evidence for the rule to exclude. In the huge number of cases in which the police make arrests but the persons arrested are not prosecuted, the exclusionary rule has, of course, no immediate application. The rule's proponents reply that the decision whether to prosecute or accept a defendant's "guilty" pleas on a lesser offense may itself be influenced by the prosecutor's estimate of the potential operation of the exclusionary rule if the case should go to trial. (In jurisdictions where separate procedures are established to rule on motions to suppress evidence, the rule normally will have operated in advance of the trial.)

Undeniably, however, the exclusionary rule has no application at all to the cases that cry out most for a remedy: cases of police misconduct against innocent persons, who are never even brought to the prosecutors' attention, and cases of illegal searches and seizures made for purposes other than collecting evidence to support prosecutions. In *Terry v. Ohio* (1968) Chief Justice Earl Warren admitted: "Regardless how effective the rule may be where obtaining conviction is an important objective of the police, it is powerless to deter invasions of constitutionally guaranteed rights where the police either have no interest in prosecuting or are willing to forego successful prosecution in the interest of serving some other goal." The police may deliberately engage in illegal searches and seizures for a number of reasons: to control crimes such as gambling or prostitution; to confiscate weapons or contraband or stolen property; or to maintain high visibility either to deter crime or to satisfy a public clamoring for aggressive police action. In none of these cases will the exclusionary rule inhibit police violations of the Bill of Rights.

The rule does not in fact significantly impede the police, despite contentions from the rule's opponents that it handcuffs the police. A 1984 report prepared for the National Center for State Courts concluded that a properly administered search warrant process can protect constitutional rights without hampering effective law enforcement. Nevertheless, police try when possible to conduct search and seizure under some exception to the warrant requirement. The overwhelming number of searches and seizures are warrantless. In 1980, for example, only about 1,000 warrants were issued in Los Angeles in about 300,000 cases. Police usually try to make consent searches or searches under what they claim to be exigent circumstances, or they conduct a search to confiscate contraband or harass criminals, without attempting a prosecution. In the few cases in which they seek warrants, they get them almost as if magistrates rubber-stamp their applications, and almost all warrants survive in court despite motions to suppress. Motions to suppress are made in about five percent of all cases but are successful in only less than one percent of all cases. Still more important is the fact that only slightly over half of one percent of all cases result in acquittals because of the exclusion of evidence.

Even when the rule does operate to exclude evidence in a criminal trial, it has no direct, personal effect on the police officer whose misconduct caused the rule to be invoked. The rule does not require discipline to be imposed by the officer's superiors, nor does either civil or criminal responsibility follow as a matter of course. Police officers are prosecuted only extremely rarely for their official misdeeds. Suits for damages by victims are inhibited not only by the defense of good faith and probable cause but also by the realization that most officers are neither wealthy nor insured against liability for their official acts. Unsurprisingly, most victims conclude that a lawsuit is not worth its trouble and expense. In the typical case of an illegal search, neither the judge who excludes the fruits of the search from evidence nor the prosecutor whose case is thereby undermined will explain to the officer the error of his ways. The intended educational effect of judicial decisions is also diminished by the time-lag between the police action and its final evaluation by the courts. Even if an officer should hear that a court has excluded the evidence he found in an illegal search some months ago, he will probably have forgotten the details of the event. Incentives and sanctions that might influence the officer's future behavior are not within the exclusionary rule's contemplation. On the other hand, advocates of the rule emphasize that it is meant to have an institutional or systemic effect on law enforcement agencies generally, not necessarily on particular officers.

The officer is apt to respond not to judicial decisions (which he may regard as unrealistic if they impede his work) but to departmental policies and the approval of his colleagues and superiors. One whose main job is the apprehension of criminals and the deterrence of crime will have a low tolerance for what he sees as procedural niceties. He may even shade the truth in making out a report on a search or when testifying in court. It is not unheard of for the police to arrange to make a valid arrest at a place where they can conduct a warrantless search incident to the arrest, and thus evade the requirement of a search warrant based on probable cause to believe that evidence of crime is in that place. To the extent that the courts have used the exclusionary rule to educate the police, then, the main things learned seem to have been the techniques for evading the rule. Summarizing the criticisms of the exclusionary rule, Dallin H. Oaks has said:

> The harshest criticism of the rule is that it is ineffective. It is the sole means of enforcing the essential guarantees of freedom from unreasonable arrests and searches and seizures by law enforcement officers, and it is a failure in that vital task.
>
> The use of the exclusionary rule imposes excessive costs on the criminal justice system. It provides no recompense for the innocent and it frees the guilty. It creates the occasion and incentive for large-scale lying by law enforcement officers. It diverts the focus on the criminal prosecution from the guilt or innocence of the defendant to a trial of the police. Only a system with limitless patience with irrationality could tolerate the fact that where there has been one wrong, the defendant's, he will be punished, but where there have been two wrongs, the defendant's and the officer's, both will go free. This would not be an excessive cost for an effective remedy against police misconduct, but it is a prohibitive price to pay for an illusory one.

Despite the severity of criticisms, the exclusionary rule's chief critics have not proposed its total abolition. However, the Supreme Court has limited the rule's application in significant ways. Thus, for the most part, only the victim of an illegal search has standing to claim the benefits of the exclusionary rule; if A's house is searched in violation of the Fourth Amendment, and evidence is found incriminating B, the evidence can be used in B's trial. (State courts are free to extend the exclusionary rule to such cases; some state courts have done so, concluding that the point of the rule is not to protect people against being convicted but to deter the police.) Similarly, in *United States v. Calandria* (1974) the Court held that illegally obtained evidence is admissible in grand jury proceedings, and it ruled in *Harris v. New York* (1971) that it can be used for the purpose of impeaching the testimony of the accused at his trial. Some uses of illegally obtained evidence have been tolerated as harmless error. More important, the good faith exception to the exclusionary rule allows the use of evidence obtained with a search warrant if the police reasonably believed the warrant to be valid, even though it later proves to be illegal. The rule has also been held inapplicable to collateral proceedings for postconviction relief such as habeas corpus. The Court's opinions in these cases have repeated the familiar criticisms of the exclusionary rule; their logic would seem to suggest abandonment of the rule altogether.

Yet the exclusionary rule remains, largely because no one has yet suggested an effective alternative means for enforcing the Bill of Rights against police misconduct. A federal statute dating from Reconstruction authorizes the award of damages against state or local officials (including police officers) who violate individuals' constitutional rights. In 1971, the Supreme Court found that the Fourth Amendment itself implicitly authorized similar damages awards against federal officers who violated the Amendment. The future effectiveness of such remedies will depend in part on the Supreme Court itself, as it spells out the victim's burden of proof in these cases and the measure of damages. Partly, however, the civil-damages alternative depends for its effectiveness on legislation to provide for real compensation to victims when the police officers are judgment-proof, and for real punishment of officers for constitutional violations when the payment of damages is unrealistic.

Meanwhile, the Supreme Court has only the exclusionary rule, which everyone agrees is an imperfect deterrent to police misbehavior. The rule survives, then, for want of better alternatives. But it also stands as a symbol that government itself is not above the law.

Bibliography

LaFave, Wayne R. 1978 *Search and Seizure: A Treatise on the Fourth Amendment*, 3 vols. St. Paul: West Publishing Co.

Oaks, Dallin H. 1970 Studying the Exclusionary Rule. *University of Chicago Law Review* 37:665–757.

Schroeder, William 1981 Deterring Fourth Amendment Violations: Alternatives to the Exclusionary Rule. *Georgetown Law Review* 68:1361–1426.

Stewart, Potter 1983 The Road to *Mapp v. Ohio* and Beyond: The Origins, Development and Future of the Exclusionary Rule in Search-and-Seizure Cases. *Columbia Law Review* 83:1365–1404.

11

Establishment of the
Fifth Amendment Right

The right against self-incrimination was but shakily or unevenly established in America by the close of the seventeenth century. But a perceptible change was occurring in the legal development of all the colonies: the English common law was increasingly becoming American law. The degree to which that was true varied from colony to colony, and the pace was not the same in each. But in all, as their political and economic systems matured, their legal systems, most strikingly in the field of criminal procedure, began more and more to resemble that of England. The consequence was a greater familiarity with and respect for the right against self-incrimination.

In the eighteenth century the legal profession, which in the early years of every colony was virtually nonexistent and distrusted, rapidly grew in size, competence, social status, and political power. The rise of a substantial propertied class and the growing complexity and prosperity of colonial business required the services of a trained legal profession; the colonial governments also found an increasing need for the special skills of lawyers, both on and off the bench. Although lay judges still dominated the colonial bench at the time of the American Revolution, they increasingly included men who, though self-educated in the law, were highly knowledgeable and respectful of professional standards. Bench and bar resorted more and more to English law and English procedure as their guide. The complex, highly technical common-law system required well-trained lawyers to administer it, and they looked to Westminster, to the English law reports and legal treatises, for their rules and even for their training. There were more and

more Americans educated at the Inns of Court with each passing decade, about sixty before 1760, triple that number by 1776. They became the leaders and teachers of the American bar and had a prodigious effect in making American law imitative of the English, by
making English cases and English legal treatises the measure of competence, the fount of inspiration, and the precedent for emulation.
Although law books, especially in the seventeenth century, had been
in short supply in the colonies, there were always enough to provide
instruction, especially in matters of criminal law and procedure. Michael
Dalton's *Countrey Justice* was the universal handbook. It was one of
the books, along with Coke's works, ordered by the General Court of
Massachusetts in 1647 "to the end that we may have better light for
making & proceeding about laws." Rhode Island relied heavily on
Dalton in framing her criminal code in 1647; Maryland in 1678 required that all her judges keep copies of Dalton at hand, and in 1723
added Hawkins's *Pleas of the Crown* and Nelson's *Justice of the Peace*
to the required list. In Virginia, where the assembly also prescribed
Dalton for the courts, gentlemen increasingly read law books as part
of their general education. A seventeenth-century Virginia lawyer named
Arthur Spicer had a private library of fifty-two law books. In the
eighteenth century the supply of law books became more and more
plentiful as their importation increased and as American printers took
to issuing local editions.[1]

The experience of New York is a good indication of the trend of the
time. Beginning in 1683 the criminal law of New York became an
extremely sophisticated duplication of the "practices and forms of the
English central courts." From the beginning of the eighteenth century,
according to Goebel and Naughton, New York's criminal courts were
peopled by men with excellent legal training who conducted their
work as skillfully as their counterparts in England. Because their "intellectual home . . . centered in the dingy streets about the Inns of Court,
they read and cited what lawyers did at home." They prized English
law books, "because it was from English precedent that provincial law
was built." The standard of practice in the highest court of the colony
became "really comparable" with that in King's Bench, while the
inferior criminal jurisdiction was "administered in much the same way
as . . . in English Quarter Sessions." Goebel and Naughton also said,
with reference to the "malignant ferocity" of the judges, "If the case of
Penn and Mead at Old Bailey was typical the proceedings were exactly similar," and presumably, therefore, they illustrate the sessions

trials in colonial New York. It is to the point then, to repeat that at that trial, Mead, on being asked an incriminating question, replied: "It is a maxim in your own law, 'Nemo tenetur accusare seipsum,' which if it be not true Latin, I am sure it is true English, 'That no man is bound to accuse himself.' And why dost thou offer to insnare me with such a question?" "Sir, hold your tongue," replied the judge, "I did not go about to insnare you, and he dropped the question.[2]

Goebel and Naughton heavily stressed the influence of English law books on the development of New York law generally and that colony's criminal procedure in particular. They pointed out that James Alexander, William Smith, Joseph Murray, John Tabor Kempe, and other New York attorneys "collected every [law] book they could lay their hands on" and subscribed to new ones as they were published. Alexander's collection of 152 law books as of 1721 was probably the largest in the colonies at the time, and he generously loaned them, making his, in effect, the first circulating library in New York. William Smith's library in 1770 contained three times as many law titles as Alexander had had. "No one," says Goebel and Naughton, "who has examined the memoranda and citations of any first-rate New York lawyer of the 1730's can doubt the general availability or spread of these sources or the competency to use them." For nearly everything done in the New York Supreme Court, precedent could be found in Hawkins's *Pleas of the Crown,* while the New York City Sessions Court trod "as closely as it may the path of the superior court," and the local justices of the peace found some manual like Dalton or Nelson to be the magistrate's vade mecum. Because the "patterns of practice were cut after the designs of Hawkins, Hale, and the *Crown Circuit Companion,"* defiance of these tutelary geniuses was "exceptional." "The course of the typical criminal trial in New York during the eighteenth century," Goebel and Naughton concluded, "can be plotted with the Office of the Clerk of Assize or the *Crown Circuit Companion* in one hand and with Hawkins' *Pleas of the Crown* in the other. . . . "[3]

In view of the fact that the right against self-incrimination had by then become entrenched and respected in England, its existence in New York and in the other colonies should be expected, its absence would be an astonishing departure from the general reception of the common law's accusatorial system of criminal procedure. Because England provided the model, English history, English law books, and English criminal practice are at the source of any understanding of the right in New York and the other colonies. And since the colonial bar so avidly followed the English treatises and precedents, Goebel and Naughton would be justified in concluding that a strong prima facie case against the existence of the right could be constructed if it were passed over in those books and cases. As noted earlier, Goebel and Naughton unequivocally stated that the right was unknown in colonial New York. And they added that, "It is obviously idle to imagine that a 'principle' which even Baron Gilbert forbears to mention, should have been cosseted in our own courts."[4]

The existence of the right against self-incrimination in English case law, especially that of the central courts at Westminster, has already been established in earlier chapters. That the right was scarcely unnoticed by English law writers might be taken for granted had not a distinctly contrary impression been spread by such impressive authority as the authors of *Law Enforcement in Colonial New York*. Baron Gilbert, as a matter of fact, by no means forbore to mention the "principle," nor was it ignored by other writers or in the law books that were relied upon by the colonial lawyers of New York or of the other colonies.[5]

Geoffrey Gilbert's *Law of Evidence,* published in 1756, was, as Goebel and Naughton say, the first work on the subject with any analytic merit. Gilbert, whose words have been fully quoted earlier, observed that while a confession was the best evidence of guilt, it must be voluntarily made because "our Law . . . will not force any Man to accuse himself; and in this we do certainly follow the Law of Nature. . . . " Gilbert's statement of the right against compulsory self-incrimination reflected the age-old English phrasing which, by his time, required no explanation. His *Law of Evidence* was used in New York even before it was published in England. On February 5, 1753, William Smith, Jr., one of the luminaries of the New York bar, received from John McEvers, a fellow attorney, a manuscript volume "supposed to be done by Baron Gilbert." Smith copied 173 pages of the manuscript, including the passage against self-accusing, and in the margin later wrote, "Note this book is now printed under title Law of Evidence in 8 vo. 1 June 1756." Smith, by the way, not only knew of the right from many sources, in addition to Gilbert, but as an historian, councilor, and lawyer, he respected the right.[6]

Gilbert's book has been singled out for special consideration only because its alleged silence on the subject has been offered by Goebel and Naughton as proof that the right was not even known in New

York's English-minded courts. Yet almost any law book that touched criminal law might be used to prove that information about the right was available to the colonists. In the most widely used English law dictionary of the eighteenth century, written by Giles Jacob, the broad proposition is stated under "Evidence" that "the witness shall not be asked any Question to accuse himself." Jacob cited Coke's *Institutes,* Hobbes's *Leviathan,* and the *State Trials* as his authorities. He restated the proposition in his popular guidebook, *Every Man His Own Lawyer,* the seventh edition of which was published in New York in 1768. In a political tract described by Clinton Rossiter as "the most popular statement of English rights during the second half of the colonial period," Henry Care condemned Star Chamber practice as contrary to all law and reason, "For No Man is bound to accuse himself." In *The Security of Englishmen's Lives,* a popular treatise on grand juries, John Somers, the Lord Chancellor of England, declared that it was lawful for witnesses before grand juries "to refuse to give Answer to some Demands which the Jury make; as where it would be to accuse themselves of Crimes." These seventeenth-century books by Care and Somers were reprinted in eighteenth-century America, each for the second time on the eve of the American Revolution.[7]

In Dalton's celebrated *Countrey Justice* the reason given to explain why the offender should not be examined under oath is that "by the Common Law, Nullus tenetur seipsum prodere." In a book on the same subject by William Nelson, also described by Goebel and Naughton as the magistrate's vade mecum, the same maxim was expressed in slightly different Latin, *"Nemo debet seipsum accusare."* The identical phrase appeared in what was probably the most widely used American manual for justices of the peace, *Conductor Generalis,* attributed to James Parker, a New Jersey justice of the peace. His book went through sixteen American editions in the eighteenth century, including eight in New York, in most of which he also stated "a general rule, that a witness shall not be asked any question, the answering of which might oblige him to accuse himself of a crime. . . . " Other manuals repeated the same words. They were identical to those used in the classic *Pleas of the Crown* by Sergeant William Hawkins, first published in 1716. William Nelson's volume on *The Law of Evidence,* published in 1735, included the rule that "a witness ought not to be examined where his evidence tends either to clear or accuse himself of a crime."

Even the works of the libertarian Continental jurists, Jean Jacques Burlamaqui and Samuel von Pufendorf, who were read in America not only by lawyers but by political theorists from John Wise to John Adams, contained the principle that a criminally accused person is under no obligation to expose himself to punishment by answering incriminating interrogatories. Pufendorf even concluded that "no Man is bound to accuse himself" in civil as well as criminal cases. While he approved of putting a defendant to his oath, a practice condemned in English law, he observed that oaths should not be administered if the consequences of confessing the truth entailed capital punishment, "any grievous inconvenience," an offense to conscience, or "very considerable Damage."[8]

Edmond Wingate's *Maxims of Reason* of 1658, which included the earliest discussion under the heading "Nemo tenetur accusare seipsum," was in the libraries of such eminent New York lawyers as James Alexander, Joseph Murray, and William Smith, who also read Pufendorf and Burlamaqui. From Wingate to William Blackstone's *Commentaries,* the principle of the right against self-incrimination was recognized by the English law writers as well as by the English courts. The logic of Goebel and Naughton leads us, therefore, to expect its recognition by the bench and bar of the colonies, especially in New York. The right was in fact so recognized, if not "cosseted" or pampered.[9]

The evidence for its recognition in the colonies is not abundant for the trial records, unfortunately, prove little. As Goebel and Naughton state, only a few trials were reported and those "execrably" so; the judgment rolls and *posteas* "are nearly always silent on what was said or proffered at trial, and the judicial minutes at best ordinarily furnish only a list of documents or the names of those who testified." Because "statements respecting testimony are rarely to be found in minutes of the provincial courts or the records of trials," a generalization based on trial records about the nonexistence of the right against self-incrimination in New York or elsewhere in the colonies, should be regarded as suspect. Historians who "cleave to a scintilla of evidence theory" are properly reprimanded by Goebel and Naughton: they disapprove of those who take a proposition as proven with the minimum of citation who base a rule on a single case, or refer to statutes only when stating a judicial practice. "This is the way of advocacy, not of scholarship. . . . The ends of legal history are not served by the mere establishment of a prima facie case."[10]

The injunction, a sound one, has not been observed by Goebel and Naughton in their discussion of the right against self-incrimination. By way of proving the nonexistence of that right, they cite the case of a man who was incriminatingly questioned at his trial about the contradictory confessions he had made in his preliminary examination. "This case of course concerned a slave [one of the defendants in the Negro Plot to burn the city in 1742], but we have not noticed any special tenderness of white persons charged with felony, and it is not unlikely that similar tactics were used against them. There are numerous cases where the minutes reveal the reading at trial of a prisoner's confession." The passage illustrates the "scintilla of evidence theory" in practice and a badly mistaken assumption that the right against self-incrimination is nonexistent in a jurisdiction that accepts in evidence the confession of the accused. Never in history has the existence of the right placed the state under an obligation to prevent a person from incriminating himself.[11]

The fact must be emphasized that the right in question was a right against *compulsory* self-incrimination, and, excepting rare occasions when judges intervened to protect a witness against incriminating interrogatories, the right had to be claimed by the defendant. Historically it has been a fighting right: unless invoked, it offered no protection. It vested an option to refuse answer but did not bar interrogation nor taint a voluntary confession as improper evidence. Incriminating statements made by a suspect at the preliminary examination or even at arraignment could always be used with devastating effect at his trial. That a man might unwittingly incriminate himself when questioned in no way impaired his legal right to refuse answer. He lacked the right to be warned that he need not answer, for the authorities were under no legal obligation to apprise him of his right. That reform did not come in England until Sir John Jervis's Act in 1848, and in the United States more than a century later the matter was still a subject of acute constitutional controversy. Yet if the authorities in eighteenth century Britain and in her colonies were not obliged to caution the prisoner, he in turn was not legally obliged to reply. His answers, although given in ignorance of his right, might secure his conviction, but by the mid-eighteenth century the courts, at least at Westminster, were willing to consider the exclusion of confessions that had been made involuntarily or under duress. The lawyers of the colonies, familiar with Gilbert's *Law of Evidence,* knew that a coerced confession was not to be trusted.[12]

After the first quarter of the eighteenth century, the history of the right in formal common-law proceedings centered upon the preliminary examination of the suspect, the legality of placing in evidence various types of forced confessions, the rights of witnesses, and the disadvantaged position of the felony defendant. He was, to be sure, excluded from the stand in the sense that he was not permitted to give testimony even if he wanted to. His interest in the case disqualified him on the theory that his evidence was unreliable. He was, nevertheless, permitted to tell his story unsworn at least in a final statement to the court. Deprived of counsel in many of the colonies, he was forced to conduct his own defense and, as a result, was vulnerable to comments and questions from the prosecution and the bench. This, at least, was the situation of the felony defendant in New York and several of the other colonies that followed English practice closely. Eighteenth century England permitted counsel to the felony defendant only at the discretion of the trial judge and usually on points of law only. The accused could make his case through witnesses whom he could subpoena and put under oath, although there is some evidence that even in usually imitative New York, witnesses for the defense were not always sworn. Deprived of counsel, however, the felony defendant was left exposed to insinuations or charges that he had to rebut or else he risked the suspicion of the jury. Yet even the right against self-incrimination has always been exercised at the same risk.[13]

In some colonies—Rhode Island after 1664, New Hampshire after 1696, Pennsylvania, Massachusetts, and Delaware after 1701, South Carolina after 1731, and Virginia after 1734—practice was well in advance of England's, because counsel was permitted even in felony cases; in misdemeanor and treason cases the right to counsel was universal in England and America. The defendant who could afford counsel to conduct his defense, who had witnesses to testify for him, and who was not himself permitted to testify, was well insulated against the possibility of incriminating himself after the preliminary hearing. In the seven colonies where the right to counsel was provided even in felony cases, the right against self-incrimination was well secured in common-law trials. It bears reiteration, however, that in all the colonies, New York included, the mere fact that neither the examining magistrate nor the trial judge were required to inform the prisoner that he could lawfully remain silent in the face of incriminating questions does not prove the nonexistence of the right against self-incrimination.

Nor does the fact that there were in New York "occasional" instances, as late as the Revolution, of the ancient practice of questioning the defendant upon his arraignment in order to secure his submission. The "scintilla of evidence theory," abhorred by Goebel and Naughton, is clearly adopted by them in the proposition that the general indifference "to any privilege of self-incrimination probably embraced witnesses generally although we have found but one case." That case may be but the exception to the rule expressed in the English law books and precedents so dear to the hearts of New York's lawyers and judges.[14]

Given the facts—that so few trials were reported, that they were reported very incompletely and rarely included testimony, and that the accused was not permitted to give formal testimony—it is not at all surprising that a scrutiny of the records of the courts that employed common-law procedures yields so little data about the emergence or existence of the right against self-incrimination. The right had arisen in England as a shield against inquisitions by prerogative courts into crimes that were essentially political and religious in nature. The investigations of the governor and council, even of the legislature—bodies that tended to employ inquisitorial procedures—might be expected to produce protests that would reveal, at the very least, knowledge of the right against self-incrimination and refusals to answer based on that right. There is something symbolic in the fact that the first glimmer of the right in America is seen in Wheelwright's case, tried in 1637 by the legislature of Massachusetts sitting in its judicial capacity, but not using common-law procedures. Even in New York itself under the Dutch, in 1661, when Townshend and Spicer refused to incriminate themselves, their judges were the governor and council. So too in the Bradford-Growden case in Pennsylvania, in the Maule case in Massachusetts, and in the Lawrence case in Maryland, all in the closing years of the seventeenth century, the accused parties invoked the right in proceedings before the governor and council. That the right first became an issue in New York under English rule as a result of the inquisitorial tactics of the same prerogative court, in a case of 1698 heavy with political implications, fits a revealing pattern.

The issue arose as a result of the Earl of Bellomont's investigation into the administration of his predecessor, Governor Benjamin Fletcher. Assemblyman Henry Beekman (or Beckman) was a victim of Bellomont's effort to discredit Fletcher. Beekman, who had been close to Fletcher, was instrumental in having secured the passage of the Bolting Act of 1694 by which New York City lost its monopoly of the bolting and packing of flour. In 1698 governor and council summoned Beekman to be examined on his connection with the charge that the approval of the act by Fletcher and certain councilors had been purchased. Instructed to answer questions under oath, Beekman refused. Threatening to imprison him "without baile or mainprize" should he persist in his contemptuous refusal to take his oath without giving a "lawful" reason, the council finally "persuaded" Beekman to swear and answer the questions. That Beekman's case was not exceptional is evident from the accusations filed with the Board of Trade in London by John Key, the London correspondent of the New York merchants. Key complained that Bellomont "has tendred extrajudicial oaths to severall of His Majtys Subjects requiring them to make answer to such questions he should ask them, and upon their refusall to swear has threatned to committ them into custody." In one case he imprisoned two merchants, accused of having "farmed the excise," for refusing to "discover upon oath what profits they had made by that farme. . . ." Counsel for these merchants denounced the oath as "illegal and arbitrary . . . a great Instance of Infringement of English liberties." Bellomont's treatment of Beekman did not go unnoticed either.[15]

The merchants of New York understandably objected to testifying against themselves, particularly when they suspected that political motives were behind the governor's inquisition. Nicholas Bayard, one of Fletcher's most intimate associates who had been ousted from the council by Bellomont, complained in London to the Board of Trade about the governor's administration. He cited Bellomont's "undue method of forcing witnesses to swear, and instanced in his requiring Colonel Beckman . . . to make oath to answer whatever should be asked him (tho' he were himself concerned in the business of that Enquiry) with threats to send him to Gaol in case he refus'd." Bayard's protest, in other words, was that Beekman had been forced to incriminate himself.[16]

Thomas Weaver, a barrister-at-law of Inner Temple who was the governor's agent in London, defended Bellomont before the Board of Trade. In rebutting Bayard's accusation, Weaver made the significant point that both he and the attorney-general of the province agreed that "Beckman was obliged (as any man might be, especially in matters of state or other high concernment) to give evidence in what did not *concerne himself criminally* (which was all required of him)." Thus Weaver, who later became attorney-general, and James Graham, Bellomont's attorney-general, explicitly acknowledged that a man might not be forced to testify against himself in a criminal matter, not even by the governor and council.[17]

In 1702 William Atwood, the Chief Justice of New York, and Samuel Shelton Broughton, the new attorney-general, also acknowledged the right in connection with the sensational treason trial of Bayard and Hutchins. The death of Bellomont had kindled Bayard's hope of returning to power against the Leislerians who controlled the government. To ingratiate himself with the new governor, Lord Cornbury, Bayard drew up addresses accusing Lieutenant-Governor John Nanfan, Chief Justice Atwood, and members of the council, of nefarious actions ranging from bribery to oppression. Nanfan retaliated by arresting Bayard on a charge of treason under a statute of 1691 loosely drawn by Bayard himself against Leisler's followers. It provided that anyone who by arms "or otherwise" endeavored to "disturb the peace" should be deemed a traitor. For a crime which at worst was a mere misdemeanor, a seditious libel, Bayard in 1702 found himself on trial for his life, along with his confederate Alderman John Hutchins. From indictment to conviction the case was a travesty of common-law procedure, a fact which saved the prisoners' heads, for their conviction was condemned as illegal on appeal to the Privy Council.[18]

In the initial stage of the case, Nanfan and the council employed inquisitorial tactics to gather evidence about the addresses. Several suspects refused to produce copies on demand. The council, after receiving a legal opinion from Attorney-General Broughton, decided to prosecute them for contempt. Broughton believed that because the addresses "were not criminal or illegal," the suspects could be forced to produce copies without incriminating themselves. Although the council thought the addresses criminal, it sought to incriminate only the authors, not those examined to betray them. Bayard, his son, and Hutchins were shortly arrested. Bayard, complaining to friends in England, noted that Hutchins had been jailed for treason, without bail, until he produced copies of the addresses which the council "were pleased to call Libells." After the conviction of the defendants, Bayard's friends petitioned the Board of Trade and charged that an attempt had been made to force Hutchins to incriminate himself in a criminal matter. Sir Edward Northey, Attorney-General of England, informed the Board of Trade that "it appears by the warrant for committing Hutchins that the Council required him to produce a libell he is charged to be author of *which was to accuse himself* and his refusal to produce it is alleged as part of his Crime." The Privy Council ruled that the convictions were illegal and ordered the annulment of the sentences.[19]

Chief Justice Atwood in an attempt to defend his conduct in the case, sought to justify the requirement of the provincial council that Hutchins produce the addresses. Although Atwood's statement of the facts differs from Bayard's, the significant point of his apologia is his denial that Hutchins had been forced to incriminate himself: "But since he was not committed for High Treason, as he might have been, and there wanted no Evidence against him; this, surely, may answer the Objection against requiring him to produce Papers which might tend to accuse himself." The right against self-incrimination may have been honored in New York in name only, but the highest officials of the colony vied with each other in denying that they had abridged it.[20]

In 1707, at the trial of Francis Makemie, a Presbyterian minister charged with preaching without a license, the defendant voluntarily, indeed, eagerly, answered all questions, however technically incriminating. His successful defense was based on the rights of conscience as protected by the Act of Toleration. In the contemporary account of his trial, which Makemie himself probably wrote, there is a heated passage against Governor Cornbury's attempt to induce Makemie's friends to incriminate each other, though not themselves. Several men were examined under oath "to discover what Discourse they had with sundry of their friends." The author of the account rages that "the practice is not to be outdone, yea, scarce parallelled by *Spanish Inquisition;* for no men are safe in their most private Conversations, if most intimate Friends can be compelled upon Oath, to betray one anothers Secrets. If this is agreeable to English Constitution and Priviledges, I confess, we have been hitherto in the Dark." It is not likely that the author would have regarded involuntary self-accusing in a better light.[21]

The right against self-incrimination next became an issue in New York politics as a result of merchant protest against Governor William Burnet's efforts to outlaw the fur trade between Albany and Quebec. When a prohibitory act of 1720 proved unenforceable because of the sheriff's inability to supervise the frontier, the legislature adopted an amendment in 1722 authorizing civil and military officers to exact from any suspected persons an oath of purgation that they had not in any way traded with the French. Refusal to take the oath automatically convicted one of the crime of illicitly trading, the penalty for which was a one hundred pound fine. The statute certainly compelled the guilty to incriminate themselves, a fact that its opponents used as the basis of their objections to the Board of Trade.[22]

Stephen DeLancey, Adolph Philipse, and Peter Schuyler cared little about abstract principle, but they recognized a good issue with which to mask their interest in the fur trade. John Sharpe, their London agent, argued that the statute of 1722 was illegal because the party suspected "was by a very extraordinary Oath, made liable either to accuse himself or to suffer very great penalties." A fur trader, John Peloquin, giving evidence at the hearing, mentioned that he had bought skins from the French and was asked when he had done so. Sharpe interposed to say that Peloquin's "answering that Question might be of ill consequences to himself, if it were since the passing of the said acts; & said he believ'd their Lordships did not expect Mr. Peloquin should accuse himself." Their Lordships changed the subject. Subsequently they recommended to the Privy Council that Governor Burnet be urged to halt the undesirable trade by other methods. The Board specified its objections: "There is an Oath impos'd upon all Traders whereby they are obliged to accuse themselves or else to be under the greatest temptation to perjury." New York enacted a new statute regulating the fur trade by a tax device. The oath was conspicuously absent from its provisions.[23]

On the other hand, the purgative oath that in effect compelled self-incrimination was a frequent feature of New York legislation during the colonial period. The right against self-incrimination was indeed an illusion, as Goebel and Naughton declared, under the acts of the Assembly from 1701 to 1759. The first act employing the oath of purgation, with a proviso that those refusing to take it should be subject to double the normal penalties imposed on the guilty, was intended to detect and deter evasion of the militia laws. Legislation of this kind was used against those suspected of selling liquor to the Indians, exporting specie, taking seamen's notes for liquor or food, entertaining slaves, stealing furs from Indians, selling liquor to servants, failing to report imported copper money, trading with the Iroquois for certain articles, and giving credit to servants. In all these cases, the statutes fixed criminal penalties for the refusal of a suspect to take the oath of purgation. Some declared that such a refusal automatically established guilt for the crime suspected; others provided for special fines and/or imprisonment. The purgative oath, like the oath *ex officio* of an earlier time, was a noose for the guilty: the mere requirement of it insured conviction for perjury, or contempt, or the crime suspected. Even the innocent could suffer, particularly conscientious objectors. However, the purgative oath was authorized by the legislature only once after 1759 and passed into disuse before the outbreak of the Revolution. The ever-increasing professionalization of the bar, the growing familiarity with "the liberty of the subject" and English rights, and the protests against self-accusing all contributed to the respectability of the right against incriminating oneself. William Smith, Jr., who had copied the passage against self-incrimination from the manuscript of Baron Gilbert's book on evidence, reflected the new spirit. A book of his own, published in 1757, contained a scathing passage against oaths of purgation. Recalling that the assembly had tendered such an oath to Robert Livingston in 1701, Smith wrote, "Mr. Livingston, who was better acquainted with English law and liberty than to countenance a practice so odious, rejected the insolent demand with disdain. . . . "[24]

The developing recognition of the right against self-incrimination in New York had its parallels elsewhere. In 1735 there was a sensational case in Pennsylvania that was unusual for that late date and place. The case involved an ecclesiastical inquiry into heresy, bringing Benjamin Franklin to the defense of the right. A special commission of the Presbyterian synod of Philadelphia examined the unorthodox beliefs of Samuel Hemphill, a Presbyterian minister with deistic notions. Franklin enjoyed his sermons largely because he preached good citizenship rather than good Presbyterianism. The commission of inquiry, however, unanimously censuring Hemphill's doctrines as "Unsound and Dangerous," suspended him from his ministry. Franklin, in an angry pamphlet which quickly sold out, reported that Hemphill had refused to submit his sermons to the commission, because "It was contrary to the common Rights of Mankind, no Man being obliged to furnish Matter of Accusation against himself." The commission, though acknowledging that it had no right to compel delivery of the sermons, had taken Hemphill's refusal as a virtual confession of guilt, provoking Franklin to denounce the commission still further. Hemphill finally decided to read his sermons to the commission, yet succeeded only in proving to its members that their worst suspicions were well founded. Bitingly, Franklin observed: "And here I am sorry, that I am obliged to say, that they have no Pattern for their Proceedings, but that hellish Tribunal the *Inquisition,* who rake up all the vile Evidences, and extort all the Confessions they can from the wretched Object of their Rage . . . and proceed to Judgment."

A defender of the synod's commission, responding to Franklin, vindicated its position that Hemphill's claim of a right not to accuse himself was "but a tacit Acknowledgement of his Guilt." Franklin, in what had become a pamphlet war—he wrote three popular tracts on the controversy—replied on the theme that Hemphill "was in the right to do so [that is, to claim the right against self-incrimination], since the . . . Commission was determin'd to find Heresy enough . . . to condemn him. . . . " Although Hemphill finally lost his case, it had provoked a public debate that educated the province on both the right against self-incrimination and freedom of religion, with which it was so closely allied in its origins.[25]

The best evidence that the right was honored in Pennsylvania derives from the conduct of the provincial Assembly. In 1756, for example, in an election-frauds case investigated by that body, counsel asked several questions of a witness who was being examined under oath. The questions, say the Assembly records, "were thought to have a Tendency to make him criminate himself. . . . " On an objection that he ought not be obliged to answer such questions, the Assembly, after debate, resolved: "That no Questions be asked the Witnesses of either Side, which may tend to make them criminate themselves; and that therfore all Questions shall be first proposed to Mr. Speaker, who is to put such of them as he judges not to have that Tendency."[26]

Two years later the same legislature conducted a drumhead trial of two leading Anglicans, William Moore, the chief judge of the Court of Common Pleas for Chester County, and William Smith, the president of the provincial college. Both men had publicly criticized the phlegmatic prosecution of the war against the French and Indians. The Quaker-dominated Assembly retaliated by publishing an address to the governor demanding Moore's removal from office on ground that he was corrupt and oppressive. Moore replied in print and with Smith's help published his self-defense in a German-language newspaper. The Assembly, deeming the publication to be a seditious reflection upon its honor, arrested and convicted both men in a proceeding that was about as fair as the trial of the Knave of Hearts for stealing the tarts in Wonderland. Moore, on being shown the manuscript of the libelous publication, written in his own hand and signed by him, incriminated himself by confessing his authorship, but refused to answer other questions on ground that the legislature had no competence to try him. Smith also faced incriminating questions, yet they were but trivial matters in his ordeal; for the House virtually convicted him before trial by adopting special rules that stripped him of every defense he might make to the charge of abetting a libel. Neither Smith nor Moore invoked the right against self-incrimination, making idle any speculation whether the House, which acted as if unaware of British justice, would have sought to compel their answers or honor the right.[27]

Hostile witnesses nevertheless received fair, if not considerate, treatment. Dr. Phineas Bond, a close friend of Judge Moore, on being asked to give whatever information he possessed about the seditious libel, evaded direct answer. The Assembly, surmising that he might be implicated, assured him that they would provide "the utmost Lenity in their Manner of taking his Evidence, and should ask him no Questions which had any Tendency to criminate that Gentleman [Moore], or himself, but only a third Person [Smith], to whom he was not publicly known to be under any Obligations." Asked whether Smith had assisted in the composition of Moore's address, Bond persisted in his refusal to answer. The Assembly then arrested him, but before acting further, formally resolved to grant him complete immunity against prosecution for any testimony that he might offer. Bond, nevertheless, continued his obstinate refusal to give evidence, though he could not incriminate himself. The Assembly therefore judged his refusal to be "an high Contempt" and imprisoned him until he relented. After a few hours behind bars, Bond's courage evaporated and he consented to giving damaging testimony in violation of "the Ties of Honour and Friendship." In a similar manner the Assembly exacted the testimony of Anthony Armbruster, the printer of the German-language newspaper.[28]

Whatever one thinks of the House's ethics, it went out of its way to protect hostile witnesses from the penalties of self-incriminatory statements, although not, of course, out of concern for them, but, rather, as a price worth paying to compel their testimony. The involuntary witness, when forced into the role of informer, does not, however, incriminate himself. Anglo-American law protected only against compulsory self-incrimination, not against the incrimination of others. What is striking about the proceedings in the Smith-Moore case is the

Assembly's respect for that protection even as it arbitrarily suspended the writ of habeas corpus, made a mockery of fair trial and due process of law, and grossly abridged the freedom of political expression.

By the mid-eighteenth century the right against self-incrimination was also firmly fixed in Massachusetts law. The *Boston Post-Boy* found newsworthy a story from Halifax concerning the investigation by governor and council into the conduct of certain trial judges who had allegedly deprived defendants of their rights to examine and cross-examine witnesses against them. The public learned that the judges had been vindicated by proving that they had merely protected witnesses against questions that might tend to make them accuse themselves. A year later, in 1754, the legislature, whose devotion to the principle against compulsory self-incrimination was less than consistent, passed a liquor excise requiring consumers to give an account to tax collectors, on oath if necessary, concerning the amount spent by them for liquor. The bill was understandably unpopular and, because of its incriminating oath, thought to be a menace to freedom. Pamphleteers quickly condemned the bill. John Lovell, a Boston schoolmaster whose pupils included John Hancock and Sam Adams, courted the wrath of the legislature by overstepping the bounds of reasonable criticism. Lovell, calling the bill "the most pernicious Attack upon *English Liberty* that was ever attempted," alleged that its methods would enslave the country. Samuel Cooper, the minister of the Brattle Church, shared Lovell's use of hyperbole but focused more precisely on the oath. If an accounting of any part of one's innocent conduct could be so "extorted," he contended, "every other Part may with equal Reason be required, and a *Political Inquisition* severe as that in Catholick Countries may inspect and controul every Step of his private Conduct." Cooper exalted the British Constitution, lamenting that the oath was a step toward its overthrow and the establishment of "Arbitrary Power." Some thought the bill not to be such a menace, he wrote, "But will any one presume to say, that *this* will be no Diminution of our Liberties, if it be an essential Part of our Constitution, that no Man is held to convict himself in any Affair whereof he is accus'd? And whoever will undertake to prove, that a Man can consistent with the Constitution, be obliged to clear himself of an innocent Action by Oath, or forfeit an heavy Penalty, may *a fortiori* prove, that this Practice is defensible in Criminal Cases. If the argument for purging by Oath in one Case, is founded upon the Advantage the Publick will receive by *knowing the Truth*, the very same Argument will hold stronger in Criminal Cases." Finally Governor William Shirley refused to sign the bill, declaring it to be an unprecedented violation of "natural Rights."[29]

That same year, in 1754, an anonymous author had published a pamphlet with the intriguing title, *The Monster of Monsters,* also satirizing the legislative debate on the recent excise bill—the allegorical monster. The House, having taken more than it could bear, promptly condemned the pamphlet as a seditious libel, ordered the hangman to burn copies, and arrested Daniel Fowle, a bookseller. At his examination before the bar of the House, Fowle asked whether he was obligated to answer an incriminating question concerning his complicity. Speaker Thomas Hubbard, evading the question, pressed him to answer, and Fowle foolishly confessed his guilt. He also named Royal Tyler, a respected merchant and future councilor, as the man who had given him his stock of copies for sale to the public. The legislature illogically concluded that Fowle, rather than Tyler, was the author and locked him up, brutally keeping him incommunicado in a stinking, bedless cell exposed to bad weather.[30]

Tyler was more knowledgable about his rights and not the sort to be intimidated. When the speaker demanded his confession, Tyler requested counsel, which the House refused. He parried all questions by invoking his right against self-incrimination: "and the only Answer he would make," the record states, "was, *Nemo tenetur seipsum Accusare; or, A Right of Silence was the Priviledge of every Englishman*"—a magnificent free translation. The legislature jailed him anyway, not for a contempt resulting from his invocation of the right but because of Fowle's testimony incriminating him. Yet Tyler was free on bail in only two days. By contrast, Fowle, who had not known the magic formula, was severely reprimanded by the speaker, ordered to pay costs, and was jailed indefinitely under the worst of conditions. In an act of mercy, the legislature released him in a week because he was needed at home to nurse his sick wife. His new pamphlet, *The Eclipse of Liberty,* vividly expressed his outrage at the House's violations of Magna Carta's guarantees of due process and personal liberty. With public sympathy on Fowle's side, the House discreetly dropped further proceedings in the case. Like its counterpart in Pennsylvania, the Massachusetts legislature had behaved in a high-handed, even tyrannical manner, seeking to suppress criticism by arbitrary proceedings, but had yielded, if begrudgingly, to a direct invocation of the right against self-incrimination.[31]

In New York, meanwhile, the course of events signalized an ever broadening respect for the right. William Smith, Jr., in 1757, had lent his influence against incriminatory oaths of purgation. In 1760 William Smith, his father, also defended the right against self-incrimination. The elder Smith, who had learned his law at the Inns of Court, was one of New York's most distinguished attorneys, had served as provincial attorney-general, and had declined the chief justiceship, although he accepted a seat on the high court in 1763. In 1760, as a member of the governor's council, he presented a report on illicit trading with the enemy by some of the colony's leading merchants. The manuscript record, though damaged by fire, shows that Smith had received his information from one of the masters of the vessels trading with the French West Indies. Smith accepted his evidence against others but did not require him to inform against himself. The master himself, "being Particeps Crimin[is] [a party to the crime] can not be compelled to answer." Offenders, said Smith, should be prosecuted only if sufficient proof of guilt could be obtained. In a case of 1702, Chief Justice Atwood had prevented David Jamison from testifying on behalf of Bayard because Jamison "is *particeps criminis* for which reason he cannot be allowed as evidence." But the case of the master in 1760 involved one who could not be *compelled.* Jamison, as an alleged party to the crime, could not be *allowed* to testify because his interest in the case had disqualified him. The master, by contrast, was not disqualified for interest; he was protected against self-incrimination.[32]

John Tabor Kempe, the attorney-general, did not wholly agree with Smith's opinion, which might deprive the prosecution of testimony needed for a conviction. In 1762, on the basis of information received from informers, Kempe obtained indictments against sixteen prominent men for trading with the enemy. In preparation for the trial of two of the merchants, he drafted a long brief in which he indicated his intention to call a number of witnesses who might be disqualified from testifying because of interest or excused because they were parties to the crime. Kempe carefully wrote out the arguments by which he intended to show that such persons were not necessarily incompetent to testify and, indeed, might even be compelled to. These witnesses, he declared, even parties to the crime, would be obliged to give evidence against others, "for the convictions of the persons on tryal will be attended with no punishment corporal or pecuniary to the witness— and he is not obliged to accuse himself." To the objection that no person should be compelled to swear against his own interest, Kempe noted: "He may—The Court of Chancery every day compels the party on oath to discover his own frauds. The rule that a witness shall not be compelled to swear to his own detriment goes not farther, than that he shall not be compelled to accuse himself of a crime." In conclusion, he wrote, "Every person being a *participis criminis,* may be a witness either for or against his accomplices, if he has not been indicted for the offence (2 Hawk. P. C. 432)." Thus, at three points in his brief, the attorney-general acknowledged the principle of the right against self-incrimination.[33]

Some of the ship captains whom Kempe had sworn as witnesses were unwilling to testify against the owners of their sloops. Captain William Dobbs, for example, simply refused to answer questions and was committed for contempt. Captain William Paulding at first was unwilling to be sworn, saying, "he understood he was not to declare anything that might affect himself." Informed that he had the king's pardon, he refused to accept it. Although he finally permitted himself to be sworn, he would not answer incriminating questions, and the court committed him also. The jury incidentally, without leaving the jury box, found the owner-defendants not guilty. The same verdict occurred in a companion case when Captain Theunis Thew refused to testify. He, too, was pardoned in order to protect him from the perils of the criminal law, but he remained silent to the questions and was committed. The court fined Dobbs, Paulding, and Thew for their respective contempts. Paulding had expressly invoked his right against self-incrimination, and the crown, eager for his testimony, immunized him against prosecution. Thew's pardon was similarly intended to safeguard him against self-incrimination. The cases scarcely bear out the allegation that the right was an illusion in New York. In Maryland at about this time the provincial court, in an action of trespass, upheld the right of a sheriff and his deputies not to be sworn as witnesses, against their will, to prove the defendant's claim that they had not given him notice of a resurvey as the duties of their office required. For the officers to have admitted their negligence would have exposed them to punishment. The court's matter-of-fact decision indicated that the law was settled in Maryland on the point that a witness in a *civil* case could not be required to answer questions that might reveal criminal liability.[34]

In the 1760's the opposition to general search warrants gave the right against self-incrimination a tremendous boost, first in England, then in America. The right was originally a "right of silence," in Royal Tyler's words, only in the sense that legal process could not force incriminating statements from the defendant's own lips. Beginning in the early eighteenth century the English courts widened that right to include protection against the necessity of producing books and documents that might tend to incriminate the accused. Thus, in a 1744 case the court refused the prosecution's request that the defendant be required to turn over the records of his corporation; that, said the court, would be forcing him to "furnish evidence against himself." Lord Mansfield summed up the law by declaring that the defendant, in a criminal case, could not be compelled to produce any incriminating documentary evidence "though he should hold it in his hands in Court." Yet it was an open question whether the government, though unable to subpoena such evidence, might lawfully seize it by a search warrant and introduce it at the trial against the accused. In the 1760's the English courts extended the right of silence to prevent the use of general warrants to seize private papers in seditious libel cases. Thus the right against self-incrimination and freedom of the press, with which it was so closely allied in its origins, were linked to a right to be free from unreasonable searches and seizures.[35]

The new departure originated in the Wilkes prosecution. John Wilkes's studied insult of the king's speech of 1763, in the forty-fifth issue of his journal, the *North Briton*, triggered the government's retaliatory instincts. Upon an information for libel filed by the attorney-general, one of the secretaries of state issued general search warrants leading to the arrest of forty-nine persons, including Wilkes, his printer, and his publisher. Within a short time about two hundred informations were filed, resulting in mass arrests, searches, and harassment of the press. In the treatment and prosecution of Wilkes the government found that it had mounted a tiger. No one since the days of John Lilburne, more than a century earlier, proved to be such a resourceful and pugnacious antagonist against the combined forces of all branches of the government. His private study had been ransacked on a general warrant and all his papers seized for incriminating evidence. The Commons voted that his *North Briton* Number 45 was a seditious libel, and Wilkes himself was expelled from the House, convicted in absentia for his criminal publications, outlawed, and, later, jailed and fined. Libertarian England rallied to his defense, spurred by Wilkes's own brilliant writings. He emerged from his persecution a popular idol, the personification of constitutional liberty in England and also in America, whose cause he championed. Although he himself held rather orthodox opinions on the subject of freedom of the press, his case touched off an intense public debate on the values and scope of that freedom and of others that were entwined. Though Wilkes focused mainly on the dangers of general warrants and the seizure of private papers, some of his supporters made notable contributions to libertarian theory, enlarging its concepts of freedom of the press and the right against self-incrimination.[36]

One pseudonymous author, a Gray's Inn lawyer calling himself "Candor," though defending the prosecution of seditious libels, blazed a fresh trail on the question of general search warrants. He described the seizure of private papers for the purpose of securing evidence of libel as an odious act comparable to "the worst sort of inquisitions . . . It is, in short, putting a man to the torture, and forcing him to give evidence against himself." Another lawyer, calling himself "Father of Candor," replied in a small book that went through three editions within as many months, seven altogether by 1771. It deserves to be ranked with Milton's *Areopagitica,* Andrew Hamilton's speech in the Zenger case, and the *Cato's Letters* of John Trenchard and Thomas Gordon, as one of the foremost expressions of English libertarian theory. "Father of Candor," who may have been either Lord Camden, the Chief Justice of the Court of Common Pleas, or Lord Ashburton, then John Dunning, one of the leading defenders of a free press, amplified what had been a passing point in "Candor's" pamphlet. Condemning the use of general search warrants as an "excruciating torture" that was inconsistent with every idea of liberty, he declared:

> The laws of England, are so tender to every man accused, even of capital crimes, that they do not permit him to be put to torture to extort a confession, nor oblige him to answer a question that will tend to accuse himself. How then can it be supposed that the law will intrust any officer of the crown, with the power of charging any man in the kingdom (or, indeed, every man by possibility and nobody in particular) at his will and pleasure, with being the author, printer or publisher of such a paper, being a libel, (however, which till a jury has determined to be so, is nothing) and that upon this charge, any common fellows under a general warrant, upon their own imaginations, or the surmises of their acquantance, or upon other worse and more dangerous intimations, may, with a strong hand, seize and carry off all his papers; and then at his trial produce these papers, thus taken by force from him, in evidence against himself; and all this on the charge of a mere misdemeanor, in a country of liberty and property. This would be making a man give evidence against and accuse himself, with a vengeance.[37]

The principle advocated by "Candor" and "Father of Candor" was destined for acceptance by the highest judicial authority on both sides of the Atlantic. Wilkes and others had urged editors, printers, and publishers whose papers had been seized to initiate suits for false arrest and trespass against the king's agents if their searches had been conducted on the authority of general warrants. *Entick* v. *Carrington,* one such suit, resulted in an opinion by Lord Camden that was later described by the Supreme Court of the United States as "one of the landmarks of English liberty."[38]

John Entick, an editor who sued for trespass, was represented by Serjeant Leigh who took his law from "Father of Candor," quite possibly the Lord Chief Justice sitting on the case. The crime, Leigh argued, was the publication, not the possession, of the libel. But even if its possession was criminal, "no power can lawfully break into a man's house and study to search for evidence against him. This would be worse than the Spanish inquisition; for ransacking a man's secret drawers and boxes, to come at evidence against him, is like racking his body to come at his secret thoughts." When opposition counsel replied that the secretary of state, having power to commit, must therefore have power to search and seize, Leigh replied tartly if illogically, "it might as well be said he has a power of torture." On the question whether the secretary of state or any crown officer had the power to search and seize under a general warrant, without parliamentary authorization, the court followed Leigh's path of reasoning. The existence of that power of search, Lord Camden declared, would open the "secret cabinets and bureaus of every subject in this kingdom" to search and seizure, whenever the government suspected a person of seditious libel. "It is very certain," he continued, "that the law obligeth no man to accuse himself; because the necessary means of compelling self-accusation, falling upon the innocent as well as the guilty, would be both cruel and unjust; and it should seem, that search for evidence is disallowed upon the same principle."[39]

Camden held that neither arrests nor general warrants could issue on executive discretion, and implied that evidence seized on the authority of a general warrant could not be used in court without violating the right against self-incrimination. Camden did not explain why, in accordance with the same principle, that same right did not also illegalize the evidence obtained by special warrants as well as general warrants, even if issued by judicial or parliamentary authority rather than executive authority; nor did Camden explain why the principle did not also apply in all cases rather than merely in seditious libel cases. Clearly, he laid the foundation of the right against unreasonable searches and seizures in order to fortify the already strained principle of the old *nemo tenetur* maxim. Never before had it extended to illegally seized evidence. The Supreme Court of the United States in 1886, relying heavily on Camden, took notice of the "intimate relation" between the Fourth and Fifth Amendments:

> They throw great light on each other. For the "unreasonable searches and seizures" condemned in the Fourth Amendment are almost always made for the purpose of compelling a man to give evidence against himself, which in criminal cases is condemned in the Fifth Amendment; and compelling a man "in a criminal case to be a witness against himself," which is condemned in the Fifth Amendment, throws light on the question as to what is an "unreasonable search and seizure" within the meaning of the Fourth Amendment. And we have been unable to perceive that the seizure of a man's private books and papers to be used in evidence against him is substantially different from compelling him to be a witness against himself.

Two centuries after *Entick* v. *Carrington,* the Supreme Court reaffirmed that the two freedoms—against unreasonable search and seizure and against compulsory self-incrimination—are complementary to, though not dependent upon, each other. At the very least, the two amendments when taken together assure that no man be convicted on unconstitutional evidence.[40]

In America, where libertarian thought, excepting on questions of religious liberty, usually lagged behind English models, the legality of general search warrants had been an earlier target of attack. Yet the American lawyers failed to make as imaginative a use of the right against self-incrimination, even though the warrants they vehemently opposed were more dangerous, that is, more general, than those associated with the prosecutions of Wilkes and Entick. The English warrants were general with respect to the objects of the search, but specific as to person, place, and time. In the colonies, the writs of assistance, as the warrants issued to customs officials were called, were general in every respect; on the other hand, they were issued by the courts on the authority of acts of Parliament. James Otis, in his famous argument against writs of assistance in 1761, described them as remnants of Star Chamber tyranny, yet he never connected them with a violation of the *nemo tenetur* principle. He might have done so had he been contesting the legality of evidence secured by an illegal search; instead, he was arguing against the re-authorization of the writs that had expired six months after the death of George II. Nevertheless, British lawyers when arguing against the principle of general search warrant, whether out of court, as in the case of "Father of Candor," or in court, even in a case of trespass, as in Serjeant Leigh's advocacy of Entick's cause, capitalized on the abhorrence of forcing a man to accuse himself. Not even in the American cases following *Entick* v. *Carrington* did the colonial lawyers copy that precedent. Their argument was that while specific search warrants might be legal if issued on probable cause, a general warrant was illegal because it threatened personal liberty by vesting arbitrary power in the officer conducting the search.[41]

The American argument brought the right against self-incrimination into play in connection with a procedure related to and following the use of writs of assistance. The writ was a device used by customs officials to search for contraband, goods that had been loaded from or smuggled into a colonial port in violation of the revenue acts or the acts regulating colonial trade. At the discretion of the customs officials, suits for penalties and forfeitures in such cases could be brought in the courts of vice admiralty. Those courts followed civil-law, rather than common-law, procedures. "The swarms of searchers, tide waiters, spies, and other underlings, with which every port in America now abounds," said a Philadelphia newspaper, "are not it seems, quite sufficient to ruin our trade, but infamous informers, like dogs of prey thirsting after the fortunes of worthy and wealthy men, are let loose and encouraged to seize and libel in the courts of admiralty the vessels of such as are advocates of the rights of America." Armed with the testimony of informers who might gain one-third of the value of ship and cargo in the event of a conviction, prosecutors initiated cases by merely bringing an accusation or "information." No grand jury indictment was necessary. The trial was without a jury. The judge held irregular sessions, used secret examinations and interrogatories, both written and oral, and then issued his decree.[42]

Admiralty procedures, Otis said in 1764, "savour more of . . . Rome and the Inquisition, than of the common law of England and the constitution of Great-Britain." Another American propagandist compared the vice-admiralty courts to the "high commission and star chamber courts." These exaggerations seemed true to anyone devoted to the common law, as were all Americans who opposed the revenue measures of the 1760's. When they damned the civil-law procedures of the vice-admiralty courts as violative of the rights of Englishmen, they knew that no jury would return a verdict of guilty against anyone accused of breaking one of Parliament's detested and allegedly unconstitutional revenue acts. In England, moreover, such cases could be tried only by the common-law Court of Exchequer.[43]

Henry Laurens, a wealthy, influential, and very conservative merchant-planter of South Carolina, fell prey to the rapacity of the customs officers and the vice-admiralty judge in Charleston. Within three months, in 1767, three of his ships were seized on insubstantial charges. In two of the cases, Judge Egerton Leigh released the vessels on ground that there was no evidence indicating intent to defraud the revenues or breach the acts of trade; yet Laurens was forced to pay court costs, including the judge's fees, in amounts exceeding the value of the ships. In the third case, for noncompliance with a technical formality of the law, Leigh condemned the ship in addition to assessing exorbitant costs. In one of these cases, he ruled that the searcher of the port, George Roupell, deputy to the collector, had acted without probable cause, leaving him open to a damage suit by Laurens. In 1768, Roupell retaliated by seizing the Ann, one of Lauren's most valuable ships, again on a highly technical charge. Leigh decreed an acquittal, though he again charged two-thirds of his fees and costs against Laurens; this time, however, the judge protected Roupell against a counter-suit by ruling that there had been probable cause for the seizure. He further protected Roupell by requiring him to swear an oath of calumny to prove that his actions were not motivated by malice. The oath of calumny brought the right against self-incrimination into play.[44]

Laurens, outraged by the injustice of oppressive suits and expensive fees, decided to expose customs racketeering and the venial admiralty judge. After publishing an article in the local press—newspapers as far away as Boston reprinted it—Laurens wrote an angry tract in 1768 detailing the history of his victimization. He denounced the vice-admiralty courts and extolled the protections of the common law. Of the various admiralty procedures that he found repugnant, none was worse than denial of trial by jury, but another, only slightly less obnoxious, was the willingness of the admiralty judge to abridge the right against self-incrimination. Laurens did not allege that Leigh had sought to force him to testify against himself. Rather, in an effort to support his argument against admiralty or civil-law procedure, he condemned Leigh for having exacted the oath of calumny from Roupell. Confusing the oath of calumny with the oath *ex officio,* Laurens warned against the dangers to liberty from that dread oath. He very effectively quoted Lord Bacon against the practice "whereby Men are inforced to accuse themselves," and in the next sentence alluded to torture. Laurens also quoted "the Learned Puffendorff" on the dangers of oaths when punishment or even "grievous Inconveniences" might be the consequence of confessing the truth. For his own part, Laurens added, he would rather have lost the case than have such an oath imposed on Roupell.[45]

Judge Leigh, replying to Laurens's many charges, exposed his accuser's confounding the oath of calumny and the oath *ex officio.* Leigh also denied that he had violated the right in question: "the benignity of our law will not suffer any man to accuse himself *criminally. . . .* " The case of the *Ann,* however, had not been a criminal one. Admiralty procedure, the admiralty judge observed, permitted the oath of calumny in order to protect the party against either the costs of the suit or a counter-action for damages in the event that probable cause for seizure were not established.[46]

The news of Laurens's ordeal reached Boston in the midst of a prosecution in the vice-admiralty court against another future president of the Continental Congress, John Hancock. In 1768 on the evidence of a confessed perjurer, the customs office in Boston libeled one of Hancock's ships for smuggling. The *Liberty,* as the ship was fatefully called, was seized, condemned, and forfeited. Then Hancock himself was sued for triple damages in a proceeding that in some respects really did savor of the inquisitorial. He was jailed and then released on bail of three thousand pounds sterling, an amount that would have been inordinately excessive in a common-law action, though in this case it was only one-third of the amount of the damages sought. Hancock's relatives, friends, employees, and business associates were privately examined and reexamined on interrogatories over a period of several months. Enemies and strangers, including pimps and informers, were paid to testify against him. His office was searched, his desk rifled, his papers seized. The patriot party launched a newspaper war against the admiralty court and in favor of common-law procedures. A special publication, *A Journal of the Times,* was issued almost daily in Boston as a news service detailing the prosecution, and newspapers in almost every colony copied or summarized its coverage of the case. *A Journal of the Times* obliquely assumed that the court violated the right against self-incrimination, as is evident from the unremitting and extravagant denunciations of "Star Chamber proceedings" by the "inquisitorial" tactics of examining men secretly and by "odious" interrogatories. In the hope that evidence could be "fished up" to sustain the prosecution, the court would stop at nothing, according to the patriot view. There were frequent references to the Laurens case, and the press asked whether the admiralty judge, being able to use interrogatories and the oath of calumny, might not next "put parties or witnesses to the torture, and extend them on the rack?"[47]

John Adams, who was Hancock's counsel, probably provided *A Journal of the Times* with its up-to-date accounts of the case, which dragged on for five months. Yet in his argument before the court, Adams was restrained both in tone and substance. He referred neither to the right against self-incrimination nor to the illegality of writs of assistance, though he did rely heavily on Magna Carta to prove that the statute authorizing trial by admiralty-court procedure in cases involving penalties and forfeiture violated the English constitution. He also argued that the case should be tried at common law, by a jury, with witnesses in open court, in the presence of the parties, face to face. "Examinations of witnesses upon Interrogatories," he added, "are only by the Civil Law. Interrogatories are unknown at common Law, and Englishmen and common Lawyers have an aversion to them if not an Abhorrence of them." Nevertheless, there is no reference to Hancock's having been examined under interrogatories, nor any real proof that they were used to incriminate the witnesses.[48]

The claim by an eminent historian that Hancock was "compelled to give evidence against himself" rests on the alleged use of his papers against him, though even that is not an established fact. Surely it is a gross exaggeration to claim, even as a probability, "that the constitutional provisions for indictment by a grand jury, trial by jury, forced self-incrimination, confronting witnesses face to face, excessive bail, depriving persons of property without due process of law, and excessive fines found in the earliest state constitutions and embodied in the fifth, sixth, seventh, and eighth amendments to the Federal Constitution are there because of the procedures of this case." On the other hand, these constitutional provisions, including the one in the Fifth Amendment, were stimulated, at least in part, by the kind of frenzied sense of injustice, real or feigned, that the Laurens and Hancock cases provoked in the patriot party. They exalted common-law procedures of criminal justice as expressions of fundamental law, and when the opportunity was theirs, they ritualistically gave constitutional embodiment to those procedures as if symbolically emancipating themselves from a tyranny, although it scarcely had existed.[49]

Despite the publicity of the Laurens and Hancock cases, in 1770 there was a move by the Customs Office in Philadelphia to question under oath every officer and seaman of a vessel that was supposed to have engaged in the smuggling of tea. But Attorney-General Andrew Allen informed the collector of the port: "I am very clear in opinion that the Court of Admiralty cannot with propriety oblige any persons to answer interrogatories which may have a tendency to criminate themselves, or subject them to a penalty, it being contrary to any principle of Reason and the Laws of England."[50]

That the right against self-incrimination was an illusion in New York is disproved by the sensational McDougall case, which occurred at this time. In December of 1769 a handbill addressed "To the Betrayed Inhabitants of New York," signed by a "Son of Liberty," was broadcast throughout the city. The author, criticizing the legislature for having voted to supply provisions for the king's troops, called upon the public to rise against unjust measures that subverted American liberties. The legislature condemned the handbill as a seditious libel and offered a reward for information leading to discovery of "Son of Liberty's" identity. A journeyman printer in the shop of James Parker, publisher of the *New York Gazette: or, the Weekly Post-Boy,* betrayed his employer as the printer of the broadside.[51]

On February 7, 1770, the governor and council summoned Parker and his employees. Having once before been jailed by the Assembly for publishing a reflection on its members, Parker was a reluctant witness. Claiming that he would be "wrecked" if he answered the council's questions, he asked for immunity in exchange for his cooperation. He remained reluctant even after being informed that he was not being asked to incriminate *himself.* The council then threatened him with the loss of his position in the post office and warned of his "danger"—punishment for contempt. Yet they did not threaten him criminally for a refusal to incriminate himself; they were after the author of the handbill. Giving Parker an opportunity to reconsider, the council brought in Anthony Carr, one of his journeymen. Carr, testifying under oath, denied knowledge of the identity of the author; however, he admitted that the offensive piece had been printed at Parker's.

Councilman William Smith recorded in his diary that Carr was then told "at my Instance as Parker had been before, that he need not answer so as to accuse himself." Nevertheless, when Carr persisted in feigning ignorance, they bullied him with threats of imprisonment. Intimidated, he finally broke down, naming as author Captain Alexander McDougall. Carr's brother, John, also a journeyman printer in Parker's office, was next sworn and "told that he was not bound to accuse himself." John Carr willingly corroborated Anthony's testimony. The Council then recalled Parker. Upon being told that they knew everything about the writing and printing of the libel, he accepted the offer of a pardon and confessed both his role and McDougall's authorship. He was then sworn and his examination taken down.[52]

McDougall, a popular leader of the patriot party during these years of controversy with Britain—subsequently he was a delegate to both Continental Congresses and then a major-general during the Revolution—was arrested for seditious libel and jailed when he refused to pay bail. He turned his arrest into a theatrical triumph, consciously posing as America's Wilkes while the Sons of Liberty converted his prosecution into a weapon for the patriot cause. William Smith anonymously supported McDougall. Smith refused Governor Cadwallader Colden's request that he assist Attorney-General Kempe in the prosecution of "an unpopular suit." Then he published in Parker's paper a defense of McDougall, based chiefly upon liberty of the press, in which he censured the Star Chamber practice of examining "even the accused." The manuscript version of the article, which Smith considerably shortened for publication, also declared that "to the eternal scandal of this inquisition they examined sometimes the Party himself & even accepted against himself."[53]

When Parker, the principal witness for the crown, died, the trial of McDougall was postponed a number of times. Finally the legislature, impatient for revenge, resolved to punish him on its own authority, and summoned McDougall before the bar of the House on December 13, 1770. Charged with having written "To the Betrayed," he was asked whether he was in fact the author. McDougall refused to answer, claiming his rights both against self-incrimination and against double jeopardy. The minutes of the Assembly's proceedings show his reply, in part, to be: "That as the Grand Jury & House of Assembly had declared the Paper in Question to be a Libel, he could not answer to the Question."[54]

In a letter to the press written from prison, McDougall more fully reported his statement as follows: "First, that the Paper just read to me, had been declared by the Honourable House to be a Libel; that the Grand Jury for ... New York, had also declared it to be a Libel, and found a Bill of Indictment against me as the Author of it; therefore that I could not Answer a Question that would tend to impeach myself, or might otherwise be improper for me to answer." Because of McDougall's insistence that the Assembly could not try him on a criminal charge still being prosecuted in the courts, they voted him guilty of contempt and remanded him to prison for the remainder of their session, which continued for nearly three months. About a week after his release, the Sons of Liberty met to celebrate the anniversary of the repeal of the Stamp Act. One of the many toasts on that festive occasion was to Alexander McDougall; another was, "No Answer to Interrogatories, when tending to accuse the Person interrogated." McDougall's case not only popularized but made respectable the right against self-incrimination.[55]

The impact of McDougall's case is evident from the history of the use of oaths against suspects after 1770. Goebel and Naughton asserted that the legislature authorized oaths of purgation "until the very eve of the Revolution." Their proof is not only inaccurate; it omitted evidence to the contrary. The last statute employing the oath of purgation had been enacted in 1759. It prescribed, characteristically, an express disclaimer to be sworn by suspects "I, A.B., do swear that I have not directly or Indirectly by myself or any other for me ... [after publication of the statute] Bought Exchanged or taken in Pawn any Arms Ammunition or Cloathing of or from any Indian or Indians Whatsoever within any of the said Counties So help me God." Goebel and Naughton cited enactments of 1770 and 1774 as evidence of the continued use of "this purgation procedure," but neither contained an oath of purgation.[56]

The 1770 act authorized the examination "on oath" of any person suspected of concealing the assets of the estate of an insolvent debtor, but the oath was simply the usual one to tell the truth. The 1774 act is supposed to illustrate strikingly the "parallel between this purgation procedure and the ecclesiastical forms against which the English Puritans had so bitterly inveighed. . . . " But this act, which was directed against "excessive and deceitful gambling," simply made winners liable to suits for the recovery of their spoils; it also obliged suspects "to answer under Oath such Bill or Bills as shall be preferred against them for discovering the Sum and Sums of Money or other Thing so won at Play as aforesaid." Goebel and Naughton, having rather freely quoted this section of the statute, moved on to the "inescapable" conclusion that in New York Province there was "no attempt made to privilege a defendant . . . but on the contrary a great deal was done to make sure that in one form or other his testimony would be secured and that it would count against him. The shadowy protection offered by the rule that a confession could not be under oath, was quite offset in the cases where he could be convicted on a confession alone and by those where he was required to trap himself by a purging oath." But the oath authorized in the 1774 act against gambling was not an oath of purgation, and the act itself was more a manifestation of Puritan morality than of the ecclesiastical forms against which the English Puritans had inveighed. More important, Goebel and Naughton neglected to inform their readers that the next paragraph of the very same act against gambling provided that a person who confessed his winnings and repaid them "shall be acquitted, indemnified and discharged from any further or other Punishment, Forfeiture, or Penalty which he or they may have incurred by the playing for or winning such Money. . . . " Confession, in other words, "purged" him of his offense; it did not trap or incriminate him, for the statute—in the section omitted by Goebel and Naughton—provided for complete immunity. Then, as now, self-incrimination meant to expose oneself to "Punishment, Forfeiture, or Penalty," in the absence of which one cannot incriminate himself.[57]

The practice of providing immunity, which protects against self-incrimination, was begun by the legislature, significantly enough, in the first statute requiring an oath—but not an oath of purgation—that was passed after the McDougall case. This act of 1772 against private lotteries authorized justices of the peace to examine suspects under oath. Those who answered truthfully were "exempted from . . . Penalty, and from all Prosecutions in virtue of this Act. . . . " In the following year there was a reenactment of an old statute against selling liquor to servants or extending them "large" credit. The original statute of 1750 had contained an oath of purgation; the re-enactment of 1773 made no mention of any kind of oath.[58]

In 1773, however, a new statute, overlooked by Goebel and Naughton, virtually authorized a purgative oath, though none was literally prescribed. To catch petty vandals, the legislature provided that a person caught in the vicinity, when a trespass such as the breaking of windows was committed, "shall be deemed guilty thereof" even if not an abettor. To absolve himself he must give evidence for the conviction of the parties "really guilty" or declare under oath that he was at the scene accidentally and did not know the identity of the real offenders. The obnoxious procedures authorized by this statute, the first and last of its kind since 1759, were the subject of a complaint to the Board of Trade, which recommended disallowance by the Privy Council. Mr. Jackson, the attorney for the crown, specifically censured the act as being "improper in that it provides for a Purgation by Oath in a criminal Matter, which is . . . contrary to the Genius of the Laws of this Country. . . . " The Privy Council, noting that Jackson's argument possessed "Weight," voted on July 6, 1774, to disallow the act despite its "useful" objective. However, the New York Assembly, on its own initiative and prior to the disallowance, re-enacted the statute against private lotteries, once again insuring immunity against prosecution to persons who confessed their guilt under a simple oath to tell the truth. In 1775 a new act on trespasses was passed without the objectionable procedures of the act of 1773 that had been disallowed—and without reference to oaths of any kind by the suspect. New York had surely come abreast the English common law. When the Revolution began, colonies and mother country differed little, if at all, on the right against self-incrimination.[59]

Notes

1. For the state of the colonial bar, see Charles Warren, *A History of the American Bar* (Cambridge, Eng., 1912), Part I; Anton-Hermann Chroust, *The Rise of the Legal Profession in America* (Norman, Okla., 1965, 2 vols.), vol. I; Paul M. Hamlin, *Legal Education in Colonial New York* (New York, 1939); and Edward Alfred Jones, *American Members of the Inns of Court* (London, 1924). On the use of Dalton and other law books by the colonial courts, see Edwin Powers, *Crime and Punishment in Early Massachusetts, 1620–1692* (Boston, 1966), 433; Carroll T. Bond, ed., with Richard B. Morris, *Proceedings of the Maryland Court of Appeals, 1695–1729* (Washington, 1933), xx, xxvii; George Athan Billias, ed., *Law and Authority in Colonial America: Selected Essays* (Barre, Mass., 1965), 13–14, 132 n. 5; Francis R. Aumann, *The Changing American Legal System: Some Selected Phases* (Columbus, Ohio, 1940), 43–8.
2. Julius Goebel, Jr., and T. Raymond Naughton, *Law Enforcement in Colonial New York: A Study in Criminal Procedure (1664–1776)* (New York, 1944), xxiii, xxvi, xxviii, 59, 556. Trial of Penn and Mead, *State Trials,* VI, 957–8 (1670).

3. Goebel and Naughton, xxviii, 56–7, 59–69, 284, 573. On Alexander and his library, see Hamlin, *Legal Education,* 76–8, 171–6. Appendix VII, in *ibid.,* lists the books in the libraries of several New York colonial lawyers. Smith's law books are enumerated at pp. 182–92.
4. Goebel and Naughton, 656–7.
5. On Gilbert, see above, ch. 10, n. 41 and related text. The fifth edition of Gilbert, *Law of Evidence by a Late Learned Judge,* was published in Philadelphia in 1788 and contained the identical passage, p. 137. Goebel and Naughton misstate that the book was used in New York "not long after publication," p. 628, n. 79, and wrongly give the date of publication as 1754. "A Treatise on Evidence," William Smith Papers, IX, 127–8, New York Public Library MSS. Smith's later relationship to the right against self-incrimination will be discussed below.
6. Giles Jacob, *A New Law-Dictionary* (London, 1732, 2nd ed.), under "Evidence." Jacob, *Every Man His Own Lawyer* (New York, 1768, 7th ed.), 93; the book was also published in Philadelphia in 1769. Henry Care, *English Liberties, or the Free born Subject's Inheritance* (London, 1691); I used the 5th edition (Boston, 1721), 198–9. There was a 6th edition published in Providence in 1774. Clinton Rossiter, *Seedtime of the Republic: The Origin of the American Tradition of Political Liberty* (New York, 1953), 457–8, n. 11. John Somers, *The Security of Englishmen's Lives, or the Trust, Power and Duty of the Grand Juries of England* (London, 1681; Boston, 1720; New York, 1773); I used the edition printed as the Appendix to [Anon.], *A Guide to the Knowledge of the Rights and Privileges of Englishmen* (London, 1757), 170. William Hawkins, *A Treatise of the Pleas of the Crown* (London, 1716), II, chap. 46, sect. 20, p. 433. William Nelson, *The Law of Evidence* (London, 1735), 51. See also Matthew Bacon, *A New Abridgment* of *the Law* (Savoy, Eng., 1731–59, 4 vols.), II, 288.
7. Michael Dalton, *The Countrey Justice* (London, 1618), 264; also in the London editions of 1619, 1677, and 1742, pp. 273, 411, and 380 respectively. William Nelson, *The Office and Authority of the Justice of the Peace* (London, 1714, 4th ed.), 253. [James Parker?] *Conductor Generalis, or the Office, Duty and Authority of Justices of the Peace* (Philadelphia, 1722), 83. In the 2nd ed. of *Conductor Generalis* (Philadelphia, 1749; also New York, 1749), an appendix on "Maxims and General Rules" included the following: "5. *Accusare Nemo se debet nisi coram Deo: No* man ought to accuse himself, unless it be before God. An Oath is not lawful whereby any Person may be compelled to confess, or accuse himself, &c. . . . The Law will not enforce any one to shew or say what is against him: for which Reason an Offender, tho' ever so culpable, may plead *Not Guilty,*" *ibid.,* 434. The New York editions appeared in 1749, 1764 (two), 1787, 1788 (two), 1790, and 1794. "A List of Legal Treatises Printed in the British Colonies and the American States before 1801," ed. Eldon Revare James, in Morton C. Campbell *et al., Harvard Legal Essays Written in Honor of and Presented to Joseph Henry Beale and Samuel Williston* (Cambridge, Mass., 1934), 159–211, proved useful, but is not complete. For passages similar to those in *Conductor Generalis,* see also [Richard Burn], *An Abridgment of Burn's Justice of the Peace* (Boston, 1773), 123; Richard Starke, *The Office and Authority of a Justice of the Peace* (Williamsburg, Va., 1774), 145, 146; J. Davis, *The Office and Authority of a Justice of the Peace* (Newbern, N.C., 1774), 160, [John F. Grimke], *The South-Carolina Justice of Peace* (Philadelphia, 1788), 191; William W. Hening, *The New Virginia Justice* (Richmond, Va., 1795), 177, 286. Most of these manuals, like *Conductor Generalis,* also included the rule from Coke, "4 *Inst.* 279" or *"Coke Litt.* 158b," that a witness should not be examined to his own infamy or turpitude. William Wyche, *A Trea-*

tise on the Practice of the Supreme Court of Judicature of the State of New-York in Civil Actions (New York, 1794), 156, citing Coke, said that a juror may be examined on oath "with regard to such causes of challenge, as are not to his dishonor or discredit, but not with regard to any crime, or any thing, which tends to his disgrace or disadvantage." The same rule was in Francis-Xavier Martin, *The Office and Authority of a Justice of the Peace . . . According to the Laws of the State of North-Carolina* (Newbern, N.C., 1791), 92.

8. J. J. Burlamaqui, *The Principles of Natural and Political Law,* trans. by T. Nugent (London, 1763, 2 vols.), II, 187–8. Baron Pufendorf, *The Law of Nature and Nations,* trans. by Basil Kenicott (London, 1729), 332, 353–4, 767.

9. Edward Wingate, *Maxims of Reason: or The Reason of the Common Law of England* (London, 1658), sect. 125, pp. 486–7. Hamlin, 173, 179, 181, 187, 194; Rossiter, 141, 217, 359, and related footnotes. Sir William Blackstone, *Commentaries on the Law of England* (Oxford, 1765–69, 4 vols.), III, ch. 7, p. 101, ch. 23, p. 370; IV, ch. 22, p. 296. Blackstone says nothing detailed or systematic about the right because he did not deal with the rules of evidence. At one point, when speaking of "established rules and maxims," he gave this illustration: "as 'that the king can do no wrong, that no man shall be bound to accuse himself' and the like," I, 68.

10. Goebel and Naughton, xxxi, 628–9, 641.

11. *Ibid.,* 654.

12. See above, ch. 10, notes 41–4 and related text.

13. Goebel and Naughton, 627, speculate that the swearing of defendant's witnesses was discretionary with the New York courts.

14. Chroust, I, 43–4, 130, 138, 296, 301; Arthur P. Scott, *Criminal Law in Colonial Virginia* (Chicago, 1930), 60, 79, 100; L. Kinvin Wroth and Hiller B. Zobel, eds., *Legal Papers of John Adams* (Cambridge, Mass., 1965, 3 vols.), II, 402–3 n. 40. Goebel and Naughton, 656, 659.

15. *Calendar of Council Minutes, 1668–1773,* ed. Berthold Fernow, New York State Library, *Bulletin 58* (March 1902) History 6 (Albany, 1902), 132; Philip L. White, *The Beekmans of New York in Politics and Commerce, 1647–1877* (New York, 1956), 87–8, 91–2; Lawrence H. Leder, *Robert Livingston, 1654–1728, and the Politics of Colonial New York* (Chapel Hill, N.C., 1961), 130–32; New York Council Minutes, June 25, 1698, VIII, 55–6, New York State Library MSS, Albany, N.Y.; John Key. "Heads of Accusation against the Earl of Bellomont," March 11, 1700, in E. B. O'Callaghan and B. Fernow, eds., *Documents Relative to the Colonial History of the State of New York* (Albany, 1853–87, 15 vols.), IV, 622; Commissioners of Statutory Revision, *The Colonial Laws of New York from the Year 1664 to the Revolution* (Albany, 1894, 5 vols.), I, 392–3; John Montague, *Arguments Offer'd to the Right Honourable the Lords Commissioners for Trade and Plantation Relating to Some Acts of Assembly Past* at New-York *in* America (London, 1701), in New-York Historical Society, *Collections* (New York, 1869), 180–83.

16. Proceedings of Lords of Trade, Jan. 20, 1699, in O'Callaghan and Fernow, eds., *Documents, IV,* 467.

17. *Ibid., IV, 648.*

18. *Rex* v. *Bayard, State Trials,* XIV, 471–506 (1702); Leder, *Livingston,* 174–7.

19. Samuel Bayard to Adderly and Lodwick, Jan. 27, 1702, in O'Callaghan and Fernow, eds., *Documents,* IV, 945; New York Council Minutes, Jan. 21, 26, 1702, VIII, 302–3; Nicholas Bayard to Adderly and Lodwick, Jan. 28, 1702, in O'Callaghan and Fernow, eds., *Documents,* IV, 947; Sir Edward Northey to Board

April 25, 1702, in *ibid.,* IV, 954 (italics added).

20. "The Case of William Atwood, Esq." (1703), New-York Historical Society, *Collections,* XIII (New York, 1881), 269.

21. [Anon.], *A Narrative of a New and Unusual American Imprisonment of Two Presbyterian Ministers: and Prosecution of Mr. Francis Makemie.* By a Learner of Law, and Lover of Liberty (1707), in Peter Force, ed., *Tracts and Other Papers Relating Principally to the Origin . . . of the Colonies of North America* (New York, 1947 ed., 4 vols.), IV, No. 4, unpaged introduction "An Epistle to the Reader."

22. Leder, *Livingston,* 251–4; *Colonial Laws of New York,* II, 8–10, 98.

23. Journal of Board of Trade, May 5, 12, 1725, and Representation of Board of Trade, June 16, 1725, in O'Callaghan and Fernow, eds., *Documents,* V, 748, 750, 763; *Colonial Laws of New York,* II, 281–7.

24. *Colonial Laws of New York,* I, 454–5 (ch. 95, Oct. 18, 1701). Goebel and Naughton, 657, state that the first statute employing a purgatory oath was passed in 1709. For the acts after 1701, see *Colonial Laws of New York,* I, 657–8 (ch. 187, May 24, 1709), 678–9 (ch. 196, Sept. 24, 1709), 681 (ch. 197, Oct. II, 1709), 764 (ch. 250, Dec. 10, 1712), 830 (ch. 282, Sept. 4, 1714), 889–90 (ch. 317, June 30, 1716); II, 245 (ch. 463, Nov. 10, 1725), 710 (ch. 568, Sept. 30, 1731), 954 (ch. 651, Dec. 16, 1737), 962 (ch. 655, Dec. 16, 1737); III, 243–4 (ch. 734, Oct. 29, 1742), 730–31 (ch. 869, July 1, 1748), 757–8 (ch. 881, Nov. 24, 1750), 1097–8 (ch. 979, July 5, 1755); IV, 349–50 (ch. 1086, Mar. 7, 1759). William Smith, *The History of the Late Province of New-York* (New York, 1829, 2 vols.), I, 139.

25. Benjamin Franklin, "Some Observations on the Proceedings against The Rev. Mr. Hemphill" (1735), in Leonard W. Labaree et al., eds., *Papers of Benjamin Franklin* (New Haven, 1959 ff., 9 vols.), II, 37, 44, 45, 47, 49; Franklin, "A Defense of the Rev. Mr. Hemphill's Observations" (1735), in *ibid.,* II, 90, 99. See also, Merton A. Christensen, "Franklin in the Hemphill Trial: Deism Versus Presbyterian Orthodoxy," *William and Mary Quarterly,* 3rd ser., X (July 1953), 422–40.

26. *Votes and Proceedings of the House of Representatives of the Province of Pennsylvania (1682–1776),* in Gertrude MacKinney and Charles F. Hoban, eds., *Pennsylvania Archives,* 8th ser. (n.p., 1931–35), VI, 4423 ff.; quotation at p. 4445.

27. The Smith-Moore case is reported in *ibid.,* VI, 4677–716.

28. *Ibid.,* VI, 4678–80, 4681–2, 4704. For a fuller discussion of the Smith-Moore case, see Leonard W. Levy, *Legacy of Suppression: Freedom of Speech and Press in Early American History* (Cambridge, Mass., 1960), 53–61.

29. *The Boston Post-Boy,* May 28, 1753. John Lovell, *Freedom, the First of Blessings* (Boston, 1754), I; Samuel Cooper, *The Crisis* (Boston, 1754), 5–6. Shirley is quoted in John F. Burns, *Controversies between Royal Governors and Their Assemblies in the Northern American Colonies* (Boston, 1923), 132–3. See also John A. Schutz, *William Shirley, King's Governor of Massachusetts* (Chapel Hill, N.C., 1961), 177.

30. Daniel Fowle, *A Total Eclipse of Liberty* (Boston, 1755), 11–14, 16–20.

31. *Ibid.,* 15, 26, 27; *Journals of the House of Representatives of Massachusetts (1754–1755),* (Boston, 1956), XXXI, 63–4; *ibid.,* Part I, XXXII, 10, 23, 58–9.

32. Report of Committee of Council, Dec. 24, 1760, New York Colonial Manuscripts, LXXXIX, 54 (5), New York State Library; *State Trials,* XIV, 503.

33. "Note of Recognizances taken by Mr. Justice Horsmanden relating to illicit trade," John Tabor Kempe Papers, Box "B" (under Augustus Bradley), New York-Historical Society, N.Y.; Manuscript Brief, "The King agt. Waddell Cunningham and Thomas White," 1763, Pleadings, Pl. K 1023, pp. 8, 10, Hall of Records, New York County, N.Y.

34. MS Minute Book of the Supreme Court of Judicature, Oct. 19, 1762, to April 28, 1764, entries for Oct. 28, 1763, pp. 273, 289, Engrossed Minutes, Hall of Records, New York County, N.Y. *Trammell v. Thomas, Harris & McHenry (M*aryland) 261 (1767); see also, *Trammell v. Hook, ibid.,* 259 (1767).

35. See cases cited above, ch. 10, n. 30. For the quotations, *Rex v. Cornelius,* 2 *Strange* 1210, at 1211 (1744), 93 *Eng. Rep.* 1133, at 1134; *Roe dem. Haldane v. Harvey,* 4 *Burrow* 2484, at 2489 (1769), 98 *Eng. Rep.* 302, at 305.

36. On the Wilkes case and related prosecutions, see Raymond Postgate, *That Devil Wilkes* (New York, 1929), George Nobbe, *The North Briton* (New York, 1939); George Rude, *Wilkes and Liberty* (New York, 1962); Robert R. Rea, *The English Press in Politics, 1760–1774* (Lincoln, Neb., 1963); and Pauline Maier, "John Wilkes and American Disillusionment with Britain," *William and Mary Quarterly,* 3rd ser., XX (July 1963), 373–95.

37. [Anon.], *A Letter from Candor to the Public Advertiser* (London 1764), signed, from "Grays-Inn." I used the third edition, of 1770, available in *A Collection of Interesting Political Tracts,* probably edited by John Almon (London, 1773, 8 vols), I, each tract separately paginated; the quotation is at pp. 22–3. The first edition of the book by "Father of Candor" bears the title, *An Enquiry into the Doctrine, Lately Propagated, concerning Libels, Warrants, and the Seizure of Papers . . . in a Letter to Mr. Almon from the Father of Candor (London,* 1764). Although I used the first edition, my citations are to the more easily obtainable seventh edition, reprinted in vol. I of the same *Collection* in which Candor's book appeared. The seventh edition bears the title, *A Letter Concerning Libels, Warrants, the Seizure of Papers, and Sureties for the Peace of Behaviour* (London, 1771); the quoted matter is at pp. 66–7. *State Trials,* XVII, 726, ascribes the identity of Father of Candor to Lord Chancellor Camden or Lord Ashburton. See also, on the matter of identity, Rea, *The English Press in Politics,* 113, 246, notes 7 and 15. On Father of Candor's contribution to the theory of a free press, see Levy, *Legacy of Suppression,* 148–57.

38. *Entick v. Carrington, State Trials,* XIX, 1029 (1765). *Boyd v. U.S.,* 116 U.S. 616, at 626 (1886).

39. *State Trials,* XIX, at 1038, 1041,1063, 1073.

40. *Boyd v. U.S.,* 116 U.S. 616, at 633. See also *Bram v. U.S.,* 168 U.S. 532, at 543–4 (1897). For the recent cases joining the Fourth and Fifth Amendments, see *Mapp v. Ohio,* 367 U.S. 655, at 656–7 (1960), and *Malloy v. Hogan,* 378 U.S. 1, at 8–9 (1964).

41. See also editorial note in Wroth and Zobel, eds., *Legal Papers of John Adams,* II, 106–23, on the argument on writs of assistance, and Adams's Minutes of the Argument, 1761, in *ibid.,* 123–44. See also Oliver M. Dickerson, "Writs of Assistance as a Cause of the American Revolution," in Richard B. Morris, ed., *The Era of the American Revolution* (New York, 1939), 40–76, and Nelson Lasson, *The History and Development of the Fourth Amendment to the United States Constitution (*Baltimore, 1937), 51–78. The best work on the subject is the unpublished dissertation of Joseph R. Frese, "Writs of Assistance in the American Colonies, 1660–1776" (Harvard College, 1951).

42. Oliver M. Dickerson, *The Navigational Acts and the American Revolution* (Philadelphia, 1951), 230, quoting the *Pennsylvania Journal,* Oct. 19, 1769.

43. Quoted matter from David S. Lovejoy, "Rights Imply Equality: the Case against Admiralty Jurisdiction in America, 1764–1776," *William and Mary Quarterly,* 3rd. ser., XVI (Oct. 1959), 466–7.

44. On Laurens's troubles with the vice admiralty courts, see David Duncan Wallace,

The Life of Henry Laurens (New York, 1915), 137–49; Dickerson, *Navigation Acts,* 224–31; Carl Ubbelohde, *The Vice Admiralty Courts and the American Revolution* (Chapel Hill, N.C., 1960), 105–14.

45. Henry Laurens, *Extracts from the Proceedings of the Court of Vice-Admiralty in Charles-Town, South-Carolina* (Philadelphia, 1768); I used the 2nd ed., published in Charlestown, 1769. The material on the oath is at pp. 31–3.

46. Sir Egerton Leigh, *The Man Unmasked: Or, the World Undeceived* (Charlestown, 1769), 77–9, 80–81, 86–8, for material on the oath; the line quoted is at p. 77.

47. The case of the *Liberty* is discussed in Dickerson, *Navigation Acts,* 231–45; Ubbelohde, *Vice Admiralty Courts,* 119–27; Wroth and Zobel, *Legal Papers,* II, 173–93. Oliver M. Dickerson, ed., *Boston under Military Rule (1768–1769) as Revealed in* A Journal of the Times (Boston, 1936), 43, 44, 46, 54, 56, 57, 64, 66, 67, 68, 72, 83, 98; the quotation on torture is at p. 72.

48. Adams's argument in "*Sewal v. Hancock*," in Wroth and Zobel, II, 194–207; the quotation is at p. 207.

49. The quotation is from Dickerson, *Navigation Acts,* 244.

50. Allen is quoted in ibid., 246–7; Dickerson cites Report of John Swift, Collector at Philadelphia, to the Commissioners of Customs, P.R.O., Treasury Papers, I, Bundle 482.

51. Levy, *Legacy of Suppression,* 78–9.

52. Dairy entry of Wed., Feb. 7, 1770, William H. W. Sabine, ed., *Historical Memoirs, from 16 March 1763 to 9 July 1776, of William Smith, Historian of the Province of New York* (New York, 1956), 74–5.

53. Levy, 81–2; [William Smith], "Copy of a late letter from an eminent Counsellor," *New-York Gazette: or, the Weekly Post-Boy,* March 19, 1770; William Smith, "Copy of a late letter from an eminent Counsellor," William Smith Papers, Folder #204–9, New York Public Library.

54. *Journal of the Votes and Proceedings of the General Assembly of the Colony of New York, 1769–1771,* P.R.O., Colonial Office Papers, Class 5, Vol. 1219, p. 8 (microfilm). The Assembly proceedings for Dec. 13, 1770, are also available in *New-York Gazette: and the Weekly Mercury,* Dec. 24, 1770.

55. Alexander McDougall, "To The Freeholders," *New-York Gazette: or, the Weekly Post-Boy,* Dec. 24, 1770; *ibid.,* March 25, 1771.

56. *Colonial Laws,* IV, 349–50.

57. Goebel and Naughton, 658, 659; *Colonial Laws,* V, 130, 621, 623; *Brown v. Walker,* 161 U.S. 591 (1896), and *Ullman v. U.S.,* 350 U.S. 422 (1956).

58. *Colonial Laws,* V, 354, 583–4; III, 757–8.

59. *Ibid.,* V, 237–9, 458, 639, 642, 874; W.L. Grant and James Monroe, *Acts of the Privy Council of England, Colonial Series* (London, 1908–12, 6 vols.), V, 399–400.

12

Framing the Fifth Amendment

In 1776 several states elevated the common-law right against self-incrimination to the status of a constitutional right. The tie with Britain having been severed by war and the Declaration of Independence, the colonies professed the quaint belief that they had been thrown back into a state of nature. Consciously acting out the social compact theory, they adopted written constitutions to provide for permanent state governments and a paramount law which, as Virginia declared, would secure the inherent rights of the people as the basis of government. Virginia blazed the trail with her celebrated Declaration of Rights as a preface to her constitution. Its author, George Mason, gratifyingly recalled, "This was the first thing of the kind upon the continent, and has been closely imitated by all the States." To Mason belongs the credit for initiating the constitutionalization of the old rule of evidence that a man cannot "be compelled to give evidence against himself." Mason not only enshrined the rule in the fundamental law; at the same time he expressed it in an ambiguous way.[1]

Out of context, the phrase had a Lilburnian resonance, proclaiming the broad principle of the *nemo tenetur* maxim. In context, it guaranteed far less than the ordinary practice of the common law. Section 8 of the Virginia Declaration of Rights stated:

That in all capital or criminal prosecutions a man hath a right to demand the cause and nature of his accusation, to be confronted with the accusers and witnesses, to call for evidence in his favor, and to a speedy trial by an impartial jury of twelve men of his vicinage, without whose unanimous consent he cannot be found guilty; nor *can he be compelled to give evidence against himself;* that no man be deprived of his liberty, except by the law of the land or the judgment of his peers.

The italicized words appear in the midst of an enumeration of the rights of the criminally accused. Therefore the constitutional right against self-incrimination was not extended to anyone but the accused, nor to any proceedings other than a criminal prosecution. Since 1677, however, the law of Virginia had required that witnesses for the prosecution must give testimony under oath, "but noe law can compell a man to sweare against himself in any matter wherein he is lyable to corporal punishment." That language protected witnesses and parties in civil, as well as criminal, proceedings against the necessity of giving testimony that might expose them to criminal penalties. Moreover, eighteenth-century manuals of trial practice showed that criminal defendants were entitled to have the sheriff subpoena witnesses to testify in their behalf under oath, subject to the exception that the witnesses need not reply to questions tending to self-incrimination.[2]

The right applied to all stages of all equity and common-law proceedings and to all witnesses as well as to the parties. It could be invoked by a criminal suspect at his preliminary examination before a justice of the peace; by a person testifying at a grand jury investigation into crime; by anyone giving evidence in a suit between private parties; and, above all perhaps, by the subject of an inquisitorial proceeding before any governmental or nonjudicial tribunal, such as a legislative committee or the governor and council, seeking to discover criminal culpability. If one's disclosures could make him vulnerable to legal peril, he could invoke his right to silence. He might even do so if his answers revealed infamy or disgrace yet could not be used against him in a subsequent prosecution. The law of Virginia at this time, as in England, shielded witnesses against mere exposure to public obloquy. The right against self-incrimination incorporated a protection against self-infamy and was as broad as the jeopardy against which it sought to guard. Yet the Virginia Declaration of Rights, though vesting a testimonial rule with the impregnability of a constitutional guarantee, provided only a stunted version of the common law.[3]

Read literally and in context, it seemed to apply only to a criminal defendant at his trial. If that was its meaning it was a superfluous guarantee, because the defendant at his trial was not even permitted to testify. If he had not confessed, the prosecution had to prove its case against him by the testimony of witnesses and other evidence; the prisoner, in turn, made his defense by witnesses, if he had them, by cross-examining the prosecution's witnesses, and by commenting on the evidence against him. If he could afford counsel, he need never open his mouth during the trial. With or without counsel, he could neither be placed on the stand by the prosecution nor take the stand if he wished. Consequently, neither George Mason nor his colleagues in the legislature, who were acting as a constitutional convention, could have meant what they said. More likely, they failed to say what they meant.[4]

The provision against self-incrimination was the result of bad draftsmanship, which is not easily explained. Mason himself, though a planter, not a lawyer, indeed not even a college graduate, was probably more learned in the law than most lawyers; what is more, he had long been a justice of the peace for Fairfax County. Section 8 of the Declaration of Rights bespoke his familiarity with criminal procedure. The Declaration, taken as a whole, reflected stylistic elegance, a philosophic cast of mind, and a knowledge of English constitutional law and American experience. Mason's draft of the Declaration, done entirely alone, was far more comprehensive than the British precedents, such as the Petition of Right and the Bill of Rights. That draft was genuinely creative, embracing as it did, rights not recognized by English law. Nevertheless, Mason's handiwork has been more praised, and justly praised, than critically analyzed. There was a certain carelessness in his work, possibly the result of haste, which the convention remedied only in part. In Section 8, for example, Mason omitted the word "impartial" before "jury," and wrote that the accused should have a right to be confronted with the accusers "or"—instead of "and"—witnesses. The final draft retained the original's reference to "capital" prosecutions, a superfluousness in view of the reference to "all . . . criminal prosecutions." The convention also retained the inadequate statement that the accused had a right to "demand" rather than to "know" the cause and nature of the accusation; indeed, he should have been guaranteed the right to have a copy of the accusation. Similarly, his right to "call" for evidence in his favor was like the right to summon spirits from the deep: there was no knowing whether they would come. Compulsory process should have been guaranteed. More importantly, the convention, thanks to James Madison, altered Mason's guarantee of "the fullest toleration in the exercise of religion" to "the free exercise of religion." Among the omissions from Mason's draft, remedied by the committee, were a provision against general search warrants, which the convention accepted, and a ban on ex post facto laws and bills of attainder, which the convention, under the influence of Patrick Henry, deleted.[5]

The impressive catalogue of rights, both as drafted and adopted, inexplicably omitted the freedoms of speech, assembly, and petition; the right to the writ of habeas corpus; grand jury proceedings; the right to counsel; and freedom from double jeopardy as well as from attainders and ex post facto laws. The rights omitted were as important and nearly as numerous as those included, making the great Virginia Declaration of Rights appear to be an erratic document compiled in slipshod fashion. Under the circumstances the constrictive guarantee of the right against self-incrimination cannot be taken as a deliberate attempt to supersede the common law's more generous practice. Thoughtlessness, rather than indifference or a purposeful narrowing, seems to be the best explanation for the self-incrimination clause.

Jefferson was unbelievably more thoughtless, omitting all the rights omitted by Mason and far more. Even in his third draft of a proposed constitution—which arrived too late in Williamsburg to be of much influence—Jefferson forgot guarantees against exclusive privileges and excessive bail, and all the positive, specific rights of the criminally accused, except trial by jury, which Mason enumerated. Jefferson would have included a ban on legislative prescription of torture, but he neglected a ban against compulsory self-incrimination. By comparison Mason's work was a model of completeness. What is so surprising is not that he was careless or thoughtless, but that the committee or the convention did not remedy his omissions or deficiencies.[6]

As for the self-incrimination clause in Section 8, there is no evidence that it was taken literally or regarded as anything but a sonorous declamation of the common-law right of long standing. Other common-law rights that had been entirely overlooked by Virginia's constitution-makers, including such vital rights as habeas corpus, grand jury indictment, and representation by counsel, continued to be observed in daily practice. Thus the great Declaration of Rights did not alter Virginia's system of criminal procedure nor express the totality of rights which actually flourished. The practice of the courts was simply unaffected by the restrictions inadvertently or unknowingly inserted in Section 8.

Section 8, nevertheless, became a model for other states and for the United States Bill of Rights. Indeed the Virginia Declaration of Rights became one of the most influential constitutional documents in our history. The committee draft was reprinted in the Philadelphia newspapers even before Independence, making it available to the delegates from all the states assembled in the Second Continental Congress. That committee draft was republished all over America, and even in England and on the Continent, in time to be a shaping force in the framing of other state constitutions. Excepting the corporate colonies of Rhode Island and Connecticut which stood pat with their old colonial charters, the other states followed Virginia's example of framing a state constitution. Eight of them, including Vermont which was technically an independent republic from 1776 until her admission to the Union in 1791, annexed separate bills of rights to their constitutions.[7]

Every one of the eight protected the right against self-incrimination, and every one in essentially the language of Virginia's Section 8, because each followed the basic formulation that no man can be "compelled to give evidence against himself." Pennsylvania in 1776 adopted Section 8 in entirety, adding only the right to be represented by counsel and retaining the self-incrimination clause verbatim. Delaware in 1776 introduced a subtle but crucial change by making that clause an independent section instead of inserting it among the enumerated rights of the criminally accused. Moreover, Delaware's guarantee, "That no Man in the Courts of common Law ought to be compelled to give Evidence against himself," extended the right against self-incrimination to witnesses, as well as parties, in civil as well as criminal cases. Maryland in the same year also placed the self-incrimination clause in a section by itself and broadened it as did Delaware, extending it not only to "a common court of law" but also to "any other court," meaning courts of equity. But Maryland simultaneously qualified the right by providing for exceptions to it "in such cases as have been usually practised in this State, or may hereafter be directed by the Legislature." That qualification, in effect, required a man to give evidence against himself if a pardon or a grant of immunity against prosecution exempted him from the penal consequences of his disclosures. North Carolina in 1776 followed Virginia's Section 8, as did Vermont in 1777. In 1780 Massachusetts slightly modified the Virginia phraseology. Referring to a criminal defendant, Massachusetts provided that he should not be compelled "to accuse, or furnish"—instead of "give"— evidence against himself. In 1784 New Hampshire followed suit. George Mason's observation that his Declaration of Rights was "closely imitated" was certainly accurate with respect to the self-incrimination clause.[8]

Of the four states—New Jersey, New York, Georgia, and South Carolina—that did not preface their constitutions with a separate bill of rights, none secured the right against self-incrimination. All, however, guaranteed some rights, even if only a few, at various points in their constitutions. New Jersey, for example had an omnibus clause that kept the common law of England in force, yet it specifically protected the right to counsel and trial by jury; New Jersey also protected freedom of religion, which the common law did not recognize. New York, too, provided that the common law, and English statutory law as well, should continue to be the law of the state, excepting the part that concerned English authority over New York or the establishment of religion. This omnibus clause has been termed a "terse bill of rights" because so many constitutional rights were embedded in the common law. Yet the right to indictment and trial by jury, which were expressly mentioned in New York's constitution, were surely secured by the common law. Why they were singled out above all other common-law rights is inexplicable, especially because the courts were enjoined to "proceed according to the course of the common law," and citizens were additionally protected by the standard "law of the land" or due process of law clause. The constitution also protected the right to vote, the free exercise of religion, representation by counsel, and a qualified freedom from bills of attainder. Perhaps these rights were singled out because they were either unprotected or, at best, inadequately protected by the common law. Yet, other rights in the same category were ignored, while trial by jury was superfluously secured. The whole process of selection in New York was baffling. No reasoned explanation nor any drawn from the evidence is available.[9]

Although the right against self-incrimination was not mentioned in New York's constitution, neither were the rights to freedom of speech and press—shade of Zenger!—nor the writ of habeas corpus. Additionally, New York ignored protections against unreasonable searches and seizures, ex post facto laws, and double jeopardy. The absence of express guarantees simply cannot be construed to indicate that these rights were not present in practice. One could no more reasonably argue that the omission of a ban against compulsory self-incrimination proved that it did not exist or was regarded without respect than he could argue that the right to the writ of habeas corpus was illusionary because it, too, was not constitutionally protected. In its enumeration of rights, New York's constitution was framed in an incredibly haphazard fashion, like New Jersey's, with no discernible principle of selection. The same observation applied to the constitutions of South Carolina and Georgia, neither of which protected the right against self-incrimination.[10]

The history of the writing of the first American bills of rights and constitutions simply does not bear out the presupposition that the process was a diligent or systematic one. Those documents, which we uncritically exalt, were imitative, deficient, and irrationally selective. In the glorious act of framing a social compact expressive of the supreme law, Americans tended simply to draw up a random catalogue of rights that seemed to satisfy their urge for a statement of first principles—or for some of them. That task was executed in a disordered fashion that verged on ineptness. The inclusion or exclusion of any particular right neither proved nor disproved its existence in a state's colonial history.

Twelve states, including Vermont but excluding Rhode Island and Connecticut, framed constitutions before the framing of the United States Bill of Rights. The only right universally secured was trial by jury in criminal cases, unless freedom of religion be added to the list even though some states guaranteed only religious toleration and others, no less than five, constitutionally permitted or provided for an establishment of religion in the form of tax supports for churches. Two states passed over a free press guarantee. Four neglected to ban excessive fines, excessive bail, compulsory self-incrimination, and general search warrants. Five ignored protections for the rights of assembly, petition, counsel, and trial by jury in civil cases. Seven omitted a prohibition on ex post facto laws, and eight skipped over the vital writ of habeas corpus. Nine failed to provide for grand jury proceedings and to condemn bills of attainder. Ten said nothing about freedom of speech, while eleven—all but New Hampshire—were silent on the matter of double jeopardy. In view of this record, the fact that every state having a separate bill of rights protected the right against self-incrimination is rather impressive. And for all their faults, the state bills of rights adopted before the federal Bill of Rights were achievements of the first magnitude compared to anything in the past, on either side of the Atlantic. The remarkable thing perhaps is that in time of war, the constructive and unprecedented task of constitution-making was successfully carried out. The enduring heroics of the Revolution were to be found in George Mason's study and in the legislative halls as well as at Valley Forge and Saratoga.[11]

Revolution and war may engender handsome statements of libertarian principle but are scarcely propitious circumstances for the nurture of personal liberties or closing the breach between profession and practice. Everywhere there was unlimited freedom to praise the American cause, but criticism of it invited a tarring and feathering by the zealots of patriotism. A Tory, after all, as Jefferson himself said, had been "properly defined to be a traitor in thought, but not in deed." Throughout the years of controversy that led to the war, and during the war itself, the patriots denied to those suspected of Tory thoughts and sympathies the rights they claimed for themselves. The maxim congenial to the spirit of liberty, let justice be done though heaven fall (*fiat justitia ruat coelum*), yielded to the maxim that in time of war the laws are silent (*inter arma silent leges*).[12]

The case of George Rome in 1773 probably foreshadowed the eclipse of the right against self-incrimination during the war. Rome was a Rhode Island Tory who wrote a private letter scathingly criticizing the Assembly and judiciary. The letter fell into the hands of the patriot party and appeared in the *Providence Gazette*. The Assembly arrested him for "vile abuse" of the government. Summoned before the bar of the house, he refused answer to the question whether the opinions expressed in the letter were his own. "I do not think," he replied, "on the privilege of an Englishman, that the question is fairly stated, because I do not consider I am to be called here to accuse myself." Rome persisted on this ground, and the Assembly, showing no respect whatever for the right against self-incrimination, voted him guilty of contempt and imprisoned him for the remainder of its session. Earlier in the same year Governor Dunmore of Virginia and his council inquisitorially examined a group of men suspected of counterfeiting. The House of Burgesses, though protesting the breach of normal criminal procedure, mentioned only the governor's failure to bring the suspects before the local court for examination. Criminals with safe political opinions fared better than law-abiding Tories. During the war Virginia imprisoned persons on mere suspicion that they might aid the enemy during some future military emergency, kept them in jail without charges or a hearing, passed a bill of attainder and outlawry, and punished traitorous opinions as well as deeds. Respect for the right against self-incrimination or for other rights would have meant to the revolutionists that their Declaration of Rights was an instrument of their destruction.[13]

In New York, where the Tories were numerically strongest, a committee "for detecting and defeating conspiracies," organized at the suggestion of Congress, used short-cut procedures in the mass trial of suspects. The function of the committee was to examine persons, and their papers, who appeared dangerous to the safety of the state, to administer loyalty oaths, and to convict the guilty. About one thousand persons were tried and sentenced and another six hundred released on bail. The legislature ignored petitions of grievance like the one stating that "the *Star Chamber Court* of commissioners for detecting & defeating conspiracies ought to be abolished." On occasion, revolutionary authorities could afford to be more respectful of procedure. The military tribunal that tried Major John André, a British spy but an officer and a gentleman, afforded him the courtesy of being at liberty to answer or deny answer to interrogatories as he chose. A more intriguing and very important case was that of Silas Deane, the American envoy whose corrupt schemes abroad, mixing profits with patriotism, set off a Congressional investigation. Deane exercised his right "not to answer questions which might tend to criminate himself," and one of his chief opponents, Henry Laurens, President of the Continental Congress, supported his right of silence, describing the inquiry as an ex-parte Inquisition." The Deane case remained controversial for several years. In 1781 "A Citizen," attacking Congressman Gouverneur Morris for having supported Deane, sought to embarrass him by asking in a newspaper letter whether he had been among those who had urged in Congress that Deane should be excused from answering questions that sought his incrimination Exempting Deane from answer, wrote "A Citizen," by permitting him to plead the right revealed "a purpose which implies a conviction in the author and abettors of it, that abuses had been committed, and could have no other end than to screen the party from detection." Morris, repudiating the implication of guilt drawn from an invocation of the right, replied in the same newspaper: " . . . and when he (Deane) prayed that he might not be bound to answer questions tending to accuse himself, I voted for granting his request. If it were to be done over I would do the same thing even if I believed him to be a villain, which I certainly did not." Morris's statement implies that Congress actually voted in favor of the lawfulness of an invocation of the right by a witness in a Congressional investigation.[14]

Four years after the Treaty of Peace that ended the war, the Constitutional Convention met in Philadelphia to form a stronger national government. No bill of rights introduced the finished work of the delegates. Only a few days before adjournment, Mason of Virginia almost perfunctorily wished "the plan had been prefaced with a Bill of Rights," because it would "give great quiet to the people," and he offered to second a motion "if made for the purpose." His belated speech persuaded Elbridge Gerry of Massachusetts to make the motion, which Mason seconded. But the delegates, voting in state units, defeated it ten to zero. Not a man present opposed a bill of rights, but having been in session for four months, the delegates were weary and eager to return home. Morover, they had planned a government of limited, enumerated powers, making unnecessary, they reasoned, a list of restraints on powers that did not exist. When, for example, there was another motion to insert a clause declaring that "the liberty of the Press should be inviolably observed," Roger Sherman of Connecticut tersely objected, "It is unnecessary. The power of Congress does not extend to the Press." The framers were also skeptical of the value of "Parchment barriers" against "overbearing majorities," as Madison put it, knowing that even an absolute constitutional prohibition, as experience had proved, dissolved in the case of an emergency or public alarm.[15]

The usually masterful politicians who dominated the Convention had seriously erred. Their arguments were plausible but neither convincing nor politic. A bill of rights could do no harm, and as Jefferson said, might do some good. The contention that declaring some rights might jeopardize others not mentioned was specious, inconsistent, and easily answerable as the Ninth Amendment showed. But there was no answer to Mason's point that a bill of rights would quiet the fears of the people. Neither was it good politics to alienate Mason and his followers or to hand them a stirring cause around which to muster opposition to ratification. Supporters of the Constitution were trapped by the fact that their principal point, "why declare that things shall not be done which there is no power to do?," might arguably apply to freedom of religion or freedom of speech, but could have no bearing on the rights of the criminally accused or personal liberties of a procedural nature. The new and, to many, very frightening national government would operate directly on individuals and be butressed by an undefined executive power and a national judiciary to enforce the laws made by Congress, and Congress had the authority to define crimes and prescribe penalties. Finally, the alleged needlessness of a bill of rights could not be squared with the fact that the proposed Constitution did explicitly protect certain rights. It tightly defined treason, provided for jury trials in criminal cases and for the writ of habeas corpus in the national courts, and banned both ex post facto laws and bills of attainder. No rational argument—and the lack of a bill of rights created a hyperemotional issue that was not amenable to rational argument—could possibly ease the fear that guaranteeing a few rights left in jeopardy others that were equally familiar and cherished but ignored. Criminal defendants might be assured of trial by jury, but what prevented the national government from seizing evidence against them by the use of general search warrants, and would they have the benefit of indictment by grand jury, a trial by a jury of the vicinage, representation by counsel, or freedom from compulsory self-incrimination, excessive bail, and cruel punishments? Security lay in the certainty of express protections, rather than the bona fides of the defenders of the Constitutions.[16]

In Pennsylvania, the second state to ratify, the Anti-Federalist minority in the state's ratifying convention indicated a willingness to accept the Constitution on condition that a number of amendments be approved. But the Federalist-dominated convention, by a vote of 46 to 23, rejected the minority propositions and even refused to enter them in the journal of the convention or in the reporter's account of the debates. Immediately after the convention adjourned, the minority published their "Address and Reasons of Dissent," which was reprinted from Richmond to Boston. Among the proposed amendment was a verbatim duplication of Virginia's Section 8, including the self-incrimination clause, made applicable "as well in the federal courts as in those of the several States" Nothing in the statement of the Pennsylvania minority, nor anything in the debates, revealed the contemporary understanding of the clause.[17]

Massachusetts, the sixth state to ratify, was the first to do so with recommended amendments. The Anti-Federalists had entered the state ratifying convention with a very substantial majority of votes. One of their spokesmen, Abraham Holmes, focused on the alleged dangers surrounding the national judicial power. Trial by jury in criminal cases had been provided for, he admitted, but the mode of trial had not been determined, nor that it be a trial in the vicinage. There was no assurance of the benefit of counsel, confrontation of accusers and witnesses, or the advantage of cross-examination. Worse still, there was nothing to prevent Congress from establishing "that diabolical institution, the Inquisition." His frenetic forebodings unleashed, Holmes declared that in the absence of constitutional checks, Congress might invent "the most cruel and unheard of punishments . . . racks and gibbets may be amongst the most mild instruments of their discipline." What was needed, Holmes advised, was something to prevent Congress from passing laws that might compel a person, accused or suspected of a crime, from furnishing evidence against himself. Without such a check, if the worst did not come to pass, "it would be owing *entirely* . . . to the goodness of the men, and not in the *least degree* owing to the goodness of the Constitution." By overstating his case, Holmes lost it. Clearly, however, he spoke of the right against self-incrimination only in connection with the criminally accused.[18]

The Reverend Samuel Stillman, in defense of the Constitution, reminded the convention that Congress was a representative body, elected by the people of the states. "Who are Congress, then? They are ourselves; the men of our own choice, in whom we can confide . . . Why is it then that gentlemen speak of Congress as some foreign body, as a set of men who will seek every opportunity to enslave us?" Stillman observed that not even a perfect Constitution could secure the liberties of the people "unless they watch their own liberties. Nothing written on paper will do this." Knowledge and freedom were inseparable. If education were widespread and Americans remained an enlightened people attached to liberty, the cause of tyranny had no hope. When John Hancock and Samuel Adams, the most influential men in the convention, threw their support to Stillman's voice of reason rather than to Holmes's hysteria, there was no chance for amendments that would do battle against the revival of the Inquisition with its racks and gibbets.

The brief list of amendments recommended by Massachusetts mentioned only two matters that belonged with a traditional bill of rights, jury trial in civil suits between citizens of different states and indictment by grand jury. Ironically, the grand-jury system, which was as strong in Massachusetts as in any common-law jurisdiction, had no place in the state constitution. No principle of selection may be discerned for the choice of the civil jury and indictment among all the rights that could have been chosen for protection. To have marked them for enumeration rather than freedom of religion, speech, or press, or bans on general warrants and compulsory self-incrimination was capricious. Yet Massachusetts led the way toward recommended amendments.[19]

Every state convention thereafter urged amendments to the Constitution, but, inexplicably, only the last four to ratify recommended comprehensive bills of rights. As a result many crucial rights received the support of only these states. All four of them urged a self-incrimination clause. The first of these four to ratify was Virginia, where Patrick Henry, the demagogic idol of the people, zealously opposed ratification as if once again combating British tyranny. The Constitution seemed to him to be a conspiracy against the liberties of the people, proof that he was right in having turned down a seat in the Constitutional Convention because he had "smelt a rat." His credentials as the champion of individual freedoms had been besmirched by his responsibility for Virginia's having enacted a bill of attainder and by his leadership of the opposition to Jefferson's Statute for Religious Freedom. But he was the master of the rhetorical thunderbolt and creator of an emotional climate of fear that alarmed rather than informed. Denouncing the omission of a bill of rights and prophesying imaginary horrors masked more practical, even ignoble, objections to the Constitution. Objections to the powers of commerce and taxation were not as easily popularized in dramatic terms. Congress, Henry warned, might replace the common law with the civil law of Europe and "introduce the practice of France, Spain, and Germany—of torturing, to extort a confession of crime." On such reasoning he recommended that the states adopt amendments to the Constitution prior to its ratification, including a bill of rights modeled on Virginia's of 1776. Neither Henry nor anyone else explained the meaning of the self-incrimination clause of Section 8, nor, for the matter, of any of the other rights that they recommended. The only reply to him by an advocate of the Constitution, on the self-incrimination issue, came from George Nicholas who cynically observed that if a bill of rights was the only protection against torture, "we might be tortured tomorrow; for it has been repeatedly infringed and disregarded." Mason, misunderstanding him to have said that there was no guarantee against torture in Virginia's Declaration of Rights, pointed out that one clause provided that no man could give evidence against himself, "and the worthy gentlemen must know that, in those countries where torture is used, evidence was extorted from the criminal himself." Another clause, Mason added, prohibited cruel and unusual punishments. The convention adopted Henry's proposals, but only in the form of recommended amendments. Nothing in the proceedings provided any illumination of the meaning of the self-incrimination clause in Virginia, except perhaps that it applied to the criminally accused and barred torture.[20]

Among the proposed amendments offered by the New York ratifying convention was one insuring "that in all criminal prosecutions, the accused . . . should not be compelled to give evidence against himself." Unfortunately the record of the state convention's debates does not illuminate the reasons for this or for any other proposal included in the suggested national bill of rights. The debates are fully reported through July 2, 1788, when a bill of rights was mentioned for the first time in a speech by Thomas Tredwell, an Anti-Federalist delegate who expressed apprehension about the danger of tyranny on the part of the new United States courts. None could say, he declared, whether their proceedings would be according to the common law or the "civil, the Jewish, or Turkish law," and he warned darkly about the history of inquisitions in the Star Chamber Court of England. Tredwell's is the last reported speech on any subject. The proceedings of the convention are thereafter reported in brief minutes. We know little more than that on July 7, John Lansing, one of the Anti-Federalist leaders, reported a proposed bill of rights, that it was debated on the nineteenth, and was passed on the twenty-sixth.[21]

New York's recommended bill of rights, which included a provision on the right against self-incrimination, was the product of an interstate Anti-Federalist committee of correspondence. As early as June 9, a letter to John Lamb, as head of "the federal Republican Committee of New York," from George Mason, chairman of the Republican Society of Virginia, concurred in Lamb's suggestion of a "free correspondence on the Subject of amendments." George Mason, Patrick Henry, and William Grayson kept Lamb informed of the nature and progress of proposed amendments in the Virginia convention, while Lamb kept in touch with Eleazer Oswald of Pennsylvania, Rawlins Lowndes of South Carolina, Joshua Atherton of New Hampshire, and Timothy Bloodworth of North Carolina, all leading Anti-Federalists. The Pennsylvania minority, whose dissenting report was circulated in New York, had proposed an amendment securing the right against self-incrimination, taken from the Virginia Declaration of Rights of 1776. Copies of Virginia's declaration were forwarded to Lamb by Patrick Henry and to Robert Yates by George Mason.[22]

The initial proposal for a bill of rights, by Lansing, consisted of three sections: one securing the rights of life and liberty in general, another vesting sovereignty in the people, and the third a verbatim statement of Section 8 of the Virginia Declaration of Rights. On July 19, Melancthon Smith proposed amendments constituting a bill of rights. Excepting a comment by John Jay to the effect that no bill of rights was needed, there appears to have been no debate on the motion. On its passage, Smith moved adoption of "the Virginia amendments," the entire package proposed by the Virginia convention which on June 25 had voted for ratification with recommended amendments, including a provision copied from Section 8. The only debate in New York occurred on the question whether the amendments were to be recommended or made conditional. Thus, under the influence of Virginia, the right against self-incrimination was recommended by the New York convention, notwithstanding its absence in the state's own constitution. Other states also recommended rights not secured by their own constitutions. Virginia, for example, urged the right to counsel and the freedoms of speech, assembly, and petition, none of which were mentioned in her celebrated Declaration of Rights. In New York, both Anti-Federalists and Federalists unquestioningly accepted the right against self-incrimination as a desideratum in the procedures to be followed in federal criminal prosecutions. There is nothing in the circumstances surrounding the New York proposal to doubt that the right was a traditional and respected part of the state's common-law system of criminal procedure. One may suspect the political motives of the anti-Federalists in demanding that a bill of rights be affixed to the new national constitution, but not the sincerity of their belief in the value of their proposals.[23]

The other two states recommending amendments that included a self-incrimination clause were North Carolina and Rhode Island. Ratification by the latter, coming after the First Congress had already drafted the Bill of Rights, was too late to be of any influence. Both states used the Virginia formula, broadly stating the principle that no man should be compelled to give evidence against himself, but placing the clause in a context that unmistakably referred only to the criminally accused. New York alone had made that reference explicit. The Fifth Amendment's clause would be closer to the Virginia formula and yet be unique.[24]

In the First Congress, Representative James Madison redeemed a campaign pledge to fight for a bill of rights as soon as the new national government went into operation. Although he had originally opposed a bill of rights for the usual Federalist reasons, Madison, even if still somewhat skeptical of the efficacy of such a bill, had become a convert to the cause. He deserves to be remembered as "father of the Bill of Rights" even more than as "father of the Constitution," his usual appellation. Jefferson, his friend and mentor, in a brilliant exchange of letters had persuaded him to surrender his initial opposition, but political expediency was not without its influence, too. In addition to the promise Madison had made to his constituents, he realized that amendments would allay the apprehensions—misapprehensions he thought them—of a large part of the American public. He meant to prove that the new national government was a friend of liberty. He even included a proposed amendment to prevent the states, which opponents of the Constitution had represented as guarantors of personal freedom, from infringing the equal rights of conscience, freedom of the press, and trial by jury. This, he declared, was "the most valuable" of all his proposals. Madison also understood that the adoption of his amendments would do more than reconcile the people who had been frightened by the anti-Federalist cry that "they're taking away your liberties!" His amendments, if adopted, would make extremely difficult the subsequent passage of proposals, so close to the hearts of the opposition party, that were intended to hamstring the substantive powers of the national government. He argued that his amendments would raise a standard of conduct for government to follow and provide a basis for judicial review on behalf of civil liberties: "If they are incorporated into the Constitution, independent tribunals of justice will consider themselves in a peculiar manner the guardians of those rights; they will be an impenetrable bulwark against every assumption of power in the Legislative or Executive; they will be naturally led to resist every encroachment upon rights expressly stipulated for in the Constitution by the declaration of rights."[25]

Madison's proposals, introduced on June 8, 1789, were, in the words of Fisher Ames of Massachusetts, "the fruit of much labor and research." He had "hunted up," said Ames, all the grievances expressed in the newspapers, the state debates, and the recommendations of state ratifying conventions. His long, masterful speech on behalf of his proposals forced an apathetic House to take action, though men of both parties were reluctant; they were more interested in attending to tonnage duties and a judiciary bill. Many Federalists still thought that a bill of rights was unnecessary, while Anti-Federalists, who so recently had urged a bill of rights with all the rhetorical powers that they could muster, sought to scuttle Madison's proposals. They began by stalling, then tried to annex amendments aggrandizing state powers, and finally depreciated the importance of the very protections of individual liberty that they had formerly demanded. Madison would not be put off. He was insistent, compelling, unyielding, and, finally, triumphant.[26]

As originally proposed by Madison, the Fifth Amendment's self-incrimination clause was part of a miscellaneous article that read: "No person shall be subject, except in cases of impeachment, to more than one punishment or trial for the same offence; nor shall be compelled to be a witness against himself; nor be deprived of life, liberty, or property, without due process of law; nor be obliged to relinquish his property, where it may be necessary for public use, without a just compensation." This proposal reflects the research and novelty that characterized Madison's work. Not a single state, for example, had a constitutional guarantee that life, liberty, or property should not be deprived but by due process of law, although New York, but only New York, had recommended such a clause. No state had recommended a just-compensation clause, though both Massachusetts and Vermont had such provisions in their constitutions. New Hampshire was the only state with a provision against double jeopardy. But no state, either in its own constitution or in its recommended amendments, had a self-incrimination clause phrased like that introduced by Madison: "no person . . . shall be compelled to be a witness against himself."[27]

Not only was Madison's phrasing original; his placement of the clause was also unusual. In the widely imitated model of his own state, the clause appeared in the midst of an enumeration of the procedural rights of the criminally accused at his trial. Only Delaware and Maryland had departed from this precedent by giving the clause independent status and applicability in all courts, thereby extending it to witnesses as well as parties and to civil as well as criminal proceedings. In presenting his amendments, Madison said nothing whatever that explained his intentions concerning the self-incrimination clause. Nor do his papers or correspondence illuminate his meaning. We have only the language of his proposal, and that revealed an intent to incorporate into the Constitution the whole scope of the common-law right. From the very meaning of its terms, Madison's proposal seemed as broad as the old *nemo tenetur* maxim in which it had its origins, while at the same time it virtually amalgamated that maxim with another that was different in origin and purpose: *nemo debet esse testis in propria causa* (no man should be a witness in his own case).

Madison's proposal certainly applied to civil as well as criminal proceedings and in principle to any stage of a legal inquiry, from the moment of arrest in a criminal case, to the swearing of a deposition in a civil one. And not being restricted to judicial proceedings, it extended to any other kind of governmental inquiry such as a legislative investigation. Moreover, the unique phrasing, that none could be compelled to be a witness against himself, was far more comprehensive than a prohibition against self-incrimination. By its terms the clause could also apply to any testimony that fell short of making one vulnerable to criminal jeopardy or civil penalty or forfeiture, but that nevertheless exposed him to public disgrace or obloquy, or other injury to name and reputation. Finally, Madison's phrasing protected third parties, those who were merely witnesses called to give testimony for one side or the other, whether in civil, criminal, or equity proceedings. According to customary procedure, witnesses, unlike parties, could in fact be compelled to give evidence, under oath, although they were safeguarded against the necessity of testifying against themselves in any manner that might open them to prosecution for a criminal offense or subject them to a forfeiture or civil penalties. By contrast, neither the criminal defendant nor the parties to a civil suit could be compelled to give testimony at all. They could furnish evidence neither for nor against themselves. The law did require mere witnesses to give evidence for or against the parties, but not against themselves. Madison, going beyond the recommendations of the states and the constitution of his own state, phrased his own proposal to make it coextensive with the broadest practice. He might have achieved the same end by retaining the language of the Virginia recommendation, that no man can be compelled to give evidence against himself, but fixing it outside of the context of criminal prosecutions.[28]

Madison's proposed amendments were sent to a select committee of which he was a member. The committee, when reporting to the House, made no change in the positioning or language of the clause protecting persons from being witnesses against themselves. The report was taken up by the Committee of the Whole after Madison fought off further delaying tactics, and debate followed seriatim on each proposed amendment. There was no debate, however, on the clause in question. Only one speaker, John Laurence, a Federalist lawyer of New York, addressed himself to what he called the proposal that "a person shall not be compelled to give evidence against himself." Interestingly, he restated Madison's phrasing in the language of the more familiar clause deriving from Section 8 of the Virginia Declaration of Rights, as if they were the same. Calling it "a general declaration in some degree contrary to laws passed," Laurence thought that it should "be confined to criminal cases," and he moved an amendment for that purpose. The amendment was adopted, apparently without discussion, not even by Madison, and then the clause as amended was adopted unanimously. We do not know whether the House debated Laurence's motion or what the vote on it was. The speed with which the House seems to have acted, without the record showing any controversy over the significant restriction of the scope of the clause, is bewildering. Simple respect for the House's own distinguished select committee, a nonpartisan group that included one member from each state, five of whom had been delegates to the Philadelphia Constitutional Convention of 1787, ought to have required some explanation. The select committee, following Madison, had intended what Laurence rightly called "a general declaration." Taken literally, the amended clause, "No person shall . . . be compelled in any criminal case, to be a witness against himself," excluded from its protection parties and witnesses in civil and equity suits as well as witnesses before nonjudicial governmental proceedings such as legislative investigations. It now applied only to parties and witnesses in criminal cases, presumably to all stages of proceedings from arrest and examination to indictment and trial.[29]

Laurence's passing remark that the committee proposal was "in some degree contrary to laws passed" was inaccurate, yet illuminated the purpose of his motion to amend. Exactly a month earlier, on July 17, the Senate had passed and sent to the House the bill that became the Judiciary Act of 1789. Thanks to Madison's efforts, the House merely read the judiciary bill for a first and second time on July 20, then tabled it indefinitely while it attended to the matter of amending the Constitution. Not until the House approved of the proposed amendments and sent them to the Senate on August 24 did the Committee of the Whole take up the judiciary bill. Its provisions, which had been fiercely contested in the Senate, contained a section to which

Laurence may have alluded when referring to "laws passed." Section 15 in the original Senate draft empowered the federal courts to compel civil parties to produce their books or papers containing relevant evidence. It also provided that a plaintiff might require a defendant, on proving to the satisfaction of a court that the defendant had deprived him of evidence to support his cause, "to disclose on oath his or her knowledge in the cause in cases and under circumstances where a respondent might be compelled to make such a disclosure on oath by the aforesaid rules of chancery." Opponents of that final clause described it as an authorization for "inquisitorial powers." Senator William Maclay of Pennsylvania argued that "extorting evidence from any person was a species of torture. . . . [H]ere was an attempt to exercise a tyranny of the same kind over the mind. The conscience was to be put on the rack; that forcing oaths or evidence from men, I consider equally tyrannical as extorting evidence by torture." The clause, he concluded, would offend his constitutents, whose state bill of rights provided that no person could be compelled to give evidence against himself. As a result of such opposition the oath provision was stricken from the bill as adopted by the Senate. Nevertheless, it retained the clause forcing the production of books or papers that contained pertinent evidence in civil cases "under circumstances where they might be compelled to produce the same by the ordinary rules of proceeding in Chancery," that is, in courts of equity.[30]

According to an early federal court ruling, this provision was intended to prevent the necessity of instituting equity suits to obtain from an adverse party the production of documents related to a litigated issue. The provision did not suspend or supersede the right against self-incrimination, but it did limit the reach of the general principle that no one could be compelled to be a witness against himself. The documents in question could be against the party without incriminating him. He might, for example, be forced to produce a deed proving plaintiff's ownership, thereby exposing himself to a civil, but not a criminal, liability. Thus Laurence, with this pending legislation in mind, may have moved the insertion of the words "in any criminal case" in order to retain the customary equity rule that compelled evidence of civil liability. To compel a civil defendant to produce records or papers "against himself," harming his case, in no way infringed his traditional right not to produce them if they could harm him criminally. The House, incidentally, passed the judiciary bill with Section 15 unchanged.[31]

In the Senate, the House's proposed amendments to the Constitution underwent further change. However, the Senate accepted the self-incrimination clause without change. The double jeopardy clause in the same article was rephrased and a clause on the grand jury, which the House had coupled with guarantees relating to the trial of crimes, was transferred to the beginning of what became the Fifth Amendment. In what was to be the Sixth Amendment the Senate clustered together the procedural rights of the criminally accused after indictment. That the self-incrimination clause did not fall into the Sixth Amendment indicated that the Senate, like the House, did not intend to follow the implication of Virginia's Section 8, the original model, that the right not to give evidence against oneself applied merely to the defendant on trial. The Sixth Amendment, referring explicitly to the accused, protected him alone. Indeed the Sixth Amendment, with the right of counsel added, was the equivalent of Virginia's Section 8 and included all of its rights except that against self-incrimination. Thus, the location of the self-incrimination clause in the Fifth Amendment rather than the Sixth proves that the Senate, like the House, did not intend to restrict that clause to the criminal defendant only nor only to his trial. The Fifth Amendment, even with the self-incrimination clause restricted to criminal cases, still put its principle broadly enough to apply to witnesses and to any phase of the proceedings.[32]

The clause by its terms also protected against more than just "self-incrimination," a phrase that had never been used in the long history of its origins and development. The "right against self-incrimination" is a short-hand gloss of modern origin that implies a restriction not in the constitutional clause. The right not to be a witness against oneself imports a principle of wider reach, applicable, at least in criminal cases, to the self-production of any adverse evidence, including evidence that made one the herald of his own infamy, thereby publicly disgracing him. The clause extended, in other words, to all the injurious as well as incriminating consequences of disclosure by witness or party. But this inference drawn from the wording of the clause enjoys the support of no proof based on American experience, as distinguished from English, before the nineteenth century. Clearly, however, to speak merely of a right against self-incrimination stunts the wider right not to give evidence against oneself, as the Virginia model put it, or not to be a witness against oneself, as the Fifth Amendment stated. The previous history of the right, both in England and America, proves that it was not bound by rigid definition. After the adoption of the Fifth Amendment, the earliest state and federal cases were in accord with that previous history, which suggests that whatever the wording of the constitutional formulation, it did not supersede or even limit the common-law right.[33]

Pennsylvania's experience is to the point. The state constitution of 1776 had followed the Virginia model by placing in the context of criminal prosecutions the principle that "no man" should be compelled to give evidence against himself. In 1790 Pennsylvania, in a new constitution, replaced the "no man" formulation with a specific reference to "the accused." Nevertheless, in the first Pennsylvania case involving this clause, the state supreme court ignored the restriction introduced in 1790 or, rather, interpreted it as expressing in the most extraordinary latitude the *nemo tenetur* maxim. The case involved a prosecution for violating an election-law that required answers on oath to questions concerning loyalty during the American Revolution. Counsel for defense argued that the constitutional clause of 1790 protected against questions the answers to which might tend to result in a prosecution or bring the party into disgrace or infamy. Chief Justice Edward Shippen, who had studied at Middle Temple and began his legal practice in Pennsylvania way back in 1750, delivered the following opinion:

> It has been objected that the questions propounded to the electors contravene an established principle of law. The maxim is, 'Nemo tenetur seipsum accusare (sen prodere).' It is founded on the best policy, and runs throughout our whole system of jurisprudence. It is the uniform practice of courts of justice as to witnesses and jurors. It is considered cruel and unjust to propose questions which may tend to criminate the party. And so jealous have the legislatures of this commonwealth been of this mode of discovery of facts that they have refused their assent to a bill brought in to compel persons to disclose on oath papers as well as facts relating to questions of mere property. And may we not justly suppose, that they would not be less jealous of securing our citizens against this mode of self-accusation? The words 'accusare' and 'prodere' are general terms, and their sense is not confined to cases where the answers to the questions proposed would induce to the punishment of the party. If they would involve him in shame or reproach, he is under no obligation to answer them.

The same court applied a similar rule in a purely civil case, holding that no one could be forced to take the oath of a witness if his testimony "tends to accuse himself of an immoral act."[34]

The state courts of the framers' generation followed the extension of the right to cover self-infamy as well as self-incrimination, although the self-infamy rule eventually fell into disuse. Both federal and state courts followed in all other respects Shippen's far-reaching interpretation of what on its face and in context was a narrow clause. In the earliest federal case on the right against self-incrimination, Justice James Iredell of the Supreme Court, on circuit duty, ruled that a *witness* was not bound to answer a question that might tend to "implicate" or criminate himself. In one of the most famous cases in our constitutional history, *Marbury v. Madison*, Attorney-General Levi Lincoln balked at a question relating to his conduct of his office as Acting Secretary of State when Jefferson first became President. Marbury's commission as a justice of the peace for the District of Columbia had been signed by the outgoing President and affixed with the seal of the United States by the then Secretary of State, John Marshall, who had had no time to deliver it. What, asked Chief Justice Marshall, had Lincoln done with that commission? Lincoln, who probably had burned it, replied that he did not think that he was bound to disclose his official transactions while acting as Secretary of State, nor should he "be compelled to answer any thing which might tend to criminate himself." Marbury's counsel, Charles Lee, who was himself a former Attorney-General of the United States, and Chief Justice Marshall were in agreement: Lincoln, who was in the peculiar position of being both a witness and counsel for the government in a civil suit, was not obliged to disclose anything that might incriminate him. In Burr's trial, Chief Justice Marshall, without referring to the constitutional clause, again sustained the right of a witness to refuse answer to an incriminating question. The courts have always assumed that the meaning of the constitutional clause is determined by the common law.[35]

Whether the framers of the Fifth Amendment intended it to be fully co-extensive with the common law cannot be proved—or disproved. The language of the clause and its framer's understanding of it may not have been synonymous. The difficulty is that its framers, from Mason to Madison and Laurence, left too few clues. Nothing but passing explication emerged during the process of state ratification of the Bill of Rights from 1789 through 1791. Indeed, in legislative and convention proceedings, in letters, newspapers, and tracts, in judicial opinions and law books, the whole period from 1776 to 1791 reveals neither sufficient explanation of the scope of such a clause nor the reasons for it. That it was a ban on torture and a security for the criminally accused were the most important of its functions, as had been the case historically, but these were not the whole of its functions. Still, nothing can be found of a theoretical nature expressing a rationale or underlying policy for the right in question or its reach.

By 1776 the principle of the *nemo tenetur* maxim was simply taken for granted and so deeply accepted that its constitutional expression had the mechanical quality of a ritualistic gesture in favor of a self-evident truth needing no explanation. The clause itself, whether in Virginia's Section 8 or the Fifth Amendment, might have been so imprecisely stated, or misstated, as to raise vital questions of intent, meaning, and purpose. But constitution-makers, in that day at least, did not regard themselves as framers of detailed codes. To them the statement of a bare principle was sufficient, and they were content to put it spaciously, if somewhat ambiguously, in order to allow for its expansion as the need might arise.

By stating the principle in the Bill of Rights, which was also a bill of restraints upon government, they were once again sounding the tocsin against the dangers of government oppression of the individual; and they were voicing their conviction that the right against self-incrimination was a legitimate defense possessed by every individual against government. Tough-minded revolutionists, the equal of any in history in the art of self-government, they were willing to risk lives and fortunes in support of their belief that government is but an instrument of man, its sovereignty held in subordination to his rights. None in history can be less justly accused than they of being soft, naive, or disregardful of the claims of law and order. They were mindful, nevertheless, that the enduring interests of the community required justice to be done as fairly as possible. The Constitution with its amendments was an embodiment of their political morality, an ever-present reminder of their view that the citizen is the master of his government, not its subject. As Abe Fortas observed, "The principle that a man is not obliged to furnish the state with ammunition to use against him is basic to this conception." The state, he acknowledged, must defend itself and, "within the limits of accepted procedure," punish lawbreakers. "But it has no right to compel the sovereign individual to surrender or impair his right of self-defense." The fundamental value reflected by the Fifth Amendment "is intangible, it is true; but so is liberty, and so is man's immortal soul. A man may be punished, even put to death, by the state; but . . . he should not be made to prostrate himself before its majesty. *Mea culpa* belongs to a man and his God. It is a plea that cannot be exacted from free men by human authority. To require it is to insist that the state is the superior of the individuals who compose it, instead of their instrument."[36]

The same point underlay the statement of another distinguished federal judge, who observed, "Our forefathers, when they wrote this provision into the Fifth Amendment of the Constitution, had in mind a lot of history which has been largely forgotten to-day." The remark applies with equal force, of course, to the right of representation by counsel, trial by jury, or any of the other, related procedural rights that are constitutionally sanctified. With good reason the Bill of Rights showed a preoccupation with the subject of criminal justice. The framers understood that without fair and regularized procedures to protect the criminally accused, there could be no liberty. They knew that from time immemorial, the tyrant's first step was to use the criminal law to crush his opposition. Vicious and ad hoc procedures had always been used to victimize nonconformists and minorities of differing religious, racial, or political persuasion. The Fifth Amendment was part and parcel of the procedures that were so crucial, in the minds of the framers, to the survival of the most treasured rights. One's home could not be his "castle," his property be his own, his right to express his opinions or to worship his God be secure, if he could be searched, arrested, tried, or imprisoned in some arbitrary or ignoble manner. As Justice Frankfurter declared, "The privilege against self-incrimination is a specific provision of which it is peculiarly true that 'a page of history is worth a volume of logic.' "[37]

The framers of the Bill of Rights saw their injunction, that no man should be a witness against himself in a criminal case, as a central feature of the accusatory system of criminal justice. While deeply committed to perpetuating a system that minimized the possibilities of convicting the innocent, they were not less concerned about the humanity that the fundamental law should show even to the offender. Above all, the Fifth Amendment reflected their judgment that in a free society, based on respect for the individual, the determination of guilt or innocence by just procedures, in which the accused made no unwilling contribution to his conviction, was more important than punishing the guilty.

Notes

1. Mason to George Mercer, Oct. 2, 1778, quoted in Kate Mason Rowland, *The Life of George Mason, 1725–1792* (New York, 1892, 2 vols.), I, 237. See also Robert A. Rutland, *The Birth of the Bill of Rights, 1776–1791* (Chapel Hill, N.C., 1955), 30–44.
2. Sect. 8, Virginia Declaration of Rights, in Francis N. Thorpe, ed., *The Federal and State Constitutions, Colonial Charters, and Other Organic Laws* (Washington, 1909, 7 vols.), VII, 3813 (italics added). William Waller Hening, ed., *The Statutes at Large Being a Collection of All the Laws of Virginia* (1619–1792) (Richmond, 1809–23, 13 vols.), 11, 442, for the act of 1677. Richard Starke, *Office and Authority of a Justice of the Peace* (Williamsburg, Va., 1774), 141, 146. See also Hugh F. Rankin, *Criminal Trial Proceedings in the General Court of Virginia* (Charlottesville, Va., 1965), 99, and Arthur P. Scott, *Criminal Law in Colonial Virginia* (Chicago, 1930), 100. Parties in civil, as well as criminal, cases were incompetent by reason of "interest" to be witnesses in their own behalf, John H. Wigmore, *A Treatise on the Anglo-American System of Evidence in Trials at Common Law* (Boston, 1940, 3rd ed., 10 vols.), II, 681–2, 693–5.
3. Starke, *Office and Authority*, 145, 146. Sir William Blackstone wrote that "no man is to be examined to prove his own infamy" and said that not even a juror could be examined as to "any thing which tends to his disgrace or disadvantage," *Commentaries on the Law of England* (Oxford, 1765–69,4 vols.), III, 364, 370.
4. In their descriptions of criminal procedure in colonial Virginia, neither Scott, 50–101, nor Rankin, 67–103, makes mention of the defendant's testifying, even unsworn, or being questioned by the prosecution, or saying anything.
5. Rowland, *Mason*, I, 239–41, 437; William T. Hutchinson and William M. E. Rachal, eds., *The Papers of James Madison* (Chicago, 1962 ff., 5 vols.), I,170–78.
6. Julian P. Boyd *et al.*, eds., *The Papers of Thomas Jefferson (Princeton, 1950 ff., 17 vols.),* I, 341, 348, 359. In a proposed constitution for Virginia, drafted in 1783, Jefferson again omitted the right against self-incrimination, but again included a provision against torture, *ibid.*, VI, 298. He believed that the Declaration of Rights and Constitution of 1776 had the status of an ordinance only because not expressly declared to be superior to statutory law; yet his proposed constitution of 1783 contained no separate bill of rights and few rights that belong in such a document. In practice, the document of 1776 was regarded as fundamental and supreme law, *ibid.*, VI, 279–80.
7. On the committee draft, which is printed in Rowland, I, 436–8, see *The Papers of Madison*, I, 171. The final draft is in Thorpe, ed., *Federal and State Constitutions*, VII, 3812–14.
8. Thorpe, ed., III, 1688 (Maryland); III, 1891 (Massachusetts); IV 2455 (New Hampshire); V, 2787 (North Carolina), 3083 (Pennsylvania); VII, 3471 (Vermont). Thorpe did not include the Delaware Declaration of Rights of 1776; it is available in *Proceedings of the Convention of the Delaware State Held at New-Castle on Tuesday the Twenty-Seventh of August, 1776* (1776, reprinted Wilmington, Del., 1927), 19.
9. Thorpe, ed., V, 2594–8 (New Jersey); V. 2623–38 (New York). Julius Goebel, Jr., and T. Raymond Naughton, *Law Enforcement in Colonial New York: A Study in Criminal Procedure (1664–1776)* (New York. 1944) xvii; see also *ibid.*, 57, 325.
10. Thorpe, ed., II, 777–85 (Georgia); VI, 3248–57 (South Carolina).
11. Edward Dumbauld, "State Precedents for the Bill of Rights," *Journal of Public Law,*

VII (1958), 323–44, includes a useful table, at pp. 343–4 showing the rights protected by state declarations of rights. But Dumbauld did not include those states that did not have a separate bill of rights, nor did he include rights guaranteed in the main body of the constitution of those that did have a separate bill. My figures include all states and Vermont. The "Table of Sources of the Provisions of the Bill of Rights" in Dumbauld's handy guide, The *Bill of Rights and What It Means Today* (Norman, Okla., 1957), 160–65, is also incomplete.

12. Thomas Jefferson, *Notes on the State of Virginia,* ed. William Peden (Chapel Hill, N.C., 1955), 155. See also Leonard W. Levy, *Jefferson and Civil Liberties: The Darker Side* (Cambridge, Mass., 1963), ch. 2.

13. For the Rome case, see David S. Lovejoy, *Rhode Island Politics and the American Revolution, 1760–1776* (Providence, 1958), 174–6, 217 n. II. For the Virginia incident, see the address of the House of Burgesses to Gov. Dunmore, March 13, 1773, in H.R. McIlwaine and J.P. Kennedy, eds., *Journals of the House of Burgesses of Virginia (1619–1776)* (Richmond, 1905–15, 13 vols.), XIII, 22. See also Rankin, 192–5. Although the Burgesses did not allude in any way to the right against self-incrimination, Pittman, "Colonial and Constitutional History of the Privilege," *Virginia Law Review,* XXI, 786, leaves a contrary impression. On Virginia's treatment of Tories during the Revolution, see Levy, *Jefferson,* ch. 2.

14. Victor Hugo Paltsits, ed., *Minutes of the Commissioners for Detecting and Defeating Conspiracies in the State of New York: Albany County Sessions, 1778–1781* (Albany, 1909, 3 vols.), I, 26. The volumes are filled, *passim,* with instances of individuals being examined under oath against themselves, but the examinations themselves are not given. The *Minutes* refer to "examinations on file," but they could not be located; they were probably burned in the fire of 1911. *The Minutes of the Committee and of the First Commission for Detecting and Defeating Conspiracies in the State of New York (1776–1778)),* New York Historical Society, *Collections* (New York, 1924–25, 2 vols.), contain similar instances. See also Claude H. Van Tyne, *The Loyalists of the American Revolution* (New York, 1902), 271. On André, see Peleg W. Chandler, ed., *American Criminal Trials* (Boston, 1841–44, 2 vols.), II, 168. On Deane, see Statement of Henry Laurens, April 21, 1779, in Edmund C. Burnett, ed., *Letters of the Members of the Continental Congress* (Washington, 1928, 5 vols.), IV, 166 n. 12, 168; *Freeman's Journal, or North-American Intelligencer* (Philadelphia), June 6 and 14, 1781. The *Journals of the Continental Congress* have nothing of relevance.

15. Max Farrand, ed., *The Records of the Federal Convention of 1787* (New Haven, 1911–37, 4 vols.), II, 587–8, 617–18, 628. Rutland, *Birth of the Bill of Rights,* ch. VI, contains a good account of the Convention in relation to civil liberties. On "parchment barriers," see Madison to Jefferson, Oct. 17, 1788, in Boyd, ed., *Papers of Jefferson, XIV,* 19. For illustrations of a similar sentiment among other Virginians, see Jonathan Elliot, ed., *The Debates in the Several State Conventions on the Adoption of the Federal Constitution* (Philadelphia, 1941, 2nd ed. rev., 5 vols.), III, 66, 70 (Randolph); 298 (Pendleton); 450–52 (Nicholas); 223, 561 (Marshall).

16. The quotation is from Hamilton in *The Federalist, #84* (var. eds.). See also James Wilson, in Elliot, ed., *Debates, IV,* 435 ff., 453 ff. On protections in the main body of the Constitution, see Farrand, ed., *Records,* II, 340–42, 344–50, 375–6, 438, 617–18.

17. The Address of the Minority is in John Bach McMaster and Frederick D. Stone, eds., *Pennsylvania and the Federal Constitution, 1787–1788* (Philadelphia, 1888), 454–83; the duplication of Section 8 is at p. 461.

18. Elliot, ed., *Debates,* II, 111.
19. *Ibid.,* II, 166–70,177.
20. *Ibid.,* III, 447–8, 451, 452, 593, 658.
21. *Ibid.,* I, 328, for the proposed amendment, and II, 400, 410–13.
22. George Mason to John Lamb, June 9, 1788; Patrick Henry to John Lamb, June 9, 1788, William Grayson to John Lamb, June 9, 1788; John Lamb to Governor Clinton, June 17, 1788; John Lamb to Joshua Atherton, June 6, 1788; Joshua Atherton to John Lamb, June 11, 1788; Rawlins Lowndes to John Lamb, June 21, 1788; Joshua Atherton to John Lamb, June 23, 1788; Timothy Bloodworth to John Lamb, July 1, 1788; Draft "Amendments to the New Constitution of Government" in the hand of Lamb's son-in-law, Charles Tillinghast: all in John Lamb Papers, Box 5, New-York Historical Society. Also, George Mason to John Mason, Sept. 2, Dec. 18, 1788, George Mason Papers, 1766–1788, pp. 245, 249, New York Public Library.
23. "Proceedings of the Convention of the State of New York in a Committee of the Whole," July 7, 1788, John McKesson Papers, Box 3, New-York Historical Society; Gilbert Livingston Papers, Box 2, New York Public Library. On the motives of the Anti-Federalists, see Levy, *Legacy,* 214–37 *passim.*
24. Elliot, ed., *Debates, IV, 243 (North Carolina); I, 334 (Rhode Island, which ratified June 16, 1790).*
25. For the exchange of letters, all in Boyd, ed., *Papers of Jefferson:* Jefferson to Madison, Dec. 20, 1787, XII, 439–40; Jefferson to Madison, July 31, 1788, XIII, 442–3; Madison to Jefferson, Oct. 17, 1788, XIV, 18–21, Madison to Jefferson, Dec. 8, 1788, XIV, 340, Jefferson to Madison, March 15, 1789, XIV, 659–61; Jefferson to Madison, Aug. 28, 1789, XV, 367–8. Speeches of Madison, June 8 and August 17, 1789, *Debates and Proceedings in the Congress of the United States* (Washington, 1834 ff.), 1st Congress, 1st Session, 431–42, 755; the quotation about judicial review is at p. 439. The latter source is commonly cited by its bookbinder's title, *Annals of Congress.*
26. Ames to Thomas Dwight, June 11, 1789, Seth Ames, ed., *The Works of Fisher Ames* (Boston, 1854, 2 vols.), I, 52–3, See also Levy, *Legacy,* 228–33.
27. Speech of Madison, June 8, 1789, *Annals of Congress,* I, 434. Madison's proposed amendment, "No State shall violate the equal rights of conscience, or the freedom of the press, or the trial by jury in criminal cases," was also original with him, *ibid.,* I, 435 Although no state had a "due process of law" clause in its constitution, several had a "law of the land" clause that was the equivalent.
28. In England, civil parties were not qualified to give testimony until an act of 1851; in the United States, Connecticut was the first state, in 1849, to abolish the incompetency of civil parties. Wigmore, *Evidence,* VIII, 695. For a different interpretation of Madison's proposed amendment that no person should be a witness against himself, see Lewis Mayers, *Shall We Amend the Fifth Amendment?* (New York, 1959), 201, 320 n. 41. Mayers assaults the policy of the right against self-incrimination and answers his title-question affirmatively. His historical background is skimpy and littered with factual errors; the American material is based mainly on Pittman's unreliable article (see above, ch. 11, n. 2) and the English material mainly on Wigmore. Sometimes Mayers seems to base his historical background on thin air and perverse logic. His interest, however, is not in history but in the recent controversy surrounding the Fifth Amendment. Mayers admits that the "common law rule as it then existed, and as it continues to be applied to this day even in states in which the privilege enjoys no constitutional protection [only Iowa and New Jersey], covers a witness in every legal proceeding, civil as

well as criminal." Yet Mayers alleges, without a shred of proof, that "to lawyers of that generation the words *against himself* applied only to a party and not to a witness. . . . " He is therefore able to argue, "The assumption is sometimes made that the use of the word 'witness' indicates that the witness was intended to be included. On the contrary, the exemption from being compelled to 'be a witness' is precisely the privilege of the accused, but *not* the privilege of the witness, who *can* be compelled to 'be a witness' but may not be compelled to 'give evidence' incriminating himself." See also Mayers, "The Federal Witness' Privilege against Self-Incrimination: Constitutional or Common Law?," *American Journal of Legal History, IV (April 1960), 111–12. The error in Mayers's argument is that he either ignores the words "against himself" or assumes incorrectly and inconsistently that "against himself" meant one thing in the case of a party and another in the case of a witness. For early cases on the words "against himself," see note 35 below.*

29. The amendments reported by the House Select Committee, July 28, 1789, are printed in *Documentary History of the Constitution of the United States of America, 1786–1870* (Washington, 1894–1905, 5 vols.), V, 186–9. In the appendices to his *Bill of Rights and What It Means Today,* Dumbauld has very conveniently brought together the amendments as proposed by Madison, as reported by the committee of the House, as passed by the House, as passed by the Senate, as agreed to after the deliberations of a joint conference committee and proposed by Congress to the states, 206–22 For Laurence's remarks, *Annals of Congress,* Aug. 17, 1789, I, 753. Mayers erroneously states that the motion to amend was adopted "by unanimous consent." The vote on the motion to amend is not given in the *Annals.* The members of the House Select Committee who had been members of the Federal Convention were Madison, Sherman of Connecticut, Abraham Baldwin of Georgia, Nicholas Gilman of New Hampshire, and George Clymer of Pennsylvania.

30. Charles Warren, "New Light on the History of the Federal Judiciary Act of 1789," *Harvard Law Review,* XXXVII (Nov. 1923), 111, 116, 118, 120, 122, 130 n. 177. [Edgar S. Maclay, ed.], *The Journal of William Maclay, United States Senator from Pennsylvania, 1789–1791,* intro. by Charles Beard (New York, 1927), 90–92, entries for June 29 and June 30, 1789. Richard Peters, ed., *The Public Statutes at Large of the United States of America* (Boston, 1861 ff.), I, 82, for the Judiciary Act of 1789, sect. 15.

31. Geyger's *Lessee v. Geyger,* 2 *Dallas* (Circ. Ct., Pa.) 332, at 333 (1795). On the non-compellability of the party opponent in a civil suit at common law and his compellability, by bill of discovery, to testify and produce documents in chancery cases, see Wigmore, *Evidence,* 168–74. The insight explaining Laurence's probable purpose in introducing the motion to amend comes from an unsigned law note, "Applicability of Privilege against Self-Incrimination to Legislative Investigations," *Columbia Law Review,* XLIX (Jan. 1949), 87, at 92–3. For early precedents, see the cases cited, above, in ch. 10, n. 30. For a later case showing the rule applying the right against self-incrimination to the production of documents in civil cases, see *Chetwind v. Marnell,* I *Bosenquet & Puller's English Common Pleas Reports* 271 (1798). See also note 35, below, for cases extending the right against self-incrimination to civil witnesses whose answers could not incriminate them.

32. *Cf.* Mayers, "The Federal Witness' Privilege," *American Journal of Legal History,* IV, 116–17, who asserts that the Fifth Amendment was intended to protect the criminal defendant only, and argues that all of the clauses of the amendment that concern criminal proceedings, *"other than the self-incrimination clause"*—indictment by grand jury, no double jeopardy, and the due process clause—"protect the

accused against executive oppression before the trial" (my italics). He adds that
the only provision of the amendment not relating to criminal proceedings, the one
guaranteeing just compensation in eminent domain cases, "is also a protection
against *executive* action." But the power of eminent domain is essentially a legislative power; the due process clause applies to non-criminal proceedings; all of
the Fifth Amendment rights were intended, primarily, to secure the people against
legislative and judicial oppression; and none of the amendment's clauses, excepting the one relating to indictment by grand jury, are restrictive in operation to pre-
trial proceedings. As for Mayers's main thesis, that the self-incrimination clause
was intended to extend only to the criminally accused and not to a witness, early
federal cases, cited in note 35, below, indicate otherwise, as does my argument at
this point in the text above. Mayers sharply distinguishes, however, between the
constitutional protection and that of the common law.

33. See Mitchell Franklin, "The Encyclopédiste Origin and Meaning of the Fifth
Amendment," *Lawyers Guild Review,* XV (Summer 1955), 41–62 Franklin, on
wholly different grounds, contends that the Fifth Amendment was intended to
protect against self-infamy as well as self-incrimination. His article was cited
approvingly by Justice Douglas, dissenting, in *Ullmann v. U.S.,* 350 U.S. 422, 450–
53 (1956). But Franklin's argument, that the Bill of Rights generally and the Fifth
Amendment in particular is of French origin, a *précis* of Encyclopédiste theory, is
a baseless concoction that defies the overwhelming evidence of English origins.
He proves that Jefferson read Beccaria and then assumes that Jefferson had an
influence in the framing of the Fifth Amendment, though he had none. The article
is a tissue of presuppositions supported by a vast amount of irrelevant, anachronistic,
and strained evidence.

34. *Respublica v. Gibbs*, 3 *Yeates* (Pa.) 429, at 437 (1802). See also *Galbreath v.
Eichelberger*, 3 *Yeates* (Pa.) 515 (1803); Bell's Case, I *Browne* (Pa.) 376 (1811).

35. For state cases showing that the common-law right protected against self-infamy,
as in the Pennsylvania cases cited in the note above, see *State v. Bailly*, 2 N.J. 396
(1807); *Vaughn v. Perrine*, 3 N.J. 299, at 303 (1811), *Miller v. Crayon*, 2 Brevard
(S.C.) 108 (1806); and *People v. Herrick*, 13 Johnson (N.Y.) 82 (1816). The English courts at this time were still applying the same rule; see *Rex v Lewis*, 4
Espinasse 225, at 226 (1802), 170 *Eng. Rep.* 700, and *Macbride v. Macbride*, 4
Espinasse 242, at 243 (1802), 170 *Eng. Rep.* 706. However, an English treatise of
1801 cast doubt on the continuing validity of the broad proposition that compulsory self-infamation or self-disgrace was illegal. The author carefully defined the
rule as having insured that "a witness shall not be rendered *infamous,* or even *dis-
graced* by his own examination, as to facts not connected with the cause in which
he is examined," and added that the bench was divided on the point, Thomas
Peake, *A Compendium of the Law of Evidence* (London, 1801), 129–30, and (London, 1813, 4th ed.), 143–4. The leading American case showing the subsequent
repudiation of the claim that the Fifth Amendment protects against compulsory
self-infamy is *Brown v. Walker*, 161 U.S. 591 (1892) See also Wigmore, *Evidence,*
IV, sect. 2255, pp. 836–9, in the 2nd ed., and the same section in the 3rd ed., VIII,
332–3, and also, III, sects. 984–7; VIII, sect. 2215. For the earliest federal case
applying the right against self-incrimination to a witness, see *U.S. v. Goosley*, Case
No. 15,230 in 25 *Fed. Cases* (Circ. Ct., Va.) 1363, at 1364 (undated, but sometime
in the 1790's; Iredell died 1799). *Marbury v. Madison,* I *Cranch* (U.S.) 137, at 144
(1803). See also, *U.S. v. Burr,* In re Willie, Case No. 14,692e, in 25 *Fed. Cases*
(Circ. Ct., Va.) 38, at 39–41 (1807). See also, Zephaniah Swift, *A System of the
Laws of the State of Connecticut* (Windham, Conn., 1795–96, 2 vols.), II, 239 and

the references to the works by Martin, Hening, and Wyche, above ch. 12, n. 7. There are dozens of early state cases in which the right against self-incrimination was extended to a witness even in civil suits where the questions asked might, if answered truthfully, "supply a link in the chain, which would lead to a conviction for a crime." See *Grannis v. Branden*, 5 *Day* (Conn.) 260, at 272–4 (1812), where the court quoted the *nemo tenetur* maxim. Some of the early state decisions in favor of the right were far-fetched, in effect taking literally the principle that a witness did not have to answer questions "against himself," whether or not his answers might incriminate him. That is, the right was illogically extended to witnesses in civil cases to protect them against answering questions that could not incriminate them but might injure their civil interests. One federal case was similar, *Carne v. McLane*, Case No. 2,416, in 5 *Fed. Cases* (Circ. Ct., D.C.), 89 (1806). In *Simons v. Payne*, 2 *Root* (Conn.) 406 (1796), the witness was "not obliged to testify against his interest as a bondsman." In *Starr v. Tracy*, 2 *Root* (Conn.) 528, at 529 (1797), the new rule was broadly given that "a witness is not obliged to disclose what will make against him." See also *Connor v. Bradey, Anthon's Nisi Prius Reports* (N.Y.) 135, at 136 (1809), extending the right to the witness though his answer to the question, revealing usury, would have exposed him "to civil injury only." In Tennessee the court acknowledged that the constitutional provision referred only to criminal cases, neglecting to notice that it also referred only to the "accused"; nevertheless the court declared, "but we think the principle existed previous to the Constitution" and applied it to a witness in a civil case who refused to answer on ground that his answer would be prejudicial to his interest civilly, *Cook v. Corn*, I *Overton* (Tenn.) 340, at 341 (1808). In Bell's Case, I *Browne* (Pa.) 376 (1811), the court said, "I have always overruled a question that would affect a witness *civilly*, or subject him to a *criminal prosecution:* I have gone farther; and where the answer to a question would cover the witness with infamy or shame, I have refused to compel him to answer it." But in *Baird v. Cochran*, 4 *Sergeant & Rawle* (Pa.) 397, at 400 (1818), the preceding case was in effect overruled on the point that the witness need not answer against his interest civilly; however, the court construed the constitutional provision, which referred only to the accused in criminal prosecutions, to apply to witnesses and to questions the answers to which "may degrade him in the public opinion" or reveal "something criminal, penal, or infamous, and not barely to matter of interest." For similar holdings, now the general rule, that the witness must answer questions against his interest though exposing himself to a civil suit, see *Taney v. Kemp*, 4 *Harris & Johnson (*Md.) 348 (1818), and *Planters' Bank v. George, 6 Martin O.S.* (La.) 670 (1819).

36.   For the 1790 Pennsylvania formulation, see Thorpe, ed., V, 3100. Delaware also, in adopting a new constitution, in 1792, made the clause refer to "the accused," *ibid.*, I, I, 569. Abe Fortas, "The Fifth Amendment: *Nemo Tenetur Prodere Seipsum,"* Cleveland Bar Association, *The Journal*, XXV (April 1954), 91, at 98-100, *passim.*

37.   The first quotation is from Chief Judge Calvert Magruder, in *Maffie v. U.S.*, 209 Fed. 2nd 225, at 237 (1954); the second, from Justice Frankfurter, in *Ullmann v. U.S.*, 350 U.S. 422, at 427 (1956). See also, to the same effect, *Quinn v. U.S.*, 349 U.S. 155, at 161 (1955).

13

Immunity Grants

"No person," the Fifth Amendment unequivocally states, "shall be ... compelled in any criminal case to be a witness against himself. ... " It does not add, "unless such person cannot be prosecuted or punished as a result of his testimony," and it does not refer to self-incrimination. Yet, if the government wants evidence concerning a crime, it can compel a witness to testify by granting immunity from prosecution. In law, such immunity means that the witness cannot incriminate himself and therefore has suffered no violation of his right against self-incrimination. The common sense of the matter is that to "incriminate" means to implicate criminally; in law, however, it means exposure to prosecution or penalties. The law indulges the fiction that when one receives a grant of immunity, removing him from criminal jeopardy, the right not to be a witness against oneself is not violated. If the witness cannot be prosecuted, the penalties do not exist for him, so that his testimony can be compelled without forcing him to incriminate himself or "be a witness against himself."

The first immunity statute in Anglo-American jurisprudence was probably the one enacted by Connecticut in 1698. That act specified that witnesses in criminal cases must give sworn evidence, on pain of punishment for refusal, "always provided that no person required to give testimonie as aforesaid shall be punished for what he doth confesse against himself when under oath." Similarly, an act that Parliament passed against gambling in 1710, which some colonies copied, guaranteed that gamblers who confessed their crimes and returned their winnings should be "acquitted, indemnified [immunized] and discharged from any further or other Punishment, Forfeiture, or Penalty which he or they may have incurred by the playing for or winning such Money. . . . " New York in 1758 obtained the king's pardon for certain ship captains in order to compel their testimony against the ships' owners. Although the pardons had eliminated the perils of the criminal law for the captains, they persisted in their claim that the law could not force them to declare anything that might incriminate them. A court fined them for contempt, on grounds that the recalcitrant captains no longer faced criminal jeopardy by giving evidence against themselves.

In modern language these colonial precedents illustrate grants of "transactional" immunity, an absolute guarantee that in return for evidence, the compelled person will not under any circumstances be prosecuted for the transaction or criminal episode concerning which he gives testimony. Absolute or transactional immunity was the price paid by the law for exacting information that would otherwise be actionable criminally. The paradox remained: one could be compelled to be a witness against oneself, but from the law's perspective the immunized witness would stand to the offense as if he had never committed it, or had received amnesty or a pardon despite having committed it.

Congress enacted its first immunity statute in 1857, granting freedom from prosecution for any acts or transactions to which a witness offered testimony in an investigation. Reacting against the immunity "baths" that enabled corrupt officials to escape from criminal liability by offering immunized testimony, Congress in 1862 supplanted the act of 1857 with one that offered only "use" immunity. Use immunity guarantees only that the compelled testimony will not be used in a criminal prosecution, but prosecution is possible if based on evidence independent from or unrelated to the compelled testimony. Under a grant of use immunity one might confess to a crime secure in the knowledge that his confession could not be used against him; however, if the prosecution had other evidence to prove his guilt, he might be prosecuted. By 1887 Congress extended the standard of use immunity from congressional investigations to all federal proceedings.

Until 1972 the Supreme Court demanded transactional rather than use immunity as the sole basis for displacing the Fifth Amendment right to remain silent. In *Counselman v. Hitchcock* (1892) the Court unanimously held unconstitutional a congressional act offering use immunity because use immunity was "not co-extensive with the constitutional provision." The compelled testimony might provide leads to evidence that the prosecution might not otherwise possess. To supplant the constitutional guarantee, an immunity statute must provide "complete protection" from all criminal perils; "in view of the constitutional provision, a statutory enactment, to be valid, must afford absolute immunity against future prosecution for the offense to which the question relates." Congress responded with a statute safeguarding against prosecution, forfeiture, or penalty for any transaction about which one might be compelled to testify. In *Brown v. Walker* (1896) the Court held that transactional immunity "operates as a pardon for the offense to which it relates," thus satisfying the constitutional guarantee. In effect the Court permitted what it had declared was impossible: congressional amendment of the Constitution. By a statute that served as a "substitute," Congress altered the guarantee that no one can be compelled to be a witness against himself criminally.

Until 1970 there were over fifty federal immunity statutes conforming with *Brown's* transactional immunity standard, which the Court reendorsed in *Ullmann v. United States* (1956). When the Court scrapped its two sovereignties rule in *Murphy v. Waterfront Commission* (1964), it held that absent an immunity grant, a state witness could not be compelled to testify unless his testimony "and its fruits" could not be used by the federal government. *Murphy* was a technical relaxation of the transactional immunity standard, as *Albertson v. Subversive Activities Control Board* (1965) proved, because a unanimous Court reconfirmed the transactional immunity standard.

Through the Organized Crime Control Act of 1970, Congress made use immunity and derivative-use immunity the standard for all federal grants of immunity, and most states copied the new standard. No compelled testimony or its "fruits" (information directly or indirectly derived from such testimony) could be used against a witness criminally, except to prove perjury. In *Kastigar v. United States* (1972) the Court relied on *Murphy,* ignored or distorted all other precedents, and upheld the narrow standard as coextensive with the Fifth Amendment, which it is not. One who relies on his right to remain silent forces the state to rely wholly on its own evidence to convict him. By remaining silent he gives the state no way to use his testimony, however indirectly. When he is compelled to be a witness against himself, his admissions assist the state's investigation against him. The burden of proving that the state's evidence derives from sources wholly independent of the compelled testimony lies upon the prosecution. But use immunity permits compulsion without removing criminality.

In *New Jersey v. Portash* (1979) the Court held that a defendant's immunized grand jury testimony could not be introduced to impeach his testimony at his trial. Whether the state may introduce immunized testimony to prove perjury has not been decided. In *Portash,* however, the Court conceded, "Testimony given in response to a grant of legislative immunity is the essence of coerced testimony." The essence of the Fifth Amendment's provision is that testimony against oneself cannot be coerced. Any grant of immunity that compels testimony compels one to be a witness against himself—except, of course, that it is "impossible," as the Court said in *Counselman,* for the constitutional guarantee to mean what it says.

Bibliography

Levy, Leonard W. 1974 *Against the Law: The Nixon Court and Criminal Justice.* Pages 165–187. New York: Harper & Row.

14

Miranda v. Arizona
384 U.S. 436 (1966)

Miranda is the best known as well as the most controversial and
maligned self-incrimination decision in the history of the Supreme
Court. Some of the harshest criticism came from the dissenters in that
case. Justice Byron R. White, for example, declared that the rule of the
case, which required elaborate warnings and offer of counsel before
the right against self-incrimination could be effectively waived, would
return killers, rapists, and other criminals to the streets and have a
corrosive effect on the prevention of crime. The facts of *Miranda,* one of
four cases decided together, explain the alarm of the four dissenters
and of the many critics of the Warren Court. The majority of five, led
by Chief Justice Earl Warren, reversed the kidnap-and-rape conviction
of Ernesto Miranda, who had been picked out of a lineup by his
victim, had been interrogated without mistreatment for a couple of
hours, and had signed a confession that purported to have been voluntarily made with full knowledge of his rights, although no one had
advised him that he did not need to answer incriminating questions or
that he could have counsel present. The Court reversed because his
confession had been procured in violation of his rights, yet had been
admitted in evidence. Warren conceded that the Court could not know
what had happened in the interrogation room and "might not find
the . . . statements to have been involuntary in traditional terms." Justice John Marshall Harlan, dissenting, professed to be "astonished" at
the decision. Yet the Court did little more than require that the states
follow what was already substantially FBI procedure with respect to
the rights of a suspect during a custodial interrogation.

The doctrinal significance of the case is that the Fifth Amendment's self-incrimination clause became the basis for evaluating the admissibility of confessions. The Court thus abandoned the traditional due process analysis that it had used in state cases since *Brown v. Mississippi* (1936) to determine whether a confession was voluntary under all the circumstances. Moreover, the Court shifted to the Fifth Amendment from the Sixth Amendment analysis of *Escobedo v. Illinois* (1964), when discussing the right to counsel as a means of protecting against involuntary confessions. *Miranda* stands for the proposition that the Fifth Amendment vests a right in the individual to remain silent unless he chooses to speak in the "unfettered exercise of his own will." The opinion of the Court lays down a code of procedures that must be respected by law enforcement officers to secure that right to silence whenever they take a person into custody or deprive him of his freedom in any significant way.

In each of the four *Miranda* cases, the suspect was not effectively notified of his constitutional rights and was questioned incommunicado in a "police-dominated" atmosphere; each suspect confessed, and his confession was introduced in evidence against him at his trial. The Court majority demonstrated a deep distrust for police procedures employed in station-house interrogation, aimed at producing confessions. The *Miranda* cases showed, according to Warren, a secret "interrogation environment," created to subject the suspect to the will of his examiners. Intimidation, even if only psychological, could undermine the will and dignity of the suspect, compelling him to incriminate himself. Therefore, the inherently compulsive character of in-custody interrogation had to be offset by procedural safeguards to insure obedience to the right of silence. Until legislatures produced other procedures at least as effective, the Court would require that at the outset of interrogation a person be clearly informed that he has the right to remain silent, that any statement he makes may be used as evidence against him, that he has the right to the presence of an attorney, and that if he cannot afford an attorney, one will be appointed to represent him.

These rules respecting mandatory warnings, Warren declared, are "an absolute prerequisite to interrogation." The presence of a lawyer, he reasoned, would reduce coercion, effectually preserve the right of silence for one unwilling to incriminate himself, and produce an accurate statement if the suspect chooses to speak. Should he indicate at any time before or during interrogation that he wishes to remain silent or have an attorney present, the interrogation must cease. Government assumes a heavy burden, Warren added, to demonstrate in court that a defendant knowingly and intelligently waived his right to silence or to a lawyer. "The warnings required and the waiver necessary in accordance with our opinion today are prerequisites," he emphasized, "to the admissibility of any statement made by a defendant."

Warren insisted that the new rules would not deter effective law enforcement. The experience of the FBI attested to that, and its practices, which accorded with the Court's rules, could be "readily emulated by state and local law enforcement agencies." The Constitution, Warren admitted, "does not require any specific code of procedures" for safeguarding the Fifth Amendment right; the Court would accept any equivalent set of safeguards.

Justice Tom C. Clark, dissenting, observed that the FBI had not been warning suspects that counsel may be present during custodial interrogation, though FBI practice immediately altered to conform to Warren's opinion. Clark, like Harlan, whose dissent was joined by Justices Potter Stewart and Byron White, would have preferred "the more pliable dictates" of the conventional due process analysis that took all the circumstances of a case into account. Harlan also believed that the right against self-incrimination should not be extended to the police station and should not be the basis for determining whether a confession is involuntary. White wrote a separate dissent, which Harlan and Stewart joined, flaying the majority for an opinion that had no historical, precedential, or textual basis. White also heatedly condemned the majority for weakening law enforcement and for prescribing rules that were rigid, but still left many questions unanswered.

Bibliography

Kamisar, Yale 1980 *Police Interrogations and Confessions.* Pages 41–76. Ann Arbor: University of Michigan Press.

Whitebread, Charles H. 1980 *Criminal Procedure.* Pages 292–310. Mineola, N.Y.: Foundation Press.

15

Testimonial and
Nontestimonial Compulsion

In the 1960s the Supreme Court ruled that the right against self-incrimination was not infringed when police compelled the driver of an accident vehicle to give a blood sample for analysis of its alcoholic content, compelled a suspect in a lineup to utter before witnesses the words used by a bank robber, and compelled another suspected bank robber to submit a sample of his handwriting for comparison with a note given to a bankteller. In the 1970s the Court held that the right against self-incrimination did not protect a person from the compulsory production of business and tax records in the possession of his or her accountant or lawyer, and did not protect a person from a court order to make a voice recording for a federal grand jury seeking to identify a criminal by the sound of a voice on a legally intercepted telephone conversation. All these decisions shared a thorny problem: if a person is compelled to provide the state with evidence to incriminate him, is he necessarily a witness against himself in the Fifth Amendment sense?

The Court prefers a different formulation: does nontestimonial compulsion force a person to be a witness against himself criminally? The consistent answer has been "no," even if there was a testimonial dimension to the forced admissions. If that testimonial dimension loomed too large, the Court loosened its distinction between testimonial and nontestimonial compulsion and relied on some other distinction. Thus, when the driver of a vehicle involved in an accident was required by state law to stop and identify himself, though doing so subjected him to criminal penalties, the Court saw no Fifth Amendment issue, only a regulation promoting the satisfaction of civil liabilities. Similarly, when a lawyer or accountant was forced to turn over a client's incriminating records, the client had not been compelled at all, though he paid the criminal penalty and lost the chance to make a Fifth Amendment plea. And when the police during the course of a lawful search found incriminating business records, the records were introduced in evidence, although they could not have been subpoenaed directly from the businessman. In these cases, where the compulsion was communicative or testimonial in character, the Court inconsistently discoursed on the need to decide as it did in order to avoid a decision against the introduction of nontestimonial evidence that had been compelled.

More often the Court relied on a supposed distinction between forcing a person to furnish evidence against himself of a testimonial nature and forcing him to be the source of nontestimonial or physical evidence against himself, usually derived from his body. The word "witness" implies giving testimony based on one's knowledge, not displaying one's person. Compulsion to reveal information other than one's physical characteristics is generally unconstitutional, especially if the information is derived directly from the party himself, though not if the police lawfully find his records. The Court's distinction between testimonial and nontestimonial compulsion is obviously a bit porous. That distinction derived from the realistic need to prevent the Fifth Amendment from disabling police identifications based on fingerprints, handwriting, photographs, blood samples, voice exemplars, and line-ups. The distinction had its origin in a passing remark by Justice Oliver Wendell Holmes in 1910, when he dismissed as "an extravagant extension of the Fifth Amendment" the claim that requiring a defendant to model a shirt for identification purposes breached the right against self-incrimination.

The trouble with the distinction, apart from the Court's own inconsistency, is that physical or identifying evidence can be communicative in character, as when a laboratory report, the result of a drunken driver's blood sample, is introduced against him, or when a grand jury indicts one whose voice identifies him as the culprit. Whether by writing, speaking, or giving blood involuntarily, an individual has been compelled to furnish evidence against himself. That he has not been forced to "testify" is a distinction less persuasive than semantically catchy. However, some such distinction seems necessary. The fundamental meaning of the Fifth Amendment is that a person need not be the unwilling instrument of his own undoing and that the state must find its own evidence against him without his involuntary cooperation, and a literal reading of the amendment would prevent the police from fingerprinting a suspect or making him stand in a lineup for identification purposes. Thus the Court must find ways around the amendment.

A minority of Justices have sought a compromise by permitting as nontestimonial that evidence which does not require volition or affirmative cooperation; thus, the lineup and taking blood, photographs, and fingerprints require merely passive conduct. If, however, incriminating evidence can be secured only by the active volition of one asked to repeat certain words, model clothing, or give a handwriting sample, these minority Justices would sustain a Fifth Amendment plea. But their distinction between volitional and passive acts is as hairsplitting as the majority's between testimonial and nontestimonial compulsion. Anyone overpowered to give a sample of his blood would scarcely think he affirmatively cooperated.

The Justices in the majority also make unreal distinctions, as between the physical properties of one's voice and the testimonial content of what he says: "This is a stickup" communicates more than pitch and resonance. If the right against self-incrimination protects a defendant at his trial from having to speak up for the benefit of witnesses, why does it not protect him in the grand jury room, the interrogation room, or the lineup?

The distinction between testimonial and nontestimonial compulsion derives from the needs of law enforcement and seems to be a permanent addition to constitutional law. The Court, which can reach whatever results it desires, probably will add to the roster of nontestimonial evidence that can be compelled and will narrow the meaning of testimonial compulsion or find exceptions to it.

Bibliography

Bauer, W. J. 1977 Formalism, Legal Realism, & Constitutionally Protected Privacy under the Fourth & Fifth Amendments. *Harvard Law Review* 90:945–991.

Koontz, Hal and Stodel, Jeffrey 1973 The Scope of Testimonial Immunity under the Fifth: *Kastigar v. United States. Loyola* (Los Angeles) *Law Review* 6:350–383.

16

The Ninth Amendment:
Unenumerated Rights

For 175 years, from 1791 to 1965, the Ninth Amendment lay dormant, a constitutional curiosity comparable in vitality to the Third Amendment (no quartering of troops in private homes) or to the privileges and immunities clause of the Fourteenth Amendment after the Supreme Court had "interpreted" the meaning out of it in the *Slaughterhouse Cases*.[1] Obscurity shrouded the meaning of the Ninth Amendment. One member of the Supreme Court, in a speech made after some reflection, acknowledged that the rights secured by the Ninth Amendment were "still a mystery."[2]

The year 1965 marks the beginning of Ninth Amendment jurisprudence. For the first time the Court mentioned the amendment, at least in part, as a basis for holding a government measure unconstitutional. Justice William O. Douglas for the Court confronted a state act that made the use of contraceptives criminal, even when counseled by a physician treating a married couple. From the First, Third, Fourth, and Fifth Amendments and in part from the Ninth Amendment, Douglas derived a "right of privacy older than the Bill of Rights" with respect to the "sacred precincts of marital bedrooms," and three Justices believed that the Ninth Amendment, unfortified by the "penumbras" and "emanations" of other provisions of the Bill of Rights, supported the voiding of the offensive state act. Justice Arthur Goldberg for the three wrote a concurring opinion based on the Ninth Amendment, buttressed by the "liberty" guaranteed by the Fourteenth Amendment.[3]

Within fifteen years the Ninth Amendment, once the subject of only incidental references, was invoked in over 1,200 state and federal cases in the most astonishing variety of matters.[4] After the Court had resuscitated the amendment, litigants found its charms compelling precisely because of its utter lack of specificity with respect to the rights that it protects. It says: "The enumeration in the Constitution, of certain rights, shall not be construed to deny or disparage others retained by the people." Those who have relied on this amendment for constitutional armament include schoolboys and police officers seeking relief from regulations that govern the length of their hair, citizens eager to preserve the purity of water and air against environmental polluters, and homosexuals claiming a right to be married. The question whether the Ninth Amendment was intended to be a cornucopia of unenumerated rights produces as many answers as there are points of view.

Oddly enough, those who advocate a constitutional "jurisprudence of original intention" and assert that the Constitution "said what it meant and meant what it said,"[5] are the ones who most vigorously deny content to the Ninth Amendment and to the concept of a "living Constitution." Presumably they would not swear fealty to a dead Constitution, not even to a static one of the sort endorsed by Chief Justice Roger Taney in the *Dred Scott* case.[6] Nevertheless they reject as absurd the idea that the Ninth Amendment could have been intended as a repository for newly discovered rights that activist judges embrace.

The fact that the Framers did not intend most, if any, of the rights that litigants read into the Ninth and would have found bizarre the notion that the Constitution protects any of those rights is really of no significance. We must remember, after all, that the Framers would have found absurd and bizarre most features of our constitutional law as well as of our politics, cities, industries, and society. Justice Hugo L. Black, in the very case of 1965 that breathed life into the Ninth Amendment, could not find much justification for the discovery of a right to privacy anywhere in the Constitution let alone in the Ninth Amendment. The judicial reading of rights into it or out of it, he cautioned, "would make of this Court's members a day-to-day constitutional convention."[7] Figuratively, however, that is what the Supreme Court is—a continuous constitutional convention. The Court has functioned as if it were that since John Marshall's time, if not earlier, and few Justices in the history of the Court have contributed so much to the Court's effectiveness as a constitutional convention as Justice Black, especially in his First and Fifth Amendment opinions.

To say that the Framers did not intend the Court to act as a constitutional convention or to shape public policies by interpreting the Constitution is, again, to assert historical truth. However, that truth does not invalidate judicial decisions that the Framers failed to foresee; it reveals, rather, their human incapacity to predict how the system that they designed would work. They did not expect the development of a judicial power that influenced public policies. They did not expect judicial activism whether conservative or liberal. Nor did they foresee political parties, administrative agencies, overwhelming executive domination of foreign policy, national governance of the economy, foreign policy made without knowledge of any elected members of the government, or management of fiscal policies by the Federal Reserve Board. The argument for or against some judicial interpretation of the Constitution progresses not at all by the allegation, even if verifiable, that the Framers would have been shocked or surprised by such an interpretation.

The starting points for interpreting the Ninth Amendment are the text itself and the rule of construction which holds that if a plain meaning exists, it should be followed. As Justice Joseph Story said, "The first and fundamental rule in the interpretation of all instruments is, to construe them according to the sense of the terms, and the intention of the parties." If a plain meaning does not exist, the language of the text must be construed so as not to contradict the document at any point, and meaning must be sought in its purposes or in the principles that it embodies as understood from "its nature and objects, its scope and design."[8] We know enough about the making of the Ninth Amendment and about its historical context to apply these rules with considerable confidence, wherever they might lead. They lead first to the indisputable fact that the amendment by force of its terms protects unenumerated rights of the people. That opens the question, What are those rights? The answer depends on a preliminary question: Why would the Framers have included an amendment that acknowledges the existence of unenumerated rights that are no more subject to abridgment than the rights that are specified in the first eight amendments?

We must remember, by way of an answer, that ratificationists, including the most sophisticated of Framers, had made the enormously unpopular and weak argument that a bill of rights was superfluous in the United States, because government derived from the people and had only delegated powers. Alexander Hamilton, James Wilson, Oliver

Ellsworth, and James Madison, among others, also argued that no need for a bill of rights existed because the government could not use its limited powers to encroach on reserved rights; no powers extended, for example, to religion or the press. That argument shriveled against contentions that Congress might exercise its delegated powers in such a way that abridged unprotected rights. The power to tax, implemented by the ominous necessary and proper clause, could be used to destroy a critical press and might be enforced by general warrants enabling the government to ransack homes and businesses for evidence of criminal evasion of the revenue laws or for evidence of seditious publications.

The Federalist #84 argued that particularizing rights was "not only unnecessary in the proposed Constitution but would even be dangerous. They would contain various exceptions to powers which are not granted; and, in this very account, would afford a colorable pretext to claim more than were granted." If no power had been granted to restrict the press, Hamilton reasoned, no need existed to declare that the liberty of the press ought not be restricted. To make such a declaration furnished "a plausible pretense for claiming that power" to violate the press. A provision "against restraining the liberty of the press afforded a clear implication that a power to prescribe proper regulations concerning it was intended to be vested in the national government." Ratificationists had also argued unconvincingly that a bill of rights would be "dangerous" because any right omitted from it might be presumed to be lost.

This argument proved far too much. First, it proved that the particular rights that the Constitution already protected—no religious test, no bills of attainder, trials by jury in criminal cases, *inter* alia—stood in grave jeopardy: specifying a right implied a power to violate it. Second, the inclusion of some rights in the original text of the constitution implied that all unenumerated ones were relinquished.

James Wilson, in the course of arguing that a bill of rights was not only unsuitable for the United States but dangerous as well, made another well-publicized statement of the ratificationist position: "A bill of rights annexed to a constitution is an enumeration of the powers reserved. If we attempt an enumeration, everything that is not enumerated is presumed to be given. The consequence is, that an imperfect enumeration would throw all implied powers into the scale of government; and the rights of the people would be rendered incomplete." Oliver Ellsworth advocated the same position.[9] Madison more carefully declared in his state's ratifying convention, "If an enumeration be made of all our rights, will it not be implied that everything omitted is given to the general government?" He too thought that "an imperfect enumeration," that is, an incomplete one, "is dangerous."[10]

Madison switched to the cause of adding amendments to the Constitution that would protect individual liberties and allay the fears of people who would likely support the Constitution, if given a sense of security about their rights. When he proposed his amendments to the House, he was mindful that proponents of ratification had warned that a bill of rights might be dangerous because the government could violate any right omitted. During the course of his great speech of June 8, 1789, Madison repeatedly reminded Congress of the need to satisfy the legitimate fears of "the great number of our constituents who are dissatisfied" with the Constitution because it seemed to put their rights in jeopardy. We must, he added, "expressly declare the great rights of mankind secured under this constitution."[11] The "great object in view," Madison declared, "is to limit and qualify the powers of Government, by excepting out of the grant of power those cases in which the Government ought not to act, or to act only in a particular mode. They [state recommendations] point these exceptions sometimes against the abuse of the executive power, sometimes against the legislative, and in some cases, against the community itself; or, in other words, against the majority in favor of the minority." Clearly, Madison was referring to constitutional prohibitions upon government to protect not only the rights of the people but even unpopular rights, such as those exercised by a minority that needed protection.[12]

Defending his recommendation that became the Ninth Amendment, Madison acknowledged that a major objection against a bill of rights consisted of the argument that "by enumerating particular exceptions to the grant of power, it would disparage those rights which were not placed in that enumeration; and it might follow, by implication, that those rights which were not singled out, were intended to be assigned into the hands of the General Government, and were consequently insecure." He called that "one of the most plausible arguments" he had even heard against the inclusion of a bill of rights. It was an argument that he himself had made, and it had become a Federalist cliché, although it self-destructed by virtue of the fact that the Constitution explicitly protected several rights, exposing all those omitted—including, by Madison's description, "the great rights of mankind"—to governmental violation.[13] He was, therefore, answering his own previous objection, not one that had been advanced by Anti-Federalists, when he devised the simple proposal that became the Ninth Amendment. It was, he said, meant to guard against the possibility that unenumerated rights might be imperiled by the enumeration of particular rights.[14] By excepting many rights from the grant of powers, no implication was intended, and no inference should be drawn, that rights not excepted from the grant of powers fell within those powers. As Madison phrased his proposal, it declared:

> The exceptions [to power] here or elsewhere in the constitution made in favor of particular rights, shall not be so construed as to diminish the just importance of other rights retained by the people, or as to enlarge the powers delegated by the constitution; but either as actual limitations on such powers, or as inserted merely for greater caution.[15]

Madison devised that proposal. No precedent for it existed. It was one of several proposals by Madison that stamped the Bill of Rights with his own creativity. Changing the flaccid verb "ought" to "shall" fell into the same category. So did his selection of particular rights for inclusion. No state, for example, had a due process of law clause in its own constitution, and only New York had recommended such a clause in place of the more familiar "law of the land" clause. Either phrasing carried the majesty and prestige of Magna Carta. Sir Edward Coke had taught, and Americans believed, that due process of law meant accordance with regularized common law procedures, especially grand jury accusation and trial by jury, both of which Madison provided for.[16] Madison also provided the basis for a radical alteration of the law of search and seizure by his choice of the broadest possible language available at the time.[17] Madison enumerated several rights whose constitutional protection was uncommon. Only New Hampshire by its state constitution provided against double jeopardy, and only Massachusetts and Vermont had constitutionally guaranteed just compensation when private property is taken for a public use. Madison's personal choice of the phrasing of several provisions of the Bill of Rights also became significant. Instead of saying that a person could not be compelled to give evidence against himself, Madison preferred to say that he could not be compelled to be a witness against himself, thereby laying the basis for a future distinction between testimonial and nontestimonial compulsion.[18] Notwithstanding the personal touch

Madison imposed on his proposed amendments, he claimed that he had recommended only the familiar and avoided the controversial. He warned against enumerating anything except "simple, acknowledged principles," saying that amendments of a "doubtful nature" might damage the constitutional system.[19]

The House did not take the time or trouble to review his recommended amendments with the attention they deserved. In committee or as a result of debate, the House added only one important right to Madison's list, freedom of speech, which Pennsylvania had constitutionally protected. Some major principles, which appropriately prefaced a bill of rights, were deleted, despite their commonplaceness Madison, for example, had urged a statement that power derives from and rests with the people, that government should be exercised for their benefit, and that they have a right to change that government when inadequate to its purposes. He had lifted his statement of those purposes from his own state's 1776 constitution and from its 1788 recommendations for inclusion in a national bill of rights. Those purposes expressed the idea that governments are instituted to secure the people, said Madison, "in the enjoyment of life and liberty, with the right of acquiring and using property, and generally of pursuing and obtaining happiness and safety."[20] The Declaration of Independence had made the points more concisely and felicitously, but not with such generosity: The Virginia version proposed by Madison (and adopted in numerous state constitutions) spoke not only about the pursuit of happiness but of obtaining it. Conceivably, the committee that eliminated Madison's prefatory principles believed them to be implicit in its streamlined version of what became the Ninth Amendment: "The enumeration in this Constitution of certain rights shall not be construed to deny or disparage others retained by the people." Both houses approved.[21]

The Ninth Amendment served as a definitive solution to the ratificationists' problem of how to enumerate the rights of the people without endangering those that might be omitted. The amendment served also as a device for Congress to avoid making a systematic enumeration when framing the Bill of Rights. Framing it was not high on Congress's agenda and, except for Madison's nagging insistence, might not have been attempted at all or, perhaps, would have been disposed of in an even more perfunctory fashion. The Ninth Amendment functioned as a sweep-it-under-the-rug means of disposing as swiftly as possible of a task embarrassing to both parties and delaying the organization of the government and providing for its revenues. And the Ninth Amendment could also serve to draw the sting from any criticism that the catalogue of personal freedoms was incomplete. Another conclusion one must draw from the text of the amendment is that the enumeration of rights in the preceding text was not meant to be exhaustive.

What rights did the Ninth Amendment protect? They had to be either "natural rights" or "positive rights," to use the terms Madison employed in the notes for the great speech of June 8 advocating amendments.[22] In that speech he distinguished "the preexistent rights of nature" from those "resulting from a social compact."[23] In his notes, he mentioned freedom of "speach" as a natural right, yet he failed to provide for it in his recommended amendments. That is an example of Madison having acknowledged the existence of important rights that he had not enumerated or believed to be included within the unenumerated category. Freedom of speech was a right that preexisted government; it was inherent in human nature and did not depend for its existence on organized society. In 1775, Alexander Hamilton wrote that "the sacred rights of mankind are not to be rummaged for among old parchments or musty records. They are written, as with a sunbeam, in the whole volume of human nature, by the hand of the divinity itself, and can never be erased or obscured by mortal power."[24] Another tough-minded American materialist had led the way to such thinking. John Dickinson, speaking of "the rights essential to happiness," rhapsodized:

> We claim them from a higher source—from the King of kings, and Lord of all the earth. They are not annexed to use by parchments and seals. They are created in us by the decrees of Providence, which establish the laws of our nature. They are born with us, exist with us; and cannot be taken from us by any human power without taking our lives. In short, they are founded on the immutable maxims of reason and justice.[25]

Such opinions were commonplace.

So, too, the directly related views expressed by Jefferson in the preamble of the Declaration of Independence reflected commonly held principles. In 1822 John Adams, who had been a member of the committee of Congress that Jefferson had chaired in 1776, observed that there was "not an idea in it [the Declaration] but what had been hackneyed."[26] Jefferson asserted that "All American whigs thought alike" on those matters. The purpose of the Declaration, he wrote, was not "to find out new principles, or new arguments . . . but to place before mankind the common sense of the subject. . . ."[27] These views are central to the meaning of the Ninth Amendment. Contrary to cynical legal scholars of today, the ideas of the preamble to the Declaration did not go out of fashion in a decade and a half; and those ideas were as appropriate for writing a frame of government as for writing a "brief."[28]

The proof derives from both text and context. The text of the Ninth Amendment does protect the unenumerated rights of the people, and no reason exists to believe that it does not mean what it says. The context consists of Madison's remarks about natural rights during the legislative history of the amendment and also the references to natural rights in the opinion of the time or what Madison called "contemporaneous interpretations." The last of the state constitutions that came out of the Revolution, that of New Hampshire, began with a bill of rights of 1783 whose language Madison might have used in his first proposed amendment, the one that included the pursuit and obtaining of happiness.[29] Virginia's 1788 recommendations for amendments to the Constitution began similarly, as had New York's and North Carolina's.[30] At the Pennsylvania ratifying convention, James Wilson, who had been second only to Madison as an architect of the Constitution, quoted the preamble of the Declaration of Independence, and he added: "This is the broad basis on which our independence was placed; on the same certain and solid foundation this system [the Constitution] is erected."[31]

The pursuit of happiness, a phrase used by Locke for a concept that underlay his political ethics, subsumed the great rights of liberty and property, which were inextricably related. Lockean thought, to which the Framers subscribed, included within the pursuit of happiness that which delighted and contented the mind, and a belief that indispensable to it were good health, reputation and knowledge.[32] There was nothing radical in the idea of the right to the pursuit of happiness. The anti-American Tory, Dr. Samuel Johnson, had used the phrase, and Sir William Blackstone, also a Tory, employed a close equivalent in his *Commentaries* in 1765, when remarking "that man should pursue his own happiness. This is the foundation of what we call ethics, or natural law."[33]

In the eighteenth century property did not mean merely the ownership of material things. Locke himself had not used the word to denote merely a right to things; he meant a right to rights. In his *Second Treatise on Government,* he remarked that people "united for the general preservation of their lives, liberties, and estates, which I call by the general name property." And, he added, "by property I must be understood here as in other places to mean that property which men have in their persons as well as goods." At least four times in his *Second Treatise,* Locke used the word "property" to mean all that belongs to a person, especially the rights he wished to preserve.[34] Americans of the founding generation understood property in this general Lockean sense, which we have lost.

This view of property as a human right is the theme of a 1792 essay by Madison on *Property.* He described what he called the "larger and juster meaning" of the term "property." It "embraces," he said, "every thing to which a man may attach a value and have a right. "In the narrow sense it meant one's land, merchandise, or money; in the broader sense, it meant that

> a man has property in his opinions and the free communication of them. He has a property of peculiar value in his religious opinions, and in the profession and practices dictated by them. He has property very dear to him in the safety and liberty of his person. He has an equal property in the free use of his faculties and free choice of the objects on which to employ them. In a word, as a man is said to have a right to his property, he may be equally said to have a property in his rights.[35]

If the Fifth Amendment incorporated this broad meaning of "property" in the due process clause (no person shall be deprived of life, liberty, or property without due process of law), then "property" had a dual meaning in that clause but only the narrower, materialistic meaning in the eminent domain or takings clause (private property shall not be taken for a public use except at a just compensation). This inconsistency in the different uses of the same word in the same amendment seems baffling. But, no matter how defined, property rights nourished individual autonomy.

Not only were liberty, property, and the pursuit of happiness deeply linked in the thought of the Framers. They also believed in the principle that all people had a right to equal justice and to equality of rights. When Lincoln at Gettysburg described the creation of a new nation "conceived in liberty and dedicated to the proposition that all men are created equal," he reminded the nation that it could not achieve freedom without equal rights for all nor could it maintain equality without keeping society free. Liberty and equality constituted the master principles of the founding, which the Framers perpetuated as constitutional ideals, even if slyly. In a society that inherited a system of human slavery, the Framers compromised by accepting political reality; they could not abolish slavery and still form a stronger Union, but they did what was feasible. Nowhere in the Constitution is any person described in derogatory terms. Nowhere is slavery even acknowledged as a human condition. The Framers in effect spoke to the future by using circumlocutions that acknowledged only the status of "persons held to service"—a term that could be applied to white indentured servants. Race was not mentioned in the Constitution not until the Fifteenth Amendment. The three-fifths rule, which applied to both direct taxation and to representation, was a device by which the Convention tied southern voting strength in Congress to southern liability for direct taxes on land and people. The Framers did not intentionally insult the humanity of blacks held to service. The same Constitution authorized Congress to extinguish the slave trade in twenty years, and thus prevented untold tens of thousands of people from being enslaved, but the authorization refers only to the "importation of such persons" as some states had thought proper to admit. The point is that the Constitution as amended by the Ninth Amendment provided a subsequent foundation for equal justice to all persons, regardless of race, sex, or religion. The Reconstruction amendments did not require the deletion or alteration of any part of the Constitution.

The Ninth Amendment is the repository for natural rights including the right to pursue happiness and the right to equality of treatment before the law. Madison, presenting his proposed amendments, spoke of "the perfect equality of mankind."[36] Other natural rights come within the protection of the amendment as well, among them the right, then important, to hunt and fish, the right to travel, and very likely the right to intimate association or privacy in matters concerning family and sex, at least within the bounds of marriage. Such rights were fundamental to the pursuit of happiness.[37] But no evidence exists to prove that the Framers intended the Ninth Amendment to protect any particular natural rights. The text expressly protects unenumerated rights, but we can only guess what the Framers had in mind. On the basis of tantalizing hints and a general philosophy of natural rights, which then prevailed, conclusions emerge that bear slight relation to the racial, sexual, or political realities of that generation.

In addition to natural rights, the unenumerated rights of the people included positive rights, those deriving from the social compact that creates government. What positive rights were familiar, when the Ninth became part of the Constitution, yet were not enumerated in the original text or the first eight amendments? The right to vote and hold office, the right to free elections, the right not to be taxed except by consent through representatives of one's choice, the right to be free from monopolies, the right to be free from standing armies in time of peace, the right to refuse military service on grounds of religious conscience, the right to bail, the right of an accused person to be presumed innocent, and the person's right to have the prosecution shoulder the responsibility of proving guilt beyond a reasonable doubt— all these were among existing positive rights protected by various state laws, state constitutions, and the common law. Any of these, among others, could legitimately be regarded as rights of the people before which the power of government must be exercised in subordination.

In addition to rights then known, the Ninth Amendment might have had the purpose of providing the basis for rights then unknown, which time alone might disclose. Nothing in the thought of the Framers foreclosed the possibility that new rights might claim the loyalties of succeeding generations. As the chief justice of Virginia's highest court mused when the Bill of Rights was being framed, "May we not in the progress of things, discover some great and important [right], which we don't now think of?"[38]

To argue that the Framers had used natural rights as a means of escaping obligations of obedience to the king but did not use natural rights "as a source for rules of decision" is hogwash.[39] One has only to read the state recommendations for a bill of rights to know that the natural rights philosophy seized the minds of the Framers as it had the minds of the rebellious patriots of 1776. One can also read natural rights opinions by members of the early Supreme Court to arrive at the same conclusion.[40] Without doubt, natural rights, if read into the Ninth Amendment, "do not lend themselves to principled *judicial* enforcement,"[41] but neither do positive rights. That is, the enumerated rights such as freedom of speech and the right to due process of law have resulted in some of the most subjective result-oriented jurisprudence in our history. That judicial decisions can be unprincipled does not detract from the principle expressed in a right, whether or not enumerated. If the Ninth Amendment instructs us to look beyond its four corners for unenumerated rights of the people, as it does, it must have some content, contrary to its detractors. Some cannot stomach the thought of such indefiniteness, and they disapprove of a license for judicial subjectivity; so they draw conclusions that violate the commonsensical premises with which they begin. John Hart Ely, for example, initially suggests that the amendment should be read for what it says and that it is the provision of the Constitution that applies the principle of equal protection against the federal government. "In fact," he wrote, "the conclusion that the Ninth Amendment was intended to signal the existence of federal constitutional rights beyond those specifically enumerated in the Constitution is the only conclusion its language seems comfortably able to support." Yet Ely ridicules natural rights theory and believes that it swiftly became passé. He ends by leaving the amendment an empty provision, significant only as a lure to judicial activism.[42]

Raoul Berger is an even more hostile critic of the amendment, but he is so eager to keep it the feckless provision that was a mystery to Justice Jackson that he confuses the Ninth and and Tenth Amendments. For example, he speaks of "the ninth's retention of rights by the states or the people," when in fact it is the Tenth Amendment, not its predecessor, that speaks of states' rights, that is, of powers retained by the states or the people. "The ninth amendment," added Berger, " . . . was merely declaratory of a basic presupposition: all powers not 'positively' granted are reserved to the people. It added no unspecified rights to the Bill of Rights. . . . "[43] But an explicit declaration of the existence of unenumerated rights is an addition of unspecified rights to the Bill of Rights, whose Tenth Amendment, not Ninth, reserved powers not granted.[44]

Confusion between the Ninth and Tenth Amendments seems to originate with two amendments proposed by Virginia in 1788. One in modified terms was modeled after Article II of the Articles of Confederation, retaining to each state every power not delegated to the United States. The second amendment concerned clauses in the Constitution declaring that Congress shall not exercise certain powers (e.g., no bills of attainder). The second proposed that such clauses should not be construed to extend the powers of Congress; rather, they should be construed "as making exceptions to the specified powers where this shall be the case, or otherwise as inserted merely for greater caution."[45] Neither proposal addressed the issue of reserving to the people unenumerated rights. Yet the Virginia Assembly, in 1789, when debating whether to ratify the amendments proposed by Congress, initially rejected what became the Ninth and Tenth Amendments. The Assembly preferred instead its two proposals of 1788. The reasoning behind the Assembly's action was confused and gave rise to the confusion between the Ninth and Tenth Amendments.

According to Hardin Burnley, a member of the Assembly who kept Madison informed about the progress of his amendments in the state legislature, Edmund Randolph, who led the opposition to the Ninth Amendment (then the eleventh), objected to the word "retained" because it was too indefinite. Randolph had argued that the rights declared in the preceding amendments (our First through Eighth) "were not all that a free people would require the exercise of; and that there was no criterion by which it could be determined whether any other particular right was retained or not." Thus Randolph argued that the Ninth was not sufficiently comprehensive and explicit. From that point he concluded, illogically, that the course of safety lay not in retaining unenumerated rights but in providing against an extension of the powers of Congress. Randolph believed that the Ninth Amendment did not reduce rights to a "definitive certainty."[46]

Madison soon after sent to Washington Burnley's information (and language) as if his own. The letter, as construed by those who find the Ninth Amendment an empty vehicle, became a means of putting Madison's authority behind the proposition that the Ninth Amendment means no more than the Tenth. Plagiarizing Burnley, Madison informed Washington that he found Randolph's distinction to be without force, because "by protecting the rights of the people & of the States, an improper extension of power will be prevented & safety made equally certain."[47] Madison did not challenge Randolph's assertion that the amendments preceding the Ninth and Tenth did not exhaust the rights of the people that needed protection against government. Nor did he challenge the assertion that the Ninth was too vague. Rather, Madison disagreed that adoption of the Virginia proposals of 1788 more effectively secured the rights deserving of protection.

In the only part of his letter that did not repeat Burnley's, Madison expressed regret that the confusion had come from Randolph, "a friend to the Constitution," and he added: "It is a still greater cause of regret, if the distinction [made by Randolph] be, as it appears to me, altogether fanciful. If a line can be drawn between the powers granted and the rights retained, it would seem to be the same thing, whether the latter be secured, by declaring that they shall not be abridged, or that the former shall not be extended. If no line can be drawn, a declaration in either form would amount to nothing."[48] The reference to "whether the latter be secured" meant the retention of a specific right. In effect, Madison argued that the line between a power granted and a right retained amounted to the same thing if a right were named. Thus to say that the government may not abridge the freedom of the press is the equivalent of saying that the government shall not abridge the freedom of the press. If, as Madison said, a line cannot be drawn between rights retained and powers denied, retaining unenumerated rights would be useless against a power of government to violate them. Whether the formulation of the First Amendment is used—"Congress shall make no law"—or whether that of the Fourth Amendment is used—"The right of the people to be secure . . . against unreasonable searches and seizures, shall not be violated"—the effect is the same. In the case of unenumerated rights, however, one can only argue that no affirmative power has been granted to regulate.

Randolph had identified a problem that remains without a solution. Madison's response was by no means a satisfactory one in all respects. Although both houses of Virginia's legislature finally ratified the Bill of Rights, the Ninth Amendment continues to bedevil its interpreters. Courts keep discovering rights that have no literal textual existence, that is, rights not enumerated, only to meet howls of denunciation from those who deplore the result—whether the right of a woman to an abortion, a right of privacy against electronic eavesdropping, or a right to engage in nude dancing.[49] Opponents have another string to their bow, which they find in a declaration by Madison in the First Congress, when he proposed his amendments. Adding a bill of rights to the Constitution, he argued, would enable courts to become "the guardians of those rights; they will be an impenetrable bulwark against every assumption of power in the legislative or executive, they will be naturally led to resist every encroachment upon rights *expressly* stipulated for in the constitution by the declaration of rights."[50] "Expressly stipulated" can be read to mean that Madison either opposed or failed to predict judicial review in cases involving unenumerated rights. And, without doubt he was not referring to the desirability of giving courts what Raoul Berger calls "a roving commission to enforce a catalog of unenumerated rights against the will of the states."[51]

Madison might well, however, have approved of courts' enforcing against the states the amendment that he thought "the most valuable amendment in the whole list"—one that prohibited the states from infringing upon the equal rights of conscience, the freedom of speech or press, and the right to trial by jury in criminal cases.[52] The House passed but the Senate defeated that proposal, making enforcement by the federal courts against the states impossible. The incorporation doctrine, drawn from the Fourteenth Amendment, superseded whatever limitations the Framers of the Bill of Rights had in mind concerning judicial review over state acts.

So long as we continue to believe that government is instituted for the sake of securing the rights of the people, and must exercise powers in subordination to those rights, the Ninth Amendment should have the vitality intended for it. The problem is not whether the rights it guarantees are as worthy of enforcement as the enumerated rights; the problem, rather, is whether our courts should read out of the amendment rights worthy of our respect, which the Framers might conceivably have meant to safeguard, at least in principle.

Notes

1. 16 Wallace 36 (1873).
2. Robert H. Jackson, *The Supreme Court in the American System of Government* (Cambridge, Mass.: Harvard University Press, 1958), pp. 74–75.
3. *Griswold v. Connecticut*, 381 U.S. 479, 484–86 (1965). Only a plurality agreed with the Ninth Amendment grounds. Chief Justice Earl Warren and Justice William Brennan were the others.
4. Raoul Berger, "The Ninth Amendment," *Cornell Law Review* 61 (1980):1, note 2, relying on a computer study.
5. Edwin Meese III, Address before the American Bar Association, Washington, D.C., July 9, 1985, Dept. of Justice typescript, pp. 13, 15.
6. *Dred Scott v. Sandford*, 19 Howard 393 (1857).
7. *Griswold v. Connecticut*, p. 520.
8. Joseph Story, *Commentaries on the Constitution of the United States* (Boston, 1833, 1st ed., 3 vols.), I, pp. 383, 387.
9. Merrill Jensen, ed., *The Documentary History of the Ratification of the Constitution*. Vol. II, *Ratification of the Constitution by States. Pennsylvania* (Madison: State Historical Society of Wisconsin, 1976–), p. 388, for Wilson. See the sixth "Landholder" essay by Ellsworth in Paul L. Ford, ed., *Essays on the Constitution of the United States . . . 1787–1789* (Brooklyn, N.Y.: 1892), p. 163.
10. Jonathan Elliot, ed., *The Debates in the Several State Conventions* (Philadelphia: Lippincott, 1941, 5 vols., reprinting the final, rev. ed.), III, p. 620.
11. Speech of June 8, 1789, reprinted in Bernard Schwartz, ed., *The Bill of Rights: A Documentary History* (New York: Chelsea House, 1971, 2 vols.), II. pp. 1023–34, quoted material at p. 1024.

12. Ibid., II, p. 1029.
13. Ibid., II, p. 1024.
14. Ibid., II, p. 1031.
15. Ibid., II, p. 1027.
16. Coke, *The Second Part of the Institutes of the Laws of England* (London, 1681, 6th ed.) chap. XXIX, p. 50. See Rodney L. Mott, *Due Process of Law* (Indianapolis: Bobbs-Merrill, 1926), pp. 75–80, and Charles H. McIlwain, "Due Process of Law in Magna Carta," *Columbia Law Review* 14 (1914):27–51. Keith Jurow, "Untimely Thoughts: A Reconsideration of the Origins of Due Process of Law," *American Journal of Legal History* 19 (1975): 265–79, straightens out the history of the matter but does not alter the fact that a tradition existed, even if ill-founded, equating due process with the law of the land and, in particular, with proceedings by grand and petty juries in criminal cases.
17. See supra, chap. 11, text connected with notes 79–80.
18. See supra, chap. 12, text connected with notes 1–2.
19. Schwartz, ed., Bill of Rights, II, p. 1096.
20. Ibid., II, p. 1026.
21. Ibid, II, pp. 1112, 1123.
22. Ibid., p. 1042.
23. Ibid., p. 1029.
24. Hamilton, "The Farmer Refuted," in *Papers of Alexander Hamilton,* ed. Harold C. Syrett et al. (New York: Columbia University Press, 1961–1981, 26 vols.), I, p. 122.
25. Dickinson, "An Address to the Committee of Correspondence in Barbados (1766), in Paul L. Ford, ed., *Writings of John Dickinson* (Philadelphia, 1895), vol. XIV of *Memoirs of the Historical Society of Pennsylvania,* p. 261.
26. John Adams to Timothy Pickering, Aug. 6, 1822, in *Works of John Adams,* ed. Charles F. Adams (Boston, 1850–1859, 10 vols.), II, p. 512.
27. Jefferson to Henry Lee, May 8, 1825, in *The Writings of Thomas Jefferson,* ed. Albert E. Bergh (Washington: Jefferson Memorial Association, 1907, 20 vols), XVI, pp. 118–19.
28. See John Hart Ely, *Democracy and Distrust: A Theory of Judicial Review* (Cambridge, Mass.: Harvard University Press, 1980), p. 49.
29. Schwartz, ed., *Bill of Rights,* I, p. 375.
30. Ibid, II, pp. 840, 911, 966.
31. Dec. 4, 1787, in Jensen, ed., *Documentary History of Ratification,* II, p. 473.
32. Locke's note on happiness in Maurice Cranston, *John Locke, a Biography* (London: Longmans, Green, 1957), p. 123. For Locke's use of "pursuit of happiness," see his *Essays Concerning Human Understanding,* ed. Alexander Campbell Fraser (Oxford: Clarendon Press, 1894, 2 vols.), I, pp. 342, 345, 348, 352.
33. Herbert L. Ganter, "Jefferson's 'Pursuit of Happiness' and Some Forgotten Men," *William and Mary Quarterly,* 2nd ser. 16 (1936), pp. 558–85, traces the pre-1776 uses of "pursuit of happiness," and quotes Johnson and Blackstone.
34. See Locke, *Second Treatise,* sections 27, 87, 123, 173; see also Laslett, ed., *Two Treatises,* p. 367, note for lines 5–6.
35. *National Gazette* (Philadelphia), March 29, 1792, reprinted in *Papers of Madison,* ed. Hutchinson et al., XIV, p. 266.
36. Ibid., XII, p. 203.
37. See Kenneth L. Karst, "Freedom of Intimate Association," in Leonard W. Levy, Kenneth L. Karst, and Dennis J. Mahoney, eds., *Encyclopedia of the American Constitution* (New York: Macmillan, 1986, 4 vols.), II, pp. 782–89, and Karst's lengthy article of the same title in *Yale Law Journal,* 89 (1980): 624–92. See also

David H. Flaherty, *Privacy in Colonial New England* (Charlottesville: University Press of Virginia, 1967), chap. 2, "The Family," chap. 3, "The Neighborhood," and chap. 6, "Government and the Law." The right to travel and the right to hunt and fish are old; precedents can be found in the Massachusetts Body of Liberties of 1641, the source, also, of equal protection of the laws and many other rights. See Richard L. Perry, ed., *Sources of Our Liberties: Documentary Origins of Individual Liberties* (Chicago: American Bar Foundation, 1959), pp. 143–61, for the document prefaced by commentary, and, especially, pp. 148 and 150.

38. Edmund Pendleton to Richard Henry Lee, June 14, 1788, in David Mayes, ed., *Letters and Papers of Edmund Pendleton* (Cambridge, Mass.: Harvard University Press, 1967, 2 vols.), II, p. 533.

39. Ely, *Democracy and Distrust*, p. 39, so argues. He relies on Robert Cover, *Justice Accused: Antislavery and the Judicial Process* (New Haven, Conn.: Yale University Press, 1975), p. 27; but Cover refers to the period before 1776. Ely extended Cover's point to the time of the Framers and later.

40. Van Horne's *Lessee v. Dorrance*, 2 Dallas 304 (1795); *Calder v. Bull*, 3 Dallas 386 (1798); *Fletcher v. Peck*, 6 Cranch 87 (1810); and *Terrett v. Taylor*, 9 Cranch 43 (1815); all discussed in chapters below; see index.

41. Ely, *Democracy and Distrust*, p. 39.

42. Ibid., pp. 49–52.

43. Berger, "Ninth Amendment," p. 16 note 95 and p. 23.

44. Russell L. Caplan, "The History and Meaning of the Ninth Amendment," *Virginia Law Review* 69 (1983): 223–68, is a desperately confused article. Most of it is a sprawling collection of historical data of no relevance. The thesis is that the Ninth Amendment derived from a provision of the Articles of Confederation, which spoke of state sovereignty and the retention by the states of all rights and powers not "expressly" delegated to the United States. Not even the Tenth Amendment, with which Caplan confuses the Ninth, speaks of powers not "expressly" delegated. Lawrence E. Mitchell, "The Ninth Amendment and the Jurisprudence of Original Intention, *Georgetown Law Journal* 74 (1986): 1719–42, focuses wholly on contemporary issues, after endorsing as good history the article by Caplan and the remarkably bad little book, Bennett Patterson's *The Forgotten Ninth Amendment* (Indianapolis: Bobbs-Merrill, 1955), which advocates that the Ninth Amendment's natural rights philosophy protects God, corporations, and patriotism. Mitchell's article is otherwise worth reading. A better article on the subject, though outdated in some respects, is Norman Redlich, "Are There Certain Rights . . . Retained by the People," *New York University Law Review* 37 (1961): 787–808. Charles L. Black, *Decision According to Law* (New York: W. W. Norton, 1981), is an 83-page essay whose principal theme is that the Ninth Amendment should be the basis for judicial decisions in favor of women's rights. Black's thesis does not rest on history or original intent.

45. Articles 1 and 17, Virginia's recommended amendments, 1788, in Schwartz, ed., *Bill of Rights,* II, pp. 842, 844.

46. Burnley to Madison, Nov. 28, 1789, in *Papers of Madison,* ed. Hutchinson et al., XII, p. 456.

47. Madison to Washington, Dec. 5, 1789, in ibid., p. 459.

48. Ibid.

49. *Roe v. Wade*, 410 U.S. 113 (1973); *Katz v. United States*, 389 U.S. 347 (1967); *Schad v. Borough of Mt. Ephraim*, 452 U.S. 61 (1981).

50. Speech of June 8, 1789, in Schwartz, ed., *Bill of Rights,* II, p. 1031, my emphasis.

51. Berger, "Ninth Amendment," p. 9.

52. Ibid., pp. 1112–13.

II

Constitutional History

17

Social Compact Theory

An invention of political philosophers, the social contract or social compact theory was not meant as a historical account of the origin of government, but the theory was taken literally in America where governments were actually founded upon contract. The words "compact" and "contract" are synonymous and signify a voluntary agreement of the people to unite as a political community and to establish a government. The theory purports to explain why individuals should obey the law: each person, in a government that exists with the consent of the governed, freely and, in effect, continuously gives consent to the Constitution of his community.

The theory hypothesizes a prepolitical state of nature in which people were governed only by the law of nature, free of human restraints. From the premise that man was born free, the deduction followed that he came into the world with God-given or natural rights. Born without the restraint of human laws, he had a right to possess liberty and to work for his own property. Born naked and stationless, he had a right to equality. Born with certain instincts and needs, he had a right to satisfy them—a right to the pursuit of happiness. These natural rights, as John Dickinson declared in 1766, "are created in us by the decrees of Providence, which establish the laws of our nature. They are born with us; exist with us; and cannot be taken from us by any human power without taking our lives."

When people left the state of nature and compacted for government, the need to make their rights secure motivated them. Alexander Hamilton observed that "Civil liberty is only natural liberty modified and secured by the sanctions of civil society. . . . The origin of all civil government, justly established, must be a voluntary compact between the rulers and the ruled, and must be liable to such limitations as are necessary for the security of the absolute rights of the latter." The most detailed exposition of this theory was by John Locke, the most brief and eloquent by Thomas Jefferson in the preamble of the Declaration of Independence. One of the self-evident truths in the latter is "That to secure these rights, Governments are instituted among Men, deriving their just powers from the consent of the governed. . . ."

The compact theory of government colored the thought and action of Americans during the colonial period and through the period of constitution making. The new world actually seemed like a state of nature, and Americans did in fact compact with each other; the theory seemed to fit the circumstances under which American political and constitutional institutions grew. Our system developed as a self-conscious working out of some of the implications of the compact theory.

The related but distinct idea, so important in Puritan thought, that people covenant with each other to make a church for their ecclesiastical polity, was extended to their secular polity. Even before the founding of Virginia a Separatist leader asked, "What agreement must there be of men? For church governors there must be an agreement of the people or commonwealth." A half century before Locke's *Second Treatise,* Thomas Hooker, a founder of Connecticut, explained that in any relationship that involved authority there must be free agreement or consent. "This," he said, "appears in all covenants betwixt Prince and People, Husband and Wife, Master and Servant, and most palpable is the expression of this in all confederations and corporations. . . . They should first freely engage themselves in such covenants. . . ." The first concrete application of the covenant theory to civil government was the Mayflower Compact (1620). The Pilgrims, putting theory into practice, solemnly did "covenant and combine . . . into a civil body politick," an experience multiplied over and again with the founding of numerous settlements in New England.

The colonists also regarded their charters as compacts. As Hamilton said later, George III was "King of America, by virtue of a compact between us and the Kings of Great Britain." These colonies, Hamilton explained, were settled under charters granted by kings who "entered into covenants with us. . . ." Over a period of a century and a half, Americans became accustomed to the idea that government existed by consent of the governed, that the people created government, that they did it by written compact, and that the compact constituted their fundamental law. From practical experience as well as from revolutionary propaganda, Americans believed in the compact theory and they acted it out.

It was a useful tool, immediately at hand and lending historical and philosophical credibility, for destroying the old order and creating a new one. William Drayton, the chief justice of South Carolina, echoed a commonplace idea when he said that George III had "unkinged" himself by subverting the "constitution of this country, by breaking the original contract. . . ." The compact theory legitimated the right of revolution, as the Declaration of Independence made clear. Even before that declaration, colonial radicals contended that the Coercive Acts have thrown us into a state of nature," and justified contracting for a new government. After Independence a town orator in Boston declared that the people had reclaimed the rights "attendant upon the original state of nature, with the opportunity of establishing a government for ourselves. . . ." The colonies became states by a practice that mirrored the theory; they drew up written constitutions, often phrased as compacts, and purposefully put formal statements of the compact theory into those documents. The Massachusetts Constitution of 1780 (still operative) declares: "The body politic is formed by a voluntary association of individuals; it is a social compact by which the whole people covenants with each citizen and each citizen with the whole people. . . ." A minister, Jonas Clark, said in a sermon that just government is founded in compact "and in compact alone." The new state constitution, he declared, was "a most sacred covenant or contract. . . ." The state Constitutional Convention that framed that constitution was devised to institutionalize the compact theory.

Although the Articles of Confederation do not formally state that theory, letters of the members of the Continental Congress that framed the Articles show that they regarded themselves as making a compact for the union of states, and *The Federalist* #21 refers to "the social compact between the States. . . ." Similarly, at the Philadelphia Constitutional Convention of 1787, James Madison declared that the delegates had assembled to frame "a compact by which an authority was created paramount to the parties, and making laws for the government of them." George Washington, on behalf of the Federal Convention, when sending the new Constitution to the Congress of the Confederation for submission to the states, drew an analogy from compact theory:

individuals left a state of nature by yielding up some liberty to preserve the rest, and the states surrendered some of their sovereignty to
consolidate the union. Some of the states, when formally ratifying the
new Constitution, considered themselves to be "entering into an explicit and solemn compact," as New Hampshire declared. Chief Justice John Jay observed, in *Chisholm v. Georgia* (1793), that every state
constitution "is a compact. . . and the Constitution of the United States
is likewise a compact made by the people of the United States to
govern themselves."

The compact theory answers one of the most profound questions of
political philosophy: why do people submit to the compulsions of
government? The answer is that when they established government
they consented to its exercise of power and agreed to obey it if it
secured their rights. The compact theory has been remarkably fecund.
From government by consent it led to political democracy. It also led
to constitutionalism as limited government, to a concept of a constitution as fundamental law, to constitutions as written documents, to the
constitutional convention as a way of writing the document, to the
right of revolution when the government is destructive of the ends of
the compact, and to concepts of civil liberty and written bill of rights.

Bibliography

McLaughlin, Andrew C. 1932 *The Foundations of American Constitutionalism.* New
York: New York University Press.
Rossiter, Clinton 1953 *Seedtime of the Republic: The Origin of the American Tradi-
tion of Political Liberty.* New York Harcourt, Brace.
Tate, Thad W. 1965 The Social Contract in America, 1774–1787: Revolutionary
Theory as a Conservative Instrument. *William and Mary Quarterly* 22:375–391.
Wood, Gordon S. 1969 *The Creation of the American Republic, 1776–1787.* Chapel
Hill: University of North Carolina Press.

18

Constitution

At the time of the Stamp Act controversy, a British lord told Benjamin Franklin that Americans had wrong ideas about the British constitution. British and American ideas did differ radically. The American Revolution repudiated the British understanding of the constitution; in a sense, the triumph in America of a novel concept of "constitution" *was* the "revolution." The British, who were vague about their unwritten constitution, meant by it their system of government, the common law, royal proclamations, major legislation such as Magna Carta and the Bill of Rights, and various usages and customs of government animating the aggregation of laws, institutions, rights, and practices that had evolved over centuries. Statute, however, was the supreme part of the British constitution. After the Glorious Revolution of 1688–1689, Parliament dominated the constitutional system and by ordinary legislation could and did alter it. Sir William Blackstone summed up parliamentary supremacy when he declared in his *Commentaries* (1766), "What Parliament doth, no power on earth can undo."

The principle that Parliament had unlimited power was at the crux of the controversy leading to the American Revolution. The American assertion that government is limited undergirded the American concept of a constitution as a fundamental law that imposes regularized restraints upon power and reserves rights to the people. The American concept emerged slowly through the course of the colonial period, yet its nub was present almost from the beginning, especially in New England where covenant theology, social compact theory, and higher law theory blended together. Thomas Hooker in 1638 preached that the foundation of authority lay in the people who might choose their governors and "set bounds and limitations on their powers." A century later Jared Elliot of Massachusetts preached that a "legal government" exists when the sovereign power "puts itself under restraints and lays itself under limitations. This is what we call a legal, limited, and well constituted government." Some liberal theologians viewed God himself as a constitutional monarch, limited in power because he had limited himself to the terms of his covenant with mankind. Moreover God ruled a constitutional universe based on immutable natural laws that also bound him. Jonathan Mayhew preached in Boston that no one has a right to exercise a wanton sovereignty over the property, lives, and consciences of the people—"such a sovereignty as some inconsiderately ascribe to the supreme governor of the world." Mayhew explained that "God himself does not govern in an absolute, arbitrary, and despotic manner. The power of this almighty king is limited by law; not indeed, by acts of Parliament, but by the eternal laws of truth, wisdom, and equity. . . ."

Political theory and law as well as religion taught that government was limited; so did history. But the Americans took their views on such matters from a highly selective and romanticized image of seventeenth-century England, which they perpetuated in America even as England changed. Seventeenth-century England was the England of the great struggle for constitutional liberty by the common law courts and Puritan parliaments against despotic Stuart kings. Seventeenth-century England was the England of Edward Coke, John Lilburne, and John Locke. It was an England in which religion, law, and politics converged with theory and experience to produce limited monarchy and, ironically, parliamentary supremacy. To Americans, however, Parliament had bound itself by reaffirming Magna Carta and passing the Habeas Corpus Act, the Bill of Rights, and the Toleration Act, among others. Locke had taught the social contract theory; advocated that taxation without representation or consent is tyranny; written that "government is not free to do as it pleases," and referred to the "bounds" which "the law of God and Nature have set to the legislative power of every commonwealth, in all forms of government."

Such ideas withered but did not die in eighteenth-century England. *Cato's Letters* popularized Locke on both sides of the Atlantic; Henry St. John (Viscount Bolingbroke) believed that Parliament could not annul the constitution; Charles Viner's *General Abridgment of Law and Equity* endorsed Coke's views in *Dr. Bonham's Case* (1610); and even as Parliament debated the Declaratory Act (1766), which asserted parliamentary power to legislate for America "in all cases whatsoever." Charles Pratt (Lord Camden) declared such a power "absolutely illegal, contrary to the fundamental laws of . . . this constitution. . . ." Richard Price and Granville Sharpe were two of the many English radicals who shared the American view of the British constitution.

Taxation without representation provoked Americans to clarify their views. James Otis, arguing against the tax on sugar, relied on *Dr. Bonham's Case* and contended that legislative authority did not extend to the "fundamentals of the constitution," which he believed to be fixed. Thomas Hutchinson, a leading supporter of Parliament, summed up the American constitutional reaction to the stamp tax duties by writing, "The prevailing reason at this time is, that the Act of Parliament is against Magna Charta and the natural rights of Englishmen, and therefore according to Lord Coke, null and void." The Townshend Act duties led to American declarations that the supreme legislature in any free state derives its power from the constitution, which limits government. John Dickinson, in an essay reprinted throughout the colonies, wrote that a free people are not those subject to a reasonable exercise of government power but those "who live under a government so constitutionally checked and controlled, that proper provision is made against its being otherwise exercised." J. J. Zubly of Georgia was another of many who argued that no government, not even Parliament, could make laws against the constitution any more than it could alter the constitution. An anonymous pamphleteer rhapsodized in 1775 about the "glorious constitution worthy to be engraved in capitals of gold, on pillars of marble; to be perpetuated through all time, a barrier, to circumscribe and bound the restless ambition of aspiring monarchs, and the palladium of civil liberty. . . ." Tom Paine actually argued that Great Britain had no constitution, because Parliament claimed to exercise any power it pleased. To Paine a constitution could not be an act of the government but of "people constituting government. . . . A constitution is a thing antecedent to a government; a government is only the creature of the constitution."

Thus, by "constitution," Americans meant a supreme law creating the government, limiting it, unalterable by it, and above it. When they said that an act of government was unconstitutional, they meant that the government had acted lawlessly because it lacked the authority to perform that act. Accordingly the act was not law; it was null and void, and it could be disobeyed. By contrast when the British spoke of a statute being unconstitutional, they meant only that it was impolitic, unwise, unjust, or inexpedient, but not that it was beyond the power of the government to enact. They did not mean that Parliament was limited in its powers and had exceeded them.

The American view of "constitution" was imperfectly understood even by many leaders of the revolutionary movement as late as 1776. The proof is that when the states framed their first constitutions, the task was left to legislatures, although some received explicit authorization from the voters. Thomas Jefferson worried because Virginia had not differentiated fundamental from ordinary law. Not until Massachusetts framed its constitution of 1780 by devising a constitutional convention did the American theory match practice. When the constitutional convention of 1787 met in Philadelphia, the American meaning of a constitution was fixed and consistent.

Bibliography

Adams, Randolph G. (1922)1958 3rd ed. *Political Ideas of the American Revolution.* New York: Barnes & Noble.

Bailyn, Bernard 1967 *Ideological Origins of the American Revolution.* Cambridge, Mass.: Harvard University Press.

Baldwin, Alice M. (1928) 1958 *The New England Clergy and the American Revolution.* New York: Frederick Ungar.

McLaughlin, Andrew C. 1932 *The Foundations of American Constitutionalism.* New York: New York University Press.

Mullett, Charles F. 1933 *Fundamental Law and the American Revolution.* New York: Columbia University Press.

19

Constitutional Convention

Constitutional conventions, like the written constitutions that they produce, are among the American contributions to government. A constitutional convention became the means that a free people used to put into practice the social compact theory by devising their fundamental law. Such a convention is a representative body acting for the sovereign people to whom it is responsible. Its sole commission is to frame a constitution; it does not pass laws, perform acts of administration, or govern in any way. It submits its work for popular ratification and adjourns. Such a convention first came into being during the American Revolution. The institutionalizing of constitutional principles during wartime was the constructive achievement of the Revolution. The Revolution's enduring heroics are to be found in constitution-making. As James Madison exultantly declared, "Nothing has excited more admiration in the world than the manner in which free governments have been established in America; for it was the first instance, from the creation of the world ... that free inhabitants have been seen deliberating on a form of government and selecting such of their citizens as possessed their confidence, to determine upon and give effect to it."

Within a century of 1776 nearly two hundred state constitutional conventions had been held in the United States. The institution is so familiar that we forget how novel it was even in 1787. At the constitutional convention, which framed this nation's constitution, Oliver Ellsworth declared that since the framing of the Articles of Confederation (1781), "a new sett [sic] of ideas seemed to have crept in.... Conventions of the people, or with power derived expressly from the people, were not then thought of. The Legislatures were considered as competent."

Credit for understanding that legislatures were not competent for that task belongs to John Lilburne, the English Leveller leader, who probably originated the idea of a constitutional convention. In his *Legall Fundamentall Liberties (1649),* he proposed that specially elected representatives should frame an Agreement of the People, or constitution, "which Agreement ought to be above Law; and therefore [set] bounds, limits, and extent of the people's Legislative Deputies in Parliament." Similarly, Sir Henry Vane, once governor of Massachusetts, proposed, in his *Healing Question* (1656), that a "convention" be chosen by the free consent of the people, "not properly to exercise the legislative power" but only to agree on "fundamentall constitutions" expressing the will of the people "in their highest state of soveraignty...." The idea, which never made headway in England, was reexpressed in a pamphlet by Obadiah Hulme in 1771, recommending that a constitution should "be formed by a convention of delegates of the people, appointed for the express purpose," and that the constitution should never be "altered in any respect by any power besides the power which first framed [it]." Hulme's work was reprinted in Philadelphia in 1776 immediately before the framing of the Pennsylvania Constitution by a specially elected convention. That convention, however, in accordance with prevailing ideas, simultaneously exercised the powers of government and after promulgating its constitution remained in session as the state legislature. Until 1780 American legislatures wrote constitutions.

The theory underlying a constitutional convention, but not the actual idea of having one, was first proposed in America by the town meeting of Pittsfield, Massachusetts, on May 29, 1776. Massachusetts then had a provisional revolutionary extralegal government. Pittsfield asked, "What Compact has been formed as the foundation of Government in this province?" The collapse of British power over the colonies had thrown the people, "the foundation of power," into "a state of Nature." The first step to restore civil government on a permanent basis was "the formation of a fundamental Constitution as the Basis & ground work of Legislation." The existing legislature, Pittsfield contended, although representative, could not make the constitution because, "They being but servants of the people cannot be greater than their Masters, & must be responsible to them." A constitution is "above the whole Legislature," so that the "legislature cannot certainly make it. . . ." Pittsfield understood the difference between fundamental and ordinary law, yet inconsistently concluded that the legislature should frame the constitution on condition that it be submitted to the people for ratification.

Pittsfield was merely inconsistent, but the Continental Congress was bewildered. The provisional government of Massachusetts, requesting advice from Congress on how to institute government, said that it would accept a constitution proposed by Congress. That was in May 1775. Many years later, when his memory was not to be trusted, John Adams recalled in his autobiography that congressmen went around asking each other, "How can the people institute government?" As late as May 1776, Congress, still lacking an answer, merely recommended that colonies without adequate governments should choose representatives to suppress royal authority and exercise power under popular authority. By then the temporary legislatures of New Hampshire and South Carolina, without popular authorization, had already framed and promulgated constitutions as if enacting statutory law, and continued to operate as legislatures. Adams, however, credited himself with knowing how to "realize [make real] the theories of the wisest writers," who had urged that sovereignty resides in the people and that government is made by contract. "This could be done," he explained, "only by conventions of representatives chosen by the people in the several colonies. . . . " How, congressmen asked him, can we know whether the people will submit to the new constitutions, and he recalled having replied, if there is doubt, "the convention may send out their project of a constitution, to the people in their several towns, counties, or districts, and the people may make the acceptance of it their own act." Congress did not follow his advice, he wrote, because of his "new, strange, and terrible doctrines."

Adams had described a procedure followed only in Massachusetts, and only after the legislature had asked the people of the towns for permission to frame a constitution, and submit it for popular ratification. Several towns, led by Concord protested that the legislature was not a competent body for the task, because a constitution had been overwhelmingly rejected in 1778. Concord had demanded a constitutional convention. In 1779 the legislature asked the towns to vote on the question whether a state constitution should be framed by a specially elected convention. The towns, voting by universal manhood suffrage, overwhelmingly approved. In late 1779 the delegates to the first constitutional convention in world history met in Cambridge and framed the Massachusetts Constitution of 1780, which the voters ratified after an intense public debate. With pride Thomas Dawes declared in an oration, "The people of Massachusetts have reduced to practice the wonderful theory. A numerous people have convened in a state of nature, and, like our ideas of the patriarchs, have authorized a few fathers of the land to draw up for them a glorious covenant." New Hampshire copied the procedure when revising its constitution in 1784, and it rapidly became standard procedure. Within a few years American constitutional theory had progressed from the belief that legislatures were competent to compose and announce constitutions, to the belief that a convention acting for the sovereign people is the only proper instrument for the task and that the sovereign must have the final word. A constitution, then, in American theory, is the supreme fundamental law that creates the legislature, authorizes its powers, and limits the exercise of its powers. The legislature is subordinate to the Constitution and cannot alter it.

Bibliography

Adams, Willi Paul 1980 *The First American Constitutions: Republican Ideology and the Making of the State Constitutions in the Revolutionary Era*. Chapel Hill: University of North Carolina Press.

Dodd, Walter F. 1910 *The Revision and Amendment of State Constitutions*. Baltimore: Johns Hopkins University Press.

Jameson, John Alexander 1887 *A Treatise on Constitutional Conventions: Their History, Powers, and Modes of Proceeding*. 4th ed. Chicago: Callahan & Co.

McLaughlin, Andrew C. 1932 *The Foundations of American Constitutionalism*. New York: New York University Press.

Wood, Gordon S. 1969 *The Creation of the American Republic, 1776–1787*. Chapel Hill: University of North Carolina Press.

20

Due Process of Law

A 1354 act of Parliament reconfirming Magna Carta paraphrased its chapter 29 as follows: "That no man . . . shall be put out of Land or Tenement, nor taken, nor imprisoned, nor disinherited, nor put to death, without being brought in Answer by due Process of Law." This was the first reference to due process in English legal history. Chapter 29 of the 1225 issue of Magna Carta originally concluded with the phrase "by the law of the land." Very probably the 1354 reconfirmation did not equate "the law of the land" with "due process of law"; the two were not synonymous. Due process in the 1354 enactment, and until the seventeenth century, meant an appropriate common law writ.

In the Five Knights Case, John Selden, the great parliamentarian, said in defense of the accused that "No freeman shall be imprisoned without due process of law," meaning that the "law of the land" was an equivalent for "either indictment or presentment." Sir Edward Coke, in his commentary on Magna Carta, also equated due process with the law of the land, meaning regularized courses of proceeding in common law prosecutions for crime. Coke's primary claim was that the law of the land was the common law, one of several rival systems of law then prevalent in England. When abolishing the courts of High Commission and Star Chamber, Parliament in 1641 quoted the due process phraseology of the act of 1354 and added that trials by "ordinary Courts of Justice and by the ordinary course of law" protected property rights against arbitrary proceedings. John Lilburne and his Levellers agreed, but they also asserted that due process signified a cluster of procedural protections of the criminally accused, including trial by jury, the right to counsel, and the right against self-incrimination. By the mid-seventeenth century due process and the law of the land referred to procedural due process in both civil and criminal cases. The "law of the land" usage, however, was the dominant one, and "due process" continued to be used in the very limited sense of a writ appropriate to a legal proceeding. A century later William Blackstone discussed various processes—original, mesne, and final—without discoursing on due process of law per se. After referring to indictment in capital cases and the principle that "no man can be put to death without being brought to answer by due process of law," Blackstone referred to the different writs that summoned an accused to trial in misdemeanor and felony cases.

In the American colonies the usage was similar. In deference to Magna Carta, the "law of the land" formulation was by far the most common, although a variety of paraphrases existed. The Massachusetts Body of Liberties (1641) guaranteed that one's life, liberty, and property could not be deprived except by "some expresse law of the Country warranting the same, established by a generall Court and sufficiently published"—that is, by known, standing law. West New Jersey protected the same substantive rights by a clause guaranteeing "due trial and judgment passed by twelve good and lawful men." New York in 1683 sought a charter that incorporated the famous chapter of Magna Carta with a clause requiring "by due course of law." Probably the first American reference to "due process of law" was in a Massachusetts act of 1692 endorsing chapter 29 of Magna Carta.

During the controversy with Great Britain leading to the American Revolution, Americans frequently spoke of trial by jury, fundamental law, the law of the land, no taxation without representation, and a gamut of civil liberties, but rarely referred to due process of law. Their references to the "law of the land" had no fixed or single meaning. They meant by it a variety of safeguards against injustice and abuses of criminal procedure; they equated it with notice, hearing, indictment, trial by jury, and, more generally, with regular forms of common law procedure and even the fundamental law itself or constitutional limitations on government. The "law of the land" was an omnibus phrase whose content ranged from specific writs to the concept of constitutionalism, and the phrase connoted protection of substantive rights—life, liberty, and property—as well as various precedural rights. Later, due process inherited all the content and connotations of law of the land.

All the first state constitutions used the "law of the land" phraseology, as did the Northwest Ordinance of 1787. No state constitution included a due process clause until New York's of 1821, although Mississippi's constitution of 1817 referred to "due course of law." Before the Civil War, only five state constitutions referred to "due process of law." All others had the older "law of the land" equivalent.

The first American constitution to include a due process clause was the Constitution of the United States in its Fifth Amendment, ratified in 1791. The clause reflected James Madison's preference. For reasons unknown, he recommended that no person should be "deprived of life, liberty, or property without due process of law." The four states which had ratified the Constitution with recommendations for a comprehensive bill of rights urged versions of chapter 29 of Magna Carta, although only one, New York, referred to "due process of law" rather than "law of the land." The due process clause of the Fifth Amendment was ratified without any discussions that illumine its meaning. Although every clause of the Constitution is supposed to have its own independent meaning, rendering no clause tautological, the due process clause was an exception. It pacified public apprehensions, bowed toward Magna Carta, and reinforced specific rights such as trial by jury.

When the Supreme Court construed the due process clause of the Fifth Amendment for the first time in *Murray v. Hoboken Land Company* (1856), it declared that although due process limited all branches of the government, it had only the procedural connotations that derived from the settled usages and modes of proceeding which characterized old English law suited to American conditions. Chief Justice Roger B. Taney's opinion in *Dred Scott v. Sandford* (1857) passingly employed substantive due process of law, which had cropped up in some state decisions and in abolitionist constitutional theory as well as proslavery theory. The Fourteenth Amendment's due process clause, taken verbatim from the Fifth's, proved to be the turning point in the national acceptance of "due process of law" as the common usage rather than the "law of the land" usage. In the last third of the nineteenth century, state constitutions finally substituted "due process" for "law of the land," and judicial decisions, state and federal, as well as legal treatises, expounded "due process of law," making it the most important and influential term in American constitutional law.

Bibliography

Howard, A. E. Dick 1968 *The Road from Runnymede: Magna Carta and Constitutionalism in America*. Charlottesville: University Press of Virginia.

Jurow, Keith 1975 *Untimely Thoughts: A Reconsideration of the Origins of Due Process of Law*. American Journal of Legal History 19:265–279.

Mott, Rodney 1926 *Due Process of Law*. Indianapolis: Bobbs-Merrill.

21

Taxation Without Representation

Taxation without representation was the primary underlying cause of the American Revolution. Taxation by consent, through representatives chosen by local electors, is a fundamental principle of American constitutionalism. From the colonial period, representation had been actual: a legislator was the deputy of his local electors. He represented a particular geographic constituency, and like his electors he had to meet local residence requirements. Thus, representation of the body politic and government by consent of the governed were structurally connected in American thought.

Taxation without representation deprived one of his property contrary to the first principles of the social compact and of the British constitution. No Englishmen endorsed the constitutionality of taxation without representation; that it violated fundamental law was the teaching of the Confirmatio Cartarum, the Petition of Right, and the Bill of Rights. Englishmen claimed, however, that Parliament "virtually" represented the colonies—every member of Parliament represented the English nation, not a locality—and therefore could raise a revenue in America. Rejecting the concept of virtual representation, Americans insisted that they were not and could not be represented in Parliament. The argument of virtual representation implicitly conceded the American contention that taxation was the function of a representative body, not merely a legislative or sovereign body. American legislatures, facing parliamentary taxation for the first times in 1764 and 1765, resolved that Parliament had no constitutional authority to raise a revenue in America. Pennsylvania's assembly, for example, resolved "that the taxation of the people of this province, by any other . . . than . . . their representatives in assembly is unconstitutional." Similarly, the Stamp Act Congress resolved that the colonies could not be constitutionally taxed except by their own assemblies. The resolutions of the colonies, individually and collectively, claimed an exemption from all parliamentary taxation including customs duties and trade regulations whose purpose was to raise revenue.

The American claims were not simply concocted to meet the unprecedented taxation levied by Parliament in 1764 and after. The experience of Virginia, the first colony, was typical. Its charter guaranteed the rights of Englishmen, which Virginia assumed included the exclusive right of its own representative assembly to tax its inhabitants; the assembly so declared in a statute of 1624. In 1652 planters in a county not represented in the assembly protested the imposition of a tax. In 1674, when Virginia sought confirmation from the crown of its exclusive right to tax its inhabitants, the crown's attorney in England endorsed "the right of Virginians, as well as other Englishmen, not to be taxed but by their consent, expressed by their representatives." The Committee for Foreign Plantations and the Privy Council approved, too, but the king withheld approval because of Bacon's Rebellion. Virginia nevertheless persisted in its position. In 1717 the imposition of a royal postal fee produced, in the words of the colony's royal governor, "a great clamor. . . . The people were made to believe that Parliament could not levy any tax (for so they called the rates of postage) here without consent of the General Assembly." In 1753, when Virginia's governor imposed a trivial fee for the use of his seal on each land patent, the assembly lectured him on the theme that subjects cannot be "deprived of the least part of their property but by their own consent: Upon this excellent principle is our constitution funded." The history of any colony would yield similar incidents, showing how entrenched were the claims that Americans advanced when Parliament first sought to tax the colonies.

When the Declaratory Act of 1766 claimed for Parliament a power to "legislate" for America "in all cases whatsoever," some members of Parliament argued the American position that Parliament could tax only in its representative capacity and therefore could not tax America. William Pitt and Lord Camden (Charles Pratt) endorsed that position. Pitt denounced virtual representation as a contemptible idea and declared that taxation "is no part of the governing or legislative power"; he also distinguished taxes levied for revenue from trade regulations that incidentally but not deliberately produced some revenue. The dominant British position, however, assumed that because taxation was inseparable from sovereignty, Parliament as the sovereign legislature in the empire had the power to tax in matters of imperial concern, even though the tax fell on unrepresented members of the empire. That position provoked Americans to distinguish the powers belonging to local governments (the idea of federalism); to develop the concepts of limited government, fundamental law, and a constitution as supreme law over all government; and to frame written constitutions that enumerated the powers of government.

Bibliography

Bailyn, Bernard 1967 *The Ideological Origins of the American Revolution.* Cambridge, Mass.: Harvard University Press.

Morgan, Edmund S. 1976 *The Challenge of the American Revolution.* Chap. 1. New York: W. W. Norton.

Morton, Richard L. 1960 *Colonial Virginia,* 2 vols. Chapel Hill: University of North Carolina Press.

22

Massachusetts Constitution
(October 25, 1780)

The "Constitution or Form of Government for the Commonwealth of Massachusetts" is the classic American state constitution and the oldest surviving written constitution in the United States (or the world), distinguished in addition by the fact that it was framed by the world's first constitutional convention. But for two states which merely modified their colonial charters, all the original thirteen states except Massachusetts had adopted their first constitutions by 1778 and in every case the body that enacted ordinary legislation framed the constitution and promulgated it. The Massachusetts legislature also framed a constitution but resorted to the novel step of submitting it to the voters for approval, and they rejected it. Then, in accordance with a proposal first advanced in the Concord Town Resolutions of 1776, a special constitutional convention elected for the sole purpose of drawing up a document of fundamental law performed the task and sent it out for ratification, article by article. Universal manhood suffrage prevailed in the vote for delegates to the convention and for popular ratification. Massachusetts, following democratic procedures for institutionalizing the social compact theory of government to devise a frame of government and a supreme law, provided the model that subsequently became common throughout the United States. The Massachusetts constitution of 1780, with amendments, still continues as the constitution of that commonwealth.

John Adams, the principal framer of the constitution, once proudly wrote, "I made a Constitution for Massachusetts, which finally made the Constitution of the United States." His exaggeration was pardonable, because no other state constitution so much influenced the framing of the national Constitution. Some earlier state constitutions had referred to the principle of separation of powers but had made their legislatures dominant, even domineering. Massachusetts not only provided the fullest statement of the principle but also put it into practice. Its judges, appointed by the governor, were to hold office "during good behavior" with undiminishable salaries. Its governor was the model for the presidency of the United States. He was to be elected by the voters, rather than by the legislature as in other states, and be a strong executive. He appointed the members of his own council or cabinet and, indeed, appointed all judicial officers down to local magistrates and registers of probate as well as sheriffs, coroners, and the state attorney general. He was commander-in-chief of the army and navy; he had the pardoning power; and he alone among the first governors of the thirteen states had a sole veto power over legislation, which could be overridden only by a two-thirds vote of both houses. The state senate and house of representatives were also precursors of the national bicameral system. No original state constitution had a better system of checks and balances than Massachusetts's.

Its constitution was divided into three parts: a preamble, a declaration of rights, and a frame of government. The preamble, on the general purposes of the state, explicitly embodied the social compact theory of the origin of the body politic. The declaration of rights, although containing little not found in constitutions previously framed by other states, was the most comprehensive compendium of its kind, and it phrased the rights which it guaranteed in language most influential in framing the Bill of Rights of the Constitution of the United States. The injunction against "unreasonable searches and seizures in the Fourth Amendment derives from the Massachusetts Declaration of Rights, and the injunction "shall not" instead of the pallid "ought not" ("liberty of the press ought not be restrained") was also a Massachusetts innovation. The one grave deficiency of the Massachusetts document was its creation of a multiple establishment of religion that was inconsistent with its guarantee of religious liberty.

Bibliography

Adams, Willi Paul 1980 *The First American Constitutions.* Chapel Hill: University of North Carolina Press.

Peters, Ronald M., Jr. 1978 *The Massachusetts Constitution of 1780: A Social Compact.* Amherst: University of Massachusetts Press.

23

Articles of Confederation

On March 1, 1781, Congress proclaimed ratification of the constitution for a confederation named "the United States of America." People celebrated with fireworks and toasts, and a Philadelphia newspaper predicted that the day would forever be memorialized "in the annals of America. . . ." Another newspaper gave thanks because the states had at last made perpetual a union begun by the necessities of war.

The war was only three months old when Benjamin Franklin proposed the first continental constitution. He called it "Articles of Confederation and Perpetual Union," a name that stuck. Because the war was then being fought to achieve a reconciliation with England on American terms, Congress would not even consider Franklin's plan. But a year later, when Congress appointed a committee to frame a Declaration of Independence, it also appointed a committee, consisting of one member from each state, to prepare "the form of a confederation to be entered into by these colonies." John Dickinson of Pennsylvania, whom the committee entrusted to draft the document, borrowed heavily from Franklin's plan and seems not to have been influenced by other committee members. One complained that Dickinson's plan involved "the Idea of destroying all Provincial Distinctions and making every thing of the most minute kind bend to what they call the good of the whole."

Dickinson was a "nationalist" in the sense that he believed that a strong central government was needed to build a union that could effectively manage its own affairs and compete with other nations. Congress, which was directing the war, became the hub of the Confederation. It was a unicameral house in which each state delegation had a single vote, making the states equal, and Dickinson proposed no change. Franklin, by contrast, had recommended that representation in Congress be apportioned on the basis of population, with each delegate having one vote. Dickinson carried over Franklin's generous allocation of powers to Congress, except for a power over "general commerce." Neither Franklin nor Dickinson recommended a general tax power. Congress requisitioned monies from each state for a common treasury, leaving each state to raise its share by taxation. Congress had exclusive powers over war and peace, armies and navies, foreign affairs, the decision of disputes between states, admiralty and prize courts, the coinage of money and its value, borrowing money on the credit of the United States, Indian affairs, the western boundaries of the states claiming lands to the Pacific, the acquisition of new territory and the creation of new states, standards of weights and measures, and the post office. Dickinson also recommended a "council of state" or permanent executive agency that would enforce congressional measures and administer financial, diplomatic, and military matters. Dickinson proposed many limitations on state power, mainly to secure effective control over matters delegated to Congress. The states could not, for example, levy imposts or duties that violated treaties of the United States. Even the sovereign power of the states over their internal concerns was limited by the qualification in Article III, the crux of the Dickinson draft: "Each colony [Dickinson always referred to "colony" and not "state"] shall retain and enjoy as much of its present Laws, Rights and Customs, as it may think fit, and reserves to itself the sole and exclusive Regulation and Government of its internal police, in all matters that shall not interfere with the Articles of Confederation." Clearly Dickinson envisioned a confederation in which the states did not master the central government.

Nationalists who supported the Dickinson draft in Congress argued, as did John Adams, that the purpose of the confederation was to meld the states into "one common mass. We shall no longer retain our separate individuality" on matters delegated to Congress. The four New England states had the same relation to Congress that "four counties bore to a single state," Adams declared. The states could build roads and enact poor laws but "they have no right to touch upon continental subjects." James Wilson, another centralist, contended that the Congress should represent all the people, not the states, because "As to those matters which are referred to Congress, we are not so many states, we are one large state." Few Congressmen were nationalists, however, and few nationalists were consistent. Congressmen from Virginia, the largest state, rejected state equality in favor of proportional representation in Congress with each delegate voting; but because Virginia claimed a western boundary on the Pacific, it rejected the nationalist contention that Congress had succeeded to British sovereignty with respect to the West and should govern it for the benefit of all. Congressmen from Maryland, a small state without western claims, adamantly held to that nationalist position but argued for state equality—one state, one vote—on the issue of representation. How requisitions should be determined also provoked dissension based on little principle other than self-interest.

The disputes over representation, western lands, and the basis for requisitions deadlocked the Congress in 1776. The next year, however, state supremacists who feared centralization won a series of victories that decisively altered the character of the confederation proposed by Dickinson and championed by Franklin, Adams, and Wilson. Dickinson's Article III was replaced by a declaration that "Each State retains its sovereignty, freedom, and independence, and every power, jurisdiction, and right, which is not by this confederation expressly delegated to the United States, in Congress assembled." Thus, colonial control over internal police became state sovereignty over all reserved powers, and the central government received only "expressly delegated" powers rather than implied powers to control even internal police involving matters of continental concern. State supremacists also restricted the power of Congress to make commercial treaties: no treaty could prohibit imports or exports, and no treaty could prevent a state from imposing retaliatory imposts. The revised Articles also scrapped Dickinson's executive branch, accepted the state sovereignty principle that each state cast an equal vote, modified Congress's judicial authority to decide all intercolonial disputes, and denied the power of Congress to fix the western boundaries of states.

Maryland, however, refused to accept the decision on the boundary issue. Although Congress completed the Articles in November 1777, unanimous ratification by state legislatures came hard. By the beginning of 1779, however, Maryland stood alone, the only state that had not ratified, and Maryland was unmovable. As unanimity was necessary, Maryland had the advantage as well as a great cause, the creation of a national domain. In 1780 New York and Connecticut ceded their western lands to the United States. Congress then adopted a report recommending the cession of western claims by other states, and in October 1780, Congress yielded to Maryland by resolving that ceded lands should be disposed of for the common benefit of the United States and be formed into "republican states, which shall become members of the federal union" on equal terms with the original states. Virginia's acceptance in January 1781 was decisive. Maryland ratified.

When Congress had submitted the Articles for ratification its accompanying letter accurately stated that its plan was the best possible under the circumstances; combining "in one general system" the conflicting interests of "a continent divided into so many sovereign . . . communities" was a "difficulty." The Articles were the product of the American Revolution and constituted an extraordinary achievement. Congress had framed the first written constitution that established a federal system of government in which the sovereign powers were distributed between the central and local governments. Those powers that unquestionably belonged to Parliament were delegated to the United States. Under the Articles Congress possessed neither tax nor commerce powers, the two powers that Americans in the final stages of the controversy with Britain refused to recognize in Parliament. Americans were fighting largely because a central government claimed those powers, which Americans demanded for their provincial legislatures. Given the widespread identification of liberty with local autonomy, the commitment to limited government, and the hostility to centralization, the states yielded as much as could be expected at the time. Because Congress represented the states and the people of the states, to deny Congress the power to tax was not logical, but the opposition to centralized powers of taxation was so fierce that even nationalists supported the requisition system. "It takes time," as John Jay remarked, "to make sovereigns of subjects."

The sovereignty claimed by the states existed—within a limited sphere of authority. The Articles made the United States sovereign, too, within its sphere of authority: it possessed "sole and exclusive" power over fundamental matters such as foreign affairs, war and peace, western lands, and Indian affairs. The reservation of some sovereign powers in the states meant the surrender of other sovereign powers to the central government. Americans believed that sovereignty was divisible and divided it. In part, federalism is a system of divided sovereign powers. The Articles had many defects, the greatest of which was that the United States acted on the states rather than the people and had no way of making the states or anyone but soldiers obey. The failure to create executive and judicial branches, the requirement for unanimity for amendments, and the refusal to concede to Congress what had been denied to Parliament resulted in the eventual breakdown of the Articles. They were, nevertheless, a necessary stage in the evolution of the Constitution of 1787 and contained many provisions that were carried over into that document. (See Constitutional History, 1776–1789.)

Bibliography

Henderson, H. James 1974 *Party Politics in the Continental Congress.* New York: McGraw-Hill.

Jensen, Merrill 1963(1940) *Articles of Confederation: An Interpretation of the Social-Constitutional History of the American Revolution.* Madison: University of Wisconsin Press.

Rakove, Jack N. 1979 *The Beginnings of National Politics: An Interpretive History of the Continental Congress.* New York: Knopf.

24

Ratifier Intent

Ratifier intent is a form of original intent or originalism that emphasizes the meanings and understandings of the Constitution possessed by those who ratified it. The ratifiers were the members of the state constitutional conventions that ratified the Constitution. The importance of ratifier intent derives from the widely held opinion that the consent of the governed, who alone were sovereign, legitimated the Constitution. The Constitutional Convention of 1787 had exceeded its instructions: to recommend revisions of the Articles of Confederation. Although the Confederation Congress transmitted the Constitution to the states for ratification, thereby implicitly agreeing to the scrapping of the Articles of Confederation, the fact remains that the Convention had violated its commission. Consequently, leading Framers of the Constitution insisted, as James Madison said, that "the legitimate meaning" of the Constitution should be sought "not in the opinions or intentions of the body which planned and proposed the Constitution, but in the sense attached to it by the people in their respective State Conventions, where it received all the authority which it possessed." Thus, as its ratification rather than its framing imbued the Constitution with its legitimacy, so ratifier intent rather than original intent (the understandings of the Framers) defined the text. This is the constitutional theory of the matter as transmitted by the Framers.

One should not have to choose between the intent of the Framers and that of the ratifiers. All contemporary expositions should be considered if they illumine a constitutional issue. Moreover, from the broadest perspective, ratifier intent and original intent almost coincided: government by consent of the governed; majority rule under constitutional restraints that limit majorities; guarantees of rights that prevail against the legislative as well as executive branch; a federal system; three branches of government, including a single executive, a bicameral legislature, and an independent judiciary; an elaborate system of checks and balances; and representative government and elections at fixed intervals. The founding generation also believed in measuring the powers of government, rather than the rights of the people, and they assumed a natural rights philosophy. They concurred on a great many fundamental matters. Without doubt, the Constitution reflects a coherent and principled political philosophy. All of this consensus bespeaks an enormously important and ascertainable set of original understandings shared by Framers and ratifiers, even by Federalists and Anti-Federalists. But none of this history enables judges to reach decisions favoring one side of a constitutional issue rather than another in real cases that come before courts.

More perplexing still is the fact that ratifier intent with respect to the meanings of particular clauses of the Constitution is more often than not unascertainable. The main reason for this is that the historical record is too skimpy to sustain a constitutional jurisprudence of ratifier intent. In a 1954 report, the National Historical Publications Commission declared that the reporters of the ratification period took notes on the debates "and rephrased those notes for publication. The shorthand in use at that time was too slow to permit verbatim transcription of all speeches, with the result that a reporter, in preparing his copy for the press, frequently relied upon his memory as well as his notes and gave what seemed to him the substance, but not necessarily the actual phraseology, of speeches. Different reportings of the same speech exhibited at times only a general similarity, and details often recorded by one reporter were frequently omitted by another." Reporters used their notes to spur their memories, and their reports were no better than their understandings.

When Jonathan Elliot began publication of his *Debates* in 1827, he collected the previously published records of the state ratifying conventions. He misleadingly called his collection *The Debates in the Several State Conventions, on the Adoption of the Federal Constitution.* In fact, Elliot unreliably reported the proceedings of only five states plus some fragments of others. He acknowledged that the debates may have been "inaccurately taken down and too faintly sketched." Elbridge Gerry, a member of the Constitutional Convention who became an Anti-Federalist leader, complained that the "debates of the State Conventions, as published by the short-hand writers, were generally partial and mutilated."

For Pennsylvania, Elliot published only the speeches of two advocates of ratification. The editor of the debates for Massachusetts apologized for his inaccuracies and omissions deriving from his inexperience. He also doctored some speeches and provided a few spurious ones. The reporter for New York made similar remarks and recorded only the debates for the first half of the convention's proceedings, reverting to a skeletal journal of motions for the remainder. In Virginia, where the debates were most fully reported and by a reporter sympathetic to ratification, James Madison and John Marshall expressed dissatisfaction with the results. Madison informed Elliot that he found passages that were "defective," "obscure," "unintelligible," and "more or less erroneous." Marshall complained that if he had not seen his name prefixed to his speeches he would not have recognized them as his own. He further declared that the speeches of Patrick Henry, the leader of the opposition, were reported worst of all. Similar criticisms apply to the proceedings of North Carolina, whose first convention rejected the Constitution and whose second was wholly unreported.

These are the five states (Pennsylvania, Massachusetts, New York, Virginia, and North Carolina) whose records provide a basis, however inadequate, for determining ratifier intent. We have only scraps of material for the other states, with the exception of Rhode Island, which ratified so late as to count for nearly nothing. Although the people acting through state ratifying conventions gave the Constitution its authority, the ratifiers' intent should not be confused or conflated with legitimacy. Ratification legitimated the text that the Constitutional Convention recommended; the Convention did not recommend its intention, only the text, and the ratifying conventions only ratified the text, without providing a basis for a constitutional jurisprudence based on ratifier intent or understanding.

Justice Joseph Story made the definitive rejection of ratifier intent in his *Commentaries on the Constitution:* "In different states and in different conventions, different and very opposite objections are known to have prevailed. Opposite interpretations, and different explanations of different provisions, may well be presumed to have been presented in different bodies, to remove local objections, or to win local favor. And there can be no certainty, either that the different state conventions in ratifying the constitution, gave the same uniform interpretation to its language, or that even in a single state convention, the same reasoning prevailed with a majority" (1st ed. 1833, I, pp. 388–389).

Story continued by noting that the terms of the Constitution impressed different people differently. Some drew conclusions that others repudiated; some understood its provisions strictly, others broadly. Ratifiers in different conventions revealed a diversity of interpretations. To Thomas Jefferson's demand that ratifier intent be honored as much as possible, Story retorted that it was not possible; he ridiculed "the utter looseness, and incoherence of this canon." No way existed to determine "what was thought of particular clauses" of the Constitution when it was ratified. "In many cases no printed debates give any account of any construction; and where any is given, different persons held different doctrines. Whose is to prevail?" Story concluded that determining ratifier intent is hopeless because "of all the state conventions, the debates of five only are preserved, and these very imperfectly. What is to be done, as to other eight states?" Ratifier intent, despite its present support by some constitutional scholars, including Robert Bork and Charles Lofgren, is as lacking in historical basis or practical application as it may be theoretically attractive.

Bibliography

Bork, Robert H. 1989 *The Tempting of America: the Political Seduction of the Law*. New York: Free Press.

Hutson, James H. 1986 The Creation of the Constitution: The Integritv of the Documentary Record. *Texas Law Review* 65:1–39.

Levy, Leonard W. 1988 *Original Intent and the Framers' Constitution*. New York: Macmillan.

Lofgren, Charles A. 1988 The Original Understanding of Original Intent. *Constitutional Commentary* 5:77–113.

25

The Supreme Court, 1789–1801

On January 8, 1801, twelve days before President John Adams appointed John Marshall as Chief Justice, a Jeffersonian newspaper reported: "John Jay, after having thru' decay of age become incompetent to discharge the duties of Governor, has been appointed to the sinecure of Chief Justice of the United States. That the Chief Justiceship is a sinecure needs no other evidence than that in one case the duties were discharged by one person who resided at the same time in England, and by another during a year's residence in France." The one in France was Oliver Ellsworth, sent there by President Adams as a special ambassador to negotiate peace. Ellsworth had recently resigned, and Jay, whose appointment as Ellsworth's successor had been confirmed by the Senate, had himself been the first Chief Justice, whom President George Washington had sent to England to negotiate a treaty that bore Jay's name. The chief justiceship was no sinecure: although the Supreme Court then met for only two short terms a year, the Justices also served as circuit court judges, and riding circuit was extremely arduous. When Jay was offered the position again, he declined it because of the circuit responsibilities and because the Court had neither "the energy, weight and dignity" necessary for it to support the national government nor "the public confidence and respect."

Jay's judgment was harsh although the Court did have problems, some of its own making. All the Justices were Federalists; their decisions en banc or on circuit seemed partisan—pro-Administration, pro-English, or procreditor—and they presided at trials under the infamous Sedition Act, whose constitutionality they affirmed. But the Court was not responsible for most of its difficulties. It had no official reporter

(Alexander J. Dallas's unofficial reports first appeared in 1798) and the press publicized only a few of the Court's decisions. The public knew little about the Court, and even members of its own bar were unfamiliar with its decisions. Nothing better symbolizes the nation's neglect of the Court than the fact that when the United States government moved to Washington, D.C., in late 1800, the Court had been forgotten. Not only did it lack a building; it had no courtroom. Congress hastily provided a small committee room in the basement of the Senate wing of the Capitol for the Court to meet.

The Court's beginnings were hardly more auspicious, however distinguished its membership. At its first term in February 1790 it had nothing to do except admit attorneys to its bar, and it shortly adjourned. It began as a court without a reporter, litigants, a docket, appeals, or decisions to make. It was chiefly an appellate court whose appellate jurisdiction scarcely matched the breadth of the judicial power of the United States stated in Article III. Congress in the Judiciary Act of 1789 had authorized the Court to review state court decisions that denied claims based on federal law, including the Constitution. Review was not authorized when the state court upheld a claim of federal right. The system of appellate jurisdiction thus permitted the Supreme Court to maintain federal law's supremacy but not its uniform interpretation. The Court's review of civil decisions of the lower federal courts was limited to cases involving more than $2,000 in controversy, and it could not review criminal cases from those courts. Congress had stingily authorized the Court to hear cases in its appellate capacity in order to keep it weak, to prevent centralization of judicial powers, to preserve the relative importance of state courts, and to insulate the Court from many matters that concerned ordinary citizens. For its first two years it heard no cases, and it made no substantive decisions until 1793. Its docket never got crowded. Dallas reported less than seventy cases for the pre-Marshall Court, and fewer than ten percent of them involved constitutional law. The Court was then first a common law court, second a court of admiralty and maritime jurisdiction.

Although its members were able, the pre-Marshall Court had difficulty attracting and keeping them. When Marshall became Chief Justice, only William Cushing of the original six Justices appointed by Washington remained. Robert H. Harrison, one of the original six, was confirmed but declined appointment, preferring instead the chancellorship of Maryland. James Iredell accepted Harrison's place, so that the first Court consisted of Chief Justice Jay and Justices Cushing, John Blair, John Rutledge, James Wilson, and Iredell. Rutledge performed his circuit duties but had never attended a session of the Court when he resigned after two years to become chief justice of South Carolina. Charles C. Pinckney and Edward Rutledge declined appointment to John Rutledge's seat, preferring to serve in their state legislature. Thomas Johnson accepted that seat but resigned it in less than two years because circuit riding was too strenuous. William Paterson succeeded him. The February 1794 term was Jay's last. That he reentered New York politics after negotiating Jay's Treaty says something about the Court's prestige at the time. So too does the fact that Alexander Hamilton preferred private practice to the chief justiceship. At that point, John Rutledge, who had quit the Court, applied for the post vacated by Jay. Washington appointed Rutledge, who attended the August 1795 term of the Court when it decided only two cases. The Senate, having reconvened, rejected him because of his opposition to Jay's Treaty. Washington offered the chief justiceship to Patrick Henry who declined it. The President then named Justice Cushing, whom the Senate confirmed; but he too declined, preferring to remain Associate Justice. In 1796, Oliver Ellsworth became Chief Justice but quit after four years. John Blair retired early in 1796 and Washington again had to fill a vacancy on the Court. After Edmund Randolph refused the position, Samuel Chase accepted. In 1798, Wilson became the first Justice to die in office. Richard Peters refused to be considered for the position, and John Marshall also declined. Adams then appointed Bushrod Washington, and after Iredell died in 1798, he appointed Alfred Moore, who resigned within five years. When Ellsworth resigned and Jay declined reappointment, even though the Senate confirmed him, Adams turned to Marshall. The rapid turnover in personnel during the Court's first decade did not ease its work or enhance its reputation.

Jeffersonians grumbled about the Court's Federalist constitutional theories, but Jay kept his Court out of politics and established its independence from the other branches of the government. That achievement and the Court's identification of its task as safeguarding the supreme law of the land kept the Court a viable institution, despite its many problems during the first decade, and laid the groundwork for the achievements of the Marshall Court.

Late in 1790, Virginia's legislature denounced as unconstitutional the bill for national assumption of state debts. Washington allowed Hamilton to send a copy of the Virginia resolves to Jay and to inquire whether the various branches of the government should employ their "collective weight ... in exploding [Virginia's strict construction] principles." Hamilton warned that Virginia had shown "the first symptom of a spirit which must either be killed or it will kill the Constitution of the United States." However, Jay, who privately advised Washington and drafted his Proclamation of Neutrality, recognized the difference between a judicial pronouncement and an extrajudicial one. The Court, strongly believing in the principle of separation of powers, would not express ex officio opinions except in judicial cases before it. Jay calmly declined the executive's invitation.

Similar principles motivated the Justices when confronted by Congress's Invalid Pensioners' Act of 1792 which required the circuit courts to pass on the pension applications of disabled veterans, subject to review by the secretary of war and Congress. Justices Wilson and Blair together with Judge Peters on circuit in the district of Pennsylvania, having refused to pass on an application from one Hayburn, explained their conduct in a letter to the President. They could not proceed because first, the business directed by the statute was not judicial in nature, there being no constitutional authority for it, and second, because the possible revision of the Court's judgment by the other branches of government would be "radically inconsistent with the independence" of the judiciary. In their circuits, Jay, Cushing, and Iredell similarly explained that a judicial decision must be a final decision. *Hayburn's Case* (1792), which was not really a "case" and in which nothing was judicially decided, was important because the Court, in Wilson's words, affirmed "a principle important to freedom," that the judicial branch must be independent of the other branches.

Similarly, Jay established another principle vital to the Court's independent, judicial, and nonpolitical character when he declined Washington's request for an advisory opinion. That request arose out of apparent conflicts between American treaty obligations to France and the Proclamation of Neutrality. The French commissioned privateers in American ports and established prize courts to condemn vessels captured by those privateers. Washington sought the Court's opinion on twenty-nine questions involving international law and treaty interpretation, in connection with the French practices. Jay, relying again on the principle of separation of powers, observed that the Court should not "extrajudicially" decide questions that might come before it in litigation. Thus, by preserving its purely judicial character, the Court was free to decide some of those questions when real cases posed them. From the beginning, the Court staked its power and prestige on its special relationship to the supreme law of the land, which it safeguarded, expounded, and symbolized.

The pre-Marshall Court also exercised the power of judicial review. The Justices on circuit quickly held state acts unconstitutional for violating the supreme law of the land. Jay and Cushing on circuit in the district of Connecticut held that that state, by adversely affecting debts owed to British creditors, had violated the treaty of peace with Britain; Iredell in Georgia and Paterson in South Carolina made similar decisions. The Justices held that United States treaties were superior to state laws. The Supreme Court confronted the issue in *Ware v. Hylton* (1796). With Iredell alone dissenting, the Court rejected the arguments of John Marshall, making his only appearance before the Justices, as counsel for the debtor interests of Virginia. He opposed "those who wish to impair the sovereignty of Virginia" and contended first that the Constitution had not authorized the Court to question the validity of state statutes and, second, that a treaty could not annul them. Seriatim opinions by Chase, Paterson, Wilson, and Cushing held otherwise.

In *Clarke* v. *Harwood* (1797) the Court ruled that *Ware* "settled" the question before it. *Clarke* was the Court's first decision against the validity of a state act in a case arising on a writ of error to a state court under section 25 of the Judiciary Act of 1789. Section 25 authorized the Court to reverse or affirm state decisions that denied rights claimed under United States treaties. Maryland's high court, relying on a state statute sequestering debts owed to British creditors, had barred a claim based on the treaty of peace with Britain. By reversing the Maryland court, the Supreme Court in effect voided the state act. However, the Court rarely heard cases on a writ of error to a state court. Indeed, it had not decided its first such case until shortly before *Clarke.* In *Olney v. Arnold* (1796) the Court had reversed a Rhode Island decision that misconstrued a revenue act of Congress. The Court's power of reviewing state decisions under Section 25 did not become controversial until 1814. (See *Martin v. Hunter's Lessee*, 1816.) During the Court's first decade, judicial review of state legislation was uncontested, and it was exercised.

On circuit the Justices also struck down state acts as violating the contract clause of the Constitution. The first such decision occurred in 1792 in *Champion and Dickason v. Casey*, which voided a Rhode Island state law. Given the hullaballoo in that state when its own judiciary was suspected of having voided a state act in *Trevett v. Weeden* (1787), the meek acceptance of the 1792 decision showed the legitimacy of judicial review over the states.

In *Hylton v. United States* (1796) the Court for the first time determined the constitutionality of an act of Congress, ruling that an excise on carriages, not being a direct tax, was valid even if not apportioned among the states. Those hoping for the Court to hold the federal excise unconstitutional were Jeffersonians; they did not then or at any time during the Court's first decade challenge the legitimacy of the Court's power to refuse to enforce an unconstitutional statute. Until the debate on the repeal of the Judiciary Act of 1801, scarcely anyone opposed judicial review, whether over state or over congressional legislation. *Hayburn's Case* in 1792 was misunderstood throughout the nation. Not only did Attorney General Randolph believe that the Court had annulled an act of Congress; so did Congress. The House established an investigating committee, "this being the first instance in which a Court of Justice had declared a law of Congress unconstitutional." Jeffersonians gleefully praised the Justices and hoped the Court would extend the precedent by holding unconstitutional other congressional legislation that promoted Hamilton's economic programs. Later, Jeffersonians in Sedition Act trials sought to persuade the Justices on circuit that they should declare the statute void. Repeatedly during the first decade, bills arose in Congress that provoked members in both houses to state that the Court should and would hold them unconstitutional. The way to the doctrine of judicial review announced in *Marbury v. Madison* (1803) was well paved, and the opposition to the Court's opinion did not derive from its assumption of a power to void an act of Congress.

Another major theme in the work of the Court during its first decade was nationalism. Once again, the Marshall Court built on what the Jay and Ellsworth Courts had first shaped. The early Courts helped vindicate the national character of the United States government, maintain the supremacy of the nation over the states, and keep the states from undermining the new constitutional system. On circuit duty the Justices frequently lectured federal grand juries, inculcating doctrines from *The Federalist*, and these grand jury charges were well publicized in the newspapers. In one of his charges, Jay, in 1790, having declared, "We had become a Nation," explained why national tribunals became necessary for the interpretation and execution of national law, especially in a nation accustomed only to state courts and state policies. Circuit court opinions striking down state laws in violation of the contract clause or federal treaties preached nationalism and national supremacy. Many of the criminal prosecutions before the federal circuit courts during the first decade were connected with national suppression of the Whiskey Rebellion and the Fries Rebellion. Similarly, prosecutions under the Sedition Act were intended to vindicate the reputations of Congress and the President.

The development of a federal common law of crimes, expanding the jurisdiction of the national courts, fit the nationalist pattern. Whether the courts could try nonstatutory offenses was a question that first arose in Henfield's case (1793). Wilson maintained that an American citizen serving on a French privateer commissioned in an American port and attacking ships of England, with whom the United States was at peace, had committed an indictable offense under the Proclamation of Neutrality, the law of nations, and the treaty with England, even though Congress had not made his act a crime.

The same nationalist pattern unified several of the Court's opinions in cases dealing with various issues. In *Chisholm v. Georgia* (1793) the Court's holding, that its jurisdiction extended to suits against a state by citizens of another state, was founded on nationalist principles as well as on the text of Article III. Wilson, for example, began with the principles that the people of the United States form a nation, making ridiculous the "haughty notions of state independence, state sovereignty, and state supremacy." "As to the purposes of the Union," he said, "therefore, Georgia is not a sovereign state." Jay's opinion also stressed "the national character" of the United States and the "inexpediency" of allowing state courts to decide questions that involved the performance of national treaties. The denunciation of the Court for its "consolidation of the Union" and its "annihilation of the sovereignty of the States" led to the Eleventh Amendment, which was intended to nullify *Chisholm*.

In *Glass v. Sloop Betsy* (1794) the Court supported the government's neutrality policy by ruling that France, after capturing a neutral ship, could not hold or award her as a prize in an American port. Only the

United States courts could determine the lawfulness of prizes brought into its ports, and no foreign nation controlled its admiralty law or could subvert American rights under international law. In *Penhallow v. Doane* (1795) the Court resolved an old dispute over the ownership of a prize. One party's claims relied on decisions of a New Hampshire court, the other's on a decision of a prize court established by the old Congress of the Confederation. Paterson, in the Supreme Court's principal opinion, upheld the lower federal courts, which had decided against the state court and claimed jurisdiction. No nation, he said, had recognized the states as sovereign for the purpose of awarding prizes. The old Congress had been the supreme council of the nation and center of the Union, he claimed, whose sovereignty was approved by the people of America and recognized by foreign nations. The federal courts succeeded to that sovereignty in prize matters. New Hampshire angrily remonstrated against the "destruction" of its sovereignty but the Court's ruling prevailed.

Its decision in *Hylton v. United States* gave life to the government's revenue powers. When the Court upheld federal treaties as paramount to state laws, in *Ware v. Hylton* (1796), Chase, in the principal opinion for the Court, indulged in fanciful nationalism when declaring, "There can be no limitation on the power of the people of the United States. By their authority the State Constitutions were made."

Other notable cases of the first decade were *Van Horne's Lessee v. Dorrance* (1794) and *Calder v. Bull* (1798), in which the Court laid the foundation for the judicial doctrine of vested rights, which it developed further in contract clause and higher law decisions during Marshall's chief justiceship. Although the Court was left out of the planning for the new national capital, it had been enunciating doctrines—of judicial review, national supremacy, and vested rights—that helped shape the United States and would in time make the judicial branch of government impossible to ignore.

Bibliography

Currie, David P. 1981 The Constitution in the Supreme Court: 1789–1801. *University of Chicago Law Review* 48:819–885.

Goebel, Julius 1971 *Antecedents and Beginnings.* Vol. I of the *Oliver Wendell Holmes Devise History of the Supreme Court,* ed. Paul Freund. New York: Macmillan.

Haines, Charles Grove 1944 *The Role of the Supreme Court in American Government and Politics, 1789–1835.* Berkeley: University of California Press.

Henderson, Dwight F. 1971 *Courts for a New Nation.* Washington, D.C.: Public
  Affairs Press.
Warren, Charles 1923 *The Supreme Court in United States History.* Vol. I. Boston:
  Little, Brown.

26

And Some Leading Cases

Chisholm v. Georgia
2 Dallas 419 (1793)

The first constitutional law case decided by the Supreme Court, *Chisholm* provoked opposition so severe that the Eleventh Amendment was adopted to supersede its ruling that a state could be sued without its consent by a citizen of another state. Article III of the Constitution extended the judicial power of the United States to all controversies "between a State and citizens of another State" and provided that the Supreme Court should have original jurisdiction in all cases in which a state should be a party. During the ratification controversy, anti-Federalists, jealous of state prerogatives and suspicious about the consolidating effects of the proposed union, had warned that Article III would abolish state sovereignty. Ratificationists, including John Marshall, James Madison, and Alexander Hamilton (*e.g., The Federalist* #81) had argued that the clause intended to cover only suits in which a state had given its sovereign consent to being sued or had instituted the suit. Here, however, with Justice James Iredell alone dissenting, the Justices in seriatim opinions held that the states by ratifying the Constitution had agreed to be amenable to the judicial power of the United States and in that respect had abandoned their sovereignty.

The case arose when Chisholm, a South Carolinian executor of the estate of a Tory whose lands Georgia had confiscated during the Revolution, sued Georgia for restitution. The state remonstrated against the

Court's taking jurisdiction of the case and refused to argue on the merits. The Justices, confronted by a question of sovereignty, discoursed on the nature of the Union, giving the case historical importance. Iredell, stressing the sovereignty of the states respecting reserved powers, believed that no sovereign state could be sued without its consent unless Congress so authorized. Chief Justice John Jay and Justice James Wilson, delivering the most elaborate opinions against Georgia, announced for the first time from the bench the ultra-nationalistic doctrine that the people of the United States, rather than the states or people thereof, had formed the Union and were the ultimate sovereigns. From this view, the suability of the states was compatible with their reserved sovereignty, and the clause in Article III neither excluded suits by outside citizens nor required state consent.

The decision, which seemed to open the treasuries of the states to suits by Tories and other creditors stirred widespread indignation that crossed sectional and party lines. A special session of the Massachusetts legislature recommended an amendment that would prevent the states from being answerable in the federal courts to suits by individuals. Virginia, taking the same action, condemned the Court for a decision dangerous to the sovereignty of the states. The Georgia Assembly would have defied the decision by a bill providing that any United States officer attempting to enforce it should "suffer death, without benefit of clergy, by being hanged." Though the state senate did not pass the bill, Georgia remained defiant. Congress too opposed the decision and finally agreed on a remedy for it that took the form of the Eleventh Amendment.

Bibliography

Mathis, Doyle 1967 Chisholm v. Georgia: Background and Settlement. *Journal of American History* 54:19–29.

Hayburn's Case

Hayburn's Case was regarded in its time and has been regarded by many historians since as the first case in which a federal court held an act of Congress unconstitutional. Congress in 1791 directed the circuit courts to rule on the validity of pension claims made by disabled

Revolutionary War veterans; the findings of the courts were to be reviewable by the secretary of war and by Congress. The circuit court in New York, presided over by Chief Justice John Jay, and the circuit court in North Carolina, presided over by Justice James Iredell, addressed letters to President George Washington explaining why they could not execute the act in their judicial capacities but that out of respect for Congress they would serve voluntarily as pension commissioners.

In the Pennsylvania circuit, Justices James Wilson and John Blair, confronted by a petition from one Hayburn, decided not to rule on his petition, and they also explained themselves in a letter to the President. They would have violated the Constitution to have ruled on the petition, they said, because the business directed by the act was not of a judicial nature and did not come within the judicial power of the United States established by Article III. They objected to the statute because it empowered officers of the legislative and executive branches to review court actions, contrary to the principle of separation of powers and judicial independence.

Hayburn's Case thus presented no suit, no controversy between parties, and, technically, no "case," and none of the courts rendered judicial decisions; they reported to the President their refusal to decide judicially. Some congressmen thought that *Hayburn's Case* was "the first instance in which a Court of Justice had declared a law of Congress to be unconstitutional," and the same opinion was delightedly trumpeted in anti-administration newspapers, which praised a precedent that they hoped would lead to judicial voiding of Hamiltonian legislation. The "case" reported in 2 Dallas 409 involved a motion for a writ of mandamus to compel the circuit court to grant a pension to Hayburn, but the court held the case over, and Congress revised the statute, providing a different procedure for the relief of pension-seeking veterans.

Calder v. Bull
3 Dallas 386 (1798)

Calder is the leading case on the meaning of the constitutional injunction against ex post facto laws. Connecticut had passed an act setting aside a court decree refusing to probate a will, and the plaintiff argued that the act constituted an ex post facto law. In the Court's main opinion Justice Samuel Chase ruled that although all ex post facto laws are necessarily "retrospective," retrospective laws adversely affecting the citizen in his private right of property or contracts are not ex post facto laws. The prohibition against the latter extended only to criminal, not civil, cases. An ex post facto law comprehends any retrospective penal legislation, such as making criminal an act that was not criminal when committed, or aggravating the act into a greater crime than at the time it was committed, or applying increased penalties for the act, or altering the rules of evidence to increase the chances of conviction.

The case is also significant in constitutional history because by closing the door on the ex post facto route in civil cases, it encouraged the opening of another door and thus influenced the course of the doctrine of vested rights. The contract clause probably would not have attained its importance in our constitutional history, nor perhaps the due process clause substantively construed, if the Court had extended the ex post facto clause to civil cases. In *Calder,* Chase endorsed the judicial doctrine of vested rights drawn from the higher law, as announced by Justice William Patterson in *Van Horne's Lessee v. Dorrance* (1795). Drawing on the very nature of our free Republican governments" and "the great first principles of the social compact," Chase declared that the legislative power, even if not expressly restrained by a written constitution, could not constitutionally violate the right of an antecedent and lawful private contract or the right of private property. To assert otherwise, he maintained, would "be a political heresy," inadmissible to the genius and spirit of our governmental system.

Justice James Iredell concurred in the judgment as well as the definition of ex post facto laws but maintained that judges should not hold an act void "merely because it is, in their judgment, contrary to the principles of natural justice," which he thought undefinable by fixed standards.

Ware v. Hylton
3 Dallas 199 (1796)

Ware established the fundamental principle of constitutional law that a state act may not violate a national treaty. An act of Virginia during the Revolution sequestered sterling debts owed by Virginians to British subjects and provided that such debts be discharged on payment (in depreciated currency) to the state. The Treaty of Paris of 1783 provided that creditors should meet with no lawful impediments to the recovery of full value in sterling, and Article VI of the Constitution made treaties of the United States the supreme law of the land. Ware, a British subject, brought an action in a federal court seeking such a recovery from Hylton, a Virginian. The prewar debts of Virginians to British creditors exceeded $2,000,000. Justice James Iredell, on circuit, ruled that the treaty did not revive any debt that had been discharged, and on the writ of error from the circuit court, John Marshall, for Hylton, argued that a United States treaty could not annul a statute passed when the state was sovereign. He also denied the authority of the Supreme Court to question the validity of a state law, arguing that the Constitution had not expressly granted such an authority.

Iredell persisted in his opinion expressed below but Justice Samuel Chase, supported by the concurring opinions of the remainder of the Justices, declared that the Supremacy Clause (Article VI), operating retroactively, nullified the state act, thereby reviving the sterling debt. Chase cloaked his opinion in sweeping nationalist doctrine that twisted history: "There can be no limitations on the power of the people to change or abolish the state constitutions, or to make them yield to the general government, and to treaties made by their authority." A treaty, he ruled, could not be supreme law if any state act could stand in its way; state laws contrary to the treaty were prostrated before it and the Constitution, which was the "creator" of the states. The *Ware* decision intensified Jeffersonian hostility to the consolidating and procreditor opinions of the federal courts. The decision's imperishable principle of the supremacy of national treaties survived its origins—no doubt in part because Jay's Treaty of 1794 had provided that the United States should assume the payment of the controversial debts.

Hylton v. United States
3 Dallas 171 (1796)

The first case in which the Supreme Court passed on the constitutionality of an act of Congress, *Hylton* stands for the principle that the only direct taxes are taxes on land and capitation taxes. The Constitution provides that no capitation "or other direct tax" be imposed except in proportion to the population of the states, but that "all duties, imposts and excises" be levied uniformly, that is, at the same rate. Congress imposed a uniform tax of $16 on all carriages (horse-drawn coaches), despite protests that the tax should have been apportioned among the states according to the census. When Congress levied a direct tax it fixed the total amount of money it intended to raise, so that in a state with ten percent of the nation's population, the parties taxed (carriage-owners) would have paid ten percent of the total. Thus, if a tax on carriages were a direct tax, the amount raised in two states of equal population would be the same, but if one state had twice as many carriages as the other, the tax rate in that state would be twice as great. The contention in this case was that the carriage tax was unconstitutional because it was a direct tax uniformly levied.

The case seems to have been contrived to obtain a Court ruling on the constitutionality of Congress's tax program. To meet the requirement that federal jurisdiction attached only if the amount in litigation came to $2,000, Hylton deposed that he owned 125 carriages for his private use, each of which was subject to a $16 tax; if he lost the case, however, his debt would be discharged by paying just $16. The United States paid his counsel, Alexander Hamilton, who defended the tax program he had sponsored as secretary of the treasury. Notwithstanding the farcical aspects of the case, its significance cannot be overestimated: if a tax on carriages were indirect and therefore could be uniform, Congress would have the utmost flexibility in determining its tax policies. As Justice Samuel Chase said, "The great object of the Constitution was to give Congress a power to lay taxes adequate to the exigencies of government." Justice William Paterson, having been a member of the Constitutional Convention of 1787, explained why the rule of apportionment applied only to capitation and land taxes, making all other taxes indirect taxes. The judgment of the Court was unanimous.

27

Freedom in Turmoil: Era of the Sedition Act

In 1798 the Fourth of July was commemorated in rather sinister fashion. While the officers of a New York military company drank to the toast "One and but one party in the United States," Federalist partisans in Newburyport, Massachusetts, publicly burned copies of the leading Republican newspaper in New England. On that same festive day the Senate, in the hope of controlling public opinion and crushing the opposition party, passed a bill making it a crime to criticize the government. The sponsor of the bill, Senator Lloyd, expressed anxiety to Washington—the bill might not be severe enough to muzzle "the lovers of Liberty, or, in other words, the Jacobins"; moreover, complained Lloyd, "I fear Congress will close the session without a declaration of War, which I look upon as necessary to enable us to lay our hands on traitors . . . " In a similar spirit the president of Yale, in his Fourth of July Sermon, warned that if the author of the Declaration of Independence, then the Vice-President of the United States, were to have his way, the country would "see the Bible cast into a bonfire . . . our wives and daughters the victims of legal prostitution . . . our sons become the disciples of Voltaire, and the dragoons of Marat . . . " Within a fortnight and even before the Sedition Act became law, the impatient administration arrested two opposition editors, Burke of the New York *Time Piece* and Bache of the Philadelphia *Aurora,* the nation's foremost Republican newspaper. A spirit of vigilantism flashed like summer lightning over a divided land that girded itself for war—abroad against the legions of Napoleon, at home against the subversion of its Jeffersonian minions. A crisis was in the making that jeopardized the nation's policies and free institutions.

The foreign crisis had been caused by French aggressions against American commerce and aggravated by Jay's Treaty. France, at war with England, not unjustifiably viewed Jay's Treaty as a pro-British instrument, a rebuff to an old ally and benefactor, even as diplomatic treachery. For Monroe, the American minister to France, had been deceived by the State Department and unwittingly misled the French on the course of Jay's mission. He had also induced them to promise compensation for their spoilations and repeal of their maritime decrees against American shipping. News of the treaty provoked France to recall her American ambassador and reinstitute her decrees with greater rigor than before, on the theory that American commerce deserved from France no greater respect than offered by England and acquiesced in by the United States. Within a year the French sank or captured over three hundred American ships and refused recognition to Charles C. Pinckney, Monroe's successor—indeed, had ordered him out of France on threat of arrest. Such was the posture of Franco-American relations when John Adams was inaugurated.

President Adams, convinced that the differences with France, however serious, might be resolved by negotiation, resolutely determined upon a policy of peace with honor. He proposed a new diplomatic mission to Paris and wisely recommended defense measures during the emergency: an increased army (then only 3500 men), creation of a permanent navy, convoys, and the arming of merchant ships. But the Republicans, despite their recent bellicosity against Great Britain, opposed all preparedness measures as unnecessarily provocative and contrary to the pacific intent of the new mission. A fierce party battle ensued in Congress. The Federalists, spurred by a war faction, tarred the obstructionist Republicans with charges of disloyalty and indulged in jingoistic saber rattling. The session ended in July with the failure of most major defense measures, chiefly because Congress was so closely divided. But the party debate had been so vituperative that a residue of hate remained. Jefferson, presiding over the Senate, commented to a friend:

> You and I have formerly seen warm debates and high political passions. But gentlemen of different politics would then speak to each other, and separate the business of the Senate from that of society. It is not so now. Men who have been intimate all their lives, cross the streets to avoid meeting, and turn their heads another way, lest they should be obliged to touch their hats.

When Congress reconvened in a tense atmosphere, partisan oratory was disrupted by a fistfight on the floor, and some Congressmen predicted "blood to be let" before the session ended.

In March of 1798 the President notified Congress that dispatches from the American envoys proved that the objects of the peace mission could not be accomplished "on terms compatible with the safety, the honor, or the essential interests of the nation." He would therefore permit merchant ships to arm for their own protection, and exhorted Congress speedily to enact defense measures proportionate to the dangers to national security. Adams neither wished war nor took any step that would provoke Congress to its declaration; but the Republicans fitfully described his message as "insane" and denounced him for incitement to belligerency on behalf of England's interests. The Republicans, however, were betrayed by their own distrust. Believing that the President had exaggerated the gravity of the situation, they induced Congress to request full disclosure of the envoys' dispatches. When Adams complied, the doubters were aghast to discover that he had muted the true state of affairs. The damning evidence of the humiliating and contumelious treatment of our envoys even alluded to a "French party in America." The envoys, after having been ignored for months, had been approached by unofficial agents of the French government—designated as Messrs. X, Y, and Z—who demanded outrageous gifts of money for high officials, an extravagant "loan" to France, and an apology for supposedly obnoxious statements made by President Adams. In addition the United States must pay all debts owed by France to American citizens and the cost of damages caused by French depredations on American commerce. Official negotiation would follow if these terms were met! After more months of degrading intrigue and diplomatic blackmail, the envoys gave up the mission as a hopeless failure.

France had been motivated by simple rapacity and arrogance, not by a desire to drive the United States into war, but she almost succeeded in doing just that. The "XYZ" disclosures, whose publication the Republicans sought to suppress, electrified the country. In the patriotic craze in support of the administration, "Millions for defense, but not one cent for tribute" became the national slogan, and the opposition dwindled to a distinctly beaten minority. War fever mounted, but no one lusted for hostilities except a small sect of ultra-Federalists who controlled the Senate. The President, the closely divided House, and the majority of the people would countenance only resistance against French aggression, not an offensive war.

Federalists of whatever hue shared a sinister understanding that national security and party supremacy might be insured if the country could be first frightened and then panicked. Both fear and panic, already present in the situation, were intensified by chilling stories in the Federalist press on the imminence of a French invasion and the dangers of subversive activities. The Republican opposition was identified as revolutionary Jacobins treasonably allied with the foreign enemy to overthrow the Constitution and cut the throats of true Americans. The Federalists were so obsessed with hate and convinced that anyone whose opinion differed must be a criminal subversive that they openly reviled even their fellow Congressmen.

For example, when Gallatin, the Republican leader of the House, discounted the possibility of an invasion, Speaker Dayton retorted that since his principles were those of "the furious hordes of democrats which threatened this country with subjugation," Gallatin could calmly watch "our dwellings burning, and might 'laugh at our calamities and mock when our fears came upon us.'" When Livingston of New York spoke against a Federalist system of tyranny that would destroy civil liberties, Allen of Connecticut lashed him for "intimate acquaintance with treason" and claimed that he "vomited" falsehood on "everything sacred, human and divine." The prime victim of abuse was the Vice-President himself, who observed: "It suffices for a man to be a philosopher and to believe that human affairs are susceptible of improvement, and to look forward, rather than back to the Gothic ages, for perfection, to mark him as an anarchist, disorganiser, atheist, and enemy of the government." To be an alien or even a naturalized citizen was equally stigmatizing. Was not Gallatin himself a Swiss, and were not Priestly, Cooper, Volney, Burk, Duane, Callender, and other foreign-born scholars and journalists the leaders of swarms of wild Irishmen, political refugees, and French apostles of sedition? It was necessary to "strike terror among these people," as Congressman Harper put it.

Between April and July of 1798, when Congress adjourned, the party program was adopted. In addition to mustering the forces of defense—enlisting an army, creating a navy, fortifying harbors, abrogating all treaties with France, authorizing the capture of armed French ships—Congress passed a series of repressive measures designed to intimidate the opposition, coerce conformity of opinion, and extend Federalist control of the government. The Naturalization Act increased the period of residence from five to fourteen years before citizenship could be granted to immigrants. The statute was a disappointment to ultra-Federalists who preferred "that nothing but birth should entitle a man to citizenship" or the right to vote and hold office. The Alien Act empowered the President to order, without assigning cause, the summary arrest and deportation of any foreigner, even the citizen of a friendly nation, whom he judged to be "dangerous" to the peace and safety of the nation or believed "suspect" of "secret machinations." A deported alien who returned without permission might be imprisoned indefinitely at the discretion of the President. The Republicans described the measure as a "refinement on despotism," while the Federalists claimed that "to *boggle* about slight forms" in time of danger courted national disaster.

The capstone of the new Federalist system was the Sedition Act, an expression of the easy rule of thumb offered by the party organ in the nation's capital, "He that is not for us, is against us." The same editor added: "Whatever American is a friend to the present administration of the American government, is undoubtedly a true republican, a true patriot . . . Whatever American opposes the administration is an anarchist, a jacobin and a traitor . . . It is *Patriotism* to write in favour of our government—it is Sedition to write against it." Given such a view of things, the Federalists believed that the government could be criminally assaulted merely by political opinions that had the supposed tendency of lowering the public esteem of the administration. Security lay in the elimination of political criticism and the creation of a one-party press, eventually a one-party system. Thus the Sedition Act made criminal any "false" or "malicious" statements against the President (but not the Vice-President), Congress, or the "government"—i.e., the administration—with intent to defame or excite the people's animosity. The Federalists had deliberately exploited the crisis in foreign relations for the sake of partisan advantage. To Jefferson, Madison explained that "the loss of liberty at home is to be charged to provisions against danger real or pretended from abroad."

As actually applied by the federal judges—all Federalists—the Sedition Act made criticism of the administration the test of criminality. Even in the course of the House debates, advocates of the measure clearly stated that the political opinion of the Republican opposition was to be outlawed. But only one congressman, Mathew Lyon of Vermont, was tried and convicted. For the crime of having published an address to his constituents in which he accused Adams of a "continual grasp for power" and an "unbounded thirst for ridiculous pomp," he was sentenced to four months and fined $1000. Lyon's cruel treatment in jail was vividly described by the editor of one of the few Jeffersonian newspapers in New England, with the result that he too became a victim of the Sedition Act.

Altogether there were only about twenty-five arrests under the Sedition Act, fourteen indictments, and a dozen trials—all ending in conviction. Though few in number the prosecutions were selectively important, for among the victims were major Jeffersonian publicists like Thomas Cooper and the editors of four of the five leading Republican papers in the nation. The administration's sedition-net also closed around several minor journalists and a few village radicals. In one farcical case a town drunk, upon hearing a sixteen-gun salute in honor of the President who had just passed by, remarked: "I do not care if they fired through his ass." Another potential Robespierre who was jailed was the itinerant speaker who so fired his Dedham audience that they put up a liberty pole with a sign proclaiming:

No Stamp Act, No sedition, No Alien Bills,
No Land Tax; downfall to the Tyrants of
America, peace and retirement to the
President, Long Live the Vice President
and the Minority.

The speaker and a local farmer who raised the liberty pole were convicted for having erected a "rallying point of insurrection and civil war."

Despite these prosecutions the repressive impact of the Sedition Act has been exaggerated. Countless citizens guarded their political expressions, but the "witchhunt" and "reign of terror" decried by the Republicans existed more by Federalist intention than by execution. Harassed Republican politicians and journalists simply refused to be intimidated and their popular support in the Middle Atlantic states and especially in the South was so great that the administration did not dare close their presses or tamper with free elections. By the time of the election of 1800 the number of Jeffersonian newspapers had even increased substantially, in spite of the Sedition Act—or perhaps because of it, as well as because of the high taxes accompanying brink-of-war defense policies. The Sedition Act was a measure of abortive tyranny. Its failure might have been predicted by any astute politician when Congressman Lyon, its first victim, was re-elected while in prison.

The policies of the government—high taxes (even a stamp tax), repression, a standing army—convinced Old Dominion leaders of the need to resist another "Anglo-monarchic-aristocratic-military government." The nation must be roused to the danger, brought to its senses. Mass petitions of protest from many states were deluging Congress, but a more effective, statesmanly appeal must be made to the voters. The device hit upon by Jefferson was the adoption of formal resolutions by state legislatures. In *The Federalist* Hamilton himself had once argued that the states were "bodies of perpetual observation . . . capable of forming and conducting plans of regular opposition" should the central government exceed its powers and invade constitutional rights. The Vice-President secretly framed a series of resolutions which were adopted by the legislature of Kentucky in November, 1798; a month later Virginia passed companion resolutions drawn by James Madison.

The Kentucky and Virginia Resolves were classic expressions of the Republican creed. They consisted of a spirited denunciation of Federalist policies, particularly the Alien and Sedition Acts, a defense of civil liberties and of the rights of a peaceable opposition, and an eloquent restatement of the most orthodox American constitutional theory, based on the concept of limited government. In a word they expressed the view that man is free because the government is not, is limited, rather, by regularized restraints upon power. What was controversial about the resolutions was their assertion that each state retained the right to judge for itself whether the central government had exceeded its powers. The other states, which were invited to join in a declaration of the unconstitutionality of the Alien and Sedition Acts, either responded adversely or not at all. In the Southern states, where public opinion was agitated by the XYZ disclosures, a discreet silence was maintained rather than give the appearance of national disunity. In the North, where the Federalists viewed the Resolutions as little short of a declaration of war against the Union, the state legislatures censured their erring Southern sisters, defended Congressional policies, and maintained that the federal judiciary was the proper body to judge infractions of the Constitution—although judicial review over Congress was not yet established. A Supreme Court decision against the Sedition Act would have been welcomed by the Jeffersonians, obviating the need for their Resolutions; but the members of the Court, on circuit duty, had been enforcing the dread statute.

The disheartening state responses impelled counter-responses, lest silence be construed as the abandonment of doctrines considered vital for the preservation of constitutional liberty. The Second Kentucky Resolves, penned by Jefferson, contained the proposition that state "nullification" was the rightful remedy for an unconstitutional act of Congress. In later years Calhoun was to subvert the constitutional theories of Jefferson and Madison when he adopted them for a defense of slavery, whereas they had been reluctantly driven to "nullification" and "interposition" in defense of human rights.

General Alexander Hamilton, who was in actual command of the army, was certain—and even hopeful—that the Virginia Jacobins were about to rise in insurrection. Given the opportunity to "subdue a *refractory* and *powerful* State," he would head the army for Virginia, enforce the national laws, and "put Virginia to the Test of resistance." Hamilton, even before the XYZ disclosures that "delighted" him, had become the principal architect of American foreign and domestic policy because of his influence on the Federalist party and his control over a Cabinet which was disloyal to Adams. As soon as the United States was armed, Hamilton, echoed by his ultra-Federalist followers, wanted war, preferably as a result of French attack. War would unify the nation, make possible the execution of traitors and the electoral destruction of the opposition party, and in the event of "internal disorder" would justify the "subdivision" of Virginia into small states that could not menace the central government. A large army, whose officers were carefully screened for party loyalty, was the *sine qua non* of his plans. He got that army, although both he and it had to be "crammed" down Adams' throat by the Cabinet and Washington, the titular commander.

Virginia, however, failed to oblige Hamilton by rebellion, and Napoleon was equally uncooperative. As early as October, 1798, Adams had predicted that there was "no more prospect of seeing a French army here than there is in Heaven." As for General Hamilton's fellow citizens, only a few Pennsylvania farmers armed to resist payment of direct taxes for the army, and they fired merely dirty looks when "conquered" by four brigades. What little satisfaction could be gained when the leaders of "Fries's Rebellion" were sentenced to death for treason was robbed by Adams' pardon.

Notwithstanding disappointments Hamilton envisioned military glories and conquests more grandiose than those of the Conquistadors. His army was not to be unused. Adams justifiably thought of him as an "artful, indefatigable and unprincipled intriguer," while a Republican journalist shrewdly wrote, "When a *little Alexander* dreams himself to be Alexander the Great . . . he is very apt to fall into miserable intrigues." Hamilton's plan, in which he was joined by Rufus King, the American minister in Great Britain, and Timothy Pickering, the Secretary of State, was the conquest and annexation of Louisiana and the Floridas. Even "the riches of Mexico and Peru," perhaps all of Latin America, beckoned invitingly for a liberator. Spain, the hapless ally of France, was to be despoiled, France herself forestalled from expansion in the Americas. Great Britain, in alliance with the United States, would provide the naval cover, while the United States would furnish the whole land force. "The command in this case," Hamilton modestly confided to Ambassador King, "would naturally fall upon me, and I hope I shall disappoint no favorable expectation." The British were ready to cooperate; Miranda, a South American revolutionary, promised the aid of his insurrectionary constituents; Pickering and McHenry, the Secretary of War, consented; and Hamilton, who did not recognize a real traitor when confronted by one, had enlisted the western commander, General Wilkinson, in the plan—Wilkinson who was a spy in the pay of Spain! All was in readiness, but John Adams had been ignored.

In February, 1799, the President stunned the country, his Cabinet, the Congress, and most of all, Hamilton and the ultra-Federalists, by announcing his intention to make peace with France. Making public a letter from Talleyrand which stated France's desire to end "existing differences" and assured that an envoy would be received on the President's own terms, "with the respect due to the representative of a free, independent, and powerful nation," Adams nominated an envoy. Disbelief soured into consternation and rage among the Hamiltonians. Their leader had planned for a declaration of war by August, but peace with France signaled the end of everything—the crisis psychology which they had manipulated for party gain, the plans for new defense measures and more taxes, the thrilling little naval war that raged at sea, the British alliance, the glorious prospects of military conquest, the army itself, the expectation of victory in the next election. All fizzled like a soggy firecracker. Hamilton still wanted "to squint at South America," but the best that he and his followers could do was delay negotiations, first by pressing for a three-man mission, then by intriguing against the departure of the envoys. The President finally issued a personal order for their sailing and did all but place them aboard himself.

In later years he wrote, "I desire no other inscription over my grave-stone than: 'Here lies John Adams, who took upon himself the respon-sibility of the peace with France . . . '" His bold and courageous stroke, placing country above partisanship, earned him the enmity of the ul-tras whose factitiousness split the party and cost Adams his re-elec-tion. But the triumph of Jefferson and the restoration of national sanity represented the triumph of moderation. In that sense the triumph be-longed also to Adams himself, a flinty, principled old patriot whom the British ambassador admitted was the last man to be "bullied into measures which he does not approve."

The crisis of 1798-99 took shape when the latent authoritarianism within the Federalist party threatened to abort the development of a free and responsible government in the United States. Deterioration of relations with France created the opportunity and the cover for a thrust for power by a high-placed political elite with little or no faith in the capacity of the people for self-government. These men, who com-posed the ultra-Federalist faction, conceived of themselves as an aris-tocracy not of land and bloodline but of political virtue and fitness to rule—rule rather than govern. Impatient with political compromise and incapable of distinguishing dissent from disloyalty, they were pre-pared to use legal and military coercion to control public opinion for party purposes. They were prepared, too, to abandon a foreign policy of neutrality and nonintervention in exchange for foreign intrigues and military conquest. Even war was planned as an instrument of party policy. Distrustful of free elections, they were intolerant of free speech, freedom of the press, and a free political opposition. Their efforts to institutionalize vigilantism and repression were noxiously at variance with the elementary principles of an open society and the development of a political democracy.

The party had been in continuous mastery since the organization of the government under the Constitution. But Washington's retirement from politics had been followed by a hairline victory in the election of

1796, jarring the Hamiltonians into a realization that their personal power and domination of the nation's destiny faced a precarious future. Unable to accept gracefully the possibility of defeat, they exploited a crisis in foreign relations by advancing an extremist program calculated to burke the opposition.

When President Adams suddenly made peace with France, he broke the Hamiltonians by destroying the basis of their program. Their savage campaign against him ended public confidence in the party which had already been weakened by the public reaction against the high cost of military preparations. A few instances of outrageous conduct on the part of soldiers against civilians gave substance to Republican propaganda which played on the popular fear of a standing army. Taxes and soldiers probably alienated more moderate voters from Federalism than the Sedition Act prosecutions.

Adams deserved the credit for the Franco-American Convention of 1800, ratified in 1801, which gave the United States a desperately needed period of peace and re-established the principle of neutrality in American foreign relations. He also paved the way for the return of national sanity. It was Jefferson, however, who reaped the credit. Certainly his election meant the conclusive repudiation of militarism and of a one-party system by the young American nation. The new President's inaugural address rechartered the national course. The will of the majority, he declared, must prevail, but to be rightful it must be reasonable, respectful of the equal rights of the political opposition.

Let us, then, fellow-citizens [said Jefferson], unite with one heart and one mind. Let us restore to social intercourse that harmony and affection without which liberty and even life itself are but dreary things. And let us reflect that, having banished from our land that religious intolerance under which mankind so long bled and suffered, we have yet gained little if we countenance a political intolerance as despotic, as wicked, and capable of as bitter and bloody persecutions ... every difference of opinion is not a difference of principle. We have called by different names brethren of the same principle. We are all Republicans, we are all Federalists. If there be any among us who would wish to dissolve this Union or change its republican form, let them stand undisturbed as monuments of the safety with which error of opinion may be tolerated where reason is left free to combat it. . . . Let us, then, with courage and confidence pursue our Federal and Republican principles, our attachment to the Union and representative government.

28

Textualism

Textualism denotes the opinion that whenever possible, judges resolving questions of constitutional law should rely primarily on the language of the Constitution itself. The text should guide decision and the text itself, rather than other considerations such as original intent, ratifier intent, history, principles inferred from the text, altered circumstances, judicial readings of societal values, or even judicial precedents. Justice Owen J. Roberts, for the Court in *United States v. Butler* (1936), manifested an allegiance to textualism when he declared that the constitutionality of a contested statute should be squared against the appropriate language of the text to see if they match.

This view of the best way to determine constitutionality was the most prevalent one at the time of the making of the Constitution. Thomas Jefferson and Alexander Hamilton differed on the question as to whether an act of Congress incorporating a bank was constitutional; but, as Hamilton said, Jefferson would agree "that whatever may have been the intention of the framers of a constitution, or of a law, that intention is to be sought for in the instrument itself, according to the usual & established rules of construction." Hamilton accurately stated the truth of the matter to the founding generation.

Despite near unanimity on the propriety of interpreting the Constitution according to established rules of construction, the Framers arrived at contradictory results when applying those rules to numerous important constitutional issues. Their belief in textualism did not prevent them from dividing on the removal power, the power to charter a corporation, the power to declare neutrality, the scope of executive powers, the power to enact excise and use taxes without apportioning

349

them on population, the power of a treaty to obligate the House to appropriate money, the power of judicial review, the power to deport aliens, the power to pass an act against seditious libel, the power to abolish judicial offices of life tenure, and the jurisdiction of the Supreme Court to decide suits against states without their consent or to issue writs of mandamus against executive officers.

Rules of constitutional construction by which to construe the text are comparable to those of statutory construction, which a current federal judge, Frank Easterbrook, called "a total jumble." For every rule, as Karl Llewellyn demonstrated in his *Common Law Tradition,* "there is an equal and opposite rule." A master commentator, Justice Joseph Story, discoursed on the rules of construction for some sixty pages in his *Commentaries on the Constitution,* yet he failed completely to convince his Jacksonian colleagues on the bench. Rules of construction in effect free, rather than fetter, judicial discretion. The fact remains, however, that textualism should be the bedrock of judicial review; as Story said, "Nothing but the text itself was adopted by the whole people." Whenever the fair or plain meaning of the Constitution can be ascertained, it should guide judgment.

The problem is that the Constitution is a brief elliptical document framed by common lawyers trained to believe that a few comprehensive and expansive principles supplementing a structural description will be infinitely adaptable and will provide guides that can serve to answer virtually any question that might arise on a case-to-case basis. In some crucial respects, the Constitution resembles Martin Chuzzlewit's grandnephew, who, Dickens said, "had no more than the first idea and sketchy notion of a face." The Framers had a genius for studied imprecision and calculated ambiguity. They relied on many general terms because common lawyers expressed themselves that way out of conviction and because politics required compromise, and compromise required ambiguity and vagueness.

The text, even with twenty-six amendments that have been added in two centuries, is scarcely 7,000 words long, and only about two percent of the verbiage possesses any significance in constitutional law. Almost without exception, these are the purposefully or unavoidably general terms: commerce among the states, obligation of contracts, necessary and proper, bills of credit, republican form of government, due process of law, privileges and immunities, direct taxes, general welfare, liberty, unreasonable searches, equal protection, and the like.

For the most part, the Constitutional Convention of 1787 designed the Constitution with the utmost diligence and attention to detail. The Convention usually chose words with craft and craftsmanship. This is the reason that constitutional law does not involve the bulk of the Constitution. It does not have to be litigated because it is clear and understandable. Consequently, the vagueness and ambiguities found in the Constitution were probably deliberate. In *The Federalist* #37, James Madison replied to the Anti-Federalist criticism that the Constitution's lack of clarity on some matters threatened the states and liberty. Obscure and equivocal language was inevitable, he contended, but its meaning would be clarified in time by adjudications. Abraham Baldwin of Georgia, another Framer, declared that some subjects were left "a little ambiguous and uncertain" for political reasons and would be settled in time by practice or by amendments. Some textual language remained open-ended to avoid giving offense by explicitness. Treaty powers, judicial powers, and rival powers of legislation fell into these categories, according to Baldwin.

Ambiguity and vagueness arise in the nonstructural sections. Ambiguous words permit different understandings; vague words do not allow for much understanding. The exceptions clause of Article III is a good example of ambiguity. It might mean that Congress may switch appellate jurisdiction to original jurisdiction, thereby adding to the Supreme Court's original jurisdiction, as counsel in *Marbury v. Madison* (1803) argued, or it might mean that the original jurisdiction of the Court is fixed, as John Marshall held. If the exceptions clause means that Congress may make exceptions to the Court's jurisdiction by diminishing its appellate jurisdiction, how far can Congress go? And how can the Court exercise the jurisdiction specified in Article III as belonging to the judicial power of the United States if it is dependent on Congress's will?

The text of Article I, section 8, poses problems too. Congress may pass no capitation or "other direct tax" unless apportioned among the states on the basis of population. Although the Framers probably regarded direct taxes as only taxes imposed on people per capita and on land, they did not say so. They left "other direct taxes" open to interpretation. Article I, section 8, on the tax power is all the more puzzling because it is not known whether the tax power connotes an equally expansive power to spend, and the meaning of the "general welfare" is equally mystifying. Constitutional government as the Framers understood it cannot survive a national power to legislate for the general welfare, nor can the federal system survive a national power authorized to spend for the general welfare, yet the text gives credibility to these views.

The term "in pursuance of" in Article VI (the supremacy clause) is also ambiguous. Usually this term is taken to mean that in order for acts of Congress to be constitutional, they must be consistent with the Constitution. The "in pursuance of" clause is a mainstay of the argument that the Supreme Court may exercise judicial review over acts of Congress. Yet at the time of the framing, the text of the Articles of Confederation showed that "in pursuance of" meant "under authority of" or "done in prosecution of."

The executive power with which the President is endowed is ambiguous too. It is not known what is meant by the executive power, apart from an obligation to execute the laws faithfully. Moreover, the text indicates that the President can call on the armed forces to suppress rebellions or repel attacks, but not whether he can engage in military hostilities without either congressional support or a congressional declaration of war. In the case of executive agreements, there is not even a vague provision of the Constitution to construe. Nothing in the document authorizes treaty-making by the President without the advice and consent of the Senate. Nothing in the document authorizes the Congress to empower the President to make international agreements that have the force of the supreme law of the land or authorizes such agreements to have this force when both branches of Congress retroactively or subsequently approve of an international agreement made by the President on the President's own initiative. Nevertheless, Presidents have been making executive agreements with foreign nations throughout U.S. history and on major matters, without successful constitutional challenge. Moreover, the text of the Constitution does not provide for the device of the joint congressional resolution. By this device, Congress has considerably augmented its powers in foreign affairs, as when it annexed Texas and then Hawaii to circumvent the requirement of a two-thirds vote of the Senate to approve treaties.

Three major provisions of the Constitution are among the vaguest: Congress has the power to regulate commerce among the states; neither the national government nor a state may take life, liberty, or property without due process of law; and no state may deny to any person the equal protection of the laws. These are the most litigated clauses in U.S. constitutional history because they are among the muddiest and most important.

Even the seemingly specific injunctions and provisions of the bill of rights are vague or ambiguous, offering little guidance for interpretation. A good example of such ambiguity is the term establishment of religion in the First Amendment. James Madison, its author, mistakenly used the term interchangeably with "religious establishment," which denotes an institution of religion such as a church or sectarian school. "Religious establishment" carries no implication of government aid to religion or government involvement with it, as does "establishment of religion." When Madison misquoted the clause as if it outlawed religious establishment, he meant that the government had no authority to legislate on religion or its institutions. Nevertheless, the term itself has no self-evident meaning. History supplies that meaning, and historians differ.

The term freedom of the press constitutes another ambiguity. In Anglo-American thought and law, it meant an exemption from prior restraint; it did not exclude liability under the criminal law for seditious, obscene, or blasphemous libel. In contrast, the Framers, who did not adopt or reject the definition of a free press under the common law, knew only a rasping, corrosive, and licentious press. They did not likely use the term "freedom of the press" without intending to protect the freedom that in fact existed and that they knew. The text itself surely lacks clarity. It declares in absolute terms that Congress shall make no law abridging the freedom of speech or press, but the copyright clause of the Constitution authorizes Congress to make laws that do abridge the freedom of speech and press of those who would infringe copyrights.

This same clause, in Article I, section 8, refers only to "authors and inventors," making a literal interpretation of it fail to protect artists, sculptors, composers, computer-software designers, television programmers, and many others who come under its protection. If only authors and inventors benefited from the clause, they could not even assign a copyright to others. The problem with the copyright clause is not that it is ambiguous or vague; it is utterly clear. But, it possesses inappropriate specificity and therefore cannot mean what it says.

The First Amendment exhibits the same problem. Assuming that its framers chose their language carefully, the fact that they failed to give adequate protection to the free exercise of religion must be confronted.

The text declares that the freedom of the press may not be abridged, but by contrast, only says that freedom of religion may not be prohibited. This is a comparatively diminished protection because freedom of religion may be abridged in many ways without being prohibited. The same amendment also suffers from terminological exactitude: Congress shall make "no law" abridging freedom of the press. A reliance on textualism would mean that neither pornography nor direct and successful verbal incitements to crime can be abridged. Yet the absolute of "no law" cannot apply to copyright laws, which can constitute abridgments.

The Fifth Amendment's self-incrimination clause cannot be taken literally either. If the text meant what it says, it meant little when framed because defendants then had no right to give sworn testimony for or against themselves. Moreover, the clause protected the right only in criminal cases, but the right existed in civil as well as criminal cases and in nonjudicial proceedings such as grand jury and legislative investigations. Finally, a person may be compelled to be a witness against himself or herself in noncriminal ways; at the time of the adoption of the Bill of Rights, the Fifth Amendment right protected persons from being forced to expose themselves to public infamy. In 1892, the Supreme Court acknowledged that the text does not mean what it says; the Court declared, "It is impossible that the meaning of the constitutional provision can only be that a person shall not be compelled to be a witness against himself in a criminal prosecution against himself."

Other examples of the text not meaning what it says appear in the Sixth Amendment, which enumerates a variety of rights of the criminally accused available to them "in all criminal prosecutions." "All" is an absolute that admits of no exceptions. Yet the Framers did not intend to extend the right of trial by jury to misdemeanants; persons accused of petty crimes were tried in a more summary manner than trial by jury. In this regard, the Sixth Amendment reinforced the provision in Article III, section 2: "The trial of all crimes, except in cases of impeachment, shall be by jury. . . ." "All crimes" here means merely all felonies; the exception for impeachments really extended to misdemeanors also. Misdemeanants are still not entitled to trial by jury unless they can be imprisoned for more than six months. The text misleads.

Similarly, the right to the assistance of counsel in all criminal prosecutions does not mean what it says: "In all criminal prosecutions, the accused . . . shall have the assistance of counsel." "Shall" conveys an imperative; but the amendment merely meant that one might have counsel if he or she could afford it. Not until 1932 did indigents receive the benefit of court-appointed counsel in capital cases in state courts; not until 1938 did all federal defendants receive the right to court-appointed counsel in any criminal prosecution. Juveniles have long been deprived of the right to trial by jury, and no one is entitled to be represented by counsel before a grand jury, which initiates a criminal prosecution. Furthermore, the text does not mean what it says in the provision that in all criminal prosecutions the accused shall be confronted with the witnesses against them; the exceptions to this, in fact, are numerous.

The problem of inappropriate specificity appears in the double jeopardy clause of the Fifth Amendment: "Nor shall any person be subject for the same offense to be twice put in jeopardy of life or limb." Here the Constitution neither means what it says, nor says what it means. It means "life or liberty," not "life or limb." The reference to "limb" is meaningless because we have long ceased to tear people apart or crop their ears. One cannot be put in jeopardy of loss of limb even if convicted by due process of law at a single trial. The double jeopardy clause implies, however, that a conviction can result in loss of limb. This would surely constitute a violation of the Eighth Amendment's guarantee against cruel and unusual punishment. The text also leads to a logical puzzle. Life may be taken if one receives due process and is not exposed to double jeopardy. But if limb may not be taken, why may life be taken?

The Second Amendment is both vague and ambiguous. Some think it upholds the collective right of state militias to bear arms, while others argue that it protects the right of individuals to bear arms. But this right existed only to maintain militias. If a standing army, even in peacetime, has succeeded militias, and if the armed forces provides weapons to those in the service, the reason for the right to bear arms may no longer be as apparent as it once was. "Arms" once meant a flintlock rifle. Does the right to bear arms include a right to bear a Saturday-night special, an assault rifle, or a bazooka?

Vagueness, not ambiguity, saturates the Fourth Amendment, which prohibits "unreasonable" search and seizure and provides that no warrants shall issue "but on probable cause." "Unreasonable" and "probable" rank high on any list of indefinite terms. It is possible, similarly, to parse every provision of the Bill of Rights and be bewildered by the meaning of the text. Terms such as speedy trial, just compensation, public use, "impartial jury," "excessive bail," "excessive fines," and "cruel and unusual" simply do not permit a constitutional jurisprudence to be based securely on textualism. To speak of strict construction is faintly ridiculous given the imprecision of the provisions of the Bill of Rights and of the Fourteenth Amendment. Ambiguity cannot be strictly construed. Strictly construing vagueness as well as inappropriately specific terms can equally lead to ludicrous, tragic, or unjust results.

The Constitution is, indeed, as Jefferson once said in exasperation, "a thing of wax that the Judiciary may twist and shape into any form they please." Unlike Humpty Dumpty, the Framers of the Constitution were unable to make words mean what they wanted them to mean. Perhaps they sensed that America would change beyond their grasp, and they did not think they could master the future. Perhaps they understood, with James Wilson, that they were representatives "not merely of the present age, but of future times; not merely of the territory along the sea-coast, but of regions immensely extended westward." This is the reason the Constitutional Convention accepted the advice of Edmund Randolph to keep the Constitution focused on "essential principles" so it can "be accomodated [*sic*] to times and events." The text is merely a point of departure; textualism as constitutional gospel is as impractical as original intent. Like original intent, however, textualism is entitled to serious attention, within its distinct limits, because Story was right: the people of the United States ratified the text, only the text, and it is the fundamental and supreme law of the land.

Bibliography

Laycock, Douglas 1984 Taking Constitutions Seriously: A Theory of Judicial Review. *Texas Law Review* 59:343–394.

Levy, Leonard W. 1988 *Original Intent and the Framers' Constitution.* New York: Macmillan.

Schauer, Frederick 1985 Easy Cases. *Southern California Law Review* 58:399–440.

Tushnet, Mark V. 1985 A Note on the Revival of Textualism in Constitutional Theory. *Southern California Law Review* 58:683–700.

29

Lemuel Shaw: America's "Greatest Magistrate" †

Lemuel Shaw served as Chief Justice of Massachusetts from 1830 to 1860, during an age which he said was remarkable for its "prodigious activity and energy in every department of life."[1] America was being transformed by the rise of railroads, steam power, the factory system, and the corporate form of business. A more complex society, urban and industrial, was superseding the older rural, agrarian one. Only a pace behind the astonishing rate of economic change came the democratization of politics and of society, while the federal system lumbered toward its greatest crisis. During this time Shaw delivered what is probably a record number of opinions for a single judge: over two thousand and two hundred, enough to fill about twenty volumes if separately collected.

At the time of his appointment to the bench, American law was still in its formative period. Whole areas of law were largely uncultivated, many unknown, and few if any settled. Although Shaw was not writing on a completely clean slate, the strategy of time and place surely presented an unrivaled opportunity for a judge of strength and vision to mold the law. His domain was the whole field of jurisprudence excepting only admiralty. No other state judge through his opinions alone had so great an influence on the course of American law.

One of the major themes of his life work was the perpetuation of what Oscar and Mary Handlin have called "the commonwealth idea"[2]— essentially a quasi-mercantilist concept of the state within a democratic framework. In Europe where the state was not responsible to the people and was the product of remote historical forces, mercantilism served the ruling classes who controlled the state. In America men put the social-contract theory into practice and actually made their government. The people were the state; the state was their "Common Wealth." They identified themselves with it and felt that they should share, as of right, in the advantages that it could bring to them as a community. The state was their means of promoting the general interest.

The Commonwealth idea precluded the laissez-faire state whose function was simply to keep peace and order, and then, like a little child, not be heard. The people of Massachusetts expected their Commonwealth to participate actively in their economic affairs. Where risk-capital feared to tread or needed franchises, powers of incorporation, or the boost of special powers like eminent domain, the duty of the state was to subsidize, grant, and supervise the whole process in the interests of the general welfare. But regulation was not restricted to those special interests which had been promoted by government aid. Banks, insurance companies, liquor dealers, food vendors, and others were all subjected to varying degrees of control, though the public trough had not been open to them. The beneficent hand of the state reached out to touch every part of the economy.

The Commonwealth idea profoundly influenced the development of law in Massachusetts. It was largely responsible for the direction taken by the law of eminent domain, for the development of the police power, and for the general precedence given by the courts to public rights over merely private ones. As employed by Shaw, the Commonwealth idea gave rise to legal doctrines of the public interest by which the power of the state to govern the economy was judicially sustained.

The idea "that some privately owned corporations are more public in character than others," as Edwin Merrick Dodd noted, "had already begun to emerge in judicial decisions before 1830."[3] The grant of powers of eminent domain to early turnpike and canal companies had been upheld because these were public highways, although privately owned. The mill acts, which originated as a means of promoting water-powered gristmills, had also been sustained in early decisions on the ground that a public purpose was served. While the earlier judges regretted the extension of the old gristmill acts to new manufacturing corporations, Shaw, by contrast, warmly accepted these acts because he believed that industrialization would bring prosperity and progress to the Commonwealth. Accordingly he declared that "a great mill-power for manufacturing purposes" was, like a railroad, a species of public works in which the public had a great interest. He even placed "steam manufactories" in the same class as water-powered mills, as devoted to a public use, although steam-powered factories were never granted powers of eminent domain.[4]

The Commonwealth idea underlay those remarkably prophetic opinions of Shaw's that established the basis of the emerging law of public utilities. The old common law of common calling had considered only millers, carriers, and innkeepers as "public employments"; it "knew no such persons as the common road-maker or the common water-supplier."[5] The "common road-maker," that is, the turnpike, bridge, and canal companies, were added to the list of public employments or public works while Shaw was still at the bar. But it was Shaw who settled the legal character of power companies,[6] turnpikes,[7] railroads,[8] and water suppliers[9] as public utilities, privately owned but subject to regulation for the public benefit. He would have included even manufacturers and banks. The Commonwealth idea left no doubt as to whether the state would master or be mastered by its creatures, the corporations, or whether the welfare of the economy was a matter of public or private concern.

The police power may be regarded as the legal expression of the Commonwealth idea, for it signifies the supremacy of public over private rights. To call the police power a Massachusetts doctrine would be an exaggeration, though not a great one. But it is certainly no coincidence that in Massachusetts, with its Commonwealth tradition, the police power was first defined and carried to great extremes from the standpoint of vested interests. Shaw's foremost contribution in the field of public law was to the development of the police-power concept.

The power of the legislature "to trench somewhat largely on the profitable use of individual property," for the sake of the common good, as Shaw expressed the police power in *Commonwealth v. Alger,*[10] was consistently confirmed over thirty years of his opinions. Three decades later, when judges were acting on the supposition that the Fourteenth Amendment incorporated Herbert Spencer's *Social Statics,* the ideas expressed in Shaw's opinions seemed the very epitome of revolutionary socialism. Shaw's name was revered, but the implications of his police-power opinions were politely evaded. In the period between Shaw and the school of Holmes and Brandeis, American law threatened to become the graveyard of general-welfare or public-interest doctrines, and doctrines of vested rights dominated.

The trend toward legal Spencerianism was so pronounced by the end of the nineteenth century that legal historians concentrated on a search for the origins of doctrines of vested rights, almost as if contrary doctrines had never existed. When touching the pre-Civil War period, it is conventional to quote Tocqueville on the conservatism of the American bench and bar, to present American law almost exclusively in terms of Marshall, Story, and Kent, and to emphasize that the rights of property claimed the very warmest affections of the American judiciary. If, however, the work of the state courts were better known, this view of our legal history might be altered. But Gibson and Ruffin and Blackford are little more than distinguished names, their work forgotten. Shaw's superb exposition of the police power is respectfully remembered, but it is usually treated as exceptional, or mistreated as an attempt to confine the police power to the common-law maxim of *sic utere tuo ut alienum non laedas.*[11]

Shaw taught that "all property . . . is derived directly or indirectly from the government, and held subject to those general regulations, which are necessary to the common good and general welfare."[12] Dean Pound, in discussing the "extreme individualist view" of the common law concerning the rights of riparian property owners, says the common law asked simply, "was the defendant acting on his own land and committing no nuisance?"[13] But Shaw believed that the common law of nuisances, which was founded on the *sic utere* maxim, inadequately protected the public, because it was restricted to the abatement of existing nuisances. He believed that the general welfare required the anticipation and prevention of prospective wrongs from the use of private property. Accordingly he held that the legislature might interfere with the use of property before its owner became amenable to the common law. So a man could not even remove stones from his own beach if prohibited by the legislature, nor erect a wharf on his property beyond boundary lines fixed by it. Even if his use of his property would be "harmless" or "indifferent," the necessity of restraints was to be judged "by those to whom all legislative power is intrusted by the sovereign authority." Similarly the "reasonableness" of such restraints was a matter of "expediency" to be determined by the legislature, not the court. The simple expedient of having a precise statutory rule for the obedience of all was sufficient reason for a finding of constitutionality.[14]

Thus Shaw, using the Commonwealth idea, established a broad base for the police power. He carried the law's conception of the public good and the power of government to protect it a long way from the straitjacketing ideas of Kent and Story. Their position may be summed up in Blackstone's language that "the public good is in nothing more essentially interested than the protection of every individual's private rights."[15]

A few other decisions of the Shaw Court on the police power will illustrate that the Chief Justice's *Alger* opinion was more than rhetoric. The authority of the legislature to shape private banking practices in the public interest was unequivocally sustained in two sweeping opinions. In one, Shaw said that a statute intended to prevent banks from "becoming dangerous to the public" was attacked as unconstitutional on the authority of Marshall, Story, and Kent. The statute allegedly operated retroactively against the bank in question; constituted a legislative assumption of judicial power because it required the Supreme Judicial Court to issue a preliminary injunction against banks on the findings of a government commission; and violated the federal contract clause by providing for a perpetual injunction against the further doing of business, in effect a revocation of the charter. Rufus Choate probably never argued a stronger case. But Shaw sustained the statute and the injunction, peppering his opinion with references to the paramountcy of "the great interests of the community," the duty of the government to "provide security for its citizens," and the legitimacy of interferences with "the liberty of action, and even with the right of property, of such institutions."[16] In a second bank case of the same year, 1839, the Court refused "to raise banks above the control of the legislature." The holding was that a charter could be dissolved at the authority of the legislature, under the reserved police power, without a judicial proceeding.[17]

It has been said that from the standpoint of the doctrine of vested rights the most reprehensible legislation ever enacted was the prohibition on the sale of liquor. Such legislation wiped out the value of existing stocks and subjected violators to criminal sanctions, their property to public destruction. Similarly, buildings used for purposes of prostitution or gambling might, on the authority of the legislature, be torn down. The question presented by such statutes was whether the police power could justify uncompensated destruction of private property which had not been appropriated for a public use. The power of the Commonwealth over the health and morals of the public provided Shaw with the basis for sustaining legislation divesting vested rights.[18] On half a dozen occasions, the New York Wynehammer doctrine of substantive due process of law was repudiated in such cases.[19]

Regulation of railroads was another subject for the exercise of the police power, according to the Shaw Court. The same principles that justified grants of eminent domain to railroads, or to canals, bridges, turnpikes, power companies, and water suppliers, also provided the basis for sustaining controls over their rates, profits, and services. Railroads, said Shaw, were a "public work, established by public authority, intended for the public use and benefit. . . ."[20] The power to charge rates was "in every respect a public grant, a franchise . . . subject to certain regulations, within the power of government, if it should become excessive."[21]

These dicta by Shaw became holdings at the first moment the railroads challenged the "reasonableness" of the rates and services fixed by government railroad commissions. "Reasonableness" was held to be a matter for determination by the legislature or the commission to which it delegated its powers. Those powers, in turn, were broadly construed. The Court would not interfere with the regulatory process if the railroads had the benefit of notice, hearing, and other fair procedures.[22] Due process of law to the Shaw Court meant according to legal forms, not according to legislation which the Court approved or disapproved as a matter of policy.

The Shaw Court's latitudinarian attitude toward the police power was influenced by the strong tradition of judicial self-restraint among Massachusetts judges, an outgrowth of the Commonwealth idea. Shaw carried on the tradition of the Massachusetts judiciary. During the thirty years that Shaw presided, there were only ten cases, one unreported, in which the Supreme Judicial Court voided legislative enactments.

Four of these cases in no way related to the police power. One involved a special legislative resolution confirming a private sale that had divested property rights of third persons without compensation.[23] The second concerned an act by which Charlestown was annexed to Boston without providing the citizens of Charlestown with representative districts and an opportunity to vote.[24] The third, an unreported case decided by Shaw sitting alone, involved the "personal liberty act," by which the state sought to evade Congress' Fugitive Slave Law.[25] Here Shaw felt bound by the national Constitution and by a decision of the Supreme Court of the United States. In the fourth case he invalidated a state act which dispensed with the ancient requirement of grand jury proceedings in cases of high Crimes.[26] In each of these four, the decisions are above any but trifling criticism.

Of the six cases bearing on the police power, three involved legislation egregiously violating procedural guarantees that are part of our civil liberties.[27] The statutes in question had validly prohibited the sale of liquor. But they invalidly stripped accused persons of virtually every safeguard of criminal justice, from the right to be free from unreasonable searches and seizures to the rights that cluster around the concept of fair trial. Shaw's decisions against these statutes, like his decisions insuring the maintenance of grand jury proceedings and the right to vote, were manifestations of judicial review in its best sense. There were also dicta by Shaw on the point that the legislature cannot restrain the use of property by ex post facto laws, by bills of attainder, or by discriminatory classifications. Thus the limitations placed upon the police power by the Shaw Court were indispensable to the protection of civil liberties.

The only exception to this generalization consists of the limitation derived from the contract clause of the United States Constitution. But there were only three cases during the long period of Shaw's Chief Justiceship in which this clause was the basis for the invalidation of statutes. In each of the three, the statutes were of limited operation and the decisions made no sacrifice of the public interest. The legislature in one case attempted to regulate in the absence of a reserved power to alter or amend public contracts; the Court left a way open for the legislature's purpose to be achieved under common law.[28] In the other two cases, regulatory powers had been reserved but were exercised in particularly faithless and arbitrary ways; in one case to increase substantially the obligations of a corporation for a second time, in effect doubling a liability which had been paid off; in the other case to repeal an explicit permission for a corporation to increase it capitalization in return for certain services rendered.[29] The legislature in all three cases had passed a high threshold of judicial tolerance for governmental interference with the sanctity of contracts. The decisions were hardly exceptional, considering the facts of the cases and their dates—they were decided between 1854 and 1860, after scores of similar decisions by Federalist, Whig, and Jacksonian jurists alike in state and federal jurisdictions.

The striking fact is that there were so few such decisions by the Shaw Court in thirty years. Handsome opportunities were provided again and again by litigants claiming impairment of their charters of incorporation by a meddlesome legislature. But the Court's decisions were characterized by judicial self-restraint rather than an eagerness to erect a bulwark around chartered rights. The three cases in which statutes were voided for conflict with the contract clause were unusual for the Shaw Court.

Generally the attitude of the Court was typified by Shaw's remark that "immunities and privileges (vested by charter) do not exempt corporations from the operations of those laws made for the general regulation. . . ."[30] He habitually construed public grants in favor of the community and against private interests. When chartered powers were exercised in the public interest, he usually interpreted them broadly; but when they competed with the right of the community to protect itself or conserve its resources, he interpreted chartered powers narrowly. He did not permit the public control over matters of health, morals, or safety, nor the power of eminent domain, to be alienated by the contract clause.

In the face of such a record it is misleading to picture state courts assiduously searching for doctrines of vested rights to stymie the police power. Certainly no such doctrines appeared in the pre-Civil War decisions of the Supreme Judicial Court of Massachusetts, except for the one doctrine derived by John Marshall from the contract clause and so sparingly used by Shaw. The sources from which vested-rights doctrines were derived by others—the higher law, natural rights, the social compact, and other sources of implied, inherent limitations on majoritarian assemblies—these were invoked by Shaw when he was checking impairments or personal liberties or traditional procedures of criminal justice.

If this picture does not fit the stereotype of conservative Whig jurists, the stereotype may need revision. On the great issue which has historically divided liberals from conservatives in politics—government controls over property and corporations—Shaw supported the government. Even when the Commonwealth idea was being eroded away by those who welcomed the give-away state but not the regulatory state, Shaw was still endorsing a concept of the police power that kept private interests under government surveillance and restraint. He would not permit the Commonwealth idea to become just a rationale for legislative subventions and grants of chartered powers, with business as the only beneficiary. To Shaw, government aid implied government control, because the aid to business was merely incidental to the promotion of the public welfare. No general regulatory statute was invalidated while he was Chief Justice. His conservatism tended to crop out in common law cases where the public interest had not been defined or suggested by statute. In such cases the law was as putty in his hands, shaped to meet the press of business needs. Nothing illustrates this better than the personal injury cases and the variety of novel cases to which railroad corporations were parties. The roar of the first locomotive in Massachusetts signaled the advent of a capitalist revolution in the common law, in the sense that Shaw made railroads the beneficiaries of legal doctrine.[31] To be sure, he believed that he was genuinely serving the general interest on the calculation that what was good for business was good for the Commonwealth.

It was when he had a free hand, in the absence of government action, that the character of his conservatism displayed itself: He construed the law so that corporate industrial interests prevailed over lesser, private ones. An individual farmer, shipper, passenger, worker, or pedestrian, when pitted against a corporation which in Shaw's mind personified industrial expansion and public prosperity, risked a rough sort of justice, whether the issue involved tort or contract.[32] Shaw strictly insisted that individuals look to themselves, not to the law, for protection of life and limb, for his beloved common law was incorrigibly individualistic. The hero of the common law was the property-owning, liberty-loving, self-reliant reasonable man. He was also the hero of American society, celebrated by Jefferson as the free-hold farmer, by Hamilton as the town-merchant, by Jackson as the frontiersman. Between the American image of the common man and the common-law's ideal Everyman, there was a remarkable likeness. It harshly and uncompromisingly treated men as free-willed, self-reliant, risk-and-responsibility taking individuals. Its spirit was, let every man beware and care for himself. That spirit, together with Shaw's belief that the rapid growth of manufacturing and transportation heralded the coming of the good society, tended to minimize the legal liabilities of business.

This was especially striking in cases of industrial accident and personal injury cases generally. For example, when an accident occurred despite all precautions, Shaw held railroads liable for damage to freight but not for injuries to passengers. They, he reasoned, took the risk of accidents that might occur regardless of due care. His opinions went a long way to accentuate the inhumanity of the common law in the area of torts, and simultaneously, to spur capitalist enterprise. Here was the one great area of law in which he failed to protect the public interest. He might have done so without stymying rapid industrialization, because the cost of accidents, if imposed on business, would have been ultimately shifted to the public by a hike in prices and rates.

The rigorous individualism of the common law was especially noticeable in the emergent doctrine of contributory negligence, of which Shaw was a leading exponent.[33] That doctrine required a degree of care and skill which no one but the mythical "prudent" or "reasonable man" of the common law could match. A misstep, however slight, from the ideal standard of conduct, placed upon the injured party the whole burden of his loss, even though the railroad was also at fault and perhaps more so. Comparative rather than contributory negligence would have been a fairer test, or perhaps some rule by which damages could be apportioned.

Probably the furthermost limit of the common law's individualism in accident cases was expressed in the rule that a right to action is personal and dies with the injured party. This contributed to the related rule that the wrongful death of a human being was no ground for an action of damages.[34] But for the intervention of the legislature, the common law would have left the relatives of victims of fatal accident without a legal remedy to obtain compensation. Shaw would also have made it more profitable for a railroad to kill a man outright than to scratch him, for if he lived he could sue.[35]

The fellow-servant rule was the most far-reaching consequence of individualism in the law as Shaw expounded it.[36] The rule was that a worker who was injured, through no fault of his own, by the negligence of a fellow employee, could not maintain a claim of damages against his employer. Shaw formulated this rule at a strategic moment for employers, because as industrialization expanded at an incredible pace, factory and railroad accidents multiplied frighteningly. Since the fellow-servant rule threw the whole loss from accidents upon innocent workers, capitalism was relieved of an enormous sum that would otherwise have been due as damages. The encouragement of "infant industries" had no greater social cost.

The fellow-servant rule was unmistakably an expression of legal thinking predicated upon the conception that a free man is one who is free to work out his own destiny, to pursue the calling of his choice, and to care for himself. If he undertakes a dangerous occupation, he voluntarily assumes the risks to which he has exposed himself. He should know that the others with whom he will have to work may cause him harm by their negligence. He must bear his loss because his voluntary conduct has implied his consent to assume it and to relieve his employer of it. On the other hand, there can be no implication that the employer has contracted to indemnify the worker for the negligence of anyone but himself. The employer, like his employees, is responsible for his own conduct, but cannot be liable without fault.

On such considerations Shaw exempted the employer from liability to his employees, although he was liable to the rest of the world for the injurious acts which they committed in the course of their employment. It is interesting to note that Shaw felt obliged to read the employee's assumption of risk into his contract of employment. This legal fiction also reflected the individualism of a time when it was felt that free men could not be bound except by a contract of their own making.

The public policy which Shaw confidently expounded in support of his reading of the law similarly expressed the independent man: safety would be promoted if each worker guarded himself against his own carelessness and just as prudently watched his neighbor; to remove this responsibility by setting up the liability of the employer would allegedly tend to create individual laxity rather than prudence. So Shaw reasoned. It seems not to have occurred to him that fear of being maimed prompted men to safety anyway, or that contributory negligence barred recovery of damages, or that freeing the employer from liability did not induce him to employ only the most careful persons and to utilize accident-saving devices. Nor, for all his reliance upon the voluntary choice of mature men, did it occure to Shaw that a worker undertook a dangerous occupation and "consented" to its risks because his poverty deprived him of real choice. For that matter, none of these considerations prompted the legislature to supersede the common law with employers' liability and workmen's compensation acts until many decades later. Shaw did no violence to the spirit of his age by the fellow-servant rule, or by the rules he applied in other personal injury cases, particularly those involving wrongful death. In all such cases his enlightened views, so evidenced in police-power cases, were absent, probably because government action was equally absent. On the other hand his exposition of the rule of implied malice in cases of homicide[37] and of the criminal responsibility of the insane[38] accorded with the growing humanitarianism of the day as well as with doctrines of individualism.

Shaw's conservatism tended to manifest itself in cases involving notable social issues of his time. For example he handed down the leading opinion on the constitutionality of the Fugitive Slave Act of 1850;[39] he originated the "separate but equal" doctrine which became the legal linchpin of racial segregation in the public schools throughout the nation;[40] and in the celebrated Abner Kneeland case,[41] he sustained a conviction for blasphemy that grossly abridged freedom of conscience and expression; still another opinion was a bulwark of the establishment of religion which was maintained in Massachusetts until 1833.[42]

But it would be misleading as well as minimally informing to conclude an analysis of Shaw's work by calling him a conservative, for the word reveals little about Shaw if it is also applied to Marshall, Kent, Story, Webster, and Choate.

When Story and Kent, steeped in the crusty lore of the Year Books, were wailing to each other that they were the last of an old race of judges and that Taney's *Charles River Bridge* decision[43] meant that the Constitution was gone,[44] Shaw was calmly noting that property was "fully subject to State regulation" in the interest of the "morals, health, internal commerce, and general prosperity of the community. . . ."[45] In 1860 at the age of eighty, in an opinion which is a little gem in the literature of the common law, he gave fresh evidence of his extraordinary talent for keeping hoary principles viable by adapting them—as he put it—"to new institutions and conditions of society, new modes of commerce, new usages and practices, as the society in the advancement of civilization may require."[46]

Shaw's mind was open to many of the liberal currents of his time. Witness his support from the bench of the free, public education movement,[47] or his public-interest doctrines,[48] or his defense of trade-union activities,[49] or his freeing sojourner slaves. While Shaw was Chief Justice all slaves whom fate brought to Massachusetts were guaranteed liberty, except for runaways. Whether they were brought by their masters who were temporarily visiting the Commonwealth or were just passing through, or whether they were cast up by the sea, they were set free by Shaw's definition of the law. Bound by neither precedent nor statute, he made that law. The principle of comity, he ruled, could not extend to human beings as property: because slavery was so odious and founded upon brute force it could exist only when sanctioned by positive, local law. There being no such law in Massachusetts, Shaw freed even slave seamen in the service of the United States Navy if they reached a port within his jurisdiction.[50]

In the area of criminal law dealing with conspiracies, Shaw seems on first glance to have run counter to individualist doctrines. He held, in what is probably his best-known opinion,[51] that a combination of workers to establish and maintain a closed shop by the use of peaceable coercion is not an indictable conspiracy even if it tends to injure employers. Shaw also indicated that he saw nothing unlawful in a peaceable, concerted effort to raise wages.

But other judges had been persuaded by the ideology of individualism, or at least used its rhetoric, to find criminality in trade-union activity and even in unions per se. Combination, labor's most effective means of economic improvement, was the very basis of the ancient doctrine of criminal conspiracy and the denial of individual effort. The closed shop was regarded as a hateful form of monopoly by labor, organized action to raise wages as coercion, and both regarded as injurious to the workers themselves, as well as to trade and the public at large. When so much store was placed in self-reliance, the only proper way in law and economics for employees to better themselves seemed to be by atomistic bargaining. Unions were thought to impede the natural operation of free competition by individuals on both sides of the labor market. Or so Shaw's contemporaries and earlier judges had believed.

Individualism, however, has many facets, and like maxims relating to liberty, the free market, or competition, can be conscripted into the service of more than one cause. If self-reliance was one attribute of individualism, the pursuit of self-interest was another. As Tocqueville noted, where individualism and freedom prevail, men pursue their self-interest and express themselves by developing an astonishing proclivity for association. As soon as several Americans of like interest "have found one another out, they combine," observed Tocqueville.

Shaw too noted the "general tendency of society in our times, to combine men into bodies and associations having some object of deep interest common to themselves. . . ."[52] He understood that freedom meant combination.

When the question arose whether it was criminal for a combination of employees to refuse to work for one who employed non-union labor, Shaw replied in the disarming language of individualism that men who are not bound by contract are "free to work for whom they please, or not to work, if they so prefer. In this state of things, we cannot perceive, that it is criminal for men to agree together to exercise their acknowledged rights, in such a manner as best to subserve their own interests."[53]

He acknowledged that the pursuit of their own interests might result in injury to third parties, but that did not in his opinion make their combination criminal in the absence of fraud, violence, or other illegal behavior. To Shaw's mind the pursuit of self-interest was a hard, competitive game in which atomistic individuals stood less chance of getting hurt by joining forces. He also seems to have considered bargaining between capital and labor as a form of competition whose benefits to society, like those from competition of any kind, outweighed the costs. Finally, he was fair enough to believe that labor was entitled to combine if business could, and wary enough to understand that if the conspiracy doctrine were not modified, it might boomerang against combinations of businessmen who competed too energetically. Thus Shaw drew different conclusions from premises which he shared with others concerning individualism, freedom, and competition. The result of his interpretation of the criminal law of conspiracies was that the newly emerging trade-union movement was left viable.

But the corporate movement was left viable too, a fact which helps reconcile the fellow-servant and trade-union decisions. To regard one as "anti-labor" and the other as "pro-labor" adds nothing to an understanding of two cases governed by different legal considerations; on the one hand tort and contract, on the other criminal conspiracy. The fellow-servant case belongs to a line of harsh personal injury decisions that were unrelated to labor as such. To be sure, labor was saddled with much of the cost of industrial accidents, but victims of other accidents hardly fared better. The fellow-servant decision also represented a departure of the maxim *respondeat superior* which might impose liability without fault; while the trade-union decision, intended in part to draw the fangs of labor's support of the codification movement, represented a departure from Hawkin's conspiracy doctrine which might impose criminality on business as well as labor.

Despite the conflicting impact of the two decisions on labor's fortunes and the fact that they are not comparable from a legal standpoint they harmonize as a part of Shaw's thought. He regarded the worker as a free agent competing with his employer as to the terms of employment, at liberty to refuse work if his demands were not met. As the best judge of his own welfare, he might assume risks, combine in a closed shop, or make other choices. For Shaw, workers possessed the same freedom of action enjoyed by employers against labor and against business rivals.

Compared to such Whig peers as Webster, Story, and Choate, Shaw was quite liberal in many respects. Indeed his judicial record is remarkably like the record one might expect from a jurist of the Jacksonian persuasion. Marcus Morton, during ten years of service as Shaw's associate, found it necessary to dissent only once, in *Kneeland's* case. No doubt the inherited legal tradition created an area of agreement among American jurists that was more influential in the decision-making process than party differences. Yet it is revealing that many of Shaw's opinions might conceivably have been written by a Gibson, but not by a Kent. It was not just the taught tradition of the common law which Shaw and Gibson shared; they shared also taught traditions of judicial self-restraint, of the positive state, and the "Commonwealth idea," a term that is meaningful in Pennsylvania's history as well as in Massachusetts'.[54]

But personality makes a difference in law as in politics. It oversimplifies to say, as Pound has, that the "chiefest factor in determining the course which legal development will take with respect to any new situation or new problem is the analogy or analogies that chance to be at hand. . . ."[55] There are usually conflicting and alternative analogies, rules, and precedents from among which judges may choose. The direction of choice is shaped by such personal factors as the judge's calculation of the community's needs, his theory of the function of government, his concept of the role of the court, inexpressible intuitions, unrecognized predilections, and perhaps doting biases. It is difficult to name a single major case decided by Shaw which might not have gone the other way had another been sitting in his place.

Shaw interpreted the received law as he understood it, and his understanding was colored by his own presuppositions, particularly in respect to those interests and values he thought the legal order should secure. Few other judges have been so earnestly and consciously concerned with the public policy implicit in the principle of a case.

Much of his greatness lay in this concern for principle and policy. "It is not enough," he observed, "to say, that the law is so established . . . The rule may be a good rule . . . But some better reason must be given for it than that, so it was enacted, or so it was decided."[56] He thought it necessary to search out the rule which governed a case; to ask "upon what principle is it founded?" and to deliver a disquisition on the subject, with copious illustrations for the guidance of the future. From the bench he was one of the nation's foremost teachers of law.

His opinions did not overlook the question *"cui bono?"* which, he believed, "applies perhaps with still greater force to the laws, than to any other subject."[57] That is why he fixed "enlightened public policy" at the root of all legal principles, along with "reason" and "natural justice."[58] He understood that American law was a functioning instrument of a free society, embodying its ideals, serving its interests. It is not surprising, then, that he tended to minimize precedent and place his decisions on broad grounds of social advantage. Justice Holmes, attributing Shaw's greatness to his "accurate appreciation of the requirements of the community," thought that "few have lived who were his equals in their understanding of the grounds of public policy to which all laws must be ultimately referred. It was this which made him . . . the greatest magistrate which this country has produced."[59] To be sure, he made errors of judgment and policy. Yet the wonder is that his errors were so few, considering the record number of opinions which he delivered, on so many novel questions, in so many fields of law.

Perhaps his chief contribution was his day-by-day domestication of the English common law. He made it plastic and practical, preserving its continuities with what was worthwhile in the past, yet accommodating it to the ideals and shifting imperatives of American life. The Massachusetts Bar made a similar evaluation of his work when honoring the "old Chief" upon his resignation. The Bar, speaking through a distinguished committee, declared:

> It was the task of those who went before you, to show that the principles of the common and the commercial law were available to the wants of communities which were far more recent than the origin of those systems. It was for you to

adapt those systems to still newer and greater exigencies; to extend them to the solution of questions, which it required a profound sagacity to foresee, and for which an intimate knowledge of the law often enabled you to provide, before they had even fully arisen for judgment. Thus it has been that in your hands the law has met the demands of a period of unexampled activity and enterprise; while over all its varied and conflicting interests you have held the strong, conservative sway of a judge, who moulds the rule for the present and the future out of the principles and precedents of the past. Thus too it has been, that every tribunal in the country has felt the weight of your judgments, and jurists at home and abroad look to you as one of the great expositors of the law.[60]

Time has not diminished the force of this observation. As Professor Chafee has noted, "Probably no other state judge has so deeply influenced the development of commercial and constitutional law throughout the nation. Almost all the principles laid down by him have proved sound. . . ."[61]

He was sound in more than his principles. Like John Quincy Adams, his fellow Bay-Statesman whom he resembled in so many ways, he made his name a synonym for integrity, impartiality, and independence. Towering above class and party, doing everything for justice and nothing for fear or favor, he was a model for the American judicial character. And none but an Adams could compare with Shaw in his overpowering sense of public service and devotion to the good of the whole community. His achievement as a jurist is to be sought in his constructive influence upon the law of our country and in the fact so perfectly summed up in a tribute to him on his death: life, liberty, and property were safe in his hands.

Notes

†   This article is based on a paper delivered by the author at the 1961 Conference of the Northeastern States Branch of the American Society for Legal History, held at Boston College Law School on September 30, 1961.
†† Dean and Earl Warren Professor of American Constitutional History Graduate School of Arts and Sciences, Brandeis University.
1. Shaw, *Profession of the Law in the United States* (Extract from an Address delivered before the Suffolk Bar, May, 1827) Amer. Jur. VII 56–65 (1832).
2. Oscar & Mary Handlin, Commonwealth. A Study of the Role of Government in the American Economy: Massachusetts, 1784–1861 31 (1947).
3. Dodd, American Business Corporations Until 1860 44 (1954).
4. See *Hazen v. Essex Co.*, 66 Mass. (12 Cush.) 475 (1853); *Palmer Co. v. Ferrill*, 34 Mass. (17 Pick.) 58 (1835).
5. Dodd, *op. cit. supra* note 3, at 161.
6. See *Gould v. Boston Duck Co.*, 79 Mass. (13 Gray) 442 (1859), *Hazen v. Essex Co.*,

66 Mass. (12 Cush.) 475 (1853), *Murdock v. Stickney*, 62 Mass. (8 Cush.) 113 (1851), *Chase v. Sutton Mfg. Co.* 58 Mass. (4 Cush.) 152 (1849); *Cary v. Daniels,* 49 Mass. (8 Met.) 466 (1844), *French v. Braintree Mfg Co.*, 40 Mass. (23 Pick.) 216 (1839); *Williams v. Nelson*, 40 Mass. (23 Pick.) 14; (1839); *Palmer Co. v. Ferrill*, 34 Mass. (17 Pick.) 58 (1835); *Fiske v. Framingham Mfg. Co.*, 29 Mass. (12 Pick.) 68 (1831).

7. *Commonwealth v. Wilkinson*, 33 Mass. (16 Pick.) 175 (1834).

8. *City of Roxbury v. Boston & Providence RR.*, 60 Mass. (6 Cush.) 424 (1850); *Newbury Tpk. Corp. v. Eastern R.R.*, 40 Mass. (23 Pick.) 326 (1839); *Boston Water Power Co. v. Boston & Worcester R.R.*, 33 Mass. (16 Pick.) 512 (1835); Wellington, Petitioners, 33 Mass. (16 Pick.) 87 (1834).

9. *Lumbard v. Stearns*, 58 Mass. (4 Cush.) 60 (1849).

10. 61 Mass. (7 Cush.) 53 (1851).

11. Corwin, The Twilight of the Supreme Court 68 (1934); Freund, The Police Power 425, § 405 (1904). For an extended discussion of the police power decisions by Shaw, see Levy, The Law of the Commonwealth and Chief Justice Shaw ch. 13 (1957).

12. *Commonwealth v. Alger*, 61 Mass. (7 Cush) 53, 83–4 (1851).

13. Pound, The Spirit of the Common Law 53–4 (1921).

14. Quotations are from Shaw's opinions in the *Alger* case and in *Commonwealth v. Tewksbury*, 52 Mass. (11 Met.) 55 (1846).

15. Quoted by Pound, The Spirit of the Common Law 53 (1921).

16. *Commonwealth v. Farmers & Mechanics Bank*, 38 Mass. (21 Pick.) 542 (1839).

17. *Crease v. Babcock*, 40 Mass. (23 Pick.) 334 (1839).

18. *Commonwealth v. Howe*, 79 Mass. (13 Gray) 26 (1859); *Brown v. Perkins* 70 Mass. (12 Gray) 89 (1858), *Fisher v. McGirr*, 67 Mass. (1 Gray) 1 (1854); *Commonwealth v. Blackington*, 41 Mass. (24 Pick.) 352 (1837). These are the leading cases among dozens.

19. *E.g., Commonwealth v. Howe*, 79 Mass. (13 Gray) 26 (1859), *Commonwealth v. Logan*, 78 Mass. (12 Gray) 136 (1859); *Commonwealth v. Murphy* 76 Mass. (10 Gray) 1 (1857); *Calder v. Kurby*, 71 Mass. (5 Gray) 597 (1856); *Commonwealth v. Hitchings*, 71 Mass. (5 Gray) 482 (1855); *Commonwealth v. Clap*, 71 Mass. (5 Gray) 97 (1855). For the Wynehammer doctrine see, *Wynehammer v. People*, 13 N.Y. 378 (1856); *People v. Toynbee*, 20 Barb. 168 (N.Y. 1855); *Wynehammer v. People*, 20 Barb. 567 (N.Y. 1855).

20. *Worcester v. Western R.R.*, 45 Mass. (4 Met.) 564, 566 (1842).

21. *B. & L. R.R. v. S. & L. R.R.*, 68 Mass. (2 Gray) 1, 29 (1854).

22. *B. & W. RR. v. Western RR.*, 80 Mass. (14 Gray) 253 (1859) and *L. & W RR. v. Fitchburg RR.*, 80 Mass. (14 Gray) 266 (1859).

23. *Sohier v. Mass. Gen. Hosp.*, 57 Mass. (3 Cush.) 483 (1849).

24. *Warren v. Mayor and Alderman of Charlestown*, 57 Mass. (3 Gray) 84 (1854).

25. *Commonwealth v. Coolidge*, Law Rep. V 482 (Mass. 1843).

26. *Jones v. Robbins*, 74 Mass. (8 Gray) 329 (1857).

27. *Robinson v. Richardson*, 79 Mass. (13 Gray) 454 (1859); *Sullivan v. Adams*, 69 Mass. (3 Gray) 476 (1855); *Fisher v. McGirr*, 67 Mass. (1 Gray) 1 (1854).

28. *Commonwealth v. New Bedford Bridge*, 68 Mass. (2 Gray) 339 (1854).

29. *Central Bridge Corp. v. City of Lowell*, 81 Mass. (15 Gray) 106 (1860); *Commonwealth v. Essex Co.*, 79 Mass. (13 Gray) 239 (1859). For an extended discussion of judicial review and of constitutional limitations under Shaw see Levy, *op. cit. supra* note 11, at ch. 14.

30. *Commonwealth v. Farmers & Mechanics Bank*, 38 Mass. (21 Pick.) 542 (1838).
31. See Levy, *op. cit. supra* note 11, at chs. 8–9 (The Formative Period of Railroad Law).
32. *Denny v. New York Central R.R.*, 79 Mass. (13 Gray) 481 (1859); *Shaw v. Boston & Worcester R.R.*, 74 Mass. (8 Gray) 45 (1857); *Lucas v. New Bedford & Taunton R.R.*, 72 Mass. (6 Gray) 64 (1856); *Nutting v. Conn. River R.R.*, 67 Mass. (1 Gray) 502 (1854); *Norway Plains Co. v. Boston & Me. R.R.*, 67 Mass. (1 Gray) 263 (1854); *Brown v. Eastern R.R.*, 65 Mass. (11 Cush.) 97 (1853) *Lichtenheim v. Boston & Providence R.R.* 65 Mass. (11 Cush.) 70 (1853); *Props. of Locks and Canals v. Nashua & Lowell R.R.*, 64 Mass. (10 Cush.) 385 (1852); *Hollenbeck v. Berkshire R.R.*, 63 Mass. (9 Cush.) 478 (1852); *Kearney v. Boston & Worcester R.R.*, 63 Mass. (9 Cush.) 108 (1851); *McElroy v. Nashua & Lowell R.R.*, 58 Mass. (4 Cush.) 400 (1849); *Cary v. Berkshire R.R.* 55 Mass. (1 Cush.) 475 (1848); *Snow v. Eastern R.R.*, 53 Mass. (12 Met.) 14 (1846); *Lewis v Western R.R.*, 52 Mass. (11 Met.) 509 (1846); *Draper v. Worcester & Norwich R.R.*, 52 Mass. (11 Met.) 505 (1846); *Worcester v. Western R.R.*, 45 Mass. (4 Met.) 564 (1842); *Thompson v. Boston & Providence R.R.*, Daily Evening Transcript (Boston) Jan. 6, 1837; *Gerry v. Boston & Providence R.R.*, Daily Evening Transcript (Boston) Dec. 29, 1836.
33. *Shaw v. B. & W. R.R.*, 74 Mass. (8 Gray) 45 (1857); *Brown v. Kendell*, 60 Mass. (6 Cush.) 292 (1850).
34. *Carey v. Berkshire R.R.*, 55 Mass. (1 Cush.) 475 (1848).
35. *Hollenbeck v. Berkshire R.R.*, 63 Mass. (9 Cush.) 478 (1852); *Kearney v. Boston & Worcester R.R.*, 63 Mass. (9 Cush.) 108 (1851).
36. *Farwell v. Boston & Worcester R.R.*, 45 Mass. (4 Met.) 49 (1842). See Levy, *op. cit. supra* note 11, at ch. 10.
37. *Commonwealth v. Hawkins*, 72 Mass. (6 Gray) 463 (1855); *Commonwealth v. Webster*, 59 Mass. (3 Cush.) 295 (1850); *Commonwealth v. York* 50 Mass. (9 Met.) 93 (1845). See Levy, *op. cit. supra* note 11, at 218–28.
38. *Commonwealth v. Rogers*, 48 Mass. (7 Met.) 500 (1844); See Levy, *op. cit. supra* note 11, at 207–18.
39. Sims' Case, 61 Mass. (7 Cush.) 285 (1851). See Levy, *Sims' Case: The Fugitive Slave Law in Boston in 1851*, J. Negro History, 35, 39–74 (1950) and Levy *op. cit. supra* note 11, at ch. 6.
40. *Roberts v. City of Boston* 59 Mass. (5 Cush.) 198 (1849). See Levy & Phillips, *The Roberts Case: Source of the 'Separate But Equal' Doctrine*, Am. Hist. Rev. 56, 510–18 (1951) and Levy, *op. cit. supra* note 11, at ch. 7.
41. *Commonwealth v. Kneeland*, 37 Mass. (20 Pick.) 206 (1838). See Levy, *Satan's Last Apostle in Massachusetts*, American Quarterly V, 16–30 (1953) and Levy, *op. cit. supra* note 11, at ch. 5.
42. *Stebbins v. Jennings*, 27 Mass. (10 Pick.) 172 (1830). See Levy, *op. cit. supra* note 11 at ch. 3.
43. *Charles River Bridge v. Warren Bridge*, 36 U.S. (11 Pet.) 420 (1837).
44. Horton, James Kent 293–95 (1939): Swisher, Roger B. Taney, 377–79 (1936).
45. *Commonwealth v. Kimball*, 41 Mass. (24 Pick.) 359, 363 (1837).
46. *Commonwealth v. Temple*, 77 Mass. (14 Gray) 69, 74 (1859).
47. Shaw, A Charge Delivered to the Grand Jury for the County of Essex, May Term 1832 15–16 (1832).
48. See notes 6 through 9, *supra*.
49. *Commonwealth v. Hunt*, 45 Mass. (4 Met.) 111 (1842).
50. The leading case is *Commonwealth v. Aves*, 35 Mass. (18 Pick.) 193 (1936). See also Betty's Case, Law Rep. XX, 455 (1857); *Commonwealth v. Fitzgerald*, Law

Rep. VII, 379 (Mass. 1844); *Commonwealth v. Porterfield,* Law Rep. VII, 256 (Mass. 1844); *Commonwealth v. Ludlum,* The Liberator (Boston) Aug. 31, 1841; *Anne v. Eames* (1836) in Report of the Holden Slave Case, Holden Anti-Slavery Society pamphlet (1839); *Commonwealth v. Howard,* Am. Jur. IX, 490 (1832).

51. *Commonwealth v. Hunt,* 45 Mass. (4 Met.) 111 (1842). See Levy, *op. cit. supra* note 11, at ch. 11.

52. Shaw, *op. cit. supra* note 47, at 7–8.

53. *Commonwealth v. Hunt,* 45 Mass. (4 Met.) 111, 130 (1842).

54. See generally Hartz, Economic Policy and Democratic Thought: Pennsylvania, 1776–1860 (1948).

55. Pound, The Spirit of the Common Law 12 (1921).

56. Shaw, *Profession of the Law in the United States.* (Extract from an address delivered before the Suffolk Bar, May, 1827) Am. Jur. VII, 56–65 (1832).

57. *Ibid*

58. *Norway Plains Co. v. Boston & Me. R.R.,* 67 Mass. (1 Gray) 263, 267 (1854).

59. Holmes, The Common Law 106 (1881).

60. Address on Chief Justice Shaw's resignation, Sept. 10, 1860, Supplement, 81 Mass. 599, 603 (1860).

61. Chafee, *Lemuel Shaw, Dictionary of American Biography.*

III

The Marshall Court

30

The Marshall Court

In 1801 the Supreme Court existed on the fringe of American awareness. Its prestige was slight, and it was more ignored than respected. On January 20, 1801, the day President John Adams nominated John Marshall for the chief justiceship, the commissioners of the District of Columbia informed Congress that the Court had no place to hold its February term. The Senate consented to the use of one of its committee rooms, and Marshall took his seat on February 4 in a small basement chamber. At the close of 1809, Benjamin Latrobe, the architect, reported that the basement had been redesigned to enlarge the courtroom and provide an office for the clerk and a library room for the Justices. In 1811, however, Latrobe reported that the Court "had been obliged to hold their sittings in a tavern," because Congress had appropriated no money for "fitting up and furnishing the Court-room. . . ." After the British burned the Capitol in 1814 Congress again neglected to provide for the Court. It held its 1815 term in a private home, and for several years after met in temporary Capitol quarters that were "little better than a dungeon." The Court moved into permanent quarters in 1819. In 1824 a New York correspondent described the Court's Capitol chamber: "In the first place, it is like going down cellar to reach it. The room is on the basement story in an obscure part of the north wing. . . . A stranger might traverse the dark avenues of the Capitol for a week, without finding the remote corner in which Justice is administered to the American Republic." He added that the courtroom was hardly large enough for a police court.

The Supreme Court, however, no longer lacked dignity or respect. It had become a force that commanded recognition. In 1819 a widely read weekly described it as so awesome that some regarded it with reverence. That year Thomas Jefferson complained that the Court had made the Constitution a "thing of wax," which it shaped as it pleased, and in 1824 he declared that the danger he most feared was the Court's "consolidation of our government." Throughout the 1820s Congress debated bills to curb the Court, which, said a senator, the people blindly adored—a "self-destroying idolatry." Alexis de Tocqueville, writing in 1831, said: "The peace, the prosperity, and the very existence of the Union are vested in the hands of the seven Federal judges. Without them, the Constitution would be a dead letter. . . ." Hardly a political question arose, he wrote, that did not become a judicial question.

Chief Justice Marshall was not solely responsible for the radical change in the Court's status and influence, but he made the difference. He bequeathed to the people of the United States what it was not in the political power of the Framers of the Constitution to give. Had the Framers been free agents, they would have proposed a national government that was unquestionably dominant over the states and possessed a formidable array of powers breathtaking in flexibility and scope. Marshall in more than a figurative sense was the supreme Framer, emancipated from a local constituency, boldly using his judicial position as an exalted platform from which to educate the nation to the true meaning, his meaning, of the Constitution. He wrote as if words of grandeur and power and union could make dreams come true. By the force of his convictions he tried to will a nation into being.

He reshaped the still malleable Constitution, giving clarification to its ambiguties and content to its omissions that would allow it to endure for "ages to come" and would make the government of the Union supreme in the federal system. Marshall is the only judge in our history whose distinction as a great nationalist statesman derives wholly from his judicial career. Justice Oliver Wendell Holmes once remarked, "If American law were to be represented by a single figure, sceptic and worshipper alike would agree without dispute that the figure could be one alone, and that one, John Marshall." That the Court had remained so weak after a decade of men of such high caliber as John Jay, Oliver Ellsworth, James Wilson, James Iredell, William Paterson, and Samuel Chase demonstrates not their weakness but Marshall's achievement in making the Court an equal branch of the national government.

Until 1807 he cast but one of six votes, and after 1807, when

Congress added another Justice, but one of seven. One Justice, one vote has always been the rule of the Court, and the powers of anyone who is Chief Justice depend more on the person than the office. From 1812, Bushrod Washington and Marshall were the only surviving Federalists, surrounded by five Justices appointed by Presidents Thomas Jefferson and James Madison; yet Marshall dominated the Court in a way that no one has ever since. During Marshall's thirty-five-year tenure, the Court delivered 1,106 opinions in all fields of law, and he wrote 519; he dissented only eight times. He wrote forty of the Court's sixty-four opinions in the field of constitutional law, dissenting only once in a constitutional case. Of the twenty-four constitutional opinions for the Court that he did not write, only two were important: *Martin v. Hunter's Lessee* (1816), a case in which he did not sit, and *Ogden v. Saunders* (1827), the case in which he dissented. He virtually monopolized the constitutional cases for himself and won the support of his associates, even though they were members of the opposing political party.

Marshall's long tenure coincided with the formative period of our constitutional law. He was in the right place at the right time, filling, as Holmes said, "a strategic place in the campaign of history." But it took the right man to make the most of the opportunity. Marshall had the character, intellect, and passion for his job that his predecessors lacked. He had a profound sense of mission comparable to a religious "calling." Convinced that he knew what the Constitution should mean and what it was meant to achieve, he determined to give its purposes enduring expression and make them prevail. The Court was, for him, a judicial pulpit and political platform from which to address the nation, to compete, if possible, with the executive and legislative in shaping public opinion.

Marshall met few of the abstract criteria for a "great" judge. A great judge should possess intellectual rectitude and brilliance. Marshall was a fierce and crafty partisan who manipulated facts and law. A great judge should have a self-conscious awareness of his biases and a determination to be as detached as human fallibility will allow. In Marshall the judicial temperament flickered weakly; unable to muzzle his deepest convictions, he sought to impose them on the nation, sure that he was right. He intoxicated himself with the belief that truth, history, and the Constitution dictated his opinions, which merely declared the law rather than made the law. A great judge should have confidence in majority rule, tempered by his commitment to personal freedom and fairness. Marshall did not think men capable of self-government and inclined to favor financial and industrial capitalism over most other interests. A great judge should have a superior technical proficiency, modified by a sense of justice and ethical behavior beyond suspicion. Marshall's judicial ethics were not unquestionable. He should have disqualified himself in *Marbury v. Madison* (1803) because of his negligent complicity. He overlooked colossal corruption in *Fletcher v. Peck* (1810) to decide a land title case by a doctrine that promoted his personal interests. He wrote the opinion in *McCulloch v. Maryland* (1819) before hearing the case. Marshall's "juridical learning," as Justice Joseph Story, his reverent admirer and closest colleague, conceded, "was not equal to that of the great masters in the profession. . . ." He was, said Story, first, last, and always, "a Federalist of the good old school," and in the maintenance of its principles "he was ready at all times to stand forth a determined advocate and supporter." He was, in short, a Federalist activist who used the Constitution to legitimate predetermined results. A great judge should have a vision of national and moral greatness, combined with respect for the federal system. Marshall had that—and an instinct for statecraft and superb literary skills. These qualities, as well as his activism, his partisanship, and his sense of mission, contributed to his inordinate influence.

So too did his qualities of leadership and his personal traits. He was generous, gentle, warm, charming, considerate, congenial, and open. At a time when members of the Court lived together in a common boarding house during their short terms in Washington, his charismatic personality enabled him to preside over a judicial family, inspire loyalty, and convert his brethren to his views. He had a cast-iron will, an astounding capacity for hard work (witness the number of opinions he wrote for the Court), and formidable powers of persuasion. He thought audaciously in terms of broad and basic principles that he expressed axiomatically as absolutes. His arguments were masterful intellectual performances, assuming that his premises were valid. Inexorably and with developing momentum he moved from an unquestioned premise to a foregone conclusion. Jefferson once said that he never admitted anything when conversing with Marshall. "So sure as you admit any position to be good, no matter how remote from the conclusion he seeks to establish, you are gone." Marshall's sophistry, according to Jefferson, was so great, "you must never give him an affirmative answer or you will be forced to grant his conclusion. Why, if he were to ask me if it were daylight or not, I'd reply, 'Sir, I don't know. I can't tell.'" Marshall could also be imperious. He sometimes gave as the opinion of the Court a position that had not mustered a majority. According to one anecdote, Marshall is supposed to have said to Story, the greatest legal scholar in our history, "That, Story, is the law. You find the precedents."

The lengthy tenure of the members of the Marshall Court also accounts for its achievements. On the pre-Marshall Court, the Justices served briefly; five quit in a decade. The Marshall Court lasted— Brockholst Livingston seventeen years, Thomas Todd nineteen, Gabriel Duvall twenty-four, William Johnson thirty, Bushrod Washington thirty-one, and Marshall outlasted them all. Story served twenty-four years with Marshall and ten more after his death; Smith Thompson served fifteen years with Marshall and eight years after. This continuity in personnel contributed to a consistent point of view in constitutional doctrine—a view that was, substantially, Marshall's. From 1812, when the average age of the Court's members was only forty-three, through 1823—twelve successive terms—the Court had the same membership, the longest period in its history without a change, and during that period the Marshall Court decided its most important cases except for *Marbury.*

Marshall also sought to strengthen the Court by inaugurating the practice of one Justice's giving the opinion of the Court. Previously the Justices had delivered their opinions seriatim, each writing an opinion in each case in the style of the English courts. That practice forced each Justice to take the trouble of understanding each case, of forming his opinion on it, and showing publicly the reasons that led to his judgment. Such were Jefferson's arguments for seriatim opinions; and Marshall understood that one official opinion augmented the Court's strength by giving the appearance of unity and harmony. Marshall realized that even if each Justice reached similar conclusions, the lines of argument and explanation of doctrine might vary with style and thought of every individual, creating uncertainty and impairing confidence in the Court as an institution. He doubtless also understood that by massing his Court behind one authoritative opinion and by assigning so many opinions to himself, his own influence as well as the Court's would be enhanced. Jefferson's first appointee, Justice Johnson, sought to buck the practice for a while. He had been surprised, he later informed Jefferson, to discover the Chief Justice "delivering all the opinions in cases in which he sat, even in some instances when contrary to his own judgment and vote." When Johnson remonstrated in vain, Marshall lectured him on the "indecency" of judges' "cutting at each other," and Johnson soon learned to acquiesce "or become such a cypher in our consultations as to effect no good at all." Story, too, learned to swallow his convictions to enhance the "authority of the Court." His "usual practice," said Story, was "to submit in silence" to opinions with which he disagreed. Even Marshall himself observed in an 1827 case, by which time he was losing control of his Court, that his usual policy when differing from majority was "to acquiesce silently in its opinion."

Like other trailblazing activist judges, Marshall squeezed a case for all it was worth, intensifying its influence. For Marshall a constitutional case was a medium for explaining his philosophy of the supreme and fundamental law, an occasion for sharing his vision of national greatness, a link between capitalism and constitutionalism, and an opportunity for a basic treatise. Justice Johnson protested in 1818, "We are constituted to decide causes, and not to discuss themes, or digest systems." He preferred, he said, to decide no more in any case "than what the case itself necessarily requires." Ordinary Justices decide only the immediate question on narrow grounds; but Marshall, confronted by some trivial question—whether a justice of the peace had a right to his commission or whether peddlers of lottery tickets could be fined—would knife to the roots of the controversy, discover that it involved some great constitutional principle, and explain it in the broadest possible way, making the case seem as if the life of the Union or the supremacy of the Constitution were at stake. His audacity in generalizing was impressive; his strategy was to take the highest ground and make unnerving use of obiter dicta; and then, as a matter of tactics, almost unnoticeably decide on narrow grounds. *Marbury* is remembered for Marshall's exposition of judicial review, not for his judicial humility in declining jurisdiction and refusing to issue the writ of mandamus. *Cohens v. Virginia* (1821) is remembered for Marshall's soaring explication of the supremacy of the judicial power of the United States, not for the decision in favor of Virginia's power to fine unlicensed lottery ticket peddlers. *Gibbons v. Ogden* (1824) is remembered for its sweeping discourse on the commerce clause of the Constitution, not for the decision that the state act conflicted with an obscure act of Congress.

Marshall's first major opinion, in *Marbury*, displayed his political cunning, suppleness in interpretation, doctrinal boldness, instinct for judicial survival, and ability to maneuver a case beyond the questions on its face. Having issued the show cause order to Madison, the Court seemingly was in an impossible position once Jefferson's supporters called that order a judicial interference with the executive branch. To decide for Marbury would provoke a crisis that the Court could not survive: Madison would ignore the Court, which had no way to enforce its decision, and the Court's enemies would have a pretext for impeachment. To decide against Marbury would appear to endorse the illegal acts of the executive branch and concede that the Court was helpless. Either course of action promised judicial humiliation and loss of independence. Marshall therefore found a way to make a tactical retreat while winning a great strategic victory for judicial power. After upbraiding the executive branch for violating Marbury's rights, Marshall concluded that the Court had no jurisdiction in the case, because a provision of an act of Congress conflicted with Article III. He held that provision unconstitutional by, first, giving it a sweeping construction its text did not bear and, second, by comparing it to his very narrow construction of Article III. Thus he reached and decided the great question, not argued by counsel, whether the Court had the power to declare unconstitutional an act of Congress. By so doing he answered from the bench his critics in Congress who, now that they were in power, had renounced judicial review during the debate on the repeal of the Judiciary Act of 1801. Characteristically Marshall relied on no precedents, not even on the authority of *The Federalist* #78. Significantly, he chose a safe act of Congress to void—section 13 of the Judiciary Act of 1789, which concerned not the province of the Congress or the President but of the Supreme Court, its authority to issue writs of mandamus in cases of original jurisdiction. But Marshall's exposition of judicial review was, characteristically, broader than the holding on section 13. Jefferson, having been given no stick with which to beat Marshall, privately fumed: "Nothing in the Constitution has given them a right to decide for the Executive, more than to the Executive to decide for them," he wrote in a letter. "The opinion which gives to the judges the right to decide what laws are constitutional, and what not, not only for themselves in their own sphere of action, but also for the Legislature and Executive also, in their spheres, would make the judiciary a despotic branch."

The Court did not dare to declare unconstitutional any other act of Congress which remained hostile to it throughout Marshall's tenure. *Stuart v. Laird* (1803), decided shortly after *Marbury,* upheld the repeal of the Judiciary Act of 1801. A contrary decision would have been institutionally suicidal for the Court. Marshall's opinion in *Marbury* was daring enough; in effect he courageously announced the Court's independence of the other branches of the government. But he was risking retaliation. Shortly before the arguments in *Marbury,* Jefferson instructed his political allies in the House to start impeachment proceedings against John Pickering, a federal district judge; the exquisite timing was a warning to the Supreme Court. Even earlier, Jeffersonian leaders in both houses of Congress openly spoke of impeaching the Justices. The threats were not idle. Two months after *Marbury* was decided, Justice Chase on circuit attacked the administration in a charge to a grand jury, and the House prepared to impeach him. Senator William Giles of Virginia the majority leader, told Senator John Quincy Adams that not only Chase "but all the other Judges of the Supreme Court," except William Johnson, "must be impeached and removed." Giles thought that holding an act of Congress unconstitutional was ground for impeachment. "Impeachment was not a criminal prosecution," according to Giles, who was Jefferson's spokesman in the Senate. "And a removal by impeachment was nothing more than a declaration by Congress to this effect: you hold dangerous opinions, and if you are suffered to carry them into effect, you will work the destruction of the Union. We want your offices for the purposes of giving them to men who will fill them better."

Intimidated by Chase's impending impeachment, Marshall, believing himself to be next in line, wrote to Chase that "impeachment should yield to an appellate jurisdiction in the legislature. A reversal of those legal opinions deemed unsound by the legislature would certainly better comport with the mildness of our character than a removal of the Judge who has rendered them unknowing of his fault." Less than a year after his *Marbury* opinion the fear of impeachment led an anguished Marshall to repudiate his reasoning and favor Congress as the final interpreter of the Constitution. Fortunately the greatest crisis in the Court's history eased when the Senate on March 1, 1805, failed to convict Chase on any of the eight articles of impeachment. Marshall and his Court were safe from an effort, never again repeated, to politicize the Court by making it subservient to Congress through impeachment.

The Court demonstrated its independence even when impeachment hung over it. In *Little v. Barreme* (1804) Marshall for the Court held that President Adams had not been authorized by Congress to order an American naval commander to seize a ship sailing from a French port. Justice Johnson on circuit vividly showed his independence of the President who had appointed him. To enforce the Embargo Acts, Jefferson had authorized port officers to refuse clearance of ships with "suspicious" cargoes. In 1808 Johnson, on circuit in Charleston, ordered the clearance of a ship and denounced the President for having exceeded the power delegated by the Embargo Acts. Jefferson could not dismiss as partisan politics Johnson's rebuke that he had acted as if he were above the law. Justice Brockholst Livingston, another Jefferson appointee, also had occasion in 1808 to show his independence of the President. Jefferson supported a federal prosecution for treason against individuals who had opposed the embargo with violence. Livingston, who presided at the trial, expressed "astonishment" that the government would resort to a theory of "constructive treason" in place of the Constitution's definition of treason as levying war against the United States and he warned against a "precedent so dangerous." The jury speedily acquitted. After the tongue-lashing from his own appointees, Jefferson won an unexpected victory in the federal courts in the case of the brig *William* (1808). Federal district judge John Davis in Massachusetts sustained the constitutionality of the Embargo Acts on commerce clause grounds. Davis, a lifelong Federalist, showed how simplistic was Jefferson's raving about judicial politics.

The evidence for the Court's nonpartisanship seems plentiful. For example, Justice Story, Madison's appointee, spoke for an independent Court in *Gelston v. Hoyt* (1818), a suit for damages against government officials whose defense was that they had acted under President Madison's orders. Story, finding no congressional authority for these orders, "refused an extension of prerogative" power and added, "It is certainly against the general theory of our institutions to create discretionary powers by implication. . . ."

On the other hand, the Court supported the theory of implied powers in *McCulloch v. Maryland* (1819), which was the occasion of

Marshall's most eloquent nationalist opinion. *McCulloch* had its antecedent in *United States v. Fisher* (1804), when the Court initially used broad construction to sustain an act of Congress that gave to the government first claim against certain insolvent debtors. Enunciating the doctrine of implied powers drawn from the necessary and proper clause, Marshall declared that Congress could employ any useful means to carry out its enumerated power to pay national debts. That the prior claim of the government interfered with state claims was an inevitable result, Marshall observed, of the supremacy of national laws. Although a precursor of *McCulloch, Fisher* attracted no opposition because it did not thwart any major state interests.

When the Court did confront such interests for the first time, in *United States v. Judge Peters* (1809), Marshall's stirring nationalist passage, aimed at states that annulled judgments of the federal courts, triggered Pennsylvania's glorification of state sovereignty and denunciation of the "unconstitutional exercise of powers in the United States Courts." The state called out its militia to prevent execution of federal judgments and recommended a constitutional amendment to establish an "impartial tribunal" to resolve conflicts between "the general and state governments." State resistance collapsed only after President Madison backed the Supreme Court. Significantly, eleven state legislatures, including Virginia's, censured Pennsylvania's doctrines and endorsed the Supreme Court as the constitutionally established tribunal to decide state disputes with the federal courts.

The *Judge Peters* episode revealed that without executive support the Court could not enforce its mandate against a hostile state, which would deny that the Court was the final arbiter under the Constitution if the state's interests were thwarted. The episode also revealed that if other states had no immediate stake in the outcome of a case, they would neither advance doctrines of state sovereignty nor repudiate the Court's supreme appellate powers. When Virginia's high court ruled that the appellate jurisdiction of the Supreme Court did not extend to court judgments and that section 25 of the Judiciary Act of 1789 was unconstitutional, the Marshall Court, dominated by Republicans, countered by sustaining the crucial statute in *Martin v. Hunter's Lessee* (1816). Pennsylvania and other states did not unite behind Virginia when it proposed the constitutional amendment initiated earlier by Pennsylvania, because *Martin* involved land titles of no interest to other states. The fact that the states were not consistently doctrinaire and became aggressive only when Court decisions adversely affected them enabled the Court to prevail in the long run. A state with a grievance typically stood alone. But for the incapacity or unwillingness of the Court's state enemies to act together in their proposals to cripple it, the great nationalist decisions of the Marshall Court would have been as impotent as the one in *Worcester v. Georgia* (1832). *Worcester* majestically upheld the supreme law against the state's despoliation of the Cherokees, but President Andrew Jackson supported Georgia, which flouted the Court. Even Georgia, however, condemned the South Carolina Ordinance of Nullification, and several state legislatures resolved that the Supreme Court was the constitutional tribunal to settle controversies between the United States and the states.

The Court made many unpopular decisions that held state acts unconstitutional. *Fletcher v. Peck,* which involved the infamous Yazoo land frauds, was the first case in which the Justices voided a state act for conflict with the Constitution itself. *Martin v. Hunter's Lessee,* which involved the title to the choice Fairfax estates in Virginia, was only the first of a line of decisions that unloosed shrill attacks on the Court's jurisdiction to decide cases on a writ of error to state courts. In *McCulloch* the Court supported the "monster monopoly," the Bank of the United States chartered by Congress, and held unconstitutional a state tax on its Baltimore branch. In *Cohens* the Court again championed its supreme appellate powers under section 25 of the Judiciary Act of 1789 and circumvented the Eleventh Amendment. In *Sturges v. Crowningshield* (1819) the Court nullified a state bankruptcy statute that aided victims of an economic panic. In *Green v. Biddle* (1821) the Court used the contract clause when voiding Kentucky acts that supported valuable land claims. In *Osborn v. Bank of the United States* (1824) it voided an Ohio act that defied *McCulloch* and raised the question whether the Constitution had provided for a tribunal capable of protecting those who executed the laws of the Union from hostile state action.

When national supremacy had not yet been established and claims of state sovereignty bottomed state statutes and state judicial decisions that the Court overthrew, state assaults on the Court were inevitable, imperiling it and the Union it defended. Virginia, the most prestigious state, led the assault which Jefferson encouraged and Spencer Roane directed. Kentucky's legislature at one point considered military force to prevent execution of the *Green* decision. State attacks were vitriolic and intense, but they were also sporadic and not united. Ten state legislatures adopted resolutions against the Marshall Court, seven of them denouncing section 25 of the 1789 Act, which was the jurisdictional foundation for the Court's power of judicial review over the states. In 1821, 1822, 1824, and 1831 bills were introduced in Congress to repeal section 25. The assault on the Court was sharpest in the Senate, whose members were chosen by the state legislatures. Some bills to curb the Court proposed a constitutional amendment to limit the tenure of the Justices. One bill would have required seriatim opinions. Others proposed that no case involving a state or a constitutional question could be decided except unanimously; others accepted a 5–2 vote. One bill proposed that the Senate should have appellate powers over the Court's decisions.

Throughout the 1820s the attempts to curb the Court created a continuing constitutional crisis that climaxed in 1831, when Marshall despondently predicted the repeal of section 25 and the dissolution of the Union. In 1831, however, the House, after a great debate, defeated a repeal bill by a vote of 138–51; Southerners cast forty-five of the votes against the Court. What saved the Court was the inability of its opponents to mass behind a single course of action; many who opposed section 25 favored a less drastic measure. The Court had stalwart defenders, of course, including Senators Daniel Webster and James Buchanan. Most important, it had won popular approbation. Although the Court had enemies in local centers of power, Americans thrilled to Marshall's paeans to the Constitution and the Union and he taught them to identify the Court with the Constitution and the Union.

A perceptible shift in the decisions toward greater tolerance for state action also helped dampen the fires under the Court in Marshall's later years. The coalition that Marshall had forged began to dissolve with the appointments of Justices Smith Thompson, John McLean, and Henry Baldwin. *Brown v. Maryland* (1827), *Martin v. Mott* (1827), *American Insurance Company v. Canter* (1828), *Weston v. Charleston* (1829), *Craig v. Missouri* (1830), and the *Cherokee Indian Cases* (1832) continued the lines of doctrine laid down by the earlier Marshall Court. But the impact of new appointments was felt in the decisions of *Ogden v. Saunders* (1827), *Willson v. Blackbird Creek Marsh Company* (1829) and *Providence Bank v. Billings* (1830). In Marshall's last decade on the Court, six decisions supported nationalist claims against seventeen for state claims. During the same decade there were ten decisions against claims based on vested rights and only one sustaining such a claim. The shift in constitutional direction may also be inferred from the inability of the Marshall Court, because of dissension and illness, to resolve *Charles River Bridge v. Warren Bridge, Mayor of New York v. Miln,* and *Briscoe v. Bank of Kentucky,* all finally decided in 1837 under Marshall's successor against the late Chief Justice's wishes. Before his last decade the only important influence on the Court resulting from the fact that Republicans had a voting majority was the repudiation of a federal common law of crimes.

What was the legacy of the Marshall Court? It established the Court as a strong institution, an equal and coordinate branch of the national government, independent of the political branches. It established itself as the authoritative interpreter of the supreme law of the land. It declared its rightful authority to hold even acts of Congress and the President unconstitutional. It maintained continuing judicial review over the states to support the supremacy of national law. In so doing, the Court sustained the constitutionality of the act of Congress chartering the Bank of the United States, laying down the definitive exposition of the doctrine of implied powers. The Court also expounded the commerce clause in *Gibbons v. Ogden* (1824), with a breadth and vigor that provided the basis for national regulation of the economy generations later. Finally, the Court made the contract clause of the Constitution into a bulwark protecting both vested rights and risk capital. *Fletcher* supported the sanctity of public land grants to private parties, encouraging capital investment and speculation in land values. *New Jersey v. Wilson* (1812) laid down the doctrine that a state grant of tax immunity constituted a contract within the protection of the Constitution, preventing subsequent state taxation for the life of the grant. *Dartmouth College v. Woodward* (1819) protected private colleges and spurred the development of state universities; it also provided the constitutional props for the expansion of the private corporation by holding that a charter of incorporation is entitled to protection of the contract clause. The Marshall Court often relied on nationalist doctrines to prevent state measures that sought to regulate or thwart corporate development. Just as national supremacy, judicial review, and the Court's appellate jurisdiction were often interlocked, so too the interests of capitalism, nationalism, and judicial review were allied. Time has hardly withered the influence and achievements of the Marshall Court.

Bibliography

Baker, Leonard 1974 *John Marshall.* New York: Macmillan.

Beveridge, Albert J. 1919 *The Life of John Marshall.* Vols. 3 and 4. Boston: Houghton Mifflin.

Corwin, Edward S. 1919 *John Marshall and the Constitution: A Chronicle of the Supreme Court.* New Haven: Yale University Press.

Haines, Charles G. 1944 *The Role of the Supreme Court in American Government and Politics, 1789–1835.* Berkeley: University of California Press.

Haskins, George Lee and Johnson, Herbert Q. 1981 *Foundations of Power: John Marshall, 1801–1815.* Volume 2 of the *Oliver Wendell Holmes Devise History of the Supreme Court of the United States.* New York: Macmillan.

Konefsky, Samuel J. 1964 *John Marshall and Alexander Hamilton.* New York: Macmillan.

Morgan, Donald G. 1954 *Justice William Johnson: The First Great Dissenter.* Columbia: University of South Carolina Press.

Warren, Charles 1923 *The Supreme Court in United States History,* 3 vols. Boston: Little, Brown.

31

Marbury v. Madison
1 Cranch 137 (1803)

Marbury has transcended its origins in the party battles between
Federalists and Republicans, achieving mythic status as the foremost
precedent for judicial review. For the first time the Court held unconstitutional an act of Congress, establishing, if only for posterity, the
doctrine that the Supreme Court has the final word among the coordinate branches of the national government in determining what is law
under the Constitution. By 1803 no one doubted that an unconstitutional act of government was null and void, but who was to judge?
What *Marbury* settled, doctrinally if not in reality, was the Court's
ultimate authority over Congress and the President. Actually, the his-
toric reputation of the case is all out of proportion to the merits of
Chief Justice John Marshall's unanimous opinion for the Court. On
the issue of judicial review, which made the case live, he said nothing
new, and his claim for the power of the Court occasioned little contemporary comment. The significance of the case in its time derived
from its political context and from the fact that the Court appeared
successfully to interfere with the executive branch. Marshall's most
remarkable accomplishment, in retrospect, was his massing of the Court
behind a poorly reasoned opinion that section 13 of the Judiciary Act
of 1789 was unconstitutional. Though the Court's legal craftsmanship
was not evident, its judicial politics—egregious partisanship and calculated expediency—was exceptionally adroit, leaving no target for
Republican retaliation beyond frustrated rhetoric.

Republican hostility to the United States courts, which were Federalist to the last man as well as Federalist in doctrine and interests, had

mounted increasingly and passed the threshold of tolerance when the Justices on circuit enforced the Sedition Act. Then the lame-duck Federalist administration passed the Judiciary Act of 1801 and, a week before Thomas Jefferson's inauguration, passed the companion act for the appointment of forty-two justices of the peace for the District of Columbia, prompting the new President to believe that "the Federalists have retired into the Judiciary as a stronghold . . . and from that battery all the works of republicanism are to be beaten down and erased." The new Circuit Court for the District of Columbia sought in vain to obtain the conviction of the editor of the administration's organ in the capital for the common law crime of seditious libel. The temperate response of the new administration was remarkable. Instead of increasing the size of the courts, especially the Supreme Court, and packing them with Republican appointees, the administration simply repealed the Judiciary Act of 1801. On taking office Jefferson also ordered that the commissions for the forty-two justices of the peace for the district be withheld, though he reappointed twenty-five, all political enemies originally appointed by President John Adams.

Marbury v. Madison arose from the refusal of the administration to deliver the commissions of four of these appointees, including one William Marbury. The Senate had confirmed the appointments and Adams had signed their commissions, which Marshall, the outgoing secretary of state, had affixed with the great seal of the United States. But in the rush of the "midnight appointments" on the evening of March 3, the last day of the outgoing administration, Marshall had neglected to deliver the commissions. Marbury and three others sought from the Supreme Court, in a case of original jurisdiction, a writ of mandamus compelling James Madison, the new secretary of state, to issue their commissions. In December 1801 the Court issued an order commanding Madison to show cause why the writ should not be issued.

A congressman reflected the Republican viewpoint when saying that the show-cause order was "a bold stroke against the Executive," and John Breckinridge, the majority leader of the Senate, thought the order "the most daring attack which the annals of Federalism have yet exhibited." When the debate began on the repeal bill, Federalists defended the show-cause order, the independence of the judiciary, and the duty of the Supreme Court to hold void any unconstitutional acts of Congress. A Republican paper declared that the "mandamus business" had first appeared to be only a contest between the judiciary and the executive but now seemed a political act by the Court to deter repeal of the 1801 legislation. In retaliation the Republicans passed the repealer and altered the terms of the Court so that it would lose its June 1802 session and not again meet until February 1803, fourteen months after the show-cause order. The Republicans hoped, as proved to be the case, that the Justices would comply with the repealer and return to circuit duty, thereby averting a showdown and a constitutional crisis, which the administration preferred to avoid.

By the time the Court met in February 1803 to hear arguments in *Marbury*, which had become a political sensation, talk of impeachment was in the air. A few days before the Court's term, Federalists in Congress moved that the Senate should produce for Marbury's benefit records of his confirmation, provoking Senator James Jackson to declare that the Senate would not interfere in the case and become "a party to an accusation which may end in an impeachment, of which the Senate were the constitutional Judges." By no coincidence, a week before the Court met, Jefferson instructed the House to impeach a U.S. District Court judge in New Hampshire, and already Federalists knew of the plan to impeach Justice Samuel Chase. Jefferson's desire to replace John Marshall with Spencer Roane was also public knowledge. Right before Marshall delivered the Court's opinion in *Marbury*, the Washington correspondent of a Republican paper wrote: "The attempt of the Supreme Court . . . by a mandamus, to control the Executive functions, is a new experiment. It seems to be no less than a commencement of war. . . . The Court must be defeated and retreat from the attack; or march on, till they incur an impeachment and removal from office."

Marshall and his Court appeared to confront unattractive alternatives. To have issued the writ, which was the expected judgment, would have been like the papal bull against the moon; Madison would have defied it, exposing the Court's impotence, and the Republicans might have a pretext for retaliation based on the Court's breach of the principle of separation of powers. To have withheld the writ would have violated the Federalist principle that the Republican administration was accountable under the law. Alexander Hamilton's newspaper reported the Court's opinion in a story headed "Constitution Violated by President," informing its readers that the new President by his first act had trampled on the charter of the peoples' liberties by unprincipled, even criminal, conduct against personal rights. Yet the Court did not issue the writ; the victorious party was Madison. But Marshall exhibited him and the President to the nation as if they were arbitrary Stuart tyrants, and then, affecting judicial humility, Marshall in obedience to the Constitution found that the Court could not obey an act of Congress that sought to aggrandize judicial powers in cases of original jurisdiction, contrary to Article III of the Constitution.

The Court was treading warily. The statute in question was not a Republican measure, not, for example, the repealer of the Judiciary Act of 1801. Indeed, shortly after *Marbury,* the Court sustained the repealer in *Stuart v. Laird* (1803) against arguments that it was unconstitutional. In that case the Court ruled that the practice of the Justices in sitting as circuit judges derived from the Judiciary Act of 1789, and therefore derived "from a contemporary interpretation of the most forcible nature," as well as from customary acquiescence. Ironically, another provision of the same statute, section 13, was at issue in *Marbury,* not that the bench and bar realized it until Marshall delivered his opinion. The offending section, passed by a Federalist Congress after being drafted by Oliver Ellsworth, one of the Constitution's Framers and Marshall's predecessor, had been the subject of previous litigation before the Court without anyone having thought it was unconstitutional. Section 13 simply authorized the Court to issue writs of *mandamus* "in cases warranted by the principles and usages of law," and that clause appeared in the context of a reference to the Court's appellate jurisdiction.

Marshall's entire argument hinged on the point that section 13 unconstitutionally extended the Court's original jurisdiction beyond the two categories of cases, specified in Article III, in which the Court was to have such jurisdiction. But for those two categories of cases, involving foreign diplomats or a state as a litigant, the Court has appellate jurisdiction. In quoting Article III, Marshall omitted the clause that directly follows as part of the same sentence: the Court has appellate jurisdiction "with such exceptions, and under such regulations as the Congress shall make." That might mean that Congress can detract from the Court's appellate jurisdiction or add to its original jurisdiction. The specification of two categories of cases in which the Court has original jurisdiction was surely intended as an irreducible minimum, but Marshall read it, by the narrowest construction, to mean a negation of congressional powers.

In any event, section 13 did not add to the Court's original jurisdiction. In effect it authorized the Court to issue writs of *mandamus* in the two categories of cases of original jurisdiction and in all appellate cases. The authority to issue such writs did not extend or add to the Court's jurisdiction; the writ of *mandamus* is merely a remedial device by which courts implement their existing jurisdiction. Marshall misinterpreted the statute and Article III, as well as the nature of the writ, in order to find that the statute conflicted with Article III. Had the Court employed the reasoning of *Stuart v. Laird* or the rule that the Court should hold a statute void only in a clear case, giving every presumption of validity in doubtful cases, Marshall could not have reached his conclusion that section 13 was unconstitutional. That conclusion allowed him to decide that the Court was powerless to issue the writ because Marbury had sued for it in a case of original jurisdiction.

Marshall could have said, simply, this is a case of original jurisdiction but it does not fall within either of the two categories of original jurisdiction specified in Article III; therefore we cannot decide: writ denied, case dismissed. Section 13 need never have entered the opinion, although, alternatively, Marshall could have declared: section 13 authorizes this Court to issue such writs only in cases warranted by the principles and usages of law; we have no jurisdiction here because we are not hearing the case in our appellate capacity and it is not one of the two categories in which we possess original jurisdiction: writ denied, case dismissed. Even if Marshall had to find that the statute augmented the Court's original jurisdiction, the ambiguity of the clause in Article III, which he neglected to quote, justified sustaining the statute.

Holding section 13 unconstitutional enabled Marshall to refuse an extension of the Court's powers and award the judgment to Madison, thus denying the administration a pretext for vengeance. Marshall also used the case to answer Republican arguments that the Court did not and should not have the power to declare an act of Congress unconstitutional, though he carefully chose an inoffensive section of a Federalist statute that pertained merely to writs of mandamus. That he gave his doctrine of judicial review the support of only abstract logic, without reference to history or precedents, was characteristic, as was the fact that his doctrine swept way beyond the statute that provoked it.

If Marshall had merely wanted a safe platform from which to espouse and exercise judicial review, he would have begun his opinion with the problems that section 13 posed for the Court; but he reached the question of constitutionality and of judicial review at the tail-end of his opinion. Although he concluded that the Court had to discharge the show-cause order, because it lacked jurisdiction, he first and most irregularly passed judgment on the merits of the case. Everything said on the merits was obiter dicta and should not have been said at all, given the judgment. Most of the opinion dealt with Marbury's unquestionable right to his commission and the correctness of the remedy he had sought by way of a writ of mandamus. In his elaborate discourse on those matters, Marshall assailed the President and his cabinet officer for their lawlessness. Before telling Marbury that he had initiated his case in the wrong court, Marshall engaged in what Edward S. Corwin called "a deliberate partisan *coup.*" Then Marshall followed with a "judicial *coup d'état,*" in the words of Albert J. Beveridge, on the constitutional issue that neither party had argued.

The partisan *coup* by which Marshall denounced the executive branch, not the grand declaration of the doctrine of judicial review for which the case is remembered, was the focus of contemporary excitement. Only the passages on judicial review survive. Cases on the removal power of the President, especially concerning inferior appointees, cast doubt on the validity of the dicta by which Marshall lectured the executive branch on its responsibilities under the law. Moreover, by statute and by judicial practice the Supreme Court exercises the authority to issue writs of mandamus in all appellate cases and in the two categories of cases of original jurisdiction. Over the passage of time *Marbury* came to stand for the monumental principle, so distinctive and dominant a feature of our constitutional system, that the Court may bind the coordinate branches of the national government to its rulings on what is the supreme law of the land. That principle stands out from *Marbury* like the grin on the Cheshire cat; all else, which preoccupied national attention in 1803, disappeared in our constitutional law. So too might have disappeared national judicial review if the impeachment of Chase had succeeded.

Marshall himself was prepared to submit to review of Supreme Court opinions by Congress. He was so shaken by the impeachment of Chase and by the thought that he himself might be the next victim in the event of Chase's conviction, that he wrote to Chase on January 23, 1804: "I think the modern doctrine of impeachment should yield to an appellate jurisdiction in the legislature. A reversal of those legal opinions deemed unsound by the legislature would certainly better comport with the mildness of our character than a removal of the judge who has rendered them unknowing of his fault." The acquittal of Chase meant that the Court could remain independent, that Marshall had no need to announce publicly his desperate plan for congressional review of the Court, and that *Marbury* remained as a precedent. Considering that the Court did not again hold unconstitutional an act of Congress until 1857, when it decided *Dred Scott v. Sandford,* sixty-eight years would have passed since 1789 without such a holding, and but for *Marbury,* after so long a period of congressional omnipotence, national judicial review might never have been established.

Bibliography

Beveridge, Albert J. 1916–1919 *The Life of John Marshall,* 4 vols. Vol. III:50–178. Boston: Houghton Mifflin.

Corwin, Edward S. 1914 *The Doctrine of Judicial Review.* Pages 1–78. Princeton, N.J.: Princeton University Press.

Haines, Charles Grove 1944 *The Role of the Supreme Court in American Government and Politics, 1789–1835.* Pages 223–258. Berkeley: University of California Press.

Van Alstyne, William W. 1969 A Critical Guide to *Marbury v. Madison. Duke Law Journal* 1969:1–47.

Warren, Charles 1923 *The Supreme Court in United States History,* 3 vols. Vol. I:200–268. Boston Little, Brown.

32

Federal Common Law of Crimes

One of the leading Jeffersonian jurists, St. George Tucker, noted with alarm that Chief Justice Oliver Ellsworth and Justice Bushrod Washington had laid down the general rule that the common law was the unwritten law of the United States government. The question whether the Constitution adopted the common law, Tucker wrote,

is of very great importance, not only as it regards the limits of the jurisdiction of the *federal courts;* but also, as it relates to the extent of the powers vested in the *federal government.* For, if it be true that the common law of England has been adopted by the United States in their national, or federal capacity, the jurisdiction of the *federal courts* must be co-extensive with it; or, in other words, *unlimited:* so also, must be the jurisdiction, and authority of the *other branches* of the federal government [Tucker, *Blackstone's Commentaries,* 1803, I, 380].

Tucker's answer to the question was that the judicial power of the United States under Article III was limited to the subjects of congressional legislative power and that common law did not give jurisdiction in any case where jurisdiction was not expressly given by the Constitution. Tucker's view eventually prevailed, but it was probably not the view of the Constitution's Framers.

Article III extends the judicial power of the United States to all cases in law and equity arising under the Constitution, treaties, and "Laws of the United States." The latter phrase could include common law crimes. At the Constitutional Convention of 1787, the Committee of Detail reported a draft declaring that the Supreme Court's jurisdiction extended to "all Cases arising under the Laws passed by the Legislature of the United States." The Convention without dissenting vote adopted a motion striking out the words "passed by the Legislature." That deletion suggests that "the Laws of the United States" comprehended the common law of crimes, as well as other nonstatutory law.

The legislative history of the Judiciary Act of 1789 suggests a similar conclusion. A draft of that statute relating to the jurisdiction of both the federal district and federal circuit courts (sections nine and eleven as enacted) gave these courts "cognizance of all crimes and offenses that shall be cognizable under the authority of the United States and *defined by the laws of the same.*" The italicized phrase, deleted from the act's final text, might have restricted criminal jurisdiction to statutory crimes. Whether a federal court was to apply a federal common law of crimes or apply the common law of the state in which a crime was committed is not clear.

What is clear is that the first generation of federal judges assumed jurisdiction in cases of nonstatutory crimes. Justice James Wilson, an influential Framer of the Constitution, at his state's ratifying convention had endorsed federal prosecutions at common law for criminal libels against the United States. In 1793 he instructed a federal grand jury on the virtues of the common law, which included, he said, the law of nations. The grand jury indicted Gideon Henfield for breaching American neutrality by assisting a French privateer in the capture of a British ship; the indictment referred to violation of the laws of nations, against the laws and constitution of the United States and against the peace and dignity of the United States. Alexander Hamilton prepared the indictment, which Attorney General Edmund Randolph (another Framer) helped prosecute. Justice Wilson, joined by Justice James Iredell and Judge Richard Peters, constituted the federal circuit court that tried Henfield's nonstatutory offense. Henfield, having been at sea when President George Washington proclaimed American neutrality, pleaded ignorance. Secretary of State Thomas Jefferson, who had urged Henfield's prosecution and endorsed Wilson's opinion as to the indictability of the offense, explained that the jury acquitted because the crime was not knowingly committed. John Marshall, in his *Life of Washington,* described the prosecution as having been based on an offense "indictable at common law, for disturbing the peace of the United States."

Subsequent common law prosecutions were not so fuzzy. In 1793 a federal grand jury indicted Joseph Ravara, a consul from Genoa, for attempting to extort money from a British diplomat. Justice Wilson, joined by Peters, ruled that the circuit court had jurisdiction, although Congress had passed no law against extortion. Justice Iredell argued that the defendant's diplomatic status brought him within the exclusive original jurisdiction of the Supreme Court. Ravara was tried in 1794 by a circuit court consisting of Jay and Peters, who instructed the jury that the offense was indictable at common law, part of the law of the land. The jury convicted. In 1795 a federal court in New York, at the instigation of Attorney General Randolph, indicted Greenleaf, the editor of the *New York Journal,* for criminal libel, a common law crime. The case was dropped, but in 1797 the editor was again indicted for the same crime and convicted by a court presided over by Chief Justice Oliver Ellsworth, an influential Framer and chief author of the Judiciary Act of 1789. In Massachusetts in 1797 Ellsworth ruled that the federal circuit court possessed jurisdiction over crimes against the common law, which the laws of the United States included, and therefore might try persons indicted for counterfeiting notes of the Bank of the United States (not then a statutory offense).

In the same year a federal grand jury followed Justice Iredell's charge and indicted a congressman, Samuel J. Cabell, for the common law crime of seditious libel, but the prosecution was aborted for political reasons. In 1798, before Congress passed the Sedition Act, prosecutions for seditious libel were begun against Benjamin Bache, who soon died, and John Burke, who fled the country before Justice William Paterson could try him. In 1799 Ellsworth and Iredell, in separate cases, told federal grand juries that the federal courts had common law jurisdiction over seditious libel and, in Ellsworth's words, over "acts manifestly subversive of the national government." He added that an indictable offense need be defined only by common law, not statute.

The sole dissenting voice in this line of decision was that of Justice Samuel Chase in *Worrall's Case* (1798), where the common law indictment was for attempted bribery of a federal official. Judge Peters disagreed with Chase's argument that no federal common law of crimes existed, and the jury convicted. Chase, however, changed his opinion in *United States v. Sylvester* (1799), when he presided over a common law prosecution for counterfeiting. Thus, Chief Justices Jay and Ellsworth and Justices Wilson, Paterson, Iredell, and Chase endorsed federal court jurisdiction over common law crimes. The Jeffersonians, by then, vehemently opposed such views, arguing that only the state courts could try common law crimes. When Jefferson was President, however, Judge Pierpont Edwards, whom he had appointed to the federal district court in Connecticut, sought and received common law indictments against several persons for seditious libel against the President and the government. Jefferson knew of the common law prosecutions by the federal court and did not criticize them or take any actions to halt them, until he learned that one of the defendants could prove the truth of his accusation that the President had once engaged in a sexual indiscretion. The prosecutions were dropped except for those against Hudson and Goodwin, editors of Hartford's *Connecticut Courant,* who challenged the jurisdiction of the federal court.

By this time the administration had a stake in a ruling against federal jurisdiction over common law crimes. After much government stalling until a majority of Jeffersonian appointees controlled the Supreme Court, *United States v. Hudson and Goodwin* was finally decided in 1812. Without hearing oral arguments and against all the precedents, a bare majority of the Court, in a brief opinion by Justice William Johnson, ruled that the question whether the federal courts "can exercise a common law jurisdiction in criminal cases" has been "settled in public opinion," which opposed such jurisdiction. Moreover, the Constitution had not expressly delegated to the federal courts authority over common law crimes. "The legislative authority of the Union must first make an act a crime, affix a punishment to it, and declare the Court that shall have jurisdiction of the offense." Justice Joseph Story, who had not made known his dissent at the time, did so in a circuit opinion in 1813 and forced a reconsideration of the rule of *Hudson and Goodwin.* In *United States v. Coolidge* (1816), decided without argument, Johnson, noting that the Court was still divided (Marshall and Washington probably supported Story), refused to review the 1812 decision in the absence of "solemn argument." Thus the great question was resolved without reasoned consideration, to the enormous detriment of the power of the United States courts to define criminal acts.

Although "judge-made" or nonstatutory federal crimes disappeared after the *Coolidge* decision, federal courts continued to exercise common law powers to enforce law and order within their own precincts and continued to employ a variety of common law techniques, forms, and writs in the enforcement of congressionally defined crimes. The Federal Rules of Criminal Procedure reflect that fact, as does *Marshall v. United States* (1959). By its "supervisory powers" over lower federal courts and, through them, over federal law enforcement officers, the Supreme Court can still be said, loosely, to exercise an interstitial common law authority with respect to federal crimes.

Bibliography

Crosskey, William W. 1953 *Politics and the Constitution in the History of the United States,* 2 vols. Chaps. 20-24. Chicago: University of Chicago Press.

Goebel, Julius, Jr. 1971—*Antecedents and Beginnings to 1801.* Volume 1 of Freund, Paul, ed., *The Oliver Wendell Holmes Devise History of the Supreme Court.* New York: Macmillan.

Presser, Stephen B. 1978 A Tale of Two Judges: Richard Peters, Samuel Chase, and the Broken Promise of Federalist Jurisprudence." *Northwestern Law Review* 73:26–111.

Tucker, St. George 1803 *Blackstones Commentaries, with Notes of Reference to the Constitution and Laws of the Federal Government of the United States and of the Commonwealth of Virginia,* 5 vols. Philadelphia: Young & Small.

Warren, Charles 1923 "New Light on the History of the Federal Judiciary Act of 1789." *Harvard Law Review* 37:49–132.

Wharton, Francis, ed. 1849(1970) *State Trials of the United States During the Administrations of Washington and Adams.* New York: Burt Franklin.

33

Three Contract Clause Cases

New Jersey v. Wilson
7 Cranch 164 (1812)

This case was the vehicle by which the Supreme Court made a breathtaking expansion of the contract clause. In the colonial period New Jersey had granted certain lands to an Indian tribe in exchange for a waiver by the Indians of their claim to any other lands. The grant provided that the new lands would be exempt from taxation in perpetuity. In 1801, over forty years later, the Indians left the state after selling their lands with state permission. The legislature repealed the tax exemption statute and assessed the new owners, who challenged the constitutionality of the repeal act.

A unanimous Supreme Court, overruling the state court, held that the grant of a tax immunity was a contract protected by the contract clause. By some species of metaphysics the Court reasoned that the tax immunity attached to the land, not to the Indians, and therefore the new holders of the land were tax exempt. Chief Justice John Marshall's opinion, voiding the state tax, gave a retroactive operation to the contract clause; the grant of tax immunity predated the clause by many years. More important, Marshall ignored the implications of his doctrine that such a grant was a contract. According to this decision, a state, by an act of its legislature, may contract away its sovereign power of taxation and prevent a successive legislature from asserting that power. The doctrine of vested rights, here converted into a doctrine of tax immunity, handicapped the revenue capabilities of the states, raising grave questions about the policy of the opinion. As a matter of political or constitutional theory, the Court's assumption that an attribute of sovereignty can be surrendered by a legislative grant to private parties or to their property was, at the least, dubious. Although Marshall restricted the states, he allowed them to cede tax powers by contract rather than thwart the exercise of those powers on rights vested by contract.

The growth of corporations revealed the significance of the new doctrine of tax immunity. States and municipalities, eager to promote the establishment of banks, factories, turnpikes, railroads, and utilities, often granted corporations tax immunity or other tax advantages as an inducement to engage in such enterprises, and the corporations often secured their special privileges by corrupt methods. This case permitted the granting of tax preferences and constitutionally sanctioned political corruption and the reckless development of economic resources. But permission is not compulsion; the legislatures, not the judiciary, granted the contracts. The Court simply extended the contract clause beyond the intentions of its framers to protect vested rights and promote business needs.

Fletcher v. Peck
6 Cranch 87 (1810)

Fletcher was the Court's point of departure for converting the contract clause into the chief link between the Constitution and capitalism. The case arose from the Yazoo land scandal, the greatest corrupt real estate deal in American history. Georgia claimed the territory within her latitude lines westward to the Mississippi, and in 1795 the state legislature passed a bill selling about two-thirds of that so-called Yazoo territory, some 35,000,000 acres of remote wilderness comprising a good part of the present states of Alabama and Mississippi. Four land companies, having bribed every voting member of the state legislature but one, bought the Yazoo territory at a penny and a half an acre. Speculation in land values was a leading form of capitalist enterprise at that time, provoking an English visitor to characterize the United States as "the land of speculation." Respectable citizens engaged in the practice; the piratical companies that bought the Yazoo included two United States senators, some governors and congressmen, and

Justice James Wilson. In a year, one of the four companies sold its Yazoo holdings at a 650 percent profit, and the buyers, in the frenzy of speculation that followed, resold at a profit. But in 1796 the voters of Georgia elected a "clean" legislature which voided the bill of sale and publicly burned all records of it but did not return the $500,000 purchase price. In 1802 Georgia sold its western territories to the United States for $1,250,000. In 1814 a Yazooist lobby finally succeeded in persuading Congress to pass a $5,000,000 compensation bill, indemnifying holders of Yazoo land titles."

Fletcher v. Peck was part of a twenty-year process of legal and political shenanigans related to the Yazoo land scandal. Georgia's nullification of the original sale imperiled the entire chain of Yazoo land speculations, but the Eleventh Amendment made Georgia immune to a suit. A feigned case was arranged. Peck of Massachusetts sold 15,000 acres of Yazoo land to Fletcher of New Hampshire. Fletcher promptly sued Peck for recovery of his $3,000, claiming that Georgia's nullification of the sale had destroyed Peck's title: the acreage was not his to sell. Actually, both parties shared the same interest in seeking a judicial decision against Georgia's nullification of the land titles—the repeal act of 1796. Thus, by a collusive suit based on diversity of citizenship, a case involving the repeal act got into the federal courts and ultimately reached the Supreme Court. The Court's opinion, by Chief Justice John Marshall, followed the contours of Justice William Paterson's charge in *Van Horne's Lessee v. Dorrance* (1795).

Although the fraud that infected the original land grants was the greatest scandal of the time, the Court refused to make an exception to the principle that the judiciary could not properly investigate the motives of a legislative body. The Court also justifiably held that "innocent" third parties should not suffer an annihilation of their property rights as a result of the original fraud. The importance of the case derives from the Court's resolution of the constitutionality of the repeal act.

Alternating in his reasoning between extraconstitutional or higher law principles and constitutional or textual ones, Marshall said that the repealer was invalid. Before reaching the question whether a contract existed that the Constitution protected, he announced this doctrine: "When, then, a law is in its nature a contract, when absolute rights have been vested under that contract, a repeal of the law cannot devest those rights. . . ." In the next sentence he asserted that "the nature of society and of government" limits legislative power. This higher law doctrine of judicially inferred limitations protecting vested rights was the sole basis of Justice William Johnson's concurring opinion. A state has no power to revoke its grants, he declared, resting his case "on a general principle, on the reason and nature of things: a principle which will impose laws even on the Deity." Explicitly Johnson stated that his opinion was not founded on the Constitution's provision against state impairment of the obligation of contracts. The difficulty, he thought, arose from the word "obligation," which ceased once a grant of lands had been executed.

The difficultly with Marshall's contract clause theory was greater than even Johnson made out. The clause was intended to prevent state impairment of executory contracts between private individuals; it had been modeled on the provision of the Northwest Ordinance, which had referred to "private contracts, or engagements *bona fide,* and without fraud previously formed." What was the contract in this case? If there was one, did its obligation still exist at the time of the repeal bill? Was it a contract protected by the contract clause, given that it was a land grant to which the state was a party? If the land grant was a contract, it was a public executed one, not a private executory one. The duties that the parties had assumed toward each other had been fulfilled, the deal consummated. That is why Johnson could find no continuing obligation. Moreover, the obligation of a contract is a creature of state law, and the state in this instance, sustained by its courts, had recognized no obligation.

Marshall overcame all difficulties by employing slippery reasoning. A contract, he observed, is either executory or executed; if executed, its object has been performed. The contract between the state and the Yazoo land buyers had been executed by the grant. But, he added, an executed contract, as well as an executory one, "contains obligations binding on the parties." The grant had extinguished the right of the grantor in the title to the lands and "implies a contract not to reassert that right." Moreover, the Constitution uses only the term "contract, without distinguishing between those which are executory and those which are executed." Having inferred from the higher law that a grant carried a continuing obligation not to repossess, he declined to make a distinction that, he said, the Constitution had not made. Similarly he concluded that the language of the contract clause, referring generally to "contracts," protected public as well as private contracts. Marshall apparently realized that the disembodied or abstract higher law doctrine on which Johnson relied would provide an insecure bastion for property holders and a nebulous precedent for courts to follow. So he found a home for the vested rights doctrine in the text of the Constitution.

Marshall seemed, however, to be unsure of the text, because he flirted with the bans on bills of attainder and ex post facto laws, giving the impression that Georgia's repeal act somehow ran afoul of those bans, too, although the suit was a civil one. Marshall's uncertainty emerged in his conclusion. He had no doubt that the repeal act was invalid, but his ambiguous summation referred to both extraconstitutional principles and the text: Georgia "was restrained, either by general principles which are common to our free institutions, or by the particular provisions of the Constitution. . . ." He did not, in the end, specify the particular provisions.

In the first contract clause decision by the Court, that clause became a repository of the higher law doctrine of vested rights and operated to cover even public, executed contracts. The Court had found a constitutional shield for vested rights. And, by expanding the protection offered by the contract clause, the Court invited more cases to be brought before the judiciary, expanding opportunities for judicial review against state legislation.

Bibliography

Magrath, C. Peter 1966 *Yazoo: Law and Politics in the New Republic, The Case of Fletcher v. Peck.* Providence, R.I.: Brown University Press.

Dartmouth College v. Woodward
4 Wheaton 518 (1819)

The most famous and influential contract clause case in our history, *Dartmouth College* was a boon to higher education and to corporate capitalism. The case established the doctrine, never overruled, that a corporation charter or the grant by a state of corporate rights to private interests comes within the protection of the contract clause. Although the case involved a small college in New Hampshire rather than a manufacturing concern, a bank, or a transportation company, the Court seized an opportunity to broaden the contract clause by making all private corporations its beneficiaries. Daniel Webster, counsel for the college, said that the judgment was a "defense of vested rights against Courts and Sovereignties," and his co-counsel, Joseph Hopkinson, asserted that it would "secure corporations . . . from legislative despotism. . . ." Corporations were still a recent innovation; James Kent, in his *Commentaries on American Law* (1826), remarked that their rapid multiplication and the avidity with which they were sought by charter from the states arose as a result of the power that large, consolidated capital gave them over business of every sort. The Court's decision in the Dartmouth College case, Kent said, more than any other act proceeding from the authority of the United States, threw "an impregnable barrier around all rights and franchises derived from the grant of government; and [gave] solidity and inviolability to the literary, charitable, religious, and commercial institutions of our country." Actually, *Fletcher v. Peck* (1810) had made the crucial and original extension of the contract clause, construing it to cover public and executed contracts as well as private executory ones. The *Dartmouth College* doctrine was a logical implication.

The college case was a strange vehicle for the doctrine that emerged from it. Dartmouth, having been chartered in 1769 in the name of the crown to christianize and educate Indians, had become a Christian college for whites and a stronghold of the Congregationalist Church, which had benefited most from the laws establishing the Protestant religion in New Hampshire. The college had become embroiled in state politics on the side of the Federalists, who supported the establishment. When in 1815 the trustees removed the president of the college, they loosed a controversy that drew to the ousted president a coalition of Jeffersonians and religious denominations demanding separation of church and state. The reformers having swept the state elections in 1816, the legislature sought to democratize the college by a series of statutes that converted it into a state university under public control, rather than a private college as provided by the original charter. The state supreme court sustained the state acts, reasoning that the institution had been established with public aid for public purposes of an educational and religious nature. The state court held that the contract clause did not limit the state's power over its own public corporations.

On appeal, the Supreme Court held that Dartmouth was a private eleemosynary corporation whose vested rights could not be divested without infringing a continuing obligation to respect inviolably the trustees' control of property given to the corporation for the advancement of its objectives. The Court held unconstitutional the state acts subjecting Dartmouth to state control and ordered Woodward, the treasurer of the institution who had sided with the state, to return to the trustees the records, corporate seal, and other corporate property which he held.

At every step of his opinion Chief Justice John Marshall misstated the facts about the history of the original charter in order to prove that it established a purely private corporation. That, perhaps, was a matter primarily of interest to the college, which, contrary to Marshall, had received its charter not from George III but from the governor of the colony; moreover, the private donations, which Marshall said had been given to Dartmouth on condition of receiving the charter, had been given unconditionally to an entirely different institution, Moor's Charity School for Indians, and had been transferred to Dartmouth over the donors' objections. Also, the funds of the college, contrary to Marshall, did not consist "entirely of private donations," because the endowment of the college at the time of the issuance of the chapter derived mainly from grants of public lands. Even if the grant of the charter were a contract, as Marshall said it "plainly" was, Parliament could have repealed it at will. The Chief Justice conceded the fact but added that a repeal would have been morally perfidious. If, however, the charter were subject to revocation at the will of the sovereign authority, or the grantor, the "contract" did not bind that party and created no obligation that could be impaired.

Marshall conceded that at the time of Independence, the state succeeded to the power of Parliament and might have repealed or altered the charter at any time before the adoption of the Constitution. The provision in Article I, section 10, preventing states from impairing the obligation of a contract, altered the situation. That clause, Marshall conceded, was not specifically intended to protect charters of incorporation: "It is," he said boldly, "more than possible that the preservation of rights of this description was not particularly in the view of the framers of the constitution," but the clause admitted no exceptions as far as private rights were concerned. "It is not enough to say that this particular case was not in the mind of the convention when the article was framed, nor of the American people when it was adopted." In the absence of proof that the language of the Constitution would have been altered had charters of incorporation been considered, the case came within its injunction against state acts impairing the obligation of contracts.

Although Marshall can be doubted when he said, "It can require no argument to prove that the circumstances of this case constitute a contract," his general doctrine, that any state charter for a private corporation is a constitutionally protected contract, was not far-fetched. The Court must construe the text, not the minds of its framers, and, as he said, "There is no exception in the constitution, no sentiment delivered by its contemporaneous expounders, which would justify us in making it." If a state granted a charter of incorporation to private interests, the charter has "every ingredient of a complete and legitimate contract," should it be made on a valuable consideration for the security and disposition of the property conveyed to the corporation for management by its trustees in perpetuity. Unless, as Justice Joseph Story stressed in his concurring opinion, the government should reserve, in the grant of the charter, a power to alter, modify, or repeal, the rights vested cannot be divested, except by the consent of the incorporators, assuming they have not defaulted. Whether, however, a modification of the charter, as in this case, impairs an obligation, if the charter be executed and by its terms should not specify a term of years for the corporation's existence, is another question. In *Fletcher v. Peck,* however, the Court had brought executed as well as public contracts within the meaning of the contract clause. Marshall construed contract rights sweepingly, state powers narrowly.

Max Lerner's comment on the case, referring to Webster's peroration, is provocative. "Every schoolboy," he wrote, "knows Webster's eloquent plea and how Marshall, whom the Yazoo land scandals had left cold, found his own eyes suffused with tears, as Webster, overcome by the emotion of his words, wept. But few schoolboys know that the case had ultimately less to do with colleges than with business corporations; that sanctity of contract was invoked to give them immunity against legislative control, and that business enterprise in America never had more useful mercenaries than the tears Daniel Webster and John Marshall are reputed to have shed so devotedly that March day in Washington. . . ." In fact, the reserved power to alter or repeal, of which Story spoke, limited corporate immunity from legislative control. Moreover, the protection given by the Court to corporate charters came into play after the legislatures, not the Court, issued these charters, often recklessly and corruptly, without consideration of the public good; Marshall's opinion should have put the legislatures and the public on guard. Finally, the case had a great deal to do with higher education as well as business. Dartmouth College is the Magna Carta of private colleges and universities, and, by putting them beyond state control, provided a powerful stimulus, not only to business corporations but also to the chartering of state institutions of higher learning. Unable to make private institutions public ones, the states established state universities.

Bibliography

Beveridge, Albert J. 1916–1919 *The Life of John Marshall,* 4 vols. Vol. IV:220–281. Boston: Little, Brown.

Haines, Charles Grove 1944 *The Role of the Supreme Court in American Government and Politics, 1789–1835.* Pages 378–419. Berkeley: University of California Press.

Shirley, John M. (1879)1971 *The Dartmouth College Causes and the Supreme Court.* New York: Da Capo Press.

Stites, Francis N. 1972 *Private Interest and Public Gain: The Dartmouth College Case, 1819.* Amherst: University of Massachusetts Press.

34

Martin v. Hunter's Lessee
1 Wheaton 304 (1816)

Appomattox ultimately settled the issue that bottomed this case: were the states or was the nation supreme? As a matter of law, the opinion of the Supreme Court supplied the definitive answer, but law cannot settle a conflict between competing governments unless they agree to abide by the decision of a tribunal they recognize as having jurisdiction to decide. Whether such a tribunal existed was the very issue in this case; more precisely the question was whether the Supreme Court's appellate jurisdiction extended to the state courts. In 1810 Virginia had supported the Court against state sovereignty advocates. Pennsylvania's legislature had resolved that "no provision is made in the Constitution for determining disputes between the general and state governments by an impartial tribunal." To that Virginia replied that the Constitution provides such a tribunal, "the Supreme Court, more eminently qualified . . . to decide the disputes aforesaid in an enlightened and impartial manner, than any other tribunal which could be erected. (See *United States v. Judge Peters,* 1809.) The events connected with the *Martin* case persuaded Virginia to reverse its position. The highest court of the state, the Virginia Court of Appeals, defied the Supreme Court, subverted the judicial power of the United States as defined by Article III of the Constitution, circumvented the supremacy clause (Article VI), and held unconstitutional a major act of Congress—all for the purpose of repudiating judicial review, or the Supreme Court's appellate jurisdiction over state courts and power to declare state acts void.

The *Martin* case arose out of a complicated and protracted legal struggle over land titles. Lord Fairfax died in 1781, bequeathing valuable tracts of his property in Virginia's Northern Neck to his nephew, Denny Martin, a British subject residing in England. During the Revolution Virginia had confiscated Loyalist estates and by an act of 1779, which prohibited alien enemies from holding land, declared the escheat, or reversion to the state, of estates then owned by British subjects. That act of 1779 did not apply to the estates of Lord Fairfax, who had been a Virginia citizen. The Treaty of Peace with Great Britain in 1783, calling for the restitution of all confiscated estates and prohibiting further confiscations, strengthened Martin's claim under the will of his uncle. In 1785, however, Virginia had extended its escheat law of 1779 to the Northern Neck, and four years later had granted some of those lands to one David Hunter. Jay's Treaty of 1794, which protected the American property of British subjects, also buttressed Martin's claims. By then a Virginia district court, which included Judge St. George Tucker, decided in Martin's favor; Hunter appealed to the state's high court. John Marshall, who had represented Martin, and James Marshall, his brother, joined a syndicate that arranged to purchase the Northern Neck lands. In 1796 the state legislature offered a compromise, which the Marshall syndicate accepted: the Fairfax devisees relinquished claim to the undeveloped lands of the Northern Neck in return for the state's recognition of their claim to Fairfax's manor lands. The Marshall syndicate accepted the compromise, thereby seeming to secure Hunter's claim, yet thereafter completed their purchase. In 1806, Martin's heir conveyed the lands to the syndicate, and in 1808 he appealed to the Court of Appeals, which decided in favor of Hunter two years later.

The Martin-Marshall interests, relying on the Treaty of 1783 and Jay's Treaty, took the case to the Supreme Court on a writ of error under section 25 of the Judiciary Act of 1789. That section provided in part that the nation's highest tribunal on writ of error might reexamine and reverse or affirm the final judgment of a state court if the state court sustained a state statute against a claim that the statute was repugnant to the Constitution, treaties, or laws of the United States, or if the state court decided against any title or right claimed under the treaties or federal authority. Chief Justice Marshall took no part in the case, and two other Justices were absent. Justice Joseph Story, for a three-member majority and against the dissenting vote of Justice William Johnson, reversed the judgment of the Virginia Court of Appeals, holding that federal treaties confirmed Martin's title. In the course of his opinion Story sapped the Virginia statutes escheating the lands of alien enemies and ignored the "compromise" of 1796. The mandate of the Supreme Court to the state Court of Appeals concluded: "You therefore are hereby commanded that such proceedings be had in said cause, as according to right and justice, and the laws of the United States, and agreeable to said judgment and instructions of said Supreme Court . . ." *(Fairfax's Devisee v. Hunter's Lessee,* 1813).

The state court that received this mandate consisted of eminent and proud men who regarded the Supreme Court as a rival; the man who dominated the state court was Spencer Roane, whose opinion Story had reversed. Roane, the son-in-law of Patrick Henry, was not just a judge; he was a state political boss, an implacable enemy of John Marshall, and the man whom Thomas Jefferson would have appointed Chief Justice, given the chance. To Roane and his brethren, Story's opinion was more than an insulting encroachment on their judicial prerogatives. It raised the specter of national consolidation, provoking the need to rally around the states' rights principles of the Virginia and Kentucky Resolutions. Roane consulted with Jefferson and James Monroe, and he called before his court the leading members of the state bar, who spoke for six days. Munford, the Virginia court reporter, observed: "The question whether this mandate should be obeyed excited all that attention from the Bench and Bar which its great importance truly merited." The reporter added that the court had its opinions ready for delivery shortly after the arguments. That was in April 1814, when the Republican political organization of Virginia dared not say anything that would encourage or countenance the states' rights doctrines of Federalist New England, which opposed the War of 1812 and thwarted national policies. Not until December 1815, when the crisis had passed and secessionism in the North had dissipated, did the Virginia Court of Appeals release its opinions.

Each of four state judges wrote opinions, agreeing that the Constitution had established a federal system in which sovereignty was divided between the national and state governments, neither of which could control the other or any of its organs. To allow the United States or any of its departments to operate directly on the states or any of their departments would subvert the independence of the states, allow the creature to judge its creators, and destroy the idea of a national government of limited powers. Although conflicts between the states and the United States were inevitable, the Constitution "has provided no umpire" and did not authorize Congress to bestow on the Supreme Court a power to pass final judgment on the extent of the powers of the United States or of its own appellate jurisdiction. Nothing in the Constitution denied the power of a state court to pass finally upon the validity of state legislation. The states could hold the United States to the terms of the compact only if the state courts had the power to determine finally the constitutionality of acts of Congress. Section 25 of the Judiciary Act was unconstitutional because it vested appellate powers in the Supreme Court in a case where the highest court of a state has authoritatively construed state acts. In sum, the position of the Court of Appeals was that the Supreme Court cannot reverse a state court on a matter of state or even federal law, but a state court can hold unconstitutional an act of the United States. Thus, Roane, with Jefferson's approval, located in the state courts the ultimate authority to judge the extent of the powers of the national government; in 1798 Jefferson had centered that ultimate authority in the state legislatures. At the conclusion of their opinions, the Virginia judges entered their judgment:

> The court is unanimously of opinion, that the appellate power of the Supreme Court of the United States does not extend to this court, under a sound construction of the constitution of the United States; that so much of the 25th section of the act of Congress to establish the judicial courts of the United States, as extends the appellate jurisdiction of the Supreme Court to this court, is not in pursuance of the constitution of the United States; that the writ of error, in this cause, was improvidently allowed, under the authority of that act; that the proceedings thereon in the Supreme Court were *Coram non judice* [before a court without jurisdiction], in relation to this court, and that obedience to its mandate be declined by the court.

When the case returned a second time to the Supreme Court on writ of error, Marshall again absented himself and Story again wrote the opinion. The *Martin* Court, consisting of five Republicans and one Federalist, was unanimous, though Johnson concurred separately. Story's forty-page opinion on behalf of federal judicial review is a masterpiece, far superior to Marshall's performance in *Marbury v. Madison* (1803) on behalf of national judicial review. In its cadenced prose, magisterial tone, nationalist doctrine, incisive logic, and driving repetitiveness, Story's opinion foreshadowed Marshall's later and magnificent efforts in *McCulloch v. Maryland* (1819), *Cohens v. Virginia* (1821), and *Gibbons v. Ogden* (1824), suggesting that they owe as much to Story as he to Marshall's undoubted influence on him. Because the Constitution, as Roane pointed out, had neither expressly empowered Congress to extend the Court's appellate jurisdiction to the state courts nor expressly vested the Court itself with such jurisdiction, Story had to justify broad construction. The Constitution, he observed, was ordained not by the sovereign states but by the people of the United States, who could subordinate state powers to those of the nation. Not all national powers were expressly given. The Constitution "unavoidably deals in general language," Story explained, because it was intended "to endure through a long lapse of ages, the events of which were locked up in the inscrutable purpose of Providence." The framers of the Constitution, unable to foresee "what new changes and modifications of power might be indispensable" to achieve its purposes, expressed its powers in "general terms, leaving to the legislature, from time to time, to adopt its own means to effectuate legitimate objects. . . ." From such sweeping premises on the flexibility and expansiveness of national powers, Story could sustain section 25. He found authority for its enactment in Articles III and VI.

Article III, which defined the judicial power of the United States, contemplates that the Supreme Court shall be primarily an appellate court, whose appellate jurisdiction shall extend to specified cases and controversies. Shall is mandatory or imperative: the Court *must* exercise its appellate jurisdiction in *"all* cases, in law and equity, arising under the Constitution, the Laws of the United States, and Treaties made. . . ." It is, therefore, the case, not the court from which it comes, that gives the Supreme Court its appellate jurisdiction, and because cases involving the Constitution, federal laws, and treaties may arise in state courts, the Supreme Court must exercise appellate jurisdiction in those cases. Contrary to Roane, that appellate jurisdiction did not exist only when the case came from a lower federal court. The Constitution required the establishment of a Supreme Court but merely authorized Congress to exercise a discretionary power in establishing lower federal courts. If Congress chose not to establish them, the Court's mandatory appellate jurisdiction could be exercised over only the state courts. The establishment of the lower federal courts meant that the appellate jurisdiction of the Supreme Court extended concurrently to both state and federal courts.

Article VI, the supremacy clause, made the Constitution itself, laws in pursuance to it, and federal treaties the supreme law of the land, binding on state courts. The decision of a state court on a matter involving the supreme law cannot be final, because the judicial power of the United States extends specifically to all such cases. To enforce the supremacy clause, the Supreme Court must have appellate jurisdiction over state court decisions involving the supreme law. That a case involving the supreme law might arise in the state courts is obvious. Story gave the example of a contract case in which a party relied on the provision in Article I, section 10, barring state impairments of the obligations of a contract, and also the example of a criminal prosecution in which the defendant relied on the provision against ex post facto laws. The Constitution, he pointed out, was in fact designed to operate on the states "in their corporate capacities." It is "crowded" with provisions that "restrain or annul the sovereignty of the States," making the Court's exercise of appellate power over unconstitutional state acts no more in derogation of state sovereignty than those provisions or the principle of national supremacy. Not only would the federal system survive the exercise of federal judicial review; it could not function without such review. The law must be uniform "upon all subjects within the purview of the Constitution. Judges . . . in different States, might differently interpret a statute, or a treaty of the United States, or even the Constitution itself: If there were no revising authority to control these jarring and discordant judgments, and harmonize them into uniformity, the laws, the treaties and the Constitution of the United States would be different in different states," and might never have the same interpretation and efficacy in any two states.

Story's opinion is the linchpin of the federal system and of judicial nationalism. It remains the greatest argument for federal judicial review, though it by no means concluded the controversy. Virginia's hostility was so intense that a case was contrived in 1821 to allow the Supreme Court to restate the principles of *Martin*. (See *Cohens v. Virginia,* 1821.) As a matter of fact, though, federal judicial review and the constitutionality of section 25 remained bitterly contested topics to the eve of the Civil War.

Bibliography

Beveridge, Albert J. 1916–1919 *The Life of John Marshall,* 4 vols. Vol. IV:145–167. Boston: Houghton Mifflin.

Crosskey, William Winslow 1953 *Politics and the Constitution,* 2 vols. Pages 785–817. Chicago: University of Chicago Press.

Haines, Charles Grove 1944 *The Role of the Supreme Court in American Government and Politics, 1789–1835.* Pages 340–351. Berkeley: University of California Press.

35

McCulloch v. Maryland
4 Wheaton 316 (1819)

Speaking for a unanimous Supreme Court, Chief Justice John Marshall delivered an opinion upon which posterity has heaped lavish encomiums. James Bradley Thayer thought "there is nothing so fine as the opinion in *McCulloch v. Maryland.*" Albert Beveridge placed it "among the very first of the greatest judicial utterances of all time," while William Draper Lewis described it as "perhaps the most celebrated judicial utterance in the annals of the English speaking world." Such estimates spring from the fact that Marshall's vision of nationalism in time became a reality, to some extent because of his vision. Beveridge was not quite wrong in saying that the *McCulloch* opinion "so decisively influenced the growth of the Nation that, by many, it is considered as only second in importance to the Constitution itself." On the other hand, Marshall the judicial statesman engaged in a judicial coup, as his panegyrical biographer understood. To appreciate Marshall's achievement in *McCulloch* and the intense opposition that his opinion engendered in its time, one must also bear in mind that however orthodox his assumptions and doctrines are in the twentieth century, they were in their time unorthodox. With good reason Beveridge spoke of Marshall's "sublime audacity," the "extreme radicalism" of his constitutional theories, and the fact that he "rewrote the fundamental law of the Nation," a proposition to which Beveridge added that it would be more accurate to state that he made of the written instrument "a living thing, capable of growth, capable of keeping pace with the advancement of the American people and ministering to their changing necessities."

The hysterical denunciations of the *McCulloch* opinion by the aged and crabbed Thomas Jefferson, by the frenetically embittered Spencer Roane, and by that caustic apostle of localism, John Taylor, may justly be discounted, but not the judgment of the cool and prudent "Father of the Constitution," James Madison. On receiving Roane's "Hampden" essays assaulting *McCulloch*, Madison ignored the threat of state nullification and the repudiation of judicial review, but he agreed with Roane that the Court's opinion tended, in Madison's words, "to convert a limited into an unlimited Government." Madison deplored Marshall's "latitude in expounding the Constitution which seems to break down the landmarks intended by a specification of the Powers of Congress, and to substitute for a definite connection between means and ends, a Legislative discretion as to the former to which no practical limit can be assigned." Few if any of the friends of the Constitution, declared Madison, anticipated "a rule of construction . . . as broad & as pliant as what has occurred," and he added that the Constitution would probably not have been ratified if the powers that Marshall claimed for the national government had been known in 1788–1789. Madison's opinion suggests how far Marshall and the Court had departed from the intentions of the Framers and makes understandable the onslaught that *McCulloch* provoked. Although much of that onslaught was a genuine concern for the prostration of states rights before a consolidating nationalism, Taylor hit the nail on the head for the older generation of Jeffersonians when he wrote that *McCulloch* reared "a monied interest."

The case, after all, was decided in the midst of a depression popularly thought to have been caused by the Bank of the United States, a private corporation chartered by Congress; and *McCulloch* was a decision in favor of the hated bank and against the power of a state to tax its branch operations. The constitutionality of the power of Congress to charter a bank had been ably debated in Congress and in Washington's cabinet in 1791, when Alexander Hamilton proposed the bank bill. Constitutional debate mirrored party politics, and the Federalists had the votes. The Court never passed judgment on the constitutionality of the original Bank of the United States Act, though it had a belated opportunity. In 1809 a case came before the Court that was remarkably similar to *McCulloch:* state officials, acting under a state statute taxing the branches of the bank, forcibly carried away from its vaults money to pay the state tax. In *Bank of the United States v. Deveaux* (1809), Marshall for the Court, deftly avoiding the questions that he confronted in *McCulloch,* found that the parties lacked the diversity of citizenship that would authorize jurisdiction. With the bank's twenty-year charter nearing expiration, a decision in favor of the bank's constitutionality might look like pro-Federalist politics by the Court, embroiling it in a dispute with President Madison, who was on record as opposing the bank's constitutionality, and with Congress, which supported Madison's policies.

The United States fought the War of 1812 without the bank to help manage its finances, and the results were disastrous. The war generated a new wave of nationalism and a change of opinion in Madison's party. In 1816 President Madison signed into law a bill chartering a second Bank of the United States, passed by Congress with the support of young nationalists like Henry Clay and John C. Calhoun and opposed by a Federalist remnant led by young Daniel Webster. The political world was turned upside down. The bank's tight credit policies contributed to a depression, provoking many states to retaliate against "the monster monopoly." Two states prohibited the bank from operating within their jurisdictions; six others taxed the operations of the bank's branches within their jurisdictions. The constitutionality of Maryland's tax was the issue in *McCulloch,* as well as the constitutionality of the act of Congress incorporating the bank.

Six of the greatest lawyers of the nation, including Webster, William Pinkney, and Luther Martin, argued the case over a period of nine days, and only three days later Marshall delivered his thirty-six-page opinion for a unanimous Court. He had written much of it in advance, thus prejudging the case, but in a sense his career was a preparation for the case. As Roane conceded, Marshall was "a man of profound legal attainments" writing "upon a subject which has employed his thoughts, his tongue, and his pen, as a politician, and an historian for more than thirty years." And he had behind him all five Jeffersonian-Republican members of the Court.

Arguing that Congress had no authority to incorporate a bank, counsel for Maryland claimed that the Constitution had originated with the states, which alone were truly sovereign, and that the national government's powers must be exercised in subordination to the states. Marshall grandiloquently turned these propositions around. When Beveridge said that Marshall the soldier wrote *McCulloch* and that his opinion echoed "the blast of the bugle of Valley Forge" (where Marshall served), he had a point. Figuratively, Old Glory and the bald eagle rise up from the opinion—to anyone stirred by a nationalist sentiment. The Constitution, declared Marshall, had been submitted to conventions of the people, from whom it derives its authority. The government formed by the Constitution proceeded "directly from the people" and in the words of the preamble was "ordained and established" in their name, and it binds the states. Marshall drove home that theme repeatedly. "The government of the Union . . . is, emphatically, and truly, a government of the people. In form and in substance it emanates from them. Its powers are granted by them, and are to be exercised directly on them, and for their benefit." A bit later Marshall declared that the government of the Union though limited in its powers "is supreme within its sphere of action. . . . It is the government of all; its powers are delegated by all; it represents all, and acts for all." And it necessarily restricts its subordinate members, because the Constitution and federal laws constitute the supreme law of the land. Reading this later, Abraham Lincoln transmuted it into "a government of the people, by the people, for the people."

Marshall's opinion is a state paper, like the Declaration of Independence, the Constitution itself, or the Gettysburg Address, the sort of document that puts itself beyond analysis or criticism. But there were constitutional issues to be resolved, and Marshall had not yet touched them. Madison agreed with Roane that "the occasion did not call for the general and abstract doctrine interwoven with the decision of the particular case," but *McCulloch* has survived and moved generations of Americans precisely because Marshall saw that the "general and abstract" were embedded in the issues, and he made it seem that the life of the nation was at stake on their resolution in the grandest way.

Disposing affirmatively of the question whether Congress could charter a bank was a foregone conclusion, flowing naturally from unquestioned premises. Though the power of establishing corporations is not among the enumerated powers, seeing the Constitution "whole," as Marshall saw it, led him to the doctrine of implied powers. The Constitution ought not have the "prolixity of a legal code"; rather, it marked only "great outlines," with the result that implied powers could be "deduced." Levying and collecting taxes, borrowing money, regulating commerce, supporting armies, and conducting war are among the major enumerated powers; in addition, the Constitution vests in Congress the power to pass all laws "necessary and proper" to carry into execution the powers enumerated. These powers implied the means necessary to execute them. A banking corporation was a means of effectuating designated ends. The word "necessary" did not mean indispensably necessary; it did not refer to a means without which the power granted would be nugatory, its object unattainable. "Necessary" means "useful," "needful," "conducive to," thus allowing Congress a latitude of choice in attaining its legitimate ends. The Constitution's Framers knew the difference between "necessary" and "absolutely necessary," a phrase they used in Article I, section 10, clause 2. They inserted the necessary and proper clause in a Constitution "intended to endure for ages to come, and, consequently, to be adapted to the various crises of human affairs." They intended Congress to have "ample means" for carrying its express powers into effect. The "narrow construction" advocated by Maryland would abridge, even "annihilate," Congress's discretion in selecting its means. Thus, the test for determining the constitutionality of an act of Congress was: "Let the end be legitimate, let it be within the scope of the Constitution, and all means which are appropriate, which are plainly adapted to that end, which are not prohibited, but consist with the letter and spirit of the Constitution, are constitutional." That formula yielded the conclusion that the act incorporating the bank was valid.

Such was the broad construction that "deduced" implied powers, shocking even Madison. The Court, he thought, had relinquished control over Congress. He might have added, as John Taylor did, that Marshall neglected to explain how and why a private bank chartered by Congress was necessary, even in a loose sense, to execute the enumerated powers. In *Construction Construed* (1820) Taylor gave five chapters to McCulloch, exhibiting the consequences of Marshall's reasoning. Congress might legislate on local agriculture and manufactures, because they were necessary to war. Roads were still more necessary than banks for collecting taxes. And:

> Taverns are very necessary or convenient for the offices of the army. . . . But horses are undoubtedly more necessary for the conveyance of the mail and for war, than roads, which may be as convenient to assailants as defenders; and therefore the principle of implied power of legislation will certainly invest Congress with a legislative power over horses. In short, this mode of construction completely establishes the position, that Congress may pass any internal law whatsoever in relation to things, because there is nothing with which war, commerce and taxation may not be closely or remotely connected.

All of which supported Taylor's contention that Marshall's doctrine of implied powers would destroy the states and lead to a government of unlimited powers, because "as ends may be made to beget means, so means may be made to beget ends, until the co-habitation shall rear a progeny of unconstitutional bastards, which were not begotten by the people."

Marshall's reasoning with respect to the second question in the case incited less hostility, though not by much. Assuming Congress could charter the bank, could a state tax its branch? Marshall treated the bank as a branch or "instrument" of the United States itself, and relying on the supremacy clause (Article VI), he concluded that if the states could tax one instrument to any degree, they could tax every other instrument as well—the mails, the mint, even the judicial process. The result would cripple the government, "prostrating it at the foot of the States." Again, he was deducing from general principles in order to defeat the argument that nothing in the Constitution prohibits state taxes on congressionally chartered instruments. Congress's power to create, Marshall reasoned, implied a power to preserve. A state power to tax was a power to destroy, incompatible with the national power to create and preserve. Where such repugnancy exists, the national power, which is supreme, must control. "The question is, in truth, a question of supremacy," with the result that the Court necessarily found the state act unconstitutional.

That was Marshall's *McCulloch* opinion. Roane and Taylor publicly excoriated it, and Jefferson spurred them on, telling Roane, who rejected even federal judicial review, "I go further than you do." The Virginia legislature repudiated implied powers and recommended an amendment to the Constitution "creating a tribunal for the decision of all questions, in which the powers and authorities of the general government and those of the States, where they are in conflict, shall be decided." Marshall was so upset by the public criticism that he was driven for the first and only time to reply in a series of newspaper articles. Still, Ohio allied itself with Virginia and literally defied, even nullified, the decision in *McCulloch*. (See *Osborn v. Bank of the United States*, 1824; *Cohens v. Virginia*, 1821.) Pennsylvania, Indiana, Illinois, and Tennessee also conducted a guerrilla war against the Court, and Congress seriously debated measures to curb its powers. Fortunately the common enemies of the Court shared no common policies. *McCulloch* prevailed in the long run, providing, together with *Gibbons v. Ogden* (1824), the constitutional wherewithal to meet unpredictable crises even to our time. *McCulloch* had unforeseen life-giving powers. Marshall, Beveridge's "supreme conservative," laid the constitutional foundations for the New Deal and the Welfare State.

Bibliography

Beveridge, Albert J. 1916–1919 *The Life of John Marshall,* 4 vols. Vol. IV: 283–339. Boston Houghton Mifflin.

Haines, Charles Grove 1944 *The Role of the Supreme Court in American Government and Politics, 1789–1835.* Pages 351–368. Berkeley: University of California Press.

Warren, Charles 1923 *The Supreme Court in United States History,* 3 vols. Vol. I:499–540. Boston: Little, Brown.

36

Cohens v. Virginia
6 Wheaton 265 (1821)

In the rancorous aftermath of *McCulloch v. Maryland* (1819), several states, led by Virginia and Ohio, denounced and defied the Supreme Court. State officers of Ohio entered the vaults of a branch of the Bank of the United States and forcibly collected over $100,000 in state taxes. Virginia's legislature resolved that the Constitution be amended to create "a tribunal for the decision of all questions, in which the powers and authorities of the general government and those of the States, where they are in conflict, shall be decided." Widespread and vitriolic attacks on the Court, its doctrine of implied powers, and section 25 of the Judiciary Act of 1789 showed that *Martin v. Hunter's Lessee* (1816) and *McCulloch* were not enough to settle the matters involved, especially as to the jurisdiction of the Court over state acts and decisions in conflict with the supreme law of the land as construed by the Court. Accordingly a case appears to have been contrived to create for Chief Justice John Marshall an opportunity to reply offlcially to his critics and to reassert both national supremacy and the supreme appellate powers of his Court.

Two brothers surnamed Cohen sold lottery tickets in Norfolk, Virginia, contrary to a state act prohibiting their sale for a lottery not authorized by Virginia. The Cohens sold tickets for a lottery authorized by an act of Congress to benefit the capital city. In Norfolk the borough court found the defendants guilty and fined them $100. By Virginia law, no appeal could be had to a higher state court. The Cohens, prosperous Baltimore merchants who could easily afford the paltry fine, claimed the protection of the act of Congress and removed the case on writ of error from the local court to the highest court of the land; moreover they employed the greatest lawyer in the nation, William Pinckney, whose usual fee was $2,000 a case, and another distinguished advocate, David B. Ogden, who commanded a fee of $1,000. More was at stake than appeared. "The very title of the case," said the Richmond *Enquirer,* "is enough to stir one's blood"—a reference to the galling fact that the sovereign state of Virginia was being hauled before the Supreme Court of the United States by private individuals in seeming violation of the Eleventh Amendment. The state governor was so alarmed that he notified the legislature, and its committee, referring to the states as "sovereign and independent nations," declared that the state judiciaries were as independent of the federal courts as the state legislatures were of Congress, the twenty-fifth section of the 1789 notwithstanding. The legislature, having adopted solemn resolutions of protest and repudiating federal judicial review, instructed counsel representing Virginia to argue one point alone: that the Supreme Court had no jurisdiction in the case. Counsel, relying on the Eleventh Amendment to argue that a state cannot be sued without its consent, also contended that not a word in the Constitution "goes to set up the federal judiciary above the state judiciary."

Marshall, for a unanimous Court dominated by Republicans, conceded that the main "subject was fully discussed and exhausted in the case of *Martin v. Hunter,"* but that did not stop him from writing a fifty-five-page treatise which concluded that under section 25 the Court had jurisdiction in the case. Marshall said little that was new, but he said it with a majestic eloquence and a forcefulness that surpassed Joseph Story's, and the fact that the Chief Justice was the author of the Court's nationalist exposition, addressed to states rights' advocates throughout the country, added weight and provocation to his utterances. He was sublimely rhapsodic about the Constitution and the Union it created, sarcastic and disparaging in restating Virginia's position. Boldly he piled inference upon inference, overwhelming every particle of disagreement in the course of his triumphs of logic and excursions into the historical record of state infidelity. And he had a sense of the melodramatic that Story lacked, as when Marshall began his opinion by saying that the question of jurisdiction "may be truly said vitally to affect the Union." The defendant in error—Virginia—did not care whether the Constitution and laws of the United States had been violated by the judgment of guilt that the Cohens sought to have reviewed. Admitting such violation, Virginia contended that the United States had no corrective. Virginia, Marshall continued, maintained that the nation possessed no department capable of restraining, peaceably and by authority of law, attempts against the legitimate powers of the nation. "They maintain," he added, "that the constitution of the United States has provided no tribunal for the final construction of itself, or of the laws or treaties of the nation; but that this power may be exercised in the last resort by the courts of every state of the Union." Virginia even maintained that the supreme law of the land "may receive as many constructions as there are states. . . ." Marshall confronted and conquered every objection.

Quickly turning to Article III, Marshall observed that it authorizes Congress to confer federal jurisdiction in two classes of cases, the first depending on the character of the case and the second on the character of the parties. The first class includes "all" cases involving the Constitution and federal laws and treaties, "whoever may be the parties," and the second includes all cases to which states are parties. By ratifying the Constitution the states consented to judicial review in both classes of cases, thereby making possible the preservation of the Union. That Union is supreme in all cases where it is empowered to act, as Article VI, the supremacy clause, insures by making the Constitution and federal law the supreme law of the land. The Court must decide every case coming within its constitutional jurisdiction to prevent the supreme law of the land from being prostrated "at the feet of every state in the Union" or being vetoed by any member of the Union. Collisions between the United States and the states will doubtless occur, but, said Marshall, "a constitution is framed for ages to come, and is designed to approach immortality as nearly as human institutions can approach it." To prevail, the government of the Union derived from the Constitution the means of self-preservation. The federal courts existed to secure the execution of the laws of the Union. History proved, Marshall declared, that the states and their tribunals could not be trusted with a power to defeat by law the legitimate measures of the Union. Thus the Supreme Court can take appellate jurisdiction even in a case between a state and one of its own citizens who relied on the Constitution or federal law. Otherwise Article III would be mere surplusage, as would Article VI. For the Court to decline the jurisdiction authorized by Article III and commanded by Congress would be "treason to the Constitution."

Although Marshall's rhetoric certainly addressed itself, grandiosely, to the question of jurisdiction, his critics regarded all that he had declared thus far as obiter dicta, for he had not yet faced the Eleventh Amendment, which Virginia thought concluded the case on its behalf. Upon finally reaching the Eleventh Amendment question, Marshall twisted a little history and chopped a little logic. The amendment, he said, was adopted not to preserve state dignity or sovereignty but to prevent creditors from initiating suits against states that would raid their treasuries. The amendment did not, therefore, apply to suits commenced by states and appealed by writ of error to the Supreme Court for the sole purpose of inquiring whether the judgment of a state tribunal violated the Constitution or federal law.

The argument that the state and federal judiciaries were entirely independent of each other considered the Supreme Court as "foreign" to state judiciaries. In a grand peroration, Marshall made his Court the apex of a single judicial system that comprehended the state judiciaries to the extent that they shared a concurrent jurisdiction over cases arising under the supreme law of the land. For most important purposes, Marshall declared, the United States was "a single nation," and for all those purposes, its government is supreme; state constitutions and laws to the contrary are "absolutely void." The states "are members of one great empire—for some purposes sovereign, for some purposes subordinate." The role of the federal judiciary, Marshall concluded, was to void state judgments that might contravene the supreme law; the alternative would be "a hydra in government."

Having sustained the jurisdiction of the Court, Marshall offered a sop to Virginia: whether the congressional lottery act intended to operate outside the District of Columbia, he suggested, depended on the words of that act. The case was then reargued on its merits, and Marshall, again for a unanimous Court, quickly sustained the Cohens' conviction: Congress had not intended to permit the sale of lottery tickets in states where such a sale was illegal.

Virginia "won" its case, just as Madison had in *Marbury v. Madison* (1803), but no one was fooled this time either. The governor of Virginia in a special message to his legislature spoke of the state's "humiliation" in having failed to vindicate its sovereign rights. A legislative committee proposed amendments to the Constitution that would cripple not only the judicial power of the United States but also (reacting to *McCulloch*) the powers of Congress in passing laws not "absolutely" necessary and proper for carrying out its enumerated powers. In the United States Senate, enemies of the Court proposed constitutional amendments that would vest in the Senate appellate jurisdiction in cases where the laws of a state were impugned and in all cases involving the federal Constitution, laws, or treaties. Intermittently for several years senators introduced a variety of amendments to curb the Court or revoke section 25, but those who shared a common cause did not share a common remedy, though *Green v. Biddle* (1823) and *Osborn v. Bank of the United States* (1824) inflamed their cause.

In Virginia, where the newspapers published Marshall's long opinion to the accompaniment of scathing denunciations, Spencer Roane and John Taylor returned to a long battle that had begun with the *Martin* case and expanded in the wake of *McCulloch*. Roane, as "Algernon Sydney," published five articles on the theme that *Cohens* "negatives the idea that the American states have a real existence, or are to be considered, in any sense, as sovereign and independent states." He excoriated federal judicial review, implied powers, and the subordination of the states, by judicial construction, to "one great consolidated government" that destroyed the equilibrium of the Constitution, leaving that compact of the states nonexistent except in name. Taylor's new book, *Tyranny Unmasked* (1822), continued the themes of his *Construction Construed* (1820), where he argued that the "federal is not a national government: it is a league of nations. By this league, a limited power only over persons and property was given to the representatives of the united nations." The "tyranny" unmasked by the second book turned out to be nationalist programs, such as the protective tariff, and nationalist powers, including the power of the Supreme Court over the states.

Thomas Jefferson read Roane and Taylor, egged them on, and congratulated them for their orthodox repudiation of the Court's "heresies." To Justice William Johnson, who had joined Marshall's opinion, Jefferson wrote that Roane's articles "appeared to me to pulverize every word which had been delivered by Judge Marshall, of the extrajudicial part of his opinion," and to Jefferson "all was extra-judicial"—and he was not wholly wrong—except the second *Cohens* opinion on the merits. Jefferson also wrote that the doctrine that courts are the final arbiters of all constitutional questions was "dangerous" and "would place us under the despotism of an oligarchy." Recommending the works of Roane and Taylor to a friend, Jefferson militantly declared that if Congress did not shield the states from the dangers originating with the Court, "the states must shield themselves, and meet the invader foot to foot." To Senator Nathaniel Macon of Virginia, Jefferson wrote that the Supreme Court was "the germ of dissolution of our federal government" and "an irresponsible body," working, he said, "like gravity, by day and night, gaining a little today and a little tomorrow, and advancing its noiseless step, like a thief over the fields of jurisdiction, until all shall be usurped from the States, the government of all becoming a consolidated one."

James Madison deplored some of the Court's tactics, especially its mingling of judgments with "comments and reasoning of a scope beyond them," often at the expense of the states; but Madison told Roane flatly that the judicial power of the United States "over cases arising under the Constitution, must be admitted to be a vital part of the System." He thought Marshall wrong on the Eleventh Amendment and extreme on implied powers, but, he wrote to Roane, on the question "whether the federal or the State decisions ought to prevail, the sounder policy would yield to the claims of the former," or else "the Constitution of the U.S. might become different in every State."

The public reaction to *Cohens* depressed Marshall, because, as he wrote to Story, the opinion of the Court "has been assaulted with a degree of virulence transcending what has appeared on any former occasion." Roane's "Algernon Sydney" letters, Marshall feared, might be believed true by the public, and Roane would be hailed as "the champion of state rights, instead of being what he really is, the champion of dismemberment." Marshall saw "a deep design to convert our government into a mere league of States. . . . The attack upon the Judiciary is in fact an attack upon the Union." The whole attack originated, he believed, with Jefferson, "the grand Lama of the mountains." An effort would be made, predicted Marshall, accurately, "to repeal the 25th section of the Judiciary Act." Doubtless the personal attacks on him proved painful. A bit of anonymous doggerel, which circulated in Virginia after *Cohens,* illuminates public feeling.

> Old Johnny Marshall what's got in ye
> To side with Cohens against Virginny.
> To call in Court his "Old Dominion."
> To insult her with your foul opinion!
> I'll tell you that it will not do
> To call old Spencer in review.

He knows the law as well as you.
And once for all, it will not do.
Alas! Alas! that you should be
So much against State Sovereignty!
You've thrown the whole state in a terror,
By this infernal "Writ of Error."

The reaction to *Cohens* proves, in part, that the Court's prose was overbroad, but Marshall was reading the Constitution in the only way that would make the federal system operate effectively under one supreme law.

Bibliography

Beveridge, Albert J. 1916–1919 *The Life of John Marshall,* 4 vols. Vol IV: 340–375. Boston: Houghton-Mifflin.

Haines, Charles Grove 1944 *The Role of the Supreme Court in American Government and Politics, 1789–1835.* Pages 427–461. Berkeley: University of California Press.

Konefsky, Samuel J. 1964 *John Marshall and Alexander Hamilton.* Pages 93–111. New York: Macmillan.

37

Gibbons v. Ogden
9 Wheaton 1 (1824)

Chief Justice John Marshall's great disquisition on the commerce clause in this case is the most influential in our history. *Gibbons* liberated the steamship business and much of American interstate commerce from the grip of state-created monopolies. More important, Marshall laid the doctrinal basis for the national regulation of the economy that occurred generations later, though at the time his opinion buttressed laissez-faire. He composed that opinion as if statecraft in the interpretation of a constitutional clause could decide whether the United States remained just a federal union or became a nation. The New York act, which the Court voided in *Gibbons,* had closed the ports of the state to steamships not owned or licensed by a monopoly chartered by the state. Other states retaliated in kind. The attorney general of the United States told the *Gibbons* Court that the country faced a commercial "civil war."

The decision produced immediate and dramatic results. Within two weeks, a newspaper jubilantly reported: "Yesterday the Steamboat *United States,* Capt. Bunker, from New Haven, entered New York in triumph, with streamers flying, and a large company of passengers exulting in the decision of the United States Supreme Court against the New York monopoly. She fired a salute which was loudly returned by huzzas from the wharves." Senator Martin Van Buren (Democrat, New York), who had recently advocated curbing the Court, declared that even those states whose laws had been nullified, including his own, "have submitted to their fate," and the Court now justly attracted "idolatry," its Chief respected as "the ablest Judge now sitting upon any judicial bench in the world." For a Court that had been under vitriolic congressional and state attack, *Gibbons* wedded a novel popularity to its nationalism.

One of the ablest judges who ever sat on an American court, James Kent of New York, whose opinion Marshall repudiated, grumbled in the pages of his *Commentaries on American Law* (1826) that Marshall's "language was too general and comprehensive for the case." Kent was right. The Court held the state act unconstitutional for conflicting with an act of Congress, making Marshall's enduring treatise on the commerce clause unnecessary for the disposition of the case. The conflict between the two statutes, Marshall said, "decides the cause." Kent was also right in stating that "it never occurred to anyone," least of all to the Congress that had passed the Coastal Licensing Act of 1793, which Marshall used to decide the case, that the act could justify national supremacy over state regulations respecting "internal waters or commerce." The act of 1793 had been intended to discriminate against foreign vessels in the American coastal trade by offering preferential tonnage duties to vessels of American registry. Marshall's construction of the statute conformed to his usual tactic of finding narrow grounds for decision after making a grand exposition. He announced "propositions which may have been thought axioms." He "assume[d] nothing," he said, because of the magnitude of the question, the distinction of the judge (Kent) whose opinion he scrapped, and the able arguments, which he rejected, by Thomas Emmett and Thomas Oakely, covering over 125 pages in the report of the case.

Except for the arguments of counsel, the Court had little for guidance. It had never before decided a commerce clause case, and the clause itself is general: "Congress shall have power to regulate commerce with foreign nations and among the several states. . . ." The power to regulate what would later be called "interstate commerce" appears in the same clause touching foreign commerce, the regulation of which is necessarily exclusive, beyond state control. But the clause does not negate state regulatory authority over interstate commerce, and the framers of the Constitution had rejected proposals for a sole or exclusive power in Congress. Interstate commerce could be, as counsel for the monopoly contended, a subject of concurrent power. Marshall had previously acknowledged that although the Constitution vested in Congress bankruptcy and tax powers, the states retained similar powers. *The Federalist* #32 recognized the principle of concurrent powers but offered no assistance on the commerce clause. Congress had scarcely used the commerce power except for the Embargo Acts, which had not come before the Supreme Court. Those acts had interpreted the power to "regulate" as a power to prohibit, but they concerned commerce with foreign nations and were an instrument of foreign policy.

Prior to *Gibbons* the prevailing view on the interstate commerce power was narrow and crossed party lines. Kent, a Federalist, differed little from the Jeffersonians. James Madison, for example, when vetoing a congressional appropriation for internal improvements, had declared in 1817 that "the power to regulate commerce among the several states cannot include a power to construct roads and canals, and to improve the navigation of water courses." In 1821, when James Monroe had vetoed the Cumberland Road Bill, whose objective was to extend national authority to turnpikes within the states, he had virtually reduced the commerce power to the enactment of duties and imports, adding that goods and vessels are the only subjects of commerce that Congress can regulate. "Commerce," in common usage at the time of *Gibbons,* meant trade in the buying and selling of commodities, not navigation or the transportation of passengers for hire. That was the business of Mr. Gibbons, who operated a steamship in defiance of the monopoly, between Elizabethtown, New Jersey, and New York City, in direct competition with Ogden, a licensee of the monopoly. Had Gibbons operated under sail, he would not have violated New York law; as it was, the state condemned his vessel to fines and forfeiture.

In *Gibbons,* then, the Court confronted a stunted concept of commerce, a strict construction of the commerce power, and an opinion bearing Kent's authority that New York had regulated only "internal" commerce. Kent had also held that the commerce power was a concurrent one and that the test for the constitutionality of a state act should be practical: could the state and national laws coexist without conflicting in their operation? Marshall "assumed nothing" and in his step-by-step "axioms" repudiated any argument based on such premises.

He began with a definition of "commerce." It comprehended navigation as well as buying and selling, because "it is intercourse." This sweeping definition prompted a disgruntled states-rightist to remark, "I shall soon expect to learn that our fornication laws are unconstitutional." That same definition later constitutionally supported an undreamed of expansion of congressional power over the life of the nation's economy. Having defined commerce as every species of commercial intercourse, Marshall, still all-embracing, defined "commerce among the several states" to mean commerce intermingled with or concerning two or more states. Such commerce "cannot stop at the external boundary line of each State, but may be introduced into the interior"—and wherever it went, the power of the United States followed. Marshall did not dispute Kent's view that the "completely internal commerce" of a state (what we call intrastate commerce) is reserved for state governance. But that governance extended only to such commerce as was completely within one state, did not "affect" other states, "and with which it is not necessary to interfere, for the purpose of executing some of the general powers of the [United States] government." Marshall's breath-taking exposition of the national commerce power foreshadowed the stream of commerce doctrine and the Shreveport doctrine of the next century. "If Congress has the power to regulate it," he added, "that power must be exercised whenever the subject exists. If it exists within the States . . . then the power of Congress may be exercised within a State."

Having so defined the reach of the commerce power, Marshall, parsing the clause, defined the power to "regulate" as the power "to prescribe the rule by which commerce is to be governed." It is a power that "may be exercised to its utmost extent and acknowledges no limitations. . . ." In *Cohens v. Virginia* (1821) he had said that the United States form, for most purposes, one nation: "In war, we are one people. In making peace, we are one people. In all commercial regulations, we are one and the same people," and the government managing that people's interests was the government of the Union. In *Gibbons* he added that because the "sovereignty of Congress" is plenary as to its objects, "the power over commerce with foreign nations, and among the several states, is vested in Congress as absolutely as it would be in a single government. . . ." Were that true, the commerce power would be as exclusive as the treaty power or war powers and could not be shared concurrently with the states.

Marshall expressly denied that the states possessed a concurrent commerce power; yet he did not expressly declare that Congress possessed an exclusive commerce power, which would prevent the states from exercising a commerce power even in the absence of congressional legislation. That was Daniel Webster's argument in *Gibbons*, against the monopoly, and Marshall found "great force" in it. Notwithstanding the ambiguity in Marshall's opinion, he implicitly adopted Webster's argument by repeatedly rejecting the theory of concurrent commerce powers. He conceded, however, that the states can reach and regulate some of the same subjects of commerce as Congress, but only by the exercise of powers distinct from an interstate commerce power. Referring to the mass of state regulatory legislation that encompassed inspection laws, health laws, turnpike laws, ferry laws, "etc.," Marshall labeled them the state's "system of police," later called the police power. But his jurisprudence-by-label did not distinguish interstate from intrastate commerce powers. Having declared that Congress might regulate a state's "internal" commerce to effectuate a national policy, he allowed the state police power to operate on subjects of interstate commerce, in subordination, of course, to the principle of national supremacy. (See *Willson v. Black-Bird Creek Marsh Co.,* 1829.)

Following his treatise on the commerce clause, Marshall turned to the dispositive question whether the New York monopoly act conflicted with an act of Congress. The pertinent act of 1793 referred to American vessels employed in the "coasting trade." It made no exception for steamships or for vessels that merely transported passengers. The New York act was therefore "in direct collision" with the act of Congress by prohibiting Gibbons's steamship from carrying passengers in and out of the state's ports without a license from the monopoly.

Justice William Johnson, although an appointee of Thomas Jefferson, was even more nationalistic than Marshall. Webster later boasted that Marshall had taken to his argument as a baby to its mother's milk, but the remark better suited Johnson. Concurring separately, he declared that the commerce clause vested a power in Congress that "must be exclusive." He would have voided the state monopoly act even in the absence of the Federal Coastal Licensing Act: "I cannot overcome the conviction, that if the licensing act was repealed tomorrow, the rights of the appellant to a reversal of the decision complained of, would be as strong as it is under this license." Johnson distinguished the police power laws that operated on subjects of interstate commerce; their "different purposes," he claimed, made all the difference. In fact, the purpose underlying the monopoly act was the legitimate state purpose of encouraging new inventions.

In a case of first impression, neither Marshall nor Johnson could lay down doctrines that settled all conflicts between state and national powers relating to commerce. Not until 1851 did the Court, after much groping, seize upon the doctrine of selective exclusiveness, which seemed at the time like a litmus paper test. (See *Cooley v. Board of Port Wardens of Philadelphia*, 1852.) Yet *Gibbons* anticipated doctrines concerning the breadth of congressional power that emerged in the next century and still govern. Marshall was as prescient as human ability allows. The Court today cannot construe the commerce clause except in certain state regulation cases without being influenced by Marshall's treatise on it. At the beginning, Justice Robert Jackson declared in *Wickard v. Filburn* (1941), "Chief Justice Marshall described the federal commerce power with a breadth never exceeded."

Bibliography

Baxter, Maurice G. 1972 *The Steamboat Monopoly: Gibbons v. Ogden*, 1824. New York: Knopf.

Beveridge, Albert J. 1916–1919 *The Life of John Marshall.* 4 vols. Vol IV:397–460. Boston: Houghton Mifflin.

Frankfurter, Felix 1937 *The Commerce Clause under Marshall, Taney and Waite.* Pages 1–45. Chapel Hill University of North Carolina Press.